CULTURAL EVENTS ARTISTS AND WRITERS	DATES	WORLD POLITICAL
MIDDLE AGES AND RENAISSANCE		
Gothic cathedrals begun (St. Denis,	**1100**	
Paris, 1144; Chartres, 1145)	**1150**	
	1200	Magna Carta signed by King John (1215)
	1250	Marco Polo leaves for Cathay (1271)
Dante's *Divine Comedy* (1307)	**1300**	Hundred Years' War begins (1337)
Chaucer's *Canterbury Tales* (1386)	**1350**	
Botticelli (1444–1510)	**1400**	Battle of Agincourt (1415)
Gutenberg Bible (1456)	**1450**	Fall of Constantinople (1453)
Michelangelo (1475–1564)		Columbus discovers America (1492)
Raphael (1483–1520)		
St. Peter's begun in Rome (1506)	**1500**	Henry VIII King of England (1509)
		Martin Luther's 95 theses (1517)
		Council of Trent (1545–1563)
	1550	Elizabeth I Queen of England (1558)
		Spanish Armada defeated (1588)

BAROQUE

CULTURAL EVENTS	DATES	WORLD POLITICAL
El Greco (1541–1614)		
William Shakespeare (1564–1616)		
Caravaggio (1573–1610)		
Peter Paul Rubens (1577–1640)		
Francesco Borromini (1599–1667)	**1600**	Jamestown settled (1607)
Cervantes, part I of *Don Quixote* (1605)		Thirty Years' War begins (1618)
Rembrandt van Rijn (1606–1669)		Mayflower Compact (1620)
Giovanni Lorenzo Bernini's		Louis XIV King of France (1643)
Ecstasy of St. Theresa (1644)		
Samuel Pepys's *Diary* (1660)	**1650**	Restoration of Charles II in England (1660)
John Milton's *Paradise Lost* (1667)		Reign of Peter the Great begins (1682)
Christopher Wren begins St. Paul's Cathedral (1675)		Salem witchcraft trials (1692)
Isaac Newton's *Principia Mathematica* (1687)	**1700**	War of the Spanish Succession begins (1702)
		Reign of Louis XV begins (1715)
Jonathan Swift's *Gulliver's Travels* (1726)		Age of Enlightened Despots (1740–1796)

CLASSICAL

CULTURAL EVENTS	DATES	WORLD POLITICAL
Francisco Goya (1746–1828)		
Jacques Louis David (1748–1825)		
Pompeii rediscovered (1748)	**1750**	Franklin's discoveries in electricity (1752)
Voltaire's *Candide* (1759)		Seven Years' War; French and Indian War (1756)
William Wordsworth (1770–1850)		Beginnings of the Industrial Revolution (ca. 1770)
J.M.W. Turner (1775–1851)		American Declaration of Independence (1776)
Immanuel Kant's *Critique of Pure Reason* (1781)		French Revolution begins (1789)
Thomas Malthus's *Essay on Population* (1798)		Bill of Rights (1791)
Eugene Delacroix (1798–1863)		Eli Whitney's cotton gin (1793)
Goethe's *Faust, Part I* (1808)	**1800**	Louisiana Purchase (1803)
Jane Austen's *Pride and Prejudice* (1813)		Battle of Waterloo (1815)

ROMANTIC

CULTURAL EVENTS	DATES	WORLD POLITICAL
Edgar Allen Poe (1809–1849)		
Goya's *Witches' Sabbath* (1815)		
Herman Melville (1818–1891)		Monroe Doctrine (1823)
Shelley's *Prometheus Unbound* (1820)	**1825**	Erie Canal opened (1825)
Victor Hugo's *Hernani* (1830)		July Revolution in France (1830)
Claude Monet (1840–1926)		Invention of telegraph (1832)
Ralph Waldo Emerson's *Essays* (1841)		Queen Victoria's reign begins (1837)
Alexander Dumas's *Count of*		California Gold Rush; Revolutions
Monte Cristo (1845)		in Europe (1848)
Karl Marx's *Communist Manifesto* (1848)		
Harriet Beecher Stowe's *Uncle Tom's Cabin* (1852)	**1850**	Opening of Japan to the West (1853)

EXPLORING MUSIC
Third Edition

ROBERT HICKOK

North Carolina School of the Arts

EXPLO

ADDISON-WESLEY PUBLISHING COMPANY   *Reading, Massachusetts*

RING MUSIC

THIRD EDITION

Menlo Park, California • London • Amsterdam • Don Mills, Ontario • Sydney

PRODUCTION EDITOR: Emily P. Arulpragasam
DESIGNER: Jean King
ILLUSTRATOR: Kris Kramer
COVER DESIGN: Gustav Szabo

The first and second editions of this text were
published under the title MUSIC APPRECIATION.

ISBN   0-201-02929-4
ABCDEFGHIJ-RN-79

For Paul and Laura

PREFACE

Exploring Music, Third Edition, is designed for introductory music courses at the college level. The book has been structured to suit a variety of course lengths. Coverage is comprehensive enough for a one-semester or full-year course. At the same time the organization affords considerable flexibility so that the instructor in a one- or two-quarter course can use the book selectively, choosing material to fit the length of time at his or her disposal.

The new title reflects a primary goal of this edition: to help the student develop an attitude of enthusiasm for and enjoyment of many types and styles of music. In order to make the beginning student's first exploration of the world of music as stimulating as possible, I have introduced a number of new elements and useful changes which are described below.

ORGANIZATION

Part I presents the fundamental elements of music in three easy-to-read, concise chapters. Simple musical examples as well as brief excerpts from works covered later in the text are used to illustrate and reinforce concepts. This section concludes with a chapter on musical instruments, including the human voice, and explores combinations of instruments: chamber and vocal ensembles, bands and wind ensembles, and the symphony orchestra. Part II introduces the music of non-Western cultures, offering the student a global perspective on music before moving to an examination of Western music in the remainder of the book. Then, using the material of Part I as a foundation, Parts III through VII examine in chronological order the periods of music history from the Middle Ages to the early twentieth century. Part VIII focuses on the American contribution to both concert and popular music, and Part IX explores developments in American and European avant-garde music since World War II.

NEW TO THIS EDITION

The third edition includes a number of changes designed to heighten student interest and increase comprehension.

• Part I has been thoroughly revised to present the basic musical elements, their relationships, and their organization in as clear a manner as possible.

• The chapter on non-Western music has been revised and reorganized and is now presented as an independent part.

• Explanations of important procedures such as sonata-allegro and fugue have been rewritten and useful diagrams added to aid understanding.

• A number of new musical analyses have been added and old ones deleted to reflect changing tastes; the choice of works analyzed is based on appeal to students and on teachability.

• Many of the musical analyses retained from earlier editions have been revised to improve their clarity. In addition, care has been taken to assure that analyses new to this edition are presented at an appropriate level for the beginning student.

• Some new biographies of composers have been added; others have been expanded or streamlined to present the most important and stimulating aspects of each composer's life and work.

• Chapters on American concert music and the new music since World War II have been revised, expanded, and updated.

• Coverage of American popular music including jazz, rock, and musical theater has been increased and updated. Of special interest is the new material on the lives and unique contributions of Louis Armstrong, Billie Holiday, and Thelonius Monk.

• Seven "Interludes" accompanied by full color plates as well as black and white photos present the historical, social, philosophical, and artistic background of each major style period. Particular emphasis is given to painting, sculpture, and architecture. The Interludes may be studied in connection with style periods, they may be assigned as supplemental material, or they may simply be omitted, depending on an instructor's own objectives for the course.

• To supplement the basic material, discographies now accompany the chapters on non-Western music and jazz, the annotated suggested listening lists at the end of each part have been expanded, and the annotated suggested reading list at the end of the book has been revised to include many recent and nontechnical books. In addition, an updated chronology of musical events, composers, cultural and political events, artists and writers is printed on the endpapers for easy reference.

• In order to enhance its visual appeal and readability, the book has an attractive new design and many new, unusual photographs.

EMPHASIS ON LISTENING

A major emphasis of the book is on listening. Music examples are representative of both the best work of each composer and specific forms or styles. For example, Bach's Fugue in G Minor illustrates fugal procedure, Mozart's Piano Concerto No. 27 illustrates the Classical concerto, Brahms's *Ein Deutsches Requiem* is an example of Romantic choral music, and Schoenberg's *Variations for Orchestra* shows the use of twelve-tone procedures. Symphonic and other orchestral music, chamber music, concerto, opera, song, piano music, and choral music are all well represented. A guide to examples by genre is included at the end of the Contents as an aid to instructors who choose to organize their courses around specific genres.

The detailed descriptions of musical works are intended to be read in conjunction with listening to the music. Divorced from the listening experience, such descriptions have little value. But when the analysis is combined with guided listening, the student becomes aware of the connection between the musical experience and the principles upon which the music is based. Listening thus becomes meaningful and pleasurable for the student, both intellectually and emotionally. Most of the pieces which are analyzed are included in the record package which supplements this book.

Musical notation is used as an aid in the listening process. It is not assumed that students can "read" music; rather, the notation is intended to give the listener some visual sense of the important musical events—particularly the major themes—as they occur.

STUDY AIDS NEW TO THIS EDITION

Several new devices have been incorporated in this edition to make the book a more useful study tool. Musical terms are now printed in boldface type and carefully defined when they first appear. New terms are also listed at the end of each chapter and included in a comprehensive glossary at the end of the text. Summaries at the end of each chapter offer a concise review of the most important material covered in the chapter. Some students may wish to read the summaries before beginning a chapter in order to get a quick overview of the major points. Review charts for each musical period have been added to reinforce the student's awareness of general distinguishing traits of the music of a particular era. Finally, there is considerably more cross-referencing than in previous editions.

SUPPLEMENTS

Three supplements have been prepared for use with the third edition. The eight-record album prepared by London Records contains many of the pieces that are analyzed in the text. In addition to concert works from each major era, examples of jazz and ethnic music are included. The *Instructor's Manual* has been streamlined for easier use and now contains an introductory section with detailed charts showing how the text material can be adapted to a one-quarter and a one-semester course. The *Student Workbook and Listening Guide* offers exercises aimed at improving listening skills and questions which test mastery of text material.

ACKNOWLEDGMENTS

I am grateful for the thoughtful criticisms and suggestions of the following reviewers, who read all or portions of the manuscript: Aldrich Adkins, Southern University; Grant Anderson, American River College; Henry Burnett, Queens College; Herbert Cecil, Weber State College; Reginald Haché, Northeastern University; Donna Dee Hardy, Point Park College; Lloyd Kaplan, Rhode Island Junior College; Lance Lehnberg; Charles L. Morey, Monroe Community College; Ammon D. Roberson, Central Missouri State University; Frederic Schoettler, Kent State University; and John Specht, Queensborough Community College. Dr. Carolyne Jordan of Salem State College revised the chapter on non-Western music. Dr. Bruce Saylor of New York University revised the chapters on American concert music and music after World War II. G. T. Sewell rewrote the Interlude essays. Deborah Polikoff assisted in the revision of Part I and in revision of the suggested listening lists. Gail Rivers updated the suggested reading list. Meredith Nightengale located the scores of new photographs that enhance this edition.

Finally, I am grateful to Kathe Golden of Addison-Wesley. Without her sensitive patience and professional expertise, this edition of the book would not have been possible.

Winston-Salem, North Carolina   R.H.
December 1978

CONTENTS

PART **IV** MUSIC OF THE BAROQUE ERA

CHAPTER 7   BAROQUE VOCAL MUSIC   109

CHAPTER 8   BAROQUE INSTRUMENTAL MUSIC   139

PART **VII** MUSIC OF THE EARLY TWENTIETH CENTURY

PART VIII MUSIC IN AMERICA

PART **IX** MUSIC OF THE LATE TWENTIETH CENTURY

INTERLUDES

A GUIDE TO MUSIC EXAMPLES BY GENRE

* Works marked with an asterisk are contained in whole or in part on the *Record Album* to accompany *Exploring Music*. Jazz and non-Western selections may be found on Record 8, Sides 1 and 2.

I

FUNDAMENTALS OF MUSIC

CHAPTER 1 | MUSICAL SOUND

WE ARE A PEOPLE SURROUNDED BY SOUNDS. THE ROAR OF AIR-planes, the rumble of automobiles, the blare of horns, the screech of sirens, and many other types of sounds constitute an ever-present aspect of the day-to-day environment in which most of us live. In addition to these random sounds, the average American is subjected to a constant flow of music. We experience music almost continuously—the phonograph as we chat, the radio while driving, Musak in the supermarket, the restaurant, and place of employment. What student lounge is without music? Indeed, from playpen to funeral parlor, we are bombarded by the sounds of music. Although we hear these sounds, we often hear them only as a vague background against which more immediate activity takes place. Most of us do not really understand or respond to such music, which is merely part of the atmosphere. To be fully alive to music, we must learn to listen with curiosity and care, with attention to the flow of musical sound. An important aid in developing skill at this kind of listening is some understanding of the nature of the materials out of which music is made.

Music, like other phenomena, is built from particular elements and described by a particular vocabulary. This vocabulary is a shortcut and convenience for anyone who wants to be an informed listener. In these first chapters, then, we will introduce the elements of music and establish the vocabulary we use to explore and discuss them.

The basic element of music is the individual musical sound itself. Any sound, musical or not, is produced by a vibrating object called a *sounding body*. A sounding body may be the string on a violin or the door of your room. When the string is plucked or the door is slammed, its vibrations set the surrounding air in motion and sound is produced.

A *musical* sound, however, is not like the random noises we experience. Rather, it is highly organized both in quality and production. In addition, it displays four different characteristics. It can be described in terms of **pitch**—the highness or lowness of the sound. It has a certain **duration**—it lasts a particular length of time. It has a quality of loudness or softness, called its **dynamic.** And it has a distinctive tonal quality that depends on what instruments are used, which is called its **tone color** or **timbre.**

Let's look at each of these aspects of sound in turn.

PITCH

If we were to pluck one of the strings on a violin, we would see it quiver, then gradually return to rest. If we could watch it in slow motion, we would observe a regular pattern of evenly timed vibrations. In the example below, A and B are fixed ends of the string and C is the point at which it is plucked:

Example 1.1

The frequency, or number of vibrations per second, determines the pitch of the sound produced. A pitch that has a steady, constant frequency is called a **tone.** A higher frequency (greater number of vibrations per second) will produce a higher pitch; a lower frequency, a lower pitch.

The frequency of vibrations can be increased by shortening the sounding body. If the distance between A and B in Example 1.1 is shortened while the tension on the string remains the same, the string will vibrate faster and the sound will have a higher pitch. The same relationship of size to sound can be seen among musical instruments. For example, the violin and the cello look alike except for their size. Because its sounding body is longer, however, the cello produces pitches lower than those of the violin.

PITCH NOTATION

Throughout history, many methods have been devised to write, or **notate,** music. The Greeks notated music with letters, the Chinese with literary script. Our modern system of notation did not reach its present form until the seventeenth century. Musical notation as we know it today is still imprecise. It continues to evolve as composers make new demands upon it.

The pitch of a sound is indicated by the position of an oval symbol (○) (♩), or (♪) called a **note** on a graphlike structure called a **staff,** consisting of five lines and four spaces.

Example 1.2

The lines and spaces of the staff represent specific pitches. The pitches are named using only the first seven letters of the alphabet—A, B, C, D, E, F, and G—this sequence being repeated over and over as one proceeds up through the range of all possible pitches. The staff location of each pitch is determined by consulting a **clef** sign at the beginning of the staff. The G or **treble clef** (𝄞) and the F or **bass clef** (𝄢) are the most commonly used in our notation system.

The G clef tells us which line has been chosen to represent the pitch G that is just above the midpoint of the piano range. Usually the G clef curves around the second line of the staff.

 *Example 1.3*

Counting up and down from G, we can then name the pitches represented by the other lines and spaces of the staff:

 *Example 1.4*

The two dots of the F clef sit on either side of the fourth line of the staff, locating the pitch F that is just below the midpoint of the piano range.

Example 1.5

If we count up and down from F, the pitches represented by the lines and spaces of the F clef are:

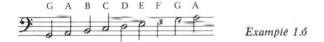 *Example 1.6*

When a pitch is too high or too low to be notated on the staff itself, extra lines called **ledger lines** are added:

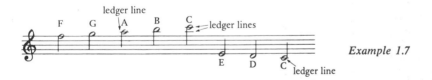 *Example 1.7*

The pitch domains of the treble and bass staffs overlap at a point called **middle C.** This pitch is notated by adding a single ledger line to either staff:

 *Example 1.8*

The treble and bass clefs are used together, as shown in Example 1.8, to notate piano music. Ordinarily, the notes written in the bass clef are played by the left hand and the notes in the treble clef by the right. In instrumental music the treble clef is used for the violin, the flute, and other instruments that play in the higher ranges. Music for instruments that sound in the lower ranges, such as the tuba or double bass, is written in the bass clef.

INTERVALS

The distance between two notes on the staff is called an **interval.** To determine the name of an interval, think of the line or space on which one of the pitches falls as "first," and then count up (or down) along lines and spaces until you come to the line or space for the other pitch. For example, the interval from C to D is called a *second.* The interval from C to E is a *third,* and so on.

Example 1.9

In Example 1.9, the *seventh* reaches from C to B. An eight-note interval—called an **octave**—would reach from C to the next C.

Example 1.10

This is easiest to visualize on the piano keyboard, with its repeated pattern of black and white keys. Notice that all the keys with the same letter name have the same position in the black-white pattern:

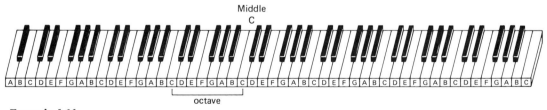

Example 1.11

Two tones that are one octave apart sound very similar. Played simultaneously on a single instrument, they sound almost like a single tone. This is because the higher tone is vibrating at exactly twice the frequency of the lower one.

The smallest difference between pitches that we can notate by traditional means is the **half step** or **semitone.** This is the smallest pitch difference used in most Western music. On the piano keyboard, all adjacent keys are one half step apart. Thus the pitch difference between any white key and a neighboring black key is always a half step. Also, since the white keys B and C are directly adjacent, without an intervening black key, they are a half step apart. The same is true of E and F. (See the keyboard diagram in Example 1.12.)

A **whole step,** or **whole tone,** is the equivalent of two consecutive half steps (again, see Example 1.12).

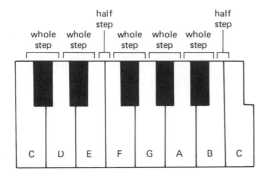

Example 1.12

ACCIDENTALS

To **sharp** a note is to raise it by one half step. To **flat** a note is to lower it by one half step.

The note that falls between C and D is one half step above C, and also one half step below D. It can be called either C-sharp (C♯) or D-flat (D♭). On the piano, all the black keys are the sharps and flats of their neighboring white keys.

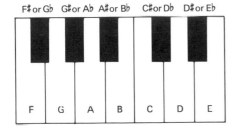

Example 1.13

To notate flats and sharps, we simply place a ♭ or a ♯ before a note on the staff.

In the course of a composition, a particular note might be sharped or flatted almost continuously. To indicate that certain notes are to be sharped (or flatted) throughout a composition, the composer may simply place sharp signs (or flat signs) on the appropriate lines and spaces at the beginning of the music. This notational device, called the key signature, is common in much of the music you will encounter in this book.

To specify that a note is to be played in its *ordinary* form, having previously been sharped or flatted, a composer will place a **natural** (♮) before the note.

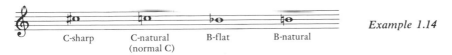

| C-sharp | C-natural (normal C) | B-flat | B-natural |

Example 1.14

SCALES

A **scale** is a progression of ascending or descending pitches. Although there are exceptions, most Western scales proceed in a pattern of whole steps, half steps, or some combination of the two. In its basic form, a scale moves from a starting note to the same note one octave away.

Most melodies are built around particular scales. There are many different scales; the examples below represent only a few of them.

The **chromatic scale** is created simply by moving up or down by half steps. It contains all twelve tones within the interval of an octave:

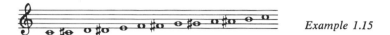

Example 1.15

The **whole-tone scale** moves by whole steps:

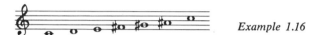

Example 1.16

The **major scale** combines both whole and half steps in a specific sequence. It is easiest to hear by playing the white keys of the piano from C to C:

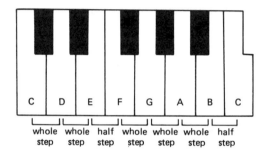

Example 1.17

Notice that the half steps fall between the third and fourth and between the seventh and eighth tones of the scale.

Example 1.18

The **minor scale** has its own structure and character. The third tone is a half step rather than a whole step above the second, which imparts the distinctive minor quality. The upper part of the scale assumes one of *several* forms, depending upon the musical context. Usually there is a half step between tones five and six, followed by whole steps between tones six and seven and between tones seven and eight. But frequently the seventh tone is raised to be just a half step below the eighth, in which case there is a one-and-a-half-step interval between tones six and seven.

Example 1.19

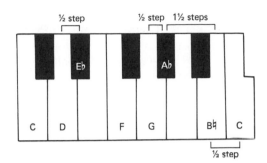

Example 1.20

Any of the scales we have described can start from any one of the twelve tones pictured on the keyboard. Each scale is recognizable by its particular design of whole and half steps. Here are the four scales beginning on C.

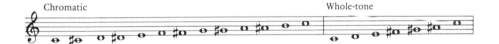

Example 1.21

Since each of these scale types has its own distinctive sound and quality, the choice of scale becomes an important aspect of any piece of music. Frequently the minor scale or mode is thought to be expressive of moods of sadness, while the major is more often used for cheerful or lighthearted emotional states. However, these are rather broad generalizations; many pieces in minor, because of other factors such as tempo, can also be relatively gay or lively; similarly, pieces in major can be rather weighty. Throughout this text we will hear many examples of how major and minor modes can be manipulated to create a great variety of moods, contrasts of mood, and other expressive effects.

The major-minor scale system is the basis for most of the music that we hear. The whole-tone scale became important in the late nineteenth and early twentieth centuries, particularly in the music of Claude Debussy (Chapter 18), and the chromatic scale is important in the development of twentieth-century music.

DURATION

Earlier, we referred to duration as the length of time a tone lasts. As long as a sounding body vibrates, the duration of the tone continues.

NOTATION OF DURATION

A system of pitch notation was developed much earlier than a system for indicating duration. We still find duration a difficult element to denote accurately.

Changes in present-day notation are still being made to accommodate the needs of some modern music.

Nevertheless, the principle underlying the basic notation of duration is fairly simple. A whole note (○) lasts twice as long as a half note (♩). A half note lasts twice as long as a quarter note (♩), and so on.

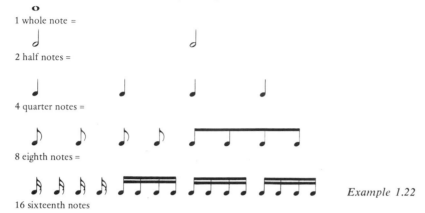

1 whole note =

2 half notes =

4 quarter notes =

8 eighth notes =

16 sixteenth notes

Example 1.22

Notice that eighth notes—which look like quarter notes with single flags attached—may be written separately or may be grouped together by a single connecting beam. Similarly, sixteenth notes may be separate (with double flags) or connected (with a double connecting beam).

Further subdivisions are possible, such as thirty-second (♪) and sixty-fourth (♪) notes. Sometimes this notation is modified. For instance, the eighth note represents half the value of the quarter note. But there is no note representing a third of its value. For this purpose a group of three eighth notes is marked with a "3." Known as the **triplet**, this grouping divides the quarter note into three equal parts.

Example 1.23

Two notes may be connected with a **tie** (♩‿♩). The second note is not articulated but is merely the continuation of the first. The two tied quarter notes (♩‿♩) sound exactly the same as a single half note (♩). A **dot** placed after a note will also serve to increase the duration of a note. Specifically, a dot extends the length of the note by half its original value.

Example 1.24

The duration of silence is as important as the duration of sound. Silences are denoted by **rests.** Rests have the same durational values as their corresponding notes.

whole   half   quarter   eighth   sixteenth

Example 1.25

DYNAMICS

Dynamics—varying degrees of loudness—depend on the relative amplitude of a vibration. (Amplitude refers to the width of a vibration.) The harder a string is plucked, the wider its vibrations, and the louder the resulting sound. Consider again the violin string of Example 1.1.

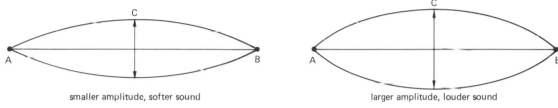

smaller amplitude, softer sound   larger amplitude, louder sound

Example 1.26

Dynamics are usually notated less precisely than pitch or duration. Indeed, long stretches of a composition may have no dynamic markings at all. The explanation for this is simple: dynamic levels are relative, and there is no absolute standard for degrees of loudness and softness. The performer therefore has some latitude in deciding how a specific dynamic is to be executed. The quality of the resulting sound is largely dependent on the performer's judgment, taste, and degree of control over the instrument.

Like most musical terms, dynamics are traditionally marked in Italian:

pianissimo	(pp)	Very soft	*mezzo forte*	(mf)	Moderately loud
piano	(p)	Soft	*forte*	(f)	Loud
mezzo piano	(mp)	Moderately soft	*fortissimo*	(ff)	Very loud

To express a gradual change from one dynamic level to another the following signs and terms are used.

crescendo		gradually louder
decrescendo or diminuendo		gradually softer
crescendo and decrescendo		gradually louder and softer

TONE COLOR

Each type of musical instrument has its own distinct kind of sound. A melody played on the oboe sounds different from the same melody played on the trumpet because the sound quality of the trumpet is clearly different from that of the oboe. As we mentioned earlier, the distinctive sound quality of an instrument is called tone color or timbre (pronounced tambr′). The elements that contribute to the tone color of an instrument are various and include the nature of the material out of which the instrument is constructed and the method by which it is made to sound (such as a plucked instrument as opposed to one that is blown into).

Instruments differ from each other in regard to tone color on several levels. The most obvious difference is between families of instruments. As a group, brass instruments (trumpet, French horn, trombone, and tuba) sound quite unlike the woodwinds (flute, oboe, clarinet, and bassoon), and both these instrument groups contrast sharply in sound with the string family (violin, viola, cello, and string bass). Within each instrument family there is a certain similarity of sound which distinguishes that family as a whole.

While the difference between the tone color of one instrument family and that of another is fairly obvious, there is a more subtle contrast in timbre among instruments in a single family. For instance, the flute and the oboe, both of which are woodwinds, sound quite distinct from each other; similarly, the violin and cello each sound unique. On a still more subtle level, a considerable variety of tone colors can be produced on a single instrument. For example, the flute can be manipulated to produce shades of tone color ranging from "bright" to "velvety" and from "piercing" to "warm."

Nineteenth-century composers were especially intrigued by the uses of tone color. It was during the Romantic era that color came to be regarded for the first time as an element as important as melody, harmony, and rhythm. Modern composers share this view and continue to explore the expressive possibilities of tone color, using not only conventional instruments but electronic media and nonmusical sounds as well.

SUMMARY

In the preceding pages we have described the qualities of musical sound—those properties that distinguish musical sounds from simple, random noises. Musical sounds have pitch, the quality of being high or low; they exist in durations of varying lengths; they can be produced at varying levels of intensity, or volume; and they are imbued with distinctive tone colors. The desired pitch, duration, and intensity of musical sound can be expressed, though not always with precision, in a system of written notation.

Thus far we have been dealing with the raw material of music, not music itself. Individual sounds achieve musical significance only when one tone relates to another and groups of tones relate to other groups, organized in the time flow they create. The next two chapters will consider musical relationships and musical organization.

NEW TERMS

pitch	ledger lines	scale
duration	middle C	chromatic scale
dynamic(s)	interval	whole-tone scale
tone color (timbre)	octave	major scale
tone	half step (semitone)	minor scale
notate	whole step (whole tone)	triplet
note	sharp	tie
staff	flat	dot (dotted note)
clef (treble and bass)	natural	rest

CHAPTER 2 | MUSICAL RELATIONSHIPS

IN CHAPTER 1 WE CONSIDERED THE CHARACTERISTICS OF INDI-vidual musical sounds. This chapter deals with the various kinds of relationships among musical sounds and the resulting musical elements known as melody, harmony, tonality, and rhythm.

MELODIC RELATIONSHIPS

When we listen to music, we are usually drawn first to a melody. We tend to follow the melodic flow with the greatest interest and ease, and, in general, it is the melody that lingers with us. When we think of a piece of music, we tend to recall the melody or melodies that for us represent the piece.

We can define a melodic line or **melody** as a series of pitches and time values that sound one after another. Melody gives music a sense of movement up and down through space as it moves forward in time. Different melodies follow different patterns of movement. For example, the following melodic line gives the strong impression of moving upward.

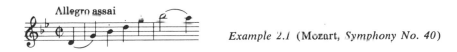

Example 2.1 (Mozart, *Symphony No. 40*)

On the other hand, a melody—even one with some upward skips—can also give a sense of moving downward:

Example 2.2 (Dvořák, *New World Symphony*)

In comparison, the following melody seems anchored in the middle. Its movement is evenly distributed around a particular tone or tones:

And the rough pla - ces   plain

Example 2.3 (Handel, *Messiah*)

Melodic movement can be smooth and even, as the preceding examples show. It can also be jerky and angular, leaping over a wide span of pitches:

Example 2.4 (Hindemith, *Kleine Kammermusik*)

Thus far we have looked at some ways pitches can be arranged to form a melodic line. But a melody consists of two inseparable, interacting elements: a succession of *pitches* and a succession of *time values* (durations). The "highs and lows" of pitch and the "longs and shorts" of duration combine to give a melody its particular shape and form, its "personality." If we change either of these ingredients, we change the melody.

For instance, this sequence of pitches

Example 2.5

combined with this sequence of time values

Example 2.6

produces the beginning of the familiar Christmas carol "Joy to the World."

Joy   to the world, the Lord is   come!

Example 2.7

If we reverse its sequence of pitches, we get quite a different melody:

Example 2.8

and if we rearrange the same pitches in another way, we get still another melody:

Example 2.9

Notice that both changes have involved only the sequence of pitches; the time values have remained the same. If we change these time values, the result will be a melody of still a different character.

The character of melody is an extremely important aspect of any piece of music. In a long work of music some melodies assume a greater importance than others. Melodies that contain central musical ideas are called **themes.** In the course of a musical composition important themes may be stated and restated in many different forms. Later in this text we will see how themes are developed in a variety of musical works.

HARMONIC RELATIONSHIPS

While a piece of music consisting of a single melodic line can be complete in and of itself (see Gregorian chant, p. 77), most Western music depends heavily on harmony to help give it structure and to enhance its expressiveness. We speak of melody as the horizontal aspect of music since it consists of pitches sounding one after another, in a linear fashion. Harmony, on the other hand, involves the vertical aspect of music, the tones that sound together. A **harmony** is a composite sound made up of two or more tones of different pitch that sound simultaneously. The smallest harmonic unit is one consisting of two tones. A harmony of three or more tones is called a **chord.**

The harmonic unit which is basic to most of the music we hear is the **triad,** a combination of three tones built on the interval of the third. For example, starting with C and adding above it two tones in a series of thirds, we produce the triad C E G:

Example 2.10

The bottom tone of this arrangement is called the **root;** the tone E is a third above the root and the tone G is a third above E. A triad may be built on any tone following this procedure of building by thirds:

Example 2.11

Triadic harmony provided the basic harmonic vocabulary for composers for hundreds of years. Indeed, as we shall see later in this book, only in the twentieth century have composers developed different methods of chord construction.

The tones that make up a harmony are heard not only individually; they also blend together into a composite sound that has its own distinctive qualities.

Harmonies can appear in "solid" form (Example 2.12) or in "broken" form, with the notes played in rapid succession (Example 2.13).

Example 2.12   *Example 2.13*

A broken chord is called an **arpeggio.** Chords on the harp are often played in broken form.

As a musical element harmony functions in a variety of ways. Harmonies are often used to support and amplify melodic lines. A particularly distinctive series of harmonies, or *harmonic progression,* often becomes an important element in its own right. Often harmonic progressions are crucial in defining large segments of musical time. The music of Claude Debussy, which we will study in Chapter 18, offers numerous examples of distinctive use of chord progressions. In addition, the harmonic qualities of consonance and dissonance contribute to the energy and interest of a piece of music.

CONSONANCE AND DISSONANCE

One important quality of a given harmony is its degree of **consonance** or **dissonance.** A consonant harmony imparts a sense of stability, simplicity, and repose. To hear this, listen as the following chord is played on the piano:

Example 2.14

In contrast, a dissonant harmony creates a feeling of complexity, instability, and the necessity of movement:

Example 2.15

Dissonance is important in creating a feeling of tension in the musical flow. Without points of tension the music would quickly become boring and lifeless. Dissonance usually occurs as a transient tension in a harmonic progression. This tension is immediately relieved by the resolution of the dissonant harmony into a consonant harmony:

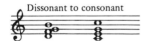

Example 2.16

Thus, the movement from dissonance to consonance contributes to the balance between movement and rest that makes the music vital and coherent.

The general character of some pieces is consonance, even though some dissonance may be employed. Haydn's *String Quartet in C,* Opus 33, No. 3 is a good example. Other works are predominantly dissonant, such as Schoenberg's *Variations for Orchestra,* Opus 31. As we move through music history from century to century, we find that the relationship of consonance and dissonance begins to change, with a gradual increase in the importance or prevalence of dissonance as we approach the twentieth century. Indeed, most of the serious concert music written today is predominantly dissonant.

TONAL RELATIONSHIPS

One of the striking characteristics of Western music is its reliance on **tonality** as an organizational element. Tonal music is characterized by its affirmation of a central tone called the **tonic** and the chord built on that tone, called the **tonic chord.** The tonic acts as a center of gravity, a kind of musical home base. It is the point of rest from which the music departs and to which it returns, creating a sense of convincing conclusion.

Although there are many ways of establishing a tonal center and creating tonality, the most familiar to concertgoers is embodied in the major-minor scale system. A composition built around the C major scale, for example, is in the tonality, or **key,** of C major. The different tones, or **degrees,** of a scale have different weights or values. The most important is the first, called the tonic. In the scale of C major, the tonic is C and the tonic chord is C major. A composition in C major will not seem finished unless the tonic, the C major chord, is arrived at to form the close of the piece.

Other tones in the scale, and other chords, have a particularly strong relationship to the tonic. In a melodic sense the seventh degree of the scale is called the **leading tone.** In the key of C major, the leading tone is B. Because of its position in the scale, a half step below the tonic, it has a strong "pull" into the tonic—it *leads* to the tonic, C. If this scale is played with the final C left out:

Example 2.17

the listener is left with an unsettled feeling. The ear *expects* to hear the last C after the leading tone. If the C is not sounded, no sense of finality, of arrival, is achieved. Once the C is supplied, however,

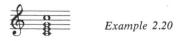

Example 2.18

"home base" has been reached and there is a convincing sense of conclusion.

While the leading tone is the strongest *melodic* tone supporting the tonic in a melody, the **dominant chord** performs the same function in the realm of *harmony.*

The dominant chord is based upon the fifth degree of the scale. In the key of C major, the dominant chord is:

Example 2.19

Notice that it contains the leading tone (B) and the dominant tone (G). The dominant chord strongly supports and implies movement to the tonic chord—which is, in C major:

Example 2.20

If we play a series of chords in C major and stop on the dominant chord, the feeling will be similar to that experienced when we stopped on the leading tone in our C scale—a feeling of suspense and lack of conclusion:

Example 2.21

Dominant

However, when the tonic chord is supplied, the feeling changes to one of rest and finality:

Example 2.22

Dominant chord | Tonic chord

This chord progression which brings the music to the point of rest is called a **cadence.** The strongest cadence involves the progression from the dominant chord to the tonic.

MODULATION

In addition to the relationships among tones and chords *within* a key, tonality also refers to the relationship *among* keys. A piece of music of any appreciable length seldom stays in one key. When we say that a piece of music is "in C major," we actually mean that the piece *begins* and *ends* in that key. Within the piece different keys are introduced, thereby providing an important aspect of variety. The process of shifting from one key to another is known as **modulation.** The diagram below illustrates one of the most frequent modulations found in Western music, that growing out of the tonic-dominant relationship.

Section A	*Section B*	*Return of Section A*
C major (tonic key)	G major (key of the dominant)	C major

All the elements discussed thus far come together and interact to create the sense of movement in time. Everyone has had the experience of being so caught up in an enjoyable activity that time seems to fly by. Similarly, the same amount of time spent doing something we dislike can seem interminable. Thus one way we experience time is on the basis of the events that occur during the course of an hour or a day. Without these events there would be less sense of the passage of time. Musical time is similar to this kind of "personal" time. It is perceived and experienced on the basis of musical events that occur. If we play a single tone over and over again for two minutes, it may seem as though a long period of time has elapsed. However, if we fill that two minutes with a cheerful and interesting melody, the same length of time will seem quite short. Although the length of time is the same, the experiences differ because the quality and character of the time are structured differently by the musical events that take place.

Like "personal" time, the passage of musical time is created by change. One tone leading to another in a melody, the progression from one harmony to another, the movement from one key to another—these and many other musical "incidents" work together to create the sense of musical time. The element that encompasses all aspects of musical time is called **rhythm.** Let's look now at some of the different aspects of rhythm and how they relate to one another.

RHYTHMIC RELATIONSHIPS

BEAT

If you were asked to clap along with the song "Scarborough Fair," you might clap with this steady pattern ($\times$ = clap):

Are you going to Scar - bor-ough Fair?   *Example 2.23*

A sequence of pulses like this one underlies most Western music. The steady pulses that mark off equal lengths of time (the points marked by $\times$'s) are called **beats.** Beats constitute the most basic unit of musical time; instead of measuring the length of individual tones in seconds, fractions of seconds and the like, we use the beat as a basic yardstick. A tone is judged as lasting one beat, several beats, or a fraction of a beat.

Once we have picked out the beat of a piece of music, we become accustomed to its regular, even flow, and we expect it to continue. Of course, the beat need not always be regular. It can be speeded up or slowed down. If the change is gradual, we can adjust to it easily. But if the change is sudden or radical, we will become confused and unsettled. Our expectation will be upset until we can adjust to the new beat.

MEASURE, METER, AND RHYTHMIC VARIATION

Let's return to "Scarborough Fair." You might also choose to clap along to it in this pattern:

Are you going to Scar - bor-ough Fair?   *Example 2.24*

Because of their longer duration, the clapped notes tend to stand out in the listener's mind. These notes are prominent also because they occur at evenly spaced intervals:

1 2 3 1 2 3 1 2 3 1 2 3   *Example 2.25*

This grouping of beats into equal units (here, units of three beats each) is called **meter** and the units themselves are called **measures.** Music which is organized on the basis of equal measures is usually referred to as **metrical.**

Being a more general term than meter, rhythm has to do with the unequal and diverse aspects of musical time. In the melody above, the *meter* is regular (three beats to a measure), but the *rhythm* involves the *unequal* note values that lend diversity to the melody, opposing the regularity of the pulsation of the beats and the regularity of the melody.

Most music maintains an almost equal balance between meter and rhythmic variation, but, some kinds of music emphasize one aspect over the other. Marches and dance music, for example, tend to be heavily metrical. In other styles—in Debussy's *Prélude à l'après-midi d'un faune,* for example—the meter is almost obscured.

Meter and rhythmic variation are the two fundamental forces continually at work in musical time. Meter imposes regularity and equality. It controls, it regulates, and it provides the basic grouping within which the listener organizes sound. Rhythmic variation opposes meter in the sense that it lends diversity and inequality to a piece of music. These two forces, however, are interdependent, with each providing the basis for the existence of the other.

NOTATING METER

A measure is usually composed of two, three, or four beats. "Scarborough Fair" has three beats per measure, or a *triple meter.* Two-beat measures are called *duple meter;* four-beat measures, *quadruple meter.* "Yankee Doodle" has a duple meter, and the folk song "This Land is Your Land," a quadruple meter.

Composers use two notational devices to indicate a particular meter, the barline and the time signature. The **barline** (a vertical line from the top to the bottom of the staff) marks the end of one measure and the beginning of the next. The **time signature,** appearing at the beginning of a section of music, is a symbol consisting of two numbers, written one above the other. The top number indicates the number of beats per measure; the bottom number indicates the note value representing one beat:

3 = 3 beats per measure   3 = 3 beats per measure
4 = ♩ (quarter note) = 1 beat   2 = 𝅗𝅥 (half note) = 1 beat

As we have notated it, "Scarborough Fair" is in ¾ time. If we write instead:

   *Example 2.26*

the durational rhythm is exactly the same. That is, the notes have the same values in relation to each other as they had in the earlier version. The only difference here is that the eighth note is the unit by which the beat is measured.

The *simple* meters are represented by such time signatures as ¼, 3/2, 2/2, 2/4, and ¾. In addition, another symbol, c, is sometimes used to represent ¼ meter, and the same symbol with a line through it (¢) to represent 2/2 meter.

In *compound* meters, five, six, seven, or more beats may make up a measure. The compound duple meters are $\frac{6}{4}$ and $\frac{6}{8}$; the compound triple meters are $\frac{9}{4}$ and $\frac{9}{8}$; and the compound quadruple meters are $\frac{12}{4}$, $\frac{12}{8}$, and $\frac{12}{16}$. When the number of beats cannot be divided by either 2 or 3 (as in $\frac{5}{4}$ or $\frac{7}{4}$), the meter is said to be irregular. Such meters are usually felt as combinations of regular meters ($\frac{5}{4} = \frac{2}{4} + \frac{3}{4}$, for example). A good example of a composition in an irregular meter is Dave Brubeck's jazz piece "Take Five," written in $\frac{5}{4}$ time.

SYNCOPATION

Ordinarily the first beat of a measure is stressed or **accented.** A piece in triple meter, for example, has a one-two-three character:

3	My	coun-	try,	'tis		of thee
4	ONE	two	three	ONE	two	three

In some pieces, however, the pulse of the meter is deliberately disturbed so that the stress does not occur where the listener expects it. When this happens the rhythm is said to be **syncopated.** This effect can be achieved in several ways. One way is to carry over a tone from one measure to the next so that the initial strong beat is not sounded:

Example 2.27

In the above example the syncopations occur at each point marked ×, where the stress occurs *before* it is expected. In the following example, the stress expected on the first beat of the measure is *delayed* at the points marked by ×, thus creating a different type of syncopation.

Example 2.28

Syncopation contributes importantly to rhythmic interest in music by creating the pleasurable element of surprise and arousing curiosity as to how the music will unfold. Syncopation is essential to African rhythms and American ragtime music. It also has been used for hundreds of years in Western concert music.

LEVELS OF TIME

We have pointed out that rhythm and meter exist simultaneously on different levels. On the most fundamental level is the beat. A succession of even beats creates a flow of equal lengths of time. But, as we have seen, some beats are more prominent than others. This regularly occurring difference in emphasis produces a second level of organization, the measure—a grouping of equal numbers of beats.

On a third level are larger segments of musical time consisting of several measures. These are called **phrases.** "Scarborough Fair" consists of four clearly delineated phrases:

Example 2.29

Notice that in this example each phrase ends with a point of rest, a pause before the next phrase begins. This pause, called a *melodic cadence,* is a common (but not universal) device in phrasing.

After sounds have been grouped and regrouped into phrases, we enter the realm of musical form. Here we are dealing with long stretches of musical time. We will explore form in music in the next chapter.

TEMPO

The length of the beat determines the speed, or **tempo,** at which a piece of music moves. If the beat is short, the tempo is fast. If the beat is relatively long, the tempo is slow. If the length of the beat falls somewhere in between these two extremes, the tempo is moderate.

Composers have traditionally marked their desired tempi (the plural of tempo) in Italian, although some have used their native language. The tempi most commonly encountered are the following, arranged in order of increasing speed.

Very slow:	*Largo* (broad)
	Grave (grave, solemn)
Slow:	*Lento*
	Adagio (leisurely; literally, at ease)
Moderate:	*Andante* (at a walking pace)
	Moderato
Fast:	*Allegretto*
	Allegro (faster than allegretto; literally, cheerful)
Very fast:	*Vivace* (vivacious)
	Presto (very quick)
	Prestissimo (as fast as possible)

These terms can be modified by adding such words as *molto* (very), *meno* (less), *poco* (a little), and *non troppo* (not too much). Thus, *molto largo* is very, very slow; *meno allegro* is less lively; *poco adagio* is just somewhat slow; and *allegro ma non troppo* is fast, but not too fast.

Once it is given, the tempo can be increased or slowed down. Gradual increases are indicated by the word *accelerando* (accelerating, getting faster), and gradual decreases by *ritardando* (slowing down, holding back). To return to the original rate of speed after such a change, the composer marks the music *a tempo.*

Tempo can also be disturbed in other ways. The word *rubato* indicates that the performer need not stay within the strict confines of the meter. Although the overall metrical pattern remains steady, the performer can lag behind or forge ahead of the beat at will. A *fermata* (⌢) tells the performer to hold a note longer than its normal time value. This usually occurs at very important moments in the music.

Since the invention of the metronome around 1816, composers have been able to indicate tempi more exactly than is possible by the use of words such as fast, slow etc. A **metronome** is a small machine that ticks the desired number of beats per minute. Thus, for example, ♩ = 80 indicates that a piece is to be played at the rate of 80 quarter notes per minute.

Melody, harmony, tonality, and rhythm constitute the basic ingredients out of which a piece of music is made. They are the building blocks which make possible the organization of a coherent piece of music. In the next chapter we will explore the topic of musical organization.

SUMMARY

Melody is the element of music we tend to follow with the greatest ease. The two components of melody are its pitch line and its durational pattern. Moving in a linear fashion through space and forward in time, melody represents the horizontal aspect of music.

Harmony is an expressive and structural element, representing the vertical aspect of music. The tones of a harmony are heard not only individually, but as a composite sound. The smallest harmony consists of two tones; chords are harmonies of three or more tones. Harmonies are usually described as consonant (in repose) or dissonant (in a state of tension).

Tonal music is characterized by the affirmation of a central tone, the tonic, which is the first degree of the scale. The principle of tonality involves relationships among tones and chords *within* a key and also relationships *among* keys. Modulations, or shifts from one key to another, are usually employed in larger works of music as one means of providing musical interest and variety.

Rhythm encompasses all aspects of musical time. It includes, but is not confined to, meter—the grouping of beats into regular units. Meter imposes equality and regularity by providing the basic groupings within which the listener organizes sound. Rhythmic variation lends diversity and inequality.

NEW TERMS

melody	tonality	beat
theme	tonic	meter (metrical)
harmony	tonic chord	measure
chord	degree	barline
triad	key	time signature
root	leading tone	accent
arpeggio	dominant chord	syncopation
harmonic progression	cadence	phrase
consonance	modulation	tempo
dissonance	rhythm	metronome

CHAPTER 3 | MUSICAL ORGANIZATION

WE HAVE SEEN THAT COMBINATIONS OF INDIVIDUAL SOUNDS PRO-
duce the elements of music: rhythm, melody, harmony, and tonality. In this chapter we will explore the ways these elements are organized to create musical texture, form, and style.

MUSICAL TEXTURE

Like cloth, music is woven of horizontal and vertical strands. We think of melody
as moving horizontally, because each tone follows the next along the flow of time.
We describe harmony as vertical, because it is based on chords of simultaneously
sounding tones.

Musical **texture** is created by the ways these vertical and horizontal strands
are interwoven. There are three basic musical textures: *monophony, polyphony,*
and *homophony.*

MONOPHONY

Monophonic music (monophony literally means "one sound") consists of a single melodic line with no accompaniment. If you sing or hum by yourself, you are

Example 3.1 Monophony, single voice

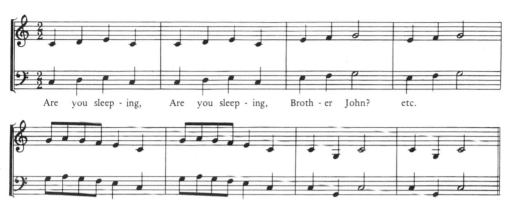

Example 3.2 Monophony, two voices an octave apart

creating monophonic music. Similarly, when many voices sing exactly the same notes at the same time (in unison) or the same notes an octave apart, the texture is also monophonic.

POLYPHONY

Music consisting of two or more "independent" melodic lines that are roughly equal in their melodic and rhythmic interest has a texture known as **polyphony** ("many sounds").

Example 3.3 Polyphony, two melodic lines

As in Example 3.2, both voices in Example 3.3 sing the same melody. But because the second voice in Example 3.3 begins singing later than the first, we hear two *independent* lines of music. It can be said that the second voice *imitates* the first—it sings exactly the same melody immediately after the first voice. Music that uses this device is known as **imitative polyphony.** A good example of the use of imitative polyphony is J. S. Bach's Fugue in G Minor ("The Little"), discussed on pp. 144–145.

Independence and equality of voices are the defining characteristics of polyphony. A **voice** is a single line of music; independence is its ability to compete with other melodic strands for the attention of the listener.

In polyphonic music we are interested in the relationship of the independent, simultaneous melodies. Our attention will shift from one melodic line to another, depending on which is most important at any given moment. The melodic lines thus enhance and enrich each other, contributing to the expressiveness of the overall sound. The interplay of melodies which characterizes polyphonic music is known as **counterpoint,** and polyphonic music is also termed **contrapuntal.** In this text we will use the three terms interchangeably.

HOMOPHONY

Homophony is the third basic type of musical texture. In homophonic music a single melodic line predominates, while the other voices provide harmonic accompaniment. The listener's attention is focused on the principal melody; the harmonic background lends it color and intensity. A singer accompanying herself on the guitar is a simple example of homophonic texture. Hymns, such as the portion of one by J. S. Bach shown in Example 3.4, are also usually homophonic in texture.

Example 3.4

In the example above, the soprano voice carries the main melodic line, while the rest of the chorus provides harmonic support.

TEXTURAL VARIETY

Actually, much music is woven of both polyphonic and homophonic textures, and frequently the texture of a piece of music alternates between the two. An essentially homophonic stretch, for example, may be followed by a polyphonic section. But even in these stretches, the distinction may not be clear-cut. One voice may dominate the polyphonic section, or, in a homophonic section, the accompaniment may assume enough interest to compete with the main melodic line. A good illustration of textural variety is the choral movement "And the glory of the Lord" from Handel's *Messiah,* analyzed on pp. 121–122.

MUSICAL FORM

Musical **form** involves the overall structuring and organization of the flow of musical time. In any piece of music, sustaining the listener's interest depends on the presence and relationship of two essential factors: unity and variety. Unity satisfies the listener's need for coherence, sameness, and familiarity. Variety sustains interest and appeals to the human enjoyment of the new, different, and unexpected. Musical variety is the result of change; musical unity is achieved by repetition. From the balance between unity and variety—repetition and change— are derived the distinguishing characteristics of the many different types of musical form.

The most obvious type of musical change is inherent in the contrast between two different musical ideas. Proceeding from one melody to a different one, or from one key to another, or from one dynamic level to another—all can contribute to change and thus to musical variety.

The most obvious form of repetition is the immediate restatement of the same musical idea in the same way, without any change.

Actually, both change and repetition vary greatly in the ways they are applied, but both are present in all types of musical form. Let us look at some common musical forms.

BINARY FORM

Binary form consists of two contrasting musical sections, A and B. Each section is usually repeated, resulting in the pattern AABB. The A section begins in the tonic key and modulates to the dominant. The B section begins in the dominant and modulates back to the tonic. In this structure, variety results from the melodic contrasts between A and B and the modulation to a new key. Unity is ensured by the return to and ending in the key in which the piece began. This form is subject to various refinements, but the basic melodic contrast and return to the original key are frequent principles of organization. The second and fourth movements of J. S. Bach's third orchestral suite in D Major (p. 147) both employ binary form.

TERNARY FORM

Ternary form also utilizes the principles of contrasting thematic material and return to the original key. However, it includes the added unifying element of returning to the original thematic material as well as the original key after the contrast. Ternary form consists of three sections: ABA. In practice, the first section is usually repeated, resulting in the pattern AABA. The final A section is a repetition of the first. In binary form, A ends in the dominant; in ternary form, by contrast, it ends in the tonic key in which it began. Then, all of the B section is in a contrasting key. With its contrasting melodic material *and* key, B supplies the element of variety. Finally, the return or *reappearance* of A in the tonic provides the unifying component. An example of a piece in ternary form which we will study later is the third movement of Wolfgang Mozart's Symphony No. 40 (pp. 165–172).

ALTERNATING FORMS

Ternary form (ABA) is the simplest example of the principle of **alternation.** Music built on this principle consists of a main section (A) alternating with contrasting sections (B,C,D, etc.):

ABA	three-part form
ABACA	five-part form
ABACABA	seven-part form

The contrasting sections and their different keys provide the element of variety, while the reappearing A section with its "home key" ensures unity. Section A may appear in a shortened or modified form (particularly in longer pieces), but it nevertheless has the unifying effect that comes from the return and recognition of familiar material.

The Baroque *aria,* the Classical *minuet and trio,* and the *rondo,* each of which we shall encounter in subsequent chapters, are forms that employ this principle of alternation.

VARIATION FORMS AND DEVELOPMENT

While alternation is based upon the contrasts among *different* musical materials, other formal procedures are based on the statement of a *single* idea and its subsequent change. *Variation* and *development* are the two principal homophonic techniques used in this type of formal structure. **Development** technique is best seen in sonata-allegro form, which we will study in detail in Chapter 9. **Variation** is most clearly demonstrated in the procedure known as **theme and variations.** A theme is stated and then is repeated several times, each time changed or varied in some particular way:

Statement	Variation[1]	Variation[2]	Variation[3]	
Theme (A)	A^1	A^2	A^3	etc.

In this procedure the restatement of the same basic thematic material is the unifying factor; the successive changes provide constant variety. The third movement of Haydn's String Quartet, Opus 33, No. 3 (p. 177) is a theme and variations.

The techniques and devices by which thematic material may be varied are numerous, and we will study them in connection with specific works. Whichever devices are employed, each variation usually utilizes the *entire theme.*

In addition to the principles of alternation, variation, and development, there are purely polyphonic techniques such as the procedures known as *canon, fugue,* and *ground bass.* In a canon a melody is strictly imitated in its entirety by another voice or voices. A round like "Brother John," Example 3.3, is a simple type of canon. We will study ground bass and fugue in connection with the music of the Baroque era (1600–1750).

Musical form and musical texture are the materials with which music is made. The specific way in which these materials are combined in any musical piece determines the style of that work.

MUSICAL STYLE

In any discussion of art the word "style" will appear in many contexts and with seemingly endless applications. Broadly defined, **style** is a manner of expression characteristic of an individual, a historical period, an artistic "school," or some other identifiable group. In speaking of musical style, we are referring to the methods of treating the elements of melody, harmony, rhythm, tone color, tonality, form, and texture.

Even in music, the term is applied in numerous ways. We speak of the style of Beethoven's Ninth Symphony as compared with that of his Second Symphony; or the style of Debussy as compared with that of Ravel; or operatic style as distinguished from oratorio style. We also speak of instrumental style, vocal style, keyboard style, German style, Italian style, or the style of Western music as contrasted with Oriental music.

In a larger sense, the word "style" is applied to periods of music history. Every age presents new problems, makes new demands, and offers new possibilities; and every artist responds in a unique way. Yet no matter how varied the stylistic traits of the individual artists of a particular era, when they are seen in historical perspective a common manner of expression binds them together. Thus we are able to identify the common practices of a specific period and talk in general terms about its style. Although scholars never completely agree on the boundary lines separating one period of style from another, the following outline of the major periods of music history provides approximate dates. Each period had a unique means of expression.

600–1450	Medieval
1450–1600	Renaissance
1600–1750	Baroque
1725–1775	Rococo
1775–1825	Classical
1820–1900	Romantic
1890–1915	Post-Romantic (includes Impressionism)
1900–	Twentieth Century

Style periods overlap; the new exists side by side with the old. Elements from an older style may be combined with new procedures to create what is sometimes called a Neoclassical (Neobaroque, etc.) style. Although Italy was the very heart of the Renaissance spirit in literature and the visual arts, Renaissance music originated and developed in northern France and Belgium. The Baroque style appeared earlier in Italy than in Germany or England. Nevertheless, the style periods listed are a useful guide in exploring developments in Western music.

SUMMARY

The relationship between the vertical and horizontal aspects of a piece of music is known as its texture. Monophonic music consists of a single melodic line with no accompaniment. Polyphonic music consists of two or more "independent" melodic lines that are roughly equal in their melodic and rhythmic interest. Homophonic music is dominated by a single melodic strand, with the other voices providing harmonic support.

Musical form refers to the structuring and organization of the musical time-flow. Forms are derived from the elements of unity and variety and the balance between them. Variety is the result of change; unity is achieved through repetition.

Alternating forms are based upon the contrasts among different musical materials, while variation and development procedures are based on the statement of a single musical idea and its subsequent alteration.

The specific way in which musical elements are combined in a piece of music determines its style. Music has evolved through a series of style periods, each with general distinguishing characteristics. In the subsequent chapters of this book, we shall trace the development of Western music from the Middle Ages to the twentieth century.

NEW TERMS

texture

monophony (monophonic)

polyphony (polyphonic)

imitative polyphony

voice

counterpoint (contrapuntal)

homophony (homophonic)

form

binary form

ternary form

alternation

development

theme and variations

style

CHAPTER 4 | MUSICAL INSTRUMENTS

WE HAVE EXAMINED THE WAY IN WHICH MUSICAL SOUNDS ARE PRO-
duced, how they are related to one another, and how they are organized in time.
This chapter examines the instruments that produce them. The first section discusses the instruments individually, and the second section deals with instrumental and vocal ensembles.

THE INSTRUMENT FAMILIES

The instruments available to composers offer a wide variety of pitch ranges,
technical capabilities, and tone colors. They are commonly grouped into four
families—strings, woodwinds, brasses, and percussion. A relatively recent development has been the use of a variety of electronic media which have had an
important impact on the course of modern music.

STRINGS

A stringed instrument produces sound when the player either plucks or bows one
of its strings. Each string is stretched between two fixed points, with one end attached to a *peg* on the neck of the instrument and the other to a *tailpiece* at the
base of the body. The midsections of the strings pass over a *bridge,* which is
mounted on the body of the instrument (Fig. 4.1).

Individual strings vary in thickness. These dimensions, plus the nature of the
material from which a particular string is made, its length, and the tension on
the string determine the frequency at which a string will vibrate and, therefore,
the pitch at which it will sound. The player can effectively reduce the portion of
a string that is free to vibrate by pressing down the string against the *fingerboard*
with the fingers of the left hand. This is known as **stopping** the string.

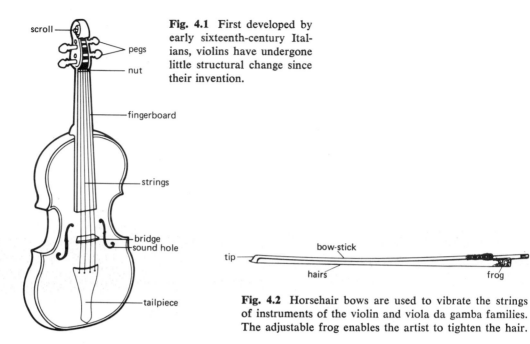

Fig. 4.1 First developed by early sixteenth-century Italians, violins have undergone little structural change since their invention.

Fig. 4.2 Horsehair bows are used to vibrate the strings of instruments of the violin and viola da gamba families. The adjustable frog enables the artist to tighten the hair.

String Techniques Many stringed instruments, including those of the violin and gamba families, are played by drawing a *bow,* held in the right hand, across the strings of the instrument, which is held with the left hand. The bow (Fig. 4.2) is a long, slender shaft of wood in which a bundle of strands of horsehair is stretched from end to end.

A variety of effects can be achieved by using legato and staccato bowing. **Legato** bowing produces a smooth, connected sound. In **staccato** playing, the notes are short and detached.

When the bow is moved rapidly back and forth across the strings, the effect called **tremolo** is produced. The bow may also be bounced off the strings, or the strings may be struck with the wooden part of the bow. **Double** and **triple stopping** are used to sound chords and intervals. To do this, the player presses two or three strings against the fingerboard at the same time while drawing the bow across them.

The player may increase the "warmth" of the tone by vibrating the left hand back and forth rapidly while pressing a string against the fingerboard. This creates a slight fluctuation in pitch that is known as **vibrato.**

A velvety tone can be achieved by clamping a device called a **mute** to the top of the bridge. The mute produces a softer and less brilliant sound without affecting the pitch.

Instead of using the bow, the player may pluck the string with the finger. This technique, known as **pizzicato,** produces short, crisp tones.

Fig. 4.3 Violins constitute an important part of the symphony orchestra and frequently perform as solo instruments as well.

Fig. 4.4 Unlike its violin and viola cousins, the cello rests on the floor. Pictured here is the late Pablo Casals, one of the outstanding cellists of our time.

The Violin Family The chief members of this family—the violin, viola, violoncello, and double bass—are among the most important instruments in all Western music. They constitute the backbone of the orchestra and are frequent members of chamber ensembles. In addition, all are solo instruments in their own right.

The highest in pitch, the *violin* is famous for its lyric and dramatic expressiveness. Its four strings are separated in pitch by the interval of a fifth. The instrument is held beneath the player's chin.

The *viola,* slightly larger than the violin, has longer, thicker, and heavier strings. Tuned a fifth lower than the violin, it is also held beneath the player's chin.

The *violoncello* is commonly called by its shortened name, *cello*. Tuned an octave below the viola, it is about twice the length of the violin. Because of its size, it rests on the floor and is held upright between the player's knees.

The *double bass,* also called the *bass viol, contrabass,* or *string bass,* is the largest and lowest-voiced member of the family. Because of its size, the player must stand to play it. The double bass is commonly used in jazz ensembles.

Other Strings Popular during the Renaissance and Baroque periods, the instruments of the *viola da gamba* family (plural, *viole da gamba*) are now being revived to play music from those periods. They are similar to the modern violin family in appearance, but they have six strings and produce a lighter, slightly more nasal tone than the members of the violin family. They are available in five sizes, and all are played in cello position, between the player's knees.

Among many instruments in which the strings are plucked instead of being played with a bow are the harp, lute, and guitar. Both the harp and the lute have ancient origins in the Near East. The modern *harp*, which is often included in the symphony orchestra, has forty-seven strings stretched vertically in a triangular frame. Seven pedals at its base are used to alter the pitch of the strings. The *lute* rose to its greatest prominence in the sixteenth century. It is generally used today in the performance of Renaissance and Baroque music. Lutes are easily recognized by their rounded backs (see photo on page 102). The *guitar* has become established as a concert instrument and is also used widely in folk, jazz, rock, and country and western music.

Fig. 4.5 The largest and lowest-voiced member of the violin family, the double bass is played standing.

Fig. 4.6 A stringed instrument played by plucking, the harp has foot pedals which alter the pitch of the strings.

Two other members of the string family are heard commonly today. The *banjo* is used in much folk-type music. The *mandolin,* a modern descendant of the lute, is encountered in Renaissance music.

WOODWINDS

Although not all woodwinds are constructed of wood, the term applies to a family of instruments in which tone is produced by a column of air vibrating through a pipe. In this group are the members of the flute, oboe, and clarinet families. Instruments such as the recorder and the saxophone are also classified as woodwinds.

All woodwinds have a pipelike shape, with fingerholes spaced along the side. The player changes the length of the column of air by closing or opening the fingerholes with fingers or with pads attached to a mechanism of keys. In stopping the fingerholes the player lengthens the air column passing through the instrument and thereby lowers the pitch.

The vibrating column of air is produced by several different methods. In all of them the position of the player's lips, or **embouchure,** is of paramount importance in controlling the amount and direction of air.

A flute is **edge-blown** in somewhat the same manner as air is blown over the top of a bottle to produce sound. The player funnels a narrow stream of air to the opposite edge of the oval-shaped mouth hole. The air in the recorder is **end-blown** into a mouthpiece resembling that of a whistle.

Other instruments produce sound by the vibrations of a thin piece of material called a **reed** (Fig. 4.7). In **single-reed** instruments, such as the clarinet, the player blows a column of air between the reed and the open side of the mouthpiece. In **double-reed** instruments, such as the oboe, the player blows the air between two reeds.

The Woodwind Family One of the oldest woodwinds, the *flute* is an extremely agile instrument, able to produce rapid scale passages and trills. The smallest and highest woodwind, the *piccolo* (*flauto piccolo* or little flute), is really a small flute. Despite its size, it produces one of the most penetrating sounds of all the instruments of the orchestra. It is pitched an octave higher than the flute.

The *oboe* has a nasal, plaintive timbre often used for pastoral or nostalgic effects.

The *English horn* is neither English nor a horn. Actually, it is an alto oboe, a double-reed instrument pitched a fifth lower than the oboe. Its timbre resembles that of the oboe.

The *bassoon* is the bass member of the oboe family. Because of its length, the instrument is bent back on itself. The bassoon has remarkably even tone color and is expressive in both its high and low ranges.

The woodwind counterpart of the double bass, the *contrabassoon,* is pitched an octave below the bassoon. Its sixteen-foot pipe is doubled back on itself three times.

The single-reed *clarinet* family has eleven members, but only four are regularly used. Fuller in tone than the oboe, the clarinet is capable of producing

oboe   clarinet

Fig. 4.7 The oboe requires a double reed, using air vibrations between its two reed parts to generate sound; the clarinet's single reed produces sound when air is blown between it and the open side of the mouthpiece.

Fig. 4.8 With an ancestry dating back to the Middle Ages, recorders have recently become popular again.

Fig. 4.9 Some of the members of the woodwind family, Front row: left, flutes; right, oboes. Back row: bassoons.

Fig. 4.10 Like the flute, the piccolo is played by blowing air across the mouth hole. This small instrument produces the highest tones in the orchestra.

rapid runs and trills. The most common instrument in this family is the *B-flat clarinet*. The *clarinet in A,* which is sometimes preferred for parts written in sharp keys, is pitched one-half step lower than the clarinet in B-flat. A fourth above the B-flat clarinet is the small *clarinet in E-flat*. An octave below the B-flat clarinet is the *bass clarinet*.

The *recorder* reached its final stage of development in the late Middle Ages. By the sixteenth century it had spawned a whole family. Today recorders are enjoying wide popularity once again. Modern recorders are available in four sizes: soprano (or descant), alto (or treble), tenor, and bass.

The *saxophone,* invented by Adolphe Sax of Brussels in the mid-nineteenth century, is a hybrid instrument. It combines the single reed and mouthpiece of the clarinet with the conical shape and key arrangement of the oboe. Its timbre is somewhere between the softness of the woodwinds and the metallic qualities of the brasses. Although it is seldom seen in symphony orchestras, the saxophone is an important instrument in jazz and dance bands.

BRASSES

Like the woodwinds, brass instruments produce sound by sending a vibrating column of air through pipe-shaped tubing. The significant difference, however, is where the vibrations come from. In a brass instrument the mouthpiece is shaped like either a cup or a funnel (Fig. 4.11). As the player blows into the mouthpiece, the vibrations of the lips function much like those of the reed in the woodwinds.

Another difference involves the valves or, in the case of the trombone, a sliding double tube. While the length of the air column in woodwinds is controlled by keys in the side of the instrument, the brasses have slides or valves to alter the length of the tubing.

Like stringed instruments, the brasses can be muted. Brass mutes look like hollow cones, which the players insert into the bells of their instruments. The mutes tend to accentuate the higher resonances, resulting in a more nasal tone color.

The modern orchestra includes trumpets, French horns, trombones, and tubas in its brass section. The highest of these, the *trumpet,* has a brilliant and penetrating timbre. Different notes are sounded by opening combinations of the three valves and by adjusting the embouchure against the cup-shaped mouthpiece. The trumpet is capable of techniques ranging from a smooth legato to a sharp staccato.

The *cornet* looks like a short version of the trumpet. It has the same range of pitch, but a unique timbre that is softer and mellower than that of the trumpet.

Descended from the hunting horn, the *French horn* produces a full, mellow tone. Its pitch is controlled by three valves and a funnel-shaped mouthpiece.

The *trombone* (which means "large trumpet" in Italian) has a cup-shaped mouthpiece, but no valves. Adjustments in pitch are made by changing the position of its long, U-shaped tubing. The tenor and bass trombones are most frequently seen in the modern orchestra, while the alto trombone is encountered less often.

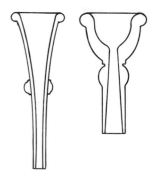

funnel-shaped   cup-shaped
mouthpiece   mouthpiece
(horn)   (trombone)

Fig. 4.11 Brass mouthpieces take one of these two shapes. Regardless of which is used, however, sound is produced by the vibrations of the player's lips rather than by reed vibrations.

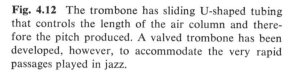

Fig. 4.12 The trombone has sliding U-shaped tubing that controls the length of the air column and therefore the pitch produced. A valved trombone has been developed, however, to accommodate the very rapid passages played in jazz.

Fig. 4.13 The highest-pitched member of an orchestra's brass section, the trumpet is also a versatile jazz instrument.

Fig. 4.14 The mellow-toned French horn tapers from a funnel-shaped mouthpiece at one end through many feet of curved tubing to the flaring bell at the other.

Fig. 4.15 With its deep, sonorous tones, the tuba helps anchor the brass section of the orchestra. It is also a popular band instrument and was widely used in early jazz.

"Ah! It's the Woodwind family!"

Drawing by Koren; © 1976 The New Yorker Magazine, Inc.

The lowest member of the brass family, the *tuba,* corresponds to the double bass and the contrabassoon in the string and woodwind families. It has a cup-shaped mouthpiece and three to five valves. Tubas come in a variety of sizes, the most common of which are the F-flat, or bass, tuba, and the BB-flat, or contra-bass.

PERCUSSION INSTRUMENTS

Instruments that produce sound by being struck or shaken are by far the oldest known. Although the principles of their construction have not altered greatly over the centuries, the number of percussion instruments has grown steadily. Today the **battery,** as the percussion section is called, consists of a variety of instruments in two categories: those that produce sounds of definite pitch and those that do not.

The most important percussion instrument of definite pitch is the *kettledrum.* Named for its copper "kettle," this instrument produces sound by the vibrations of its calfskin **head** (today the head is often made of a synthetic material). The tension on the head can be adjusted by screws around the edge of the kettle and by pedals.

Kettledrums, also called *timpani,* are available in a number of sizes, each with a basic range of a fifth. The kettledrum's roll, produced by rapid bouncing strokes of the drumsticks, can grow in intensity from a soft rumble to an awesome thunder.

The *glockenspiel* consists of two rows of tuned steel slabs of varying sizes. The sound, produced by striking the slabs with a mallet, is crisp and bell-like. The *celesta,* a keyboard glockenspiel that looks like a small, upright piano, is used

Fig. 4.16 Percussion instruments that form the battery of the modern symphony orchestra still employ the oldest sound-generating principles known. The percussionist can produce sounds of either definite or indefinite pitch by selecting the appropriate instrument.

for a soft, light effect. The *xylophone* has wooden bars and produces a dry, hollow sound. The *marimba,* a softer-sounding xylophone of African and South American origin, is used primarily for the performance of dance music. The *vibraphone* (also called *vibraharp*) has metal bars and an electric mechanism that produces its unique vibrato. It is prominent in jazz music and is increasingly used by contemporary composers for the orchestra.

The *chimes* are a set of metal tubes suspended vertically in a frame. Struck with one or two wooden mallets, they are often used to imitate church bells.

Among the drums of indefinite pitch are the *bass drum,* the *snare* (or *side*) *drum,* and the *tenor drum.*

The other instruments that produce sounds of indefinite pitch include the *tambourine,* which is played by shaking and striking the head; the *castanets,* which are clicked together; the *triangle,* which is struck by a metal rod; the *gong,* which is struck with a soft-headed stick; and the *cymbals,* which are struck together or hit by a stick.

KEYBOARD INSTRUMENTS

Although they can be classified in the wind, string, or percussion groups, keyboard instruments have a sufficient number of features in common to be considered separately.

Because it is capable of playing both loud and soft notes, the *piano* was originally named the *pianoforte* (meaning soft-loud). The piano has some 230 strings. The strings are set in motion when they are struck by small hammers. Technically, therefore, it is classified as a percussion instrument.

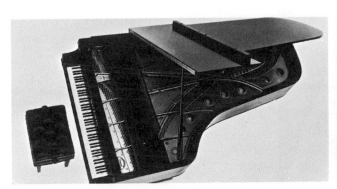

Fig. 4.17 Technically a percussion instrument, the piano has the greatest range of all the instruments. The piano's extraordinary versatility is to be found not only in its range of pitch, but also in its pedal structure and its range of volume.

Fig. 4.18 The plucked strings of the harpsichord produce much softer sounds than those of a piano. Some modern composers are now writing especially for the harpsichord, although it is primarily popular for its part in Renaissance and Baroque music.

A complex chain of mechanisms connects the key on the keyboard to the strings, which then vibrate and produce the sound. The piano's range is greater than that of any other instrument, usually extending for more than seven octaves, and its dynamic capabilities are exceeded only by those of the organ.

Since the end of the eighteenth century the piano has been extremely popular in homes and concert halls. It is technically suited for lyric melodies, rapid scales and trills, and massive chordal combinations. Its lyric, harmonic, and percussive qualities make the piano a favorite instrument for solos, accompaniment, and ensembles alike.

The *organ* is a wind instrument in which air is released from a blower into a series of pipes. The player operates one or more keyboards with the hands, and another keyboard, in the form of pedals, with the feet. By activating different stops and combinations of stops, a variety of sounds can be achieved.

The *harpsichord* has been revived in this century to play music from the Renaissance and Baroque periods. Because its strings are plucked by plectra of quill or leather, the harpsichord is classified as a stringed instrument. As one might expect, its tone is quite unlike that of the piano, in which the strings are struck.

THE VOICE

Because it produces sound by air under pressure, the human voice is fundamentally a wind instrument. Individual voices vary in their range of pitches, but generally male and female voice types are divided into high, middle, and low pitch

Fig. 4.19 Beverly Sills, star of the Metropolitan Opera, is probably America's most popular "classical" musician.

registers. The list that follows shows the basic categories arranged from highest to lowest.

Female	*Male*
Soprano	Tenor
Mezzo soprano	Baritone
Contralto	Bass

In opera and other vocal music calling for solo parts, these categories are further divided, with roles being written for specific voice types.

ELECTRONIC MEDIA

Music that is produced, modified, or amplified by electronic means has become increasingly important since World War II. Instruments range from the electronic organ, which simulates the sound produced by the pipe organ, to the computer. (Electronic music is covered in Chapter 24.)

ENSEMBLES

Throughout the history of music, composers have written works that call for the use of instruments in a great variety of numbers, combinations, and groupings. These range from the solo, unaccompanied instrument to the large orchestra, consisting of more than a hundred players, often combined with a chorus and solo voices. Instrumental music falls into two broad categories: chamber music, in which one player executes each part; and orchestral music, which requires sections with more than one performer. Within the category of orchestral music there are again two major divisions: the small chamber orchestra and the large symphony orchestra.

CHAMBER ENSEMBLES

Chamber music is classified by the number of instruments for which it is written. Thus we have *duos* for two performers, *trios* for three, *quartets, quintets, sextets, octets,* and so on. The combinations may be for a single type of instrument (such as a flute trio), instruments of the same family (such as a brass quintet consisting of trumpets, French horn, trombone, and tuba), or assortments of instruments.

The most important chamber combination, the **string quartet,** has been widely used by composers from the middle of the eighteenth century into the modern period. The string quartet consists of a first and a second violin, a viola, and a cello.

Frequently a fifth instrument is added to the string quartet to create a quintet; ensembles of this type are named after the added instrument. Thus, a *clarinet quintet* is a string quartet plus a clarinet; a *piano quintet* is a string quartet plus a piano. Clarinet quintets have been written by Mozart and Brahms; and piano quintets by Schubert, Brahms, Dvořák, and Fauré. A quintet consisting of five strings is also common. Mozart, Beethoven, Mendelssohn, and Brahms have written works of this type for ensembles consisting of two violins, two violas, and a cello. Chamber groupings, some for larger ensembles, have continued to the present day. Igor Stravinsky, for example, wrote his *Octet for Wind Instruments* for two bassoons, two trombones, two trumpets, a flute, and a clarinet.

THE ORCHESTRA

Throughout its history the **orchestra** has varied in size and composition. As the creature of the composer, it is an ever-changing unit, not only in size but also in makeup.

One of the earliest orchestral ensembles was established in Paris by Jean-Baptiste Lully in the mid-seventeenth century. His orchestra consisted mainly of strings. During the first quarter of the eighteenth century, wind instruments, trumpets, and kettledrums were added.

In the mid-eighteenth century, the orchestra became more standardized. The strings remained dominant, but the woodwinds took on an increasingly important role.

In the early decades of the nineteenth century, many of the woodwinds and brasses underwent significant technical improvements. Composers were quick to take advantage of the greater versatility of these instruments. In the second half of the nineteenth century, the orchestra grew extensively in both size and makeup. Today's symphony orchestra consists of a nucleus of about one hundred players,

Fig. 4.20 The chamber ensemble requires teamwork and instrumental balance. Violinist Kyung-Wha Chung, cellist Myung-Wha Chung, and pianist Myung-Whun Chung (all members of one Korean family) have solo careers but also perform chamber concerts together.

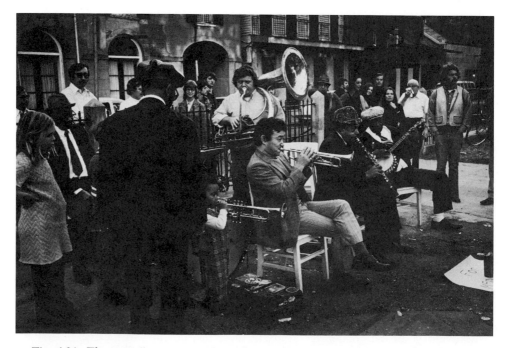

Fig. 4.21 The term "ensemble" encompasses many instrumental combinations and groupings. Here a jazz ensemble performs on the streets of New Orleans.

with additions and subtractions being made to suit the requirements of individual pieces. The players are distributed according to the plan shown in Fig. 4.22.

BANDS AND WIND ENSEMBLES

The word "band" has many applications. Marching band, military band, stage band, jazz band, hillbilly band, and the rhythm band that many of us played in as children give an idea of the variety of bands possible. For much of its history the band has been associated with summer concerts in the park. Today the term is most often applied to two types of musical organizations: the marching band and the concert band.

We are all familiar with the **marching bands** that play at high school and college sports events, march in military parades, and participate in municipal celebrations. The **concert band,** often referred to as a **symphonic band** or **wind ensemble,** is perhaps less familiar. It became an important musical force in the years following World War II. It differs from the marching band in its smaller size, its emphasis on performing original compositions, and the fact that it was intended for indoor concerts. The wind ensemble, with its lighter, more cerebral sound, has attracted the attention of several serious modern composers: Darius Milhaud, Paul Hindemith, and Ralph Vaughan Williams are among those who have written original works for wind ensemble.

Whereas the members of the violin family form the mainstay of the symphony orchestra, concert bands rely primarily on wind and percussion instruments to produce their unique tone colors. Concert bands generally contain no violins, violas, or cellos, but do employ the string bass.

VOCAL ENSEMBLES

Chamber vocal ensembles vary in size and makeup in much the same way that chamber instrumental ensembles do. There are vocal trios, quartets, quintets, sextets, and so on. The vocal quartet usually consists of soprano, alto, tenor, and bass. So long as only one or two singers sing each part, the ensemble is essentially of chamber music proportions. However, when there are four or five or more singers in each section, the ensemble is referred to as a **chorus** or **choir.** Several types of choruses are possible. A *women's chorus* usually consists of two soprano parts (first and second) and one or two alto sections—SSAA. A *men's chorus* is made up of two tenor sections (first and second), baritone, and bass—TTBB. The mixed chorus consists of both female and male voices, divided into soprano, alto, tenor, and bass. In church choirs before the nineteenth century, female voices were not generally used; soprano and alto parts were sung by boys whose voices had not yet changed.

Choral music is sometimes intended for voices alone, without instrumental accompaniment, a style of performance called **a cappella.** But choral music is also frequently performed with instruments, for example, piano, organ, or orchestra.

CONDUCTOR

Large ensembles usually require the leadership of a conductor. Standing in front of the orchestra or chorus, usually on a podium, the conductor directs the en-

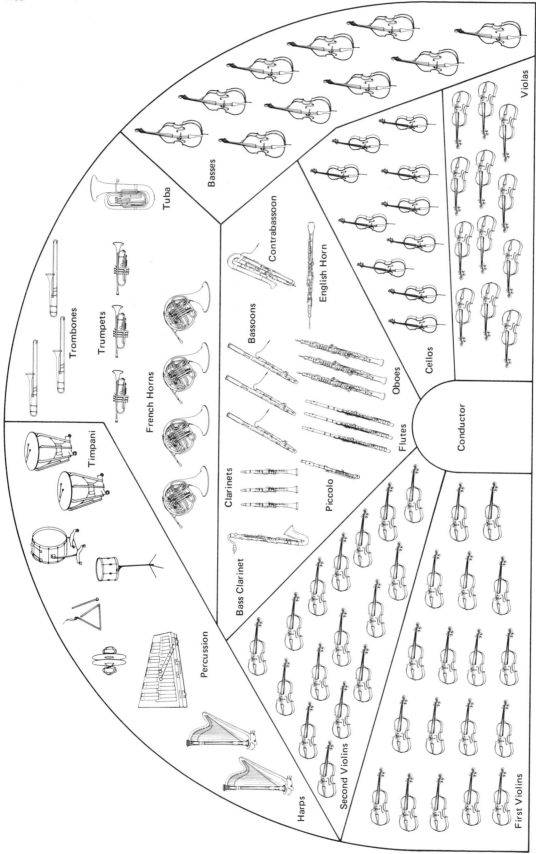

Fig. 4.22 The seating arrangement of the orchestra varies according to the preferences of the conductor, but generally the strings are to the front, the woodwinds in the middle, and the brasses and percussion to the back. The numbers of each kind of instrument also vary slightly from orchestra to orchestra. (Adapted from the *Boston Globe*, October 16, 1977.)

H ow does a conductor give instructions for dynamic shadings and other expressive nuances to the orchestra? Mstislav Rostropovich, engaging and irrepressible Russian-
born conductor of the National Symphony Orchestra of Washington, uses a highly personal,
colloquial, and often hilarious approach, as the following excerpts show:*

Sforzando (forceful attack): "Four old women in the audience must have heart attacks."
A Brahms variation: "Play this line like little crawling lousies."
To a violinist: "Your fingers are like spughetti cooked ten hours."
To a cello student: "You must opening the windows on your playing." Later: "Ahhh,
I see you opening the windows, but air coming in is polluted."
Softly: "Whisper like a lady moving in a silk dress."
To the violin section: "You play this like apple pie with separate pieces. All together,
please."
Accented notes: "Play like one shoe fits, and the other is a little small."
Cuing the string section: "Like an airplane pilot. Instead of landing 'Boom!' pilot comes
landing so slow . . . so slow . . . all of a sudden wheels are on the ground."
Diminuendo: "With expression—not like when you are turning radio down because
neighbors complaining."
Marked rhythm: "Like cowboy riding a horse."
A loud cymbal crush: "Like breaking all the glasses in Washington."
A crescendo in the brass section: "Sounds like a million devils."
A passage in Prokofiev: "You must make it like two bugs fighting."
A constantly repeated phrase: "Like blowing up a balloon."
To a cello student: "You play too serious, like you are being condemned. It should be
like singing to yourself."
Tremolo: "Like a hag who has false teeth and she is chewing caramels."

*   Reprinted by permission from *Time,* The Weekly Newsmagazine; copyright Time Inc. 1977.

Fig. 4.23 A page from the complete score of Dvořák's Symphony No. 9 in E Minor (to be discussed in Chapter 15), showing how all the instrumental parts are combined for the conductor. The individual players normally use partial scores, showing only the music to be played by their particular instruments. Note that the trombones and viola use a special clef (called the C clef); the intersection of the two backward C's in the clef sign locates the position of middle C.

semble and is responsible for all aspects of the performance. The craft of conducting is a complex one, and conducting techniques and styles are highly individual and vary widely. In general, the conductor's right hand indicates the tempo and basic metrical structure of the music. With the left hand, the conductor cues the entrances of instruments, guides the shadings or dynamics, and indicates other nuances relating to the expressive character of the music.

SUMMARY

In this chapter we have examined, both individually and in groups, some of the most important instruments in Western music.

Orchestral instruments are usually classified into four groups—strings, woodwinds, brasses, and percussion. Although they can be classified as wind, string, or percussion instruments, keyboard instruments are often considered separately. Operated by air under pressure, the human voice is technically a wind instrument. In recent times the computer and other electronic media have emerged as new means of producing music.

A great number of combinations and groupings are possible with both instrumental and vocal music. Chamber ensembles include trios, quartets, and a number of other small groups, with usually one voice or instrument assigned to a part. Larger groupings, such as the orchestra and chorus, have several voices or instruments performing a single part. Bands come in many varieties, the two principal types being the marching band and the concert band.

In the next chapter we will look at some instruments used in the performance of non-Western music.

NEW TERMS

String Terms and Techniques

legato
staccato
tremolo
stopping (double and triple)
vibrato
mute
pizzicato

Woodwind Terms and Techniques

embouchure
edge-blown
end-blown
reed (single reed, double reed)

Brass Terms and Techniques
mute

Percussion Terms and Techniques

battery
head

Ensembles

chamber music
string quartet
chorus (choir)
a cappella
orchestra
marching band
concert band (symphonic band;
    wind ensemble)

II
THE MUSIC OF
WORLD CULTURES

Bronze figure of a trumpeter, from Benin, British Nigeria.

CHAPTER 5 | THE MUSIC OF WORLD CULTURES: AN INTRODUCTION

EACH OF US IS, TO SOME EXTENT, A PRODUCT OF THE CULTURE INTO which he or she is born. Our physical, intellectual, and emotional lives are affected continuously by our surrounding social environment. The foods we consider most succulent, the art we enjoy, our patterns of friendship, family solidarity, and group identity are influenced by the cultural standards we absorb.

The same is true of music. A people's sense of their history, of their relationship to a deity, of their joy in life and sorrow in death are revealed by the use they make of musical materials. And ideas of what music should be—how it should sound, when it should be heard, and who should perform it—are related directly to cultural backgrounds. In short, the "ear" of the listener is very much conditioned by his or her culture.

SOME PRELIMINARY COMMENTS

In this chapter we will consider examples of musical cultures outside the Western European tradition. Although there are many fundamental differences between Western and non-Western music, certain similarities appear to be a common heritage of all humanity. In every culture music plays an important role in rites and ceremonies; and for all people music has an emotional content that satisfies certain deeply felt needs. Yet the resulting sounds are often so diverse that the music of one group may not be recognized as music at all by other groups. A significant degree of contrast also exists between the relative positions of music in the social fabric of various cultures. For example, the traditional work music of some African tribes is so closely integrated into daily life that it is not even recognized by its members as basically the same phenomenon as the European-derived music which they hear on transistor radios. Thus, any study of the music of non-

---

The revision of Chapter 5 was contributed by Dr. Carolyne Jordan of Salem State College.

Western cultures must include a description of not only its technical nature, but also its role and function in society.

Let us begin by clarifying some terms. The music described in this chapter is variously called "ethnic," "folk," and "traditional." Although these terms are not synonymous, the distinctions among them are sometimes unclear. *Ethnic* music usually refers to the music of a group of people who have shared a common cultural history over many generations. *Traditional* music, which can also be considered "classical" or "sophisticated," is classified by its use. In this category are included official music, such as the imperial court music of ancient China, Japan, and Vietnam, and ceremonial music used in all cultures for specific rites and festivals. Traditional (or classical) music is often formal, following more or less rigorous principles of content, style, and performance. It is usually performed by artists who have refined the music through continued use or disciplined training. *Folk* music is the music of everyday life—work songs, children's songs, lullabies, love songs, and ballad-story songs sung and played by ordinary people. In contrast to traditional music, folk music is available for all to learn, enjoy, and modify as occasion demands. In this chapter we will consider representative examples of both traditional and folk types of ethnic music.

WRITTEN AND ORAL TRADITIONS

The music we will spend most of our time exploring in this text—the concert music of Western Europe and the United States—is based on a tradition of written notation through which the artistic expression of individual composers is carefully preserved. This written music is usually recreated in performance by highly trained musicians at scheduled concerts and recitals. While the performer may take some liberties with the score, using a variety of musical techniques and resources to interpret and enrich the music, the final role of performance is to recreate sounds as intended by individual composers.

The musical heritages of many world cultures, by contrast, are usually transmitted orally. Young musicians learn by carefully listening to, observing, and imitating elder musicians. While music composition is treated with seriousness and reverence, in many cultures the name of an individual composer is not attached to the piece. In ancient cultures music was linked with supernatural beings and mythical gods and was considered a reflection of universal order and spiritual purity.

MUSICAL ELEMENTS IN NON-WESTERN MUSIC

In Part I was discussed many of the elements common to all music, emphasizing how these elements are organized in the practice of Western music. Now let us look briefly at how some of these elements are organized in non-Western music.

PITCH AND SCALE SYSTEMS

The scales employed in many non-European cultures are unfamiliar and strange to Western ears. While certain cross-culture similarities do occur, such as the significance applied by many cultures to the intervals of the octave and the fifth, octaves frequently have more, or fewer, than twelve subdivisions, and the smallest pitch differences found in non-European music may be larger or smaller than the European semitone (half step).

One of the most prevalent combinations of pitches is the **pentatonic scale**—a series of five tones. Pentatonic scales are found in the music of North and South American Indians and in African and Far Eastern cultures. If we play the pentatonic scale CDEGA(C) on the piano, we Westerners will quickly hear a characteristic "oriental" quality. It is the same scale structure as that produced by playing the five black keys of the piano. A subtle difference will be noted if we play instead the scale CDE♭GA♭. This scale is one of several pentatonic scales used commonly in Japanese music, while the first scale is typical of Chinese music.

African cultures south of the Sahara use, in addition to pentatonic scales, a variety of **tritonic** (three-tone) and **heptatonic** (seven-tone) scales, including patterns of whole and half steps that are common in Western music. Japanese music also employs heptatonic scales. In the classical music of India, sequences of pitches known as **ragas** are employed. The basic tones of a raga are modified by the use of **microtones**—intervals smaller than a half step. Microtones cannot be played on the piano, but can be produced on any stringed instrument such as a guitar, violin, or Indian sitar.

HARMONY

In most cultures there is some use of simultaneous sounds. As we shall see in succeeding chapters, Western music is governed by a long tradition of rules of harmonic organization. In non-Western music there is little use of harmony per se, particularly in countries such as India, where melodic intricacies are far more important. One prominent form of harmonic texture in Indian music is provided by a **drone**—a stationary tone or tones of constant pitch played throughout a piece. The four-stringed dulcimer used in performing Appalachian folk music also makes use of the drone, sustaining a continuous tone on one of its strings. Some cultures employ **heterophony:** two or more individuals perform a single melody, adding their own rhythmic or melodic modifications. And in some non-Western cultures textural variety is provided by changes in tone quality and vocal inflection. Such vocal or instrumental variations as slides, trills, and vibrato are among the techniques through which the effect of varying textures is achieved.

RHYTHM

Much Western music is based on symmetrical rhythmic patterns and uniform time intervals. Many world cultures, however, use complex, irregular, and free rhythms. Many cultures use primarily vocal forms; in these cultures rhythms conform to the stress patterns of the words sung. In African music, **polyrhythms**—two or more contrasting and independent rhythms used at the same time—are common, and the sophistication of use of rhythm in Africa is unmatched in any other culture. Polyrhythms have increasingly fascinated and influenced Western jazz and concert music composers. A good example of their adaptation in Western music is Stravinsky's *The Rite of Spring* (see p. 349).

EXAMPLES OF TRADITIONAL AND FOLK MUSIC

Rarely have any cultures lived in complete isolation for many centuries. As a result, the music of the dominant culture of a region has often been influenced by contacts through trade, exploration, and migration. Thus, the music in world cultures today has often been transformed to some degree from its original character. The examples we will survey here represent music of ancient origin in which many indigenous characteristics have been preserved.

MUSIC OF CHINA

Background From its beginnings, Chinese music was conceived of as a system that would reflect the order of the universe. Musicians and philosophers in ancient China believed in the existence of one true "foundation tone" upon which the whole edifice of musical composition should be built. This foundation tone, or *huang chung,* was thought to have social, cosmological, and mystical significance. For many centuries, the disappearance of a dynasty was attributed to its inability to find the true *huang chung.* Several methods were used to discover the elusive tone. One method prescribed that the correct height of the pipe that would produce the true *huang chung* would be equal to ninety average-size grains of millet laid end to end. From this tone the pitches of the other tones in the Chinese musical system were derived. Small bamboo tubes, sized through an exact mathematical formula, were used to produce twelve tones, or *lü,* which were roughly comparable to the twelve months of the year, so that each month had its tone. Musicians selected five tones from these twelve to form a pentatonic scale based on the hours of day and night and the revolving cycle of months in the yearly calendar.

Because each tone was invested with mystical significance, Chinese music developed as a system in which the perfect performance of individual tones was regarded as the highest art. The philosopher Confucius (ca. 551–479 B.C.) played a stone slab on which only one note could be produced. Yet he is said to have played it with such a full heart that its sound was captivating. The sophistication needed to enjoy subtle colorations and inflections on only one tone was, of course, not a universal gift among the ancient Chinese. Popular discontent with "scholarly music" led to the development of more accessible forms that could be enjoyed by everyone. The most enduring secular form was Chinese opera.

Chinese Opera Presented originally in teahouses or outdoor arenas, Chinese opera evolved in an atmosphere of noisy informality. Today, the uniform loudness with which the operas are performed is thought to be a stylistic holdover from the days when players had to complete with squalling babies and clattering rickshaws for audience attention. To involve the audiences emotionally, singers and musicians presented operas in which characterization was the overriding concern.

To portray three basic emotional moods, three corresponding musical styles became customary. For scenes involving agitated emotions such as happiness, gaiety, or temporary distress a quick, light style was employed. Music written in

Fig. 5.1 Chinese operas today have rejected traditional themes in favor of themes of the Communist revolution, such as the struggles of peasants against oppressive landlords. Costumes and sets are simple, in keeping with socialist ideology. As in ancient times, acrobats continue to enhance the performance.

another style portrayed subdued, contemplative moods, whereas a character's despair or depression was conveyed through a third style of composition.

Similarly, various dramatic situations came to be associated with certain melodic patterns. These stereotyped melodic formulas are still available to any composer who wishes to communicate one of the standard dramatic incidents common to Chinese operatic plots. Consequently, in a number of operas the same melodic material forms the basis for any set aria (vocal piece) describing the anguish of the abandoned wife, a villain's intended vengeance, or the final triumph of good over evil.

The vocal quality and range in these arias also depends, to a large extent, on the type of character to be portrayed. Heroes are required to sing with a tight, controlled rasp, whereas heroines often produce a high, nasal sound that originated with the male singers who until recently played the female roles.

The scenes of an opera generally begin with percussion overtures. Percussive devices are used to accompany the recitative (dialogue that is half spoken and half sung) and to mark off one character's words from another's. In melodic passages, instruments of the orchestra—bowed and plucked lutes, fiddles, and flutes —play the main melody either in unison or at various pitches. The crashing of cymbals emphasizes the end of a melody. As the Chinese opera form developed, energetic acrobatic displays and dances were introduced, adding greatly to audience enjoyment.

In modern China, the traditional music, which was associated with the old aristocratic society, has been systematically suppressed. Classical Chinese instruments are very rarely played today and it is feared that much knowledge of the traditional performance styles used in Confucian rituals and imperial court music has been irretrievably lost. Yet the Chinese opera continues to thrive with the sanction of the Communist regime (although themes acceptable to the ideology of the revolutionary government have replaced traditional ones) because of its origins as the theater of common people.

Traditional Chinese Instruments   The musical instruments of China are classified according to the material from which they are made; metal, stone, silk, and bamboo are among the most common. Metal instruments include bells, gongs, chimes, and the carillon (a set of chromatically tuned bells). The stone chime, rarely used today, is constructed of small L-shaped plates.

Of the silk instruments, the *ch'in,* or silk-stringed zither, is considered the most prestigious. Used as both a solo instrument and to accompany solo songs, the ch'in dates back to the Confucian period.

The transverse flute and the panpipe are bamboo instruments. The wood and skin instruments include a rich variety of percussive devices. The globular flute, an instrument similar to our ocarina (a simple wind instrument) is defined as a clay instrument, while the *sheng* mouth organ (Fig. 5.2) fits into the category of gourd instruments. Important in the Chinese orchestra, the sheng consists of seventeen pipes set into a gourd wind chest. Its sound is said to imitate the cry of a phoenix bird and its shape resembles a phoenix with folded wings. (The phoenix was a legendary bird which was said to have risen from its own ashes to live again.)

Fig. 5.2   An important instrument in Chinese orchestras, the sheng mouth organ consists of seventeen pipes set into a gourd wind chest.

Ancient Chinese orchestras were immense in size and diverse in instrumentation. The orchestra of the Temple of the Ancestors at Peking included over 150 players. Some musicologists have come to believe that the Chinese use of a variety of instrumental timbres represented an attempt to provide harmonic density (texture) to their music. The existence of such a variety of instruments also encouraged "programmatic" styles, in which the instruments were used to create realistic sound effects such as animal cries or roaring gales.

THE MUSIC OF INDIA

Background The cultural heritage of India is divided between two basic traditions: the Moslem culture of the north and the Hindu tradition of the south. Indian music, too, reflects this cultural split; for example, the two systems use different instruments and different naming systems. Yet they also hold many things in common, including the philosophic premise that music is intimately connected with the spiritual world. In our discussion we will generally refer to the music of the southern, Hindu tradition.

The Hindu religion influences many forms of musical expression in India. The majority of Indian songs are devotional, expressing a love for the deity. The religious spirit expresses itself throughout a wide range of subjects, from the most personal and familiar to esoteric, abstract philosophy. Even the songs of erotic love convey the bliss of union with the divine.

The basis for Indian melodies is the ancient religious music of the Aryan-speaking peoples of West Asia who migrated to India as early as the third or fourth century B.C. About 1500 B.C. the music began to be recorded in sacred books or *vedas* ("knowledge") containing prayers, chants, hymns, and other religious knowledge. Sung as incantations to the divinities or as sacred sacrificial formulas, the hymns were performed to ensure the order and stability of the universe. The oldest known treatise on classical Hindu musical theory, the *Natya Sastra,* dating from about 200 B.C., provides the bridge that connects the ancient musical heritage of India with forms still in use today.

The basic motive force of Indian music has remained constant: Music must reflect the inherent order and majesty of the universe and contribute to a performer's own spiritual development. This deep and sustaining motivation, which anchors Indian music to its mystical, philosophic framework, is reflected in the ordering of the melodic modes known as *ragas.* Each raga is related to a certain time of day or night. Indian historians tell of a musician at the court of the sixteenth-century emperor Akbar who sang a night raga at midday with such power and beauty that "darkness fell on the place where he stood." Each raga is associated also with a definite mood, a color, a festival, a deity, and certain specific natural events. Sexual differentiation of the ragas into male ragas and female *raginis* completes the unification of Indian music with the total surrounding cosmology.

A teacher of Indian music is considered a true guru, responsible not only for his students' musical progress but also for their spiritual development. The guru receives no money for his services. The knowledge and wisdom he imparts are thought to be priceless and far beyond any conceivable financial remuneration. Often, a student binds himself to one guru for a period of ten years or more. During that time he will be expected to memorize over sixty ragas and rhythmic cycles called **talas.** The memorization is demanded not to ensure perfect reproduction of the ragas as such but to promote the complete familiarity and understanding needed to master the pinnacle of Indian musical art—the art of improvisation.

Pitch, Scales, and Harmony The Hindu scale consists of seven tones or *svars—sa, ra, ga, ma, pa, dha,* and *ni,* each of which represents a basic mood. *Sa* and *ma* are associated with tranquility, *re* connotes harsh feelings, joy or gaiety is expressed in *pa,* sorrow is shown in *ni,* and solemn moods expressed through *ga* and *dha.*

These seven tones, which correspond approximately to the Western diatonic scale, are modified through the use of microtones called *srutis.* Srutis alter the basic tones in much the way that accidentals in Western music change the tones. The srutis can prescribe that a tone be played in its natural state, flat, very flat, sharp, or very sharp. These srutis are very difficult for even the well-trained Western ear to distinguish.

From the seven basic tones and their modifications, the ragas have been developed. Ragas are governed by a complex musical system in which certain tonal combinations are permitted while others are strongly prohibited. For example, some ragas do not allow the tones *re* and *dha* to be used in an ascending melodic progression but permit their use in descending melodic progressions. Occasionally, a tone that does not belong in the raga at all is sounded intentionally to heighten the tension and the poignancy of the melody.

To set off the melody of Indian ragas, a harmonic drone is played almost constantly throughout the piece. This drone consists of the key tone for the raga, the tone a fifth above, and the higher octave. For example, if the raga is played in C, the drone would include the tones C, G, and C. Or if the raga is constructed in E, the drone would be E, B, and E. This drone supplies the only harmonic element of Indian music. It serves an extremely important function by providing a harmonic frame of reference for both the audience and the performer.

Rhythm: The Tala As the drone holds an Indian raga together harmonically, the rhythmic cycle, or tala, unifies it metrically. Talas comprise a fixed number of beats, or *matras,* which are grouped together in an orderly arrangement. The tala known as *tintal* refers to a cycle of sixteen beats grouped in four (4-4-4-4). Save for a rhythmically free prelude known as the *alapana,* this rhythmic arrangement is continued throughout the raga. Another popular tala is *jhaptal,* in which ten beats are divided into four bars (2-2-2-3). In *sultal,* the same ten beats are divided into five bars (2-2-2-2-2). Although there are twenty talas in common use, the most frequently employed tala is tintal.

While maintaining the strict division of the tala, the players are free to explore and improvise on their own rhythms, competing with each other in a contest of rhythmic skill. The rhythmic tension is increased only by the requirement that all players reach the *saman,* or first beat of the cycle, exactly together. As the players attempt more and more daring cross-rhythms, and yet still manage to come out together on the saman, the audience begins to assist the performers by clapping out the beats of the tala.

The tempo, or speed, at which a raga is performed does not vary within a section. South Indian music is played from beginning to end at a constant tempo and is generally performed in only one of three tempos: slow, moderate, and fast. The moderate tempo is exactly twice as fast as the slow tempo; the fast tempo is precisely twice as fast as the moderate tempo.

Performance The ability of a performer to improvise and create his or her own music within the strict structure of the raga and tala is the standard by which

Indian audiences judge the art of a musician. In order to leave room for the performer to improvise, the forms of Indian music have remained quite flexible. In a rhapsodic, rather free introduction to the raga, the performer gradually reveals the main notes of the raga. At some time during this introduction (the alapana) the drone softly begins to intone the raga's harmonic structure. Not until the rhythmic cycle, or tala, is set into motion does the main section of the raga get underway. Then, using an individual style of *gamaka,* or melodic ornamentation, the performer begins the raga, varying and elaborating it with a variety of technical resources.

The master performer is always bound by the rules of the raga, which govern not only the tones that may be used, but the relative importance of each tone and the way in which each tone is normally approached. The musician is usually expected to center the performance on one important tone at a time, presenting the tones in the prescribed ascending or decending order.

If the raga is being performed by more than one musician, the competitive, improvisational rhythmic exploration of the tala cycle often becomes predominant. For an Indian audience, these feats of rhythmic and musical daring are more than mere pyrotechnics. Each time the performers reach the saman, or first beat of the tala cycle, with exact precision, it is as though the reality of universal order has been reaffirmed.

Musical Instruments of India Musical instruments of India fall into four general categories: *tata* ("taut"—stringed instruments), *avanaddha* ("covered"—drums), *susira* ("perforated"—wind instruments), and *ghana* ("fixed"—solids that are beaten).

The oldest of the Indian stringed instruments is the *vina,* which is associated with Saraswati, the Indian goddess of music and learning. Still used in southern India, it is a large lute constructed of jackwood, rosewood, or ebony. It is strung with seven strings (four playing strings and three drone strings) controlled by pegs and two sets of movable bridges. The main playing strings are pulled sideways on the frets to produce the characteristic ornamentation. Two hemispheric resonators fashioned from gourds amplify the sound. When played, the vina is either placed horizontally across the performer's knee or laid slanting against the left shoulder (see Fig. 5.3).

Fig. 5.3 The vina is the oldest of the Indian stringed instruments. It is used today in southern India but in the north it has been supplanted by the smaller sitar. (Courtesy The Metropolitan Museum of Art; gift of Alice E. Getty, 1946.)

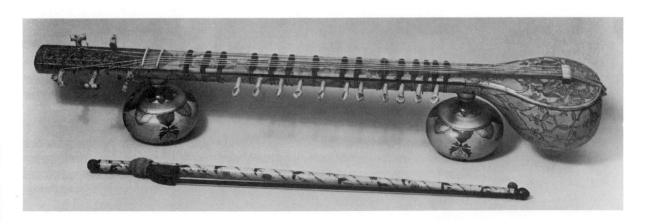

Fig. 5.4 A tabla of northern India. (Courtesy The Metropolitan Museum of Art; The Crosby Brown Collection of Musical Instruments, 1901.)

In the northern regions of India the vina has been supplanted by the *sitar,* which is smaller and simpler to play. The sitar has a track of twenty metal frets, above which are the seven main strings. Below the frets, a set of thirteen "sympathetic" strings can be tuned to the pitches that will most advantageously pick up the main notes of the raga to be performed.

The drums of India are fashioned so that they will reinforce the most important tonal pitches of the raga. In the south, the *mridanga,* a single-piece drum with two heads, is treated with tuning pastes so that various areas on the playing surface produce differing pitches. The *tabla* of the north (Fig. 5.4) is a right-hand drum which is often tuned to the tonic. A single performer plays the tabla simultaneously with the *banya,* a left-hand bass drum.

MUSIC OF AFRICA

Background In this discussion we shall be concerned only with those cultures found in the area south of the Sahara Desert (see Fig. 5.5). Many diverse cultures inhabit this vast area, representing a wide variety of musical styles. Nowhere in the world is music more a part of the very process of living than in Africa. Almost all communal activities are accompanied by singing, dancing, and drumming. These three are rarely separated: they are interdependent. As a whole the music is characterized by sophisticated and complex rhythmic structures, a wide range of indigenous instruments, a strong oral tradition of songs, and a vast store of dances to accompany and celebrate all aspects of life.

These African cultures are based on the power of the spoken word, which is believed to be the "life force" called *nommo* in Bantu languages. The languages are often inflective, and common speech assumes musiclike qualities. Musical sounds produced most often are percussive and players use bodily gestures to enhance a performance. Polyphonic textures are employed and polyrhythms are common.

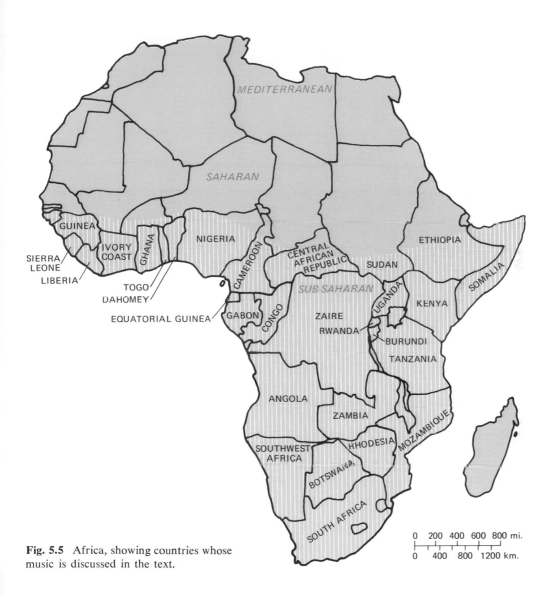

Fig. 5.5 Africa, showing countries whose music is discussed in the text.

Uses of African Music The abundance of songs may be classified into two broad categories: secular (nonreligious) and sacred (religious). Secular music is usually a common property of the people and may be performed for pure entertainment (Fig. 5.6) or as an accompaniment to daily tasks. Religious music may be either ceremonial or *esoteric*. Ceremonial music is heard on such diverse occasions as the end of harvest or fishing season; at weddings and funerals, and at installations of heads of state or rulers. Esoteric music is played only by the particular religious cult for which it is designed. These cult organizations have a repertoire of drummings, dances, and songs which are performed only by their members.

Much African music is meant to be heard by the deity. The Dagon of Mali believe that music, specifically that of the drums, is the vehicle through which the

Fig. 5.6 An impromptu cultural "happening" in the village of Juffure, Gambia, where the story of *Roots* began. Village women celebrate with improvised dancing and drumming.

sacred word is brought to humans. More commonly, music is used to lift up prayers to a divinity. To ensure the delivery of a healthy baby, special songs are sung during the hours of childbirth. After birth, thankfulness of the family finds expression in chants and dancing. The naming of the baby, the loss of a first tooth, and other incidents in the life of the child from infancy through puberty are celebrated with music.

In addition to marking the stages of life, music also deepens and defines African existence. Through songs and dances young men and women are taught the language of the tribe, the traditions of family living, the obligations they will be expected to fulfill, even the "facts of life." Communal holidays and festivals are celebrated through seasonal musical offerings. In some West African cultures, political music is considered so important to the general welfare that select groups of musicians, known as *griots,* specialize in songs of governmental and social information. Each event has a consciously selected musical program, the use of which is strictly adhered to. For example, among the Banum people of the Cameroons, a specific piece of music is traditionally performed only at the hanging of a governmental minister.

To ease the strain of monotonous labor, peoples everywhere have sung work songs. Today in Africa work songs coordinate communal efforts such as the closing of the fish net after a day's harvest, counter the dreariness of repetitive agricultural tasks, and provide diversions from the dangers of gold and diamond mining.

Tonality and Styles of African Music Africa's vocal and instrumental music exhibits a variety of styles and scale patterns. Much music is composed on a foundation of pentatonic (five-tone) or heptatonic (specially derived seven-tone) scales. In addition, a large body of African songs is based on the diatonic pattern found in Western music. A characteristic song style is based on the repetition of a short melodic phrase. This style, known as **call and response,** is found in much West African music. Repetitions of a phrase sung by a leader alternate with repetitions of the responding phrase of the chorus. Call-and-response singing is done in unison or with two and three parts sounded simultaneously in the chorus. The following example of call-and-response style is a song of exhilaration of the Akan people.

Example 5.1

African harmony differs from Western harmony. Where it occurs, it exists mainly as a by-product of melodic elaboration. Some African folk songs carry over into a round type of polyphony or a simple harmonic structure in which one group of performers sustains the key tone of a melody while another group repeats the tune. At times both groups will sing the same melody at different pitches in heterophonic style. While the interval of the third is common, harmonic intervals of a fourth, fifth, sixth, seventh, and octave may be heard in *kple* music of the Ga people (a music also based on the pentatonic scale).

The unvarying pace with which Africans sing and play their music is both legendary and amazing. For long periods of time, even hours, African musicians are able to maintain an exact and constant beat. Within this framework of a steady, changeless tempo groups of musicians drum, sing, and play in spontaneous patterns of "rhythmic polyphony." Drums beat out rhythms that are imitated and varied by voices. Instruments play in one meter, while a singer chants in another. This use of polyrhythm is customary in much African music.

Musical Instruments of Africa   The basic types of instruments found in all areas of Africa include *idiophones* (solid instruments that are beaten, such as gourds, and instruments combining both string and percussive qualities); *aerophones* (wind instruments), *membranophones* (drums), and *chordophones* (string instruments).*

The idiophones include some of the most common instruments found in West Africa. The most popular of these is the *mbira,* which also has many other African names, depending on the culture in which it is found. It is said to be second only to the drum in popularity. The soft and gentle sound of the *mbira* is produced when metal reeds, constructed of varying lengths and attached to a wooden

---

*   The terms used here describe general types of instruments and thus are not unique to instruments of Africa.

Fig. 5.7 A village boy sings and plays an mbira near Ibadan, Nigeria.

sounding board, are plucked. Figure 5.7 shows an example of an mbira from Nigeria.

A song of the Shona people of Rhodesia entitled "Gumbukumbu" uses the mbira and the *hosho,* a rattle made out of a gourd with a network of beads encircling it. The text, a proverb sung perhaps by a mother to a child, states simply:

Gumbukumbu, my mother's child, we are climbing a hill and must keep fit and strong to go on climbing. If you don't take it seriously, you will never make it, or you may, but your children will not make it as you did.

Fig. 5.8 Basketry rattles and gourd rattle from Liberia.

Fig. 5.9 Boys of the Birom tribe in North Nigeria play the calabash (gourd) xylophone.

Many Indian songs are
beauty and economy of expr
entire story or trigger a who
it is not considered import
scheme. The words are si
frighteningly fierce.

An Arapaho vision-son,

The star-child is here.
It is through him that
our people are living.

A Sioux warrior's song to h

My horse be swift in fli,
Even like a bird;
My horse be swift in fli
Bear me now in safety
Far from the enemy's i
And you shall be rewa
With streamers and rit

Indian songs also use meai
function is to complete the
do in the English carol "D
nicate specific meanings th
For the most part, their
Peyote text uses the follow

Another popular African instrument possessing both percussive and tonal qualities is the xylophone. Used both in instrumental ensembles and alone as a solo instrument, the African xylophone is constructed in one of many ways. In some xylophones, wooden planks or keys are set across banana trunks, while in others wooden keys, each with its own gourd or calabash resonator, rest in a wooden frame (Fig. 5.9).

The string instruments (chordophones) of Africa include lutes, zithers, harps, and lyres. Two of the most unique chordophones are the *musical mouth bow,* a single string attached to a bow which is resonated in the mouth, and the *gonje,* a small fiddle of which both bow and fiddle strings are made of animal hair.

The membranophones are the most important of African musical instruments. The need for drums that can produce a variety of tones is nowhere felt more keenly than in Africa. Intricate and complex messages are relayed by drumbeat. Because many African languages are tonal, or inflected, languages, in which the meanings of words are changed by delicate alterations of pitch, drums tuned to higher and lower tones can imitate the talking voice. The "talking drums" of the Ashanti people in Ghana are used to transmit messages as varied as the announcement of emergencies to the greeting given to the people at the opening of a ceremony or the heralding of the chief. The "talking drums" are also used as a vehicle for communicating literature and poetry. On state occasions poems of honor are drummed and danced to the chief and to the community as a whole.

One of the most tonally flexible drums, the hourglass drum (called the *donno* in Ghana and *dundun* in Nigeria) is a double-headed drum held in the player's left armpit. By applying pressure with the arm, the player alters the length of the strings that hold the two drum heads together, and is thus able to raise and lower the drum pitch.

Th
ent
anc
gec
dit
po
of
de
pr
wa

ea
in
to
ai
na

in
na
be
th
A
p
w
m

a
v
t

s
b
s
c
r
\
\
t

'

6 | MEDIEVAL AND RENAISSANCE MUSIC

THE BEGINNINGS OF OUR WESTERN MUSICAL HERITAGE ARE LOST IN the shadows of prehistoric times. But relics of musical instruments and pictures of musical performances indicate the central role music played in the earliest societies. The Bible, too, makes frequent reference to music: David singing psalms while accompanying himself on the harp, the trumpets leveling the walls of Jericho. Ancient Greek philosophers wrote endlessly about music, and Greek and Roman art abounds with illustrations concerning music and dance.

The earliest preserved fragments of written music are scattered, indecipherable, and impossible to date precisely. It was not until around 1000 A.D. that the melodies of the Roman Catholic church, known as Gregorian chants, began to be written down in a decipherable notation and preserved for posterity.

GREGORIAN CHANT

Gregorian chant was the music that accompanied the Roman Catholic Mass. It was named after Pope Gregory I, who was pope from 590 to 604 A.D. Gregory's papacy saw the codification of nearly three thousand melodies, particular chants assigned to specific services in the Church calendar. At the time they were codified, however, the melodies were not written down. At first they were passed on by oral tradition to the priests and monks of succeeding generations. Finally, in the eleventh century, a notational system capable of preserving the melodies in fixed form was devised. When we listen to the chants today, it is impossible to know what changes may have taken place during the intervening centuries.

THE CHANT MELODIES

The chants, also known as **plainsong** or **plainchant,** are *monophonic,* or single-line melodies, sung without instrumental accompaniment. The texts are in Latin and are taken from the Bible, particularly from the Book of Psalms.

The rhythm of Gregorian chant is unmeasured. The tempos are flexible and follow the natural accents that the text would have if it were spoken.

The chant melodies are based on an elaborate system of scales now referred to as **church modes.** There were four pairs of modes, each pair having its own structure and qualities. The church modes are similar to the major and minor scales which were developed in the Baroque period (see page 110), but are different from those scales in that the church modes do not express a strong, functional tonal center (tonic) as do the scales that make up the major-minor system. In addition, they do not convey a strong contrast between major and minor, as do the later scales.

The modes provided the raw material out of which thousands of compositions were fashioned well into the late Renaissance and early Baroque periods, and had a profound effect on musical literature and its history.

The chant melodies are built by stringing together short groups of two, three, and four notes. The melodic range is not great, usually encompassing no more than an octave.

The melodies achieve their esthetic beauty with the barest of means. They have an undulating, wavelike quality, and a simplicity that is wholly in keeping with their religious intent. They were written not for musical performance per se, but to serve as a functional part of early Christian worship.

Fig. 6.1 Today as in medieval times, the Mass is the most solemn service of the Roman Catholic church. Portions of the Ordinary have been set to music since the·fourteenth century.

THE MASS

The Mass is the most solemn service of the Roman Catholic church. It is the commemoration and symbolic reenactment of the Last Supper of Christ. The *liturgy* of the Mass, the prescribed ceremony, is divided into two parts: the *Ordinary* (using those texts that do not change from day to day) and the *Proper* (using those texts that vary according to the religious nature of the specific day in the church year). The Mass combines the items from the Ordinary and the Proper according to the plan shown in Fig. 6.2.

Fig. 6.2 The liturgy of the Mass.

Proper	*Ordinary*
1. *Introit* (processional)	
	2. *Kyrie eleison* "Lord have mercy on us"
	3. *Gloria in excelsis Deo* "Glory to God in the highest"
4. *Collect* (prayer on behalf of the congregation)	
5. *Epistle* (from the Epistles of the New Testament)	
6. *Gradual* (a psalm verse)	
7. *Alleluia* (or *Tract*) (During times of penitence, such as Lent, the Alleluia is replaced by a psalm, called the Tract.)	
8. *Sequence* (a form of hymn)	
9. *Gospel* (from one of New Testament Gospels)	
	10. *Credo* (*in unum Deum*) "I believe in one God"
11. *Offertory*	
	12. *Sanctus* "Holy, holy, holy"
	13. *Benedictus qui venit* "Blessed is he that cometh"
	14. *Canon* (a series of prayers said by the priest in a low voice during the consecration of the bread and wine)
	15. *Angus Dei* (*qui tollis peccata mundi*) "Lamb of God, who taketh away the sins of the world"
16. *Communion*	
17. *Post-Communion* (a prayer of prayers)	
	18. *Ite missa est* "Go" (the congregation is dismissed)

Over time, five of the texts from the Ordinary came to be the favorite items to set to music: Kyrie, Gloria, Credo, Sanctus, and Agnus Dei. These texts, which the public knows today as the musical setting of the Mass, have been a source of inspiration for composers since the fourteenth century. Bach, Mozart, Haydn, Beethoven, and Stravinsky are among those who have created great choral works based on these portions of the Ordinary.

Many of the items for the Ordinary and the Proper were sung to a chant melody. Chants were also composed for the *Office Hours,* or prayer services, that were held at specified times throughout the day. From a musical point of view, the most important Offices were *matins, lauds, vespers,* and *compline.*

THE CHANTS AS SOURCE MATERIALS

The chant melodies were important in their own right and were a rich source of materials used by composers throughout the Middle Ages and Renaissance. Composers used the chants as the basis for longer polyphonic compositions. Even when they made melodic and rhythmic changes, the essential melodic outlines usually remained intact.

SALVE REGINA The chant *Salve Regina* illustrates the typical manner in which a text was set to a chant melody. A hymn of praise to the Virgin, it was sung during the Church year from the week following Pentecost to Advent Sunday. It was customarily sung during vespers (evening worship). The *Salve Regina* attracted the greatest composers of the Renaissance, who used the melody for polyphonic compositions.

The melody and text were written by Hermannus Contractus, a Benedictine monk who lived during the first half of the eleventh century. The grave and expressive melody was cast in the *Dorian mode,* which begins on D and extends upward for an octave.

As Example 6.1 shows, the piece is made up of six sections. The first section (A) consists of a phrase and its immediate restatement with different words. Each subsequent section (B through F) consists of a line of text with its own melodic phrase. Two types of melodic phrases alternate freely: **syllabic,** in which each syllable of text is given one note, and **melismatic,** in which one syllable is spread over several notes. The concluding section (F) is of particular interest because of the expressiveness resulting from the melismatically extended "O," the last statement of which constitutes the longest melisma in the entire piece.

MEDIEVAL SECULAR MUSIC

In addition to the music of the Church, the Middle Ages witnessed the growth of a rich tradition of nonreligious, or *secular,* music. Gregorian chants used only Latin, but secular texts came to be written in the vernacular (everyday) language of the country of origin. Like today's popular music, these texts often concerned the subject of love. Other texts were humorous or obscene; some were about political subjects or told stories of vagabonds.

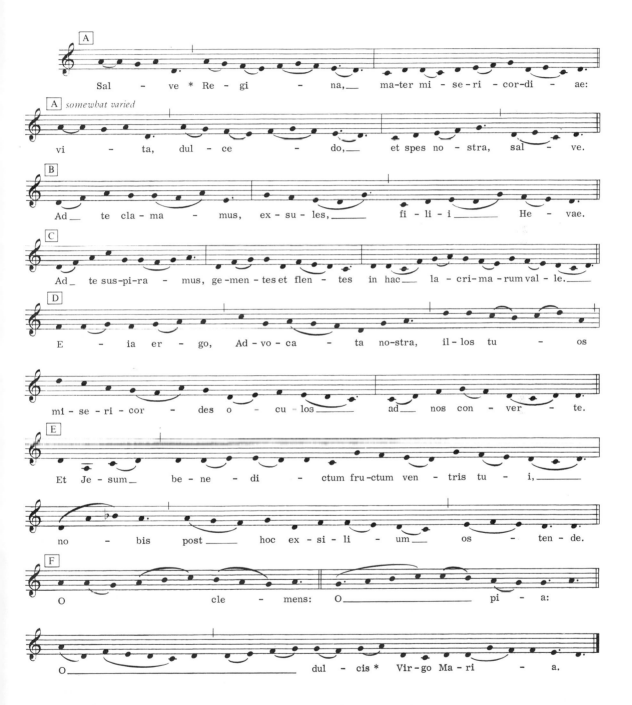

Hail, Holy Queen, Mother of mercy, our life, our sweetness, and our hope. To thee do we cry, poor banished children of Eve. To thee do we send up our sighs, mourning and weeping in this valley of tears. Turn then, most gracious advocate, thine eyes of mercy toward us; and after this our exile, show unto us the blessed fruit of thy womb, Jesus. O clement, O loving, O sweet Virgin Mary!

Example 6.1 (Hermannus Contractus, *Salve Regina*)

The most important early secular vocal music was created and performed by poet-musicians called *trouvères* in northern France, *troubadours* in southern France, and *minnesingers* in Germany. Their ranks included many members of the nobility, who traversed the countryside as court musicians, poets, and sometimes even jugglers. The number of musical and poetic works created by these wanderers is enormous. The melodies of their songs, like the melodies of the chant, were monophonic and simple in design. But they were probably sung with some kind of instrumental accompaniment. The songs were mainly **strophic;** that is, all the stanzas were sung to the same music.

POLYPHONY AND MEASURED RHYTHM

Both sacred and secular music remained monophonic until the tenth century, when two or more voice parts began appearing in combination. This new method of composition, called *polyphony,* went through a number of stages over a long period of time. At first, two melodic lines simply duplicated each other at different pitch levels. They moved in *parallel motion;* that is, at the same time and in the same melodic direction. If one line went up, the other line went up, and so forth. Gradually *contrary motion* was introduced to provide variety—one voice might move up, the other would move down. The two voice parts began to be *melodically* independent; that is, they moved in different directions, but at the same time. These early polyphonic compositions were called **organa** (singular, **organum**).

The rhythm of the earliest organa was, like that of the monophonic chant, unmeasured. It remained so as long as the two melodies moved at the same time. But eventually the two voices assumed *rhythmic* independence. They not only moved in parallel and contrary melodic motion, but in *different time patterns.* This diversity between the two parts made it necessary to develop a new type of rhythmic notation so that each voice could be accurately coordinated with the other. *Mensural notation* appeared, in which the precise length of time of each part was indicated (see Fig. 6.3). Later organa employed three and even four voice parts.

Thus, two major changes took place in Western music: (1) the change from monophony to polyphony and (2) the change from unmeasured, relatively "free" rhythm to **measured rhythm,** in which precise time values were related to each other. These principles of polyphony and measured rhythm were fully developed in the motet and in the polyphonic setting of the Mass.

THE MOTET

Much as the organa had added an independent line of music to the chant, the **motet** added a second set of words (the name *motet* comes from the French word *mot,* meaning word). Originally a form of religious music, it grew out of the two-part organa in the thirteenth century. While the lower voice continued to sing the words and music of the chant, a second text was sung in the upper voice. The second text at first paraphrased the chant text being sung below.

The motet was soon also employed for secular occasions. As its form evolved, the upper voice began to sing in the vernacular. The subject matter was usually secular, and sometimes obscene. Gradually, composers added a third and even a fourth voice part.

1. Codex 339 der Bibliothek zu St. Gallen (10. Jahrhundert).

2. Neumen und Buchstaben. — Antiphonar von Montpellier (11. Jahrhundert).

3. Neumen auf einer geritzten Linie ohne Farbe. — Graduale von Albi (11. Jahrhundert).

4. Neumen auf vier Linien. — Graduale aus dem 12.—13. Jahrhundert.

5. Auf Linien gesetzte Neumen mit viereckigem Notenkörper [Nota quadriquarta] seit dem 12. Jahrhundert bis heute.

6. Schwarzrote Mensuralnote des 14.—15. Jahrhunderts. — Tenor einer 3 stimmigen Chanson von G. Binchois.

7. Weiß-schwarze Mensuralnote des 15.—17. Jahrhunderts. Dasselbe Stück.

8. Dasselbe Stück mit heutigen Noten ohne Verkürzung der Werte.

9. Dasselbe, die Werte auf den vierten Teil verkürzt.

Fig. 6.3 The evolution of the writing of musical notes has taken nearly a thousand years. Not only has the style changed, but the indications for durational values have become increasingly precise. Time periods for the examples shown are: line 1, tenth century; lines 2 and 3, eleventh century; line 4, twelfth to thirteenth century; line 5, twelfth century onward; line 6, fourteenth to fifteenth century (mensural notation); line 7, fifteenth to seventeenth century (mensural notation); lines 8 and 9, modern notation.

QUANT VOI   The French motet *Quant voi** was typical of those written in the thirteenth century. In it the top voice carries a secular text in the vernacular and the bottom two voices carry religious texts in Latin. The chant melody is incorporated in the bottom part.

TRIPLUM, OR TOP PART:

Quant voi revenir	*When I see returning*
D'este la saison	*The summer season*
Que le bois font retenir	*And all the little birds*
Tuit cil oisillon,	*Make the woods resound,*
Adonc pleur et souspir	*Then I weep and sigh*
Pour le grant desir	*For the great desire*
Qu'ai de la belle Marion,	*Which I have for the fair Marion,*
Qui mon cuer a en prison.	*Who holds my heart imprisoned.*

MOTET, OR MIDDLE PART:

Virgo virginum	*Virgin of virgins,*
Lumen luminum,	*Light of lights,*
Restauratrix hominum,	*Restorer of men,*
Qui portasti Dominum:	*Who bore the Lord:*
Per te Maria,	*Through Thee, Mary,*
Detur venia	*Let grace be given*
Angelo nunciante,	*As the angel announced,*
Virgo es post et ante.	*Thou art Virgin before and after.*

TENOR, OR BOTTOM PART:

Hec dies	*This is the day (which the Lord hath made)*

By the fourteenth century the motet had increased in length and had become more elaborate in its melodic and rhythmic structure. But even with the increased number of melodic lines and texts the range of voices remained narrow, and the chant was almost always retained in some form in the lowest voice part. Without question, the most important composer of the fourteenth century was Guillaume de Machaut (Ma-sho´, ca. 1300–ca. 1377). In addition to large quantities of secular music and motets, he wrote the earliest polyphonic setting of the entire Ordinary of the Mass.

By the fifteenth century the motet had evolved full circle. Once again it became primarily a religious form, using one text for all voices. The text was almost always taken from the Bible. One of the leading motet composers of the fifteenth century was Guillaume Dufay (ca. 1400–1474).

In its return to a sacred form, the motet became a primary source for the polyphonic setting of the Mass. At first the Proper and isolated portions of the

---

*   This motet may be found in *Harvard Anthology of Music*, Vol. I, p. 33, Harvard University Press (Cambridge, Mass.: 1950).

Ordinary appeared in polyphonic form. Later the entire Ordinary was set in polyphony.

During the Renaissance, secular melodies were introduced into the Mass and the traditional chant forms were moved freely from one part of the Liturgy to another.

RENAISSANCE SACRED MUSIC

The Renaissance in literature and the visual arts began in the fourteenth century and centered in Italy. The Renaissance in music began in the fifteenth century in what is today northern France, Holland, and Belgium. The Franco-Flemish style developed in these countries and then became international and spread to all parts of the Continent.

In addition to Guillaume Dufay, the outstanding members of this early Flemish school were Johannes Ockeghem (ca. 1430–1495), Jacob Obrecht (1452–1505), and Josquin des Prez (ca. 1450–1521). In their Masses and motets, four-part writing became standard. An independent bass part was added beneath the chant for the first time, so that the chant was no longer the lowest voice part. In addition, the use and treatment of the chant as a basic material became much freer and at times was abandoned altogether. The practice of using secular tunes as the musical raw material for sacred compositions became extremely popular. The polyphonic style emphasized the true independence of each of the four parts.

JOSQUIN DES PREZ

The greatest representative of the Franco-Flemish school was Josquin des Prez (Zhoss-can' day Pray), who spent most of his creative life outside his native country, Belgium. In 1475 he was a member of the choir at the court of the Duke of Szorfa in Milan and later he joined the Papal Choir in Rome. He was also active in the Italian cities of Florence, Ferrara, and Modena. In the last years of his life he returned to northern Europe.

Josquin was acknowledged by his contemporaries to be the greatest master of the time, and he developed the complex Franco-Flemish style to its highest point. In much of his secular music he employed a lighter, more homophonic style, then popular in Italy. His polyphonic style is distinguished by the use of *imitation,* wherein a melodic fragment stated in one voice is repeated or imitated by another voice a measure or two later. Examples of imitative polyphony appear earlier than Josquin, but he was the first to apply the principle consistently.

Josquin's motet *Ave Maria (Hail Mary;* a portion is shown in Example 6.2) is typical of his motet writing in the following ways:

AVE MARIA
RECORD 1/SIDE 1

1. The melodic material is freely based on a Gregorian chant, in this case *Ave Maria, gratia plena.*

Hail Mary, full of grace, the Lord (is with thee).

Example 6.2 (Josquin des Prez, *Ave Maria*)

2. It is a four-part composition in which the voices are often paired, the two upper voices being pitted against the two lower voices.

3. The text is **through-composed,** which means that each unit is given a separate musical setting. (This contrasts to *strophic* music, where each stanza of text is sung to the same melody.) A feeling of continuity is achieved through overlapping phrases: before one phrase ends, another voice begins a new phrase, so that there is seldom a cadence when all four voices come to a stop. This continuous flow is characteristic of later Renaissance polyphony.

4. Contrapuntal passages alternate with homophonic sections, another hallmark of Josquin's style. Despite the complexity of the contrapuntal writing, the text remains clear, for Josquin assigns to the homophonic sections the expressive parts of the text.

Josquin left many motets, many Masses, and a considerable amount of secular music. He was also a gifted teacher, and many of his pupils became outstanding figures in the next generation of composers.

PALESTRINA

One of the most distinguished of Josquin's successors was Giovanni Pierluigi da Palestrina (1524–1594), who spent the greater part of his life as choirmaster of St. Peter's in Rome. Palestrina's great contribution was to return church music to the simplicity and purity of earlier times. Although his motets are masterpieces of composition, his Masses constitute his most important work.

Palestrina lived and worked during the Counter-Reformation, the reaction by the Catholic church to the spread of Protestantism. Central to this reaction was the Council of Trent, which met from 1545 to 1563 to formulate and execute the means by which church reform could be accomplished. The Council investigated every aspect of religious discipline, including church music. It was the opinion of the Council that sacred music had become corrupted by complex polyphonic devices that obscured the text and diverted attention from the act of worship. To remedy this situation the Council called for a return to a simpler vocal style, one that would preserve the sanctity of the text and discourage frivolous displays of virtuosity by the singers. (A **virtuoso** is one who has extraordinary technical skill in performing.)

Legend has it that Palestrina, in order to prevent the Council from abolishing the polyphonic style entirely, composed a Mass of such beauty and simplicity that he was able to dissuade the cardinals from taking this drastic step. Without abandoning polyphony, Palestrina created a style that was less intricate than that of his predecessors.

A prolific composer, Palestrina wrote more than a hundred Mass settings. One of his relatively late Masses was based on the chant melody *Salve Regina*. The *Missa Salve Regina,* which is an excellent example of late Renaissance polyphony, employs elements of the chant in each movement.

MISSA SALVE REGINA

Notice in Example 6.3 that the notes of the chant, marked with an ×, are used as the basic melodic material. The Mass also exhibits the following characteristics:

1. All the voice parts (five in this case) are of equal importance. Each participates fully in singing the text.
2. The general style is imitative polyphony, with occasional homophonic sections.
3. Strong cadences set off sections from each other.
4. The text is treated in the simplest and most sensitive way permitted by the polyphonic texture.

Palestrina's sacred music was performed *a cappella,* without instruments, but this was the exception rather than the rule. Although no instrumental parts were written, it is well known that instruments frequently played along with or substituted for a voice in one or more of the parts.

Lord have mercy on us.

✕ = notes of the chant incorporated into each vocal part.

Example 6.3 (Palestrina, *Missa Salve Regina*)

ROLAND DE LASSUS

Palestrina's great contemporary, Roland de Lassus (1532–1594), was born in Mons, Belgium, and began his musical career as a member of the choir in the Mons Cathedral. So beautiful was his voice that he was kidnapped three times to sing in other choirs. A truly international musical figure, he was equally well known by the Italian and Latin forms of his name—Orlando di Lasso and Orlandus Lassus. Lassus's music included all the national genres of the time. He wrote Latin motets and Masses, Italian madrigals, German lieder, and French chansons. His sacred style is most clearly shown in his motets.

Lassus's setting of *Salve Regina* demonstrates the fact that his music is less imitative and has a richer harmonic quality than Josquin's. (See Example 6.4.)

SALVE REGINA
RECORD 1/SIDE 1

Hail Queen of mercy.
✗ = notes of the chant melody occurring in the bass voice.

Example 6.4 (Roland de Lassus, *Salve Regina*)

RENAISSANCE SECULAR MUSIC

In addition to being a period of great piety, the sixteenth century was also a period of bawdy earthiness, irreverent humor, and celebration of sensual love. The same composers who created works "for the greater glory of God" also wrote compositions of an entirely different character. In Italy and England the principal form of secular music was the *madrigal;* in France it was the *chanson;* in Germany it was the *lied*.

THE MADRIGAL

The Renaissance **madrigal** is a poem set to music. It had its beginnings in the fourteenth century among the aristocrats of the small Italian courts. The texts, written in the vernacular, were often twelve-line poems whose subject was sentimental or erotic love. The early madrigal was written in a predominantly homophonic style. It was usually in three, but sometimes four, parts, and its expressive qualities were subdued and restrained. The so-called *classical madrigal* of the mid-sixteenth century was written usually for five and sometimes for four or six voices. Its texture was more polyphonic than the early madrigal, and a greater attempt was made to capture in the music the expressive possibilities of the words.

(*Continued on page 100.*)

INTERLUDE | THE CULTURE OF THE MIDDLE AGES AND RENAISSANCE

In 1907, a well-known art historian, writing of the Middle Ages, declared that art and society ". . . degenerated into coarse decoration and vulgar copying. Learning was forgotten. The sun set in a somber sky, and civilization settled down to a millenium of sleep." Nothing could be further from the truth. Medieval Europe was a place of great artistic production, work later dismissed undeservedly as barbaric or "Gothic." Perhaps medieval design still suffers from being judged by classical standards of beauty—that is, by the values of Greek and Roman artists before, and Renaissance artists after. And indeed, if we use realism as a criterion in assessing the quality of art, medieval work will look inferior. The symbolic nature of medieval art made the accurate representation of humanity and nature irrelevant.

THE MIDDLE AGES

The period of a thousand years known as the Middle Ages grew out of the slow disintegration of the Roman Empire. The once invincible empire was weakened by administrative disarray in its far-flung holdings, invasions from the north and east, the spread of Christian doctrine, and the removal of the imperial capital to Greek-speaking lands in the east, to Constantinople. Problems began before 300 A.D.; by the fifth century Rome had faded into a town where cows grazed on the once great forums and avenues, and a tiny fraction of its earlier population lived squalidly in the shadow of the past. In the seventh century, with the Islamic sweep of the Mediterranean, the last traces of Roman culture vanished in the west.

There is no easy explanation for a decline that took centuries. Clearly, however, the most threatening challenge to imperial values was Christianity, a religion that rejected both materialism and reason. The Christian faith advanced its mystical Son of God as an object of faith. Christians maintained that all people were brothers and sisters in the eyes of God; they were drawn toward a Heavenly City where earthly matters were of no consequence.

It was the Church, though—one church, linked by common language and doctrine—that acted as the central agent of culture and knowledge in the Middle Ages. The monasteries, particularly before the revival of towns in the twelfth century, were the principal patrons of art and architecture. They were the vehicles for the preservation of literacy and of great literary works. In the monasteries music, in the form of liturgical chants that we call Gregorian, was used in the recitation of the psalms. After the ninth century monks composed new music for feast days.

Between the seventh and twelfth centuries Europe turned into a mosaic of self-sufficient farms and manors that were controlled by secular lords or by the

90

Plate 1. This Cross Page from the Lindisfarne Gospels (700 A.D.) was painted by Irish monks and demonstrates the movement of Christianity into northern Europe in the early Middle Ages. The interlace design shows distinguished craftsmanship but no interest in representing the visible world. (Cotton Ms. Nero D IV, F. 26v, reproduced by permission of the British Library Board.)

Plate 2. Sainte Chapelle, the royal chapel in Paris, is a culmination of the Gothic style of the thirteenth century. Between 1140 and 1240, French designers developed a system of supports and pointed arches that made masonry merely a skeleton for colored glass. The result was highly spiritual and elegant. (Courtesy Ciccione/Photo Researchers, Inc.)

Plate 3. This fifteenth-century Flemish *Annunciation*, center panel of the Merode Alterpiece (ca. 1425–1428), shows a setting similar to a contemporary townhouse. It is not abstract like earlier medieval painting, but its lack of linear perspective and its distorted figures make clear the difference between ''late Gothic'' painting in Flanders and the Renaissance style being developed at that time in Italy. (Courtesy The Metropolitan Museum of Art; The Cloisters Collection, Purchase.)

Plate 4. *The Small Cowper Madonna,* by Raphael (1505). This masterpiece displays the quiet, powerful dignity of the High Renaissance style as well as the clarity, stability, draughtsmanship, and subtle emotions that made Raphael a paragon for artists of succeeding generations. (Courtesy The National Gallery of Art, Washington; Widener Collection.)

Church. Cities disappeared. Many areas that had been productive farmland became forest and wilderness. As written communication and road systems broke down, people (especially outside the Church) became less mobile. Peasants living in Burgundy had no concept of the ocean. They would all probably live their lives never traveling beyond their valley.

Europe remained on the whole rude, agrarian, and poor for hundreds of years. The arts could not flourish in an environment where survival and nourishment were daily preoccupations. Yet in spite of the small artistic output—illumination of sacred books, small sculptured reliefs, and jewelry—the quality of the art was sometimes miraculous.

In the eleventh and twelfth centuries, however, interregional trade once again became common. Villages developed into towns and cities. Great universities were established at Paris and Bologna. Bishops, using cities as administrative centers for a wealthy and powerful Church, built great cathedrals that in the later Middle Ages replaced monasteries as the focal buildings of the Christian West. A small but important new class of merchants and artisans acted as the spearhead for economic recovery. After 1100 the economic foundations of the Renaissance began to set.

No artists of the Middle Ages thought that their abilities or achievements were anything more than a gift of God. But many artists in the later Middle Ages thought that these gifts could beautify God's universe. This attitude, along with the new money in towns and the Church, explains the fine church building of the twelfth century and later. The first phase of this new architecture we call Romanesque, a loose term that suggests a style closer to the Roman Empire than to the ninth-century empire of Charlemagne. These solid, monumental churches were built mainly by rich monasteries. They were the first large-scale, stone-vaulted buildings in the West since the days of the Roman Empire; they were decorated by splendid, complicated sculpture of biblical subjects, often crowned by the awesome subject of the Last Judgment.

The second (and much longer lasting) phase of later medieval architecture we call Gothic. By contemporaries it was called the "royal French style," because it was given its impetus by the brilliant Abbot Suger at the royal abbey of St. Denis in the 1140s. Gothic architecture borrowed from earlier buildings in the Romanesque style, but it used pointed rather than rounded arches, a change that allowed higher ceilings, and it used flying buttresses, which threw the weight of those ceilings outside the buildings. The combination of these techniques produced an entirely different appearance from that of the Romanesque. Thick, massive walls became unnecessary with the new arches and supports. Naves were built higher and higher. Walls disappeared as the mason's work became lighter, more verticalized, and more elegantly slender. The rich, translucent colors of stained glass replaced the solid wall surfaces of the Romanesque. The century after the 1140s was the time when the great French cathedrals were built—Laon, Paris, Chartres, Reims, and Amiens. In Sainte Chapelle, built in the 1240s, the masonry became merely a skeleton for brilliant colored light (Plate 2).

In the thirteenth century the Gothic style radiated from the area around Paris to become the predominant style in European art for the next 300 years. It became an "international" style with ingenious local variations. It was applied to

Plate 6. The west facade of the cathedral at Reims, built in the thirteenth century, exemplifies the height, grandeur, and sculptural magnificence of Gothic architecture. The nave of the cathedral is 125 feet high, with a drive upward that is reinforced by the slenderness of its proportions. (Courtesy Marburg/Art Reference Bureau.)

Plate 5. The sculpture on the west portals of Chartres Cathedral, done in the middle of the twelfth century, demonstrates the greater order and realism of Gothic design as compared with Romanesque work. The three-dimensionality of the figures suggests the growing independence of sculpture from architecture. (Courtesy Bulloz/Art Reference Bureau.)

Plate 7. Andrea Palladio's Villa Rotunda (begun 1550) exhibits the balance, symmetry, and simplicity of Renaissance architecture in the fifteenth and sixteenth centuries. Inspired by the architectural structures and details of Roman antiquity, proponents of this new style rejected the soaring towers, flying buttresses, sculptured pinnacles, and pointed arches of the Gothic era. (Courtesy Alinari/Art Reference Bureau.)

secular (nonreligious) buildings in the great towns: in Flanders, France, and Germany we have excellent guild houses, town halls, and townhouses constructed in the Gothic style.

The west facade of the Gothic cathedral often displayed an ambitious sculptural program with a wealth of carved designs (Plate 6). In contrast to the sculpture of the previous 800 years, Gothic sculpture rapidly assumed a more realistic, ordered, and three-dimensional appearance, particularly in the representation of human figures. Sculpture remained, however, a handmaiden of architecture and overwhelmingly religious in content.

THE RENAISSANCE

The raw materials of the Renaissance are visible in European culture from the twelfth century. But it was the 1400s when the Renaissance came "out of the oven." New literary and design values, discontent in the Church, exploratory ventures in Asia and the Western Hemisphere, and the consolidation of nations under powerful monarchs—all this would completely reshape the nature of European life before 1600. The cultural future was being redefined, however, in Italian towns where artists and intellectuals were passionately admiring the achievements of ancient Rome.

These Italians, especially in Florence, were contemptuous of the recent past. They called the Gothic style "the merest travesty of art" and felt that only "in our own day . . . men dare to boast that they see the dawn of better things." Over a very short period of time—less than two generations—Florentine masters transformed the look of art. Masaccio developed systematic perspective in painting; Donatello sculpted bodies based on the proportions of Roman statues; Brunelleschi reintroduced an architecture of clear plan and classical forms. Florentine discoveries and innovations were imitated, first by Italians and later by northern Europeans. In the early sixteenth century Italian artists were imported wholesale by the French king: Leonardo da Vinci died in a chateau in the Loire Valley. Italian principles became doctrine in the training of artists. The Gothic pinnacle and tower were replaced by the Renaissance capital and dome.

What captured the Italian mind of the early Renaissance was a sense of the tremendous power and beauty of the human being. While medieval Europe idealized meditative withdrawal, the Renaissance stressed activity and worldly excellence. In this climate, portraiture and the ideal nude—kinds of art that had vanished in Western art for a millenium—again became the fashion. Humanistic literature examined the state of the world instead of heaven. Reason replaced faith as the intellectual norm.

Music, like the other art forms, developed in new directions. Composers of religious music drew on the Gregorian chants as source materials for longer, more complex polyphonic works. The more worldly outlook of the Renaissance was expressed in the composition and performance of secular vocal music, especially the English madrigals, French chansons, and German lieder.

The northern Renaissance of the sixteenth century brought less change than the Italian Renaissance, being more a blend of the old and new. Yet it was two

Germans who revolutionized the European conception of humanity's place in the cosmos. Copernicus advanced the thesis that the earth revolved around the sun, and thus was not the center of the universe. Martin Luther broke with the Roman Church on the grounds of corruption in the Church and disagreement with doctrine, thus igniting a firestorm of conflict in which Protestants saw themselves as individually responsible for their spiritual destinies, not subject to papal authority. The Renaissance not only revised the look of European art, but with its emphasis on things secular, individual, and objectively observed, also transformed the assumptions of European society.

Plate 8. *The Annunciation*, by Botticelli (1490). In this Florentine painting the beautiful, linear figures interact in a nearly bare room drawn through the principles of perspective. This kind of design resulted in a far more accurate, naturalistic image than in earlier centuries. (Courtesy Alinari/Art Reference Bureau.)

99

Plate 9. Michelangelo dominated Italian art during the sixteenth century. His athletic figures, often in highly imaginative, complicated poses, were copied and paraphrased by later artists throughout Europe. *The Dying Slave* (1513–1516), shown here, was meant for a papal tomb that was never completed. (Courtesy Musées Nationaux, Paris.)

(*Continued from page 89.*)

The final flowering of the madrigal took place during the closing decades of the sixteenth century. The late madrigal was an elaborate composition, invariably through-composed, with a mixture of homophonic and polyphonic textures. It used notes from the chromatic scale (all twelve notes in the octave) for bold effects, often to express sadness. The compositions also used coloristic and dramatic effects. One of the most interesting elements of the madrigal style was **word painting,** which attempted to represent the literal meaning of the text through music. Thus, the melody would ascend for the word "heaven," and a wavelike melody would depict the word "water."

Around the middle of the sixteenth century the Italian madrigal was brought to England. There it flourished under a variety of names—song, sonnet, canzonet, and ayre. William Byrd (1543–1623) and Thomas Morley (1557–1603) were the first English composers to cultivate the genre. Morley wrote simplified versions of the madrigal, known as *balletts*. Adapted from the Italian *belletti,* they were usually characterized by a *fa-la-la* refrain of the type that appears in the English carol "Deck the Halls." Enlivened by accents and a regular beat, the music was largely homophonic.

Fig. 6.4 During the Renaissance, music became a popular leisure time activity for both the educated middle class and the aristocracy. This detail of a fresco in the Este palace, Ferrara, Italy, depicts the musical and sensual delights of spring.

THE CHANSON

In the sixteenth century the **chanson** (the French word for "song") was to France what the madrigal was to Italy and England. Early chansons developed with the work of Clement Jannequin (ca. 1485–ca. 1560), Claudin de Sermisy (ca. 1490–1562), and Pierre Certon (ca. 1510–1572).

Chansons modified the motet style with strong accented rhythms, frequent repetitions, and short phrases ending simultaneously in all parts. They were usually sung by three, four, or five voices, and sections of simple imitation alternated with sections that were essentially homophonic.

Word painting occurred frequently in the early chansons. Jannequin wrote several *program chansons,* in which the music imitates a nonmusical idea. An example is his *Chant des oiseaux* (*Song of the Birds*), in which the singers' voices imitate the sounds of birds such as the cuckoo:

CHANT DES OISEAUX

RECORD 1/SIDE 1

Example 6.5 (Jannequin, *Chant des oiseaux*)

THE LIED

In Germany the counterpart to the French chanson was the **lied** (pronounced "leet"), also meaning "song." The lied (plural, **lieder,** pronounced "leader") dates from the middle of the fifteenth century, when both monophonic melodies and three-part settings appeared. The early lieder, which were heavily influenced by the Netherlands' polyphonic style, later provided the Lutheran church with many melodies for chorale tunes (see Chapter 9). The first important lied composer was Heinrich Isaac (ca. 1450–1517).

In the sixteenth century Germany looked to Italy and France for musicians to staff her courts and municipalities. As a result, lied composers turned from the Franco-Flemish styles to the chanson and madrigal as their new models. In these lieder the text was treated in the manner of the madrigals, and the various melodies were set in imitative counterpoint.

RENAISSANCE INSTRUMENTAL MUSIC

Although most of the music of the Renaissance was written for voices, the role of instrumental music should not be underestimated. Instruments were used in church, at many festive and social occasions, as part of theatrical productions, and in private homes.

The earliest music played on instruments was sacred or secular vocal music. During the Renaissance some music was written specifically for instruments. Most of it was dance music, as dancing was an important part of Renaissance social life. A fairly large collection of this music has been preserved, but apparently much of it was improvised on well-known or harmonic bass patterns, much as jazz is today.

The most popular instrument of the fifteenth and sixteenth centuries was the lute. The earliest lute music consisted of transcriptions (a **transcription** is an arrangement of a composition for a medium other than that for which it was originally written) of vocal pieces and dance music, but in the sixteenth century composers began to write original pieces for lute. These **ricercari,** or **fantasias,** were elaborate, difficult, and often polyphonic pieces that demonstrated the vir-

Fig. 6.5 The lute was the most popular Renaissance stringed instrument. During the sixteenth century, volumes of solo music for lute were published all over Europe. (Courtesy The National Gallery of Art, Washington; Ailson Mellon Bruce Fund.)

tuosity of the performer, who was often the composer. Beginning in the 1530s, volumes of solo music for the lute were published in Italy, France, Germany, England, and Spain.

Keyboard instruments, especially the harpsichord and the organ, were also popular during the Renaissance. Keyboard music evolved through the same states as lute music, from vocal music to dance music, and then to original compositions, which were increasingly complex.

Small chamber music ensembles, called consorts, were favored among those who performed music in their homes. One of the favorite groupings, especially in England, was a consort of several viole da gamba. Polyphonic pieces for such consorts of two to five or more were written by some of England's greatest composers, including William Byrd and Orlando Gibbons (1583–1625). Similar pieces were also played by consorts of recorders and other woodwinds. Music for brass and reed instruments was popular for outdoor occasions and for festive church ceremonies.

CHARACTERISTICS OF MEDIEVAL AND RENAISSANCE MUSIC

	MEDIEVAL	RENAISSANCE
Texture	Gregorian chants and troubador songs were monophonic; medieval motet employed polyphony	Polyphonic
Tonality	Church modes	Church modes
Rhythm	Gregorian chant employed unmeasured rhythm; secular music employed measured rhythm	Measured
Singing Style	Sacred music: solemn, expressive, small voice range Secular music: simple, strophic, more rhythmic	Four-part singing common, some virtuoso singing Late madrigal used "word painting"
Large Vocal Works	None	Polyphonic Mass
Small Vocal Works	Gregorian chant, organum, medieval motet	Motet, madrigal, chanson, lied
Musical Instruments	Instruments (lute) accompanied troubador songs	Lute, keyboard, chamber consorts (especially viole da gamba), recorder, organ
Instrumental Music	Sacred music: arrangements of vocal pieces Secular music: isolated dances	Ricercari, fantasias, dance forms

SUMMARY

Western music grew out of the religious music of the Middle Ages. Chants, closely allied with the Roman Catholic Liturgy, were codified and compiled during the time of Pope Gregory. In the following centuries the simple, monophonic form of these chants evolved into the more complex, polyphonic forms of the organum and the motet. These forms, in turn, were further developed by Machaut and Dufay, and the sacred music of the Renaissance culminated in the works of Josquin des Prez, Lassus, and Palestrina.

Together with the sacred music, secular music was also developing. Early vocal music was performed by trouvères in northern France, troubadours in southern France, and minnesingers in Germany. The vernacular and sometimes bawdy tradition of their songs was preserved in the madrigals, chansons, and lieder of the Renaissance.

Instrumental music of the Renaissance evolved from vocal music to dance music, and then to more complex original compositions. The most popular Renaissance instrument was the lute, with keyboard music and chamber consorts also coming into use.

NEW TERMS

Gregorian chant (plainsong; plainchant)
church modes
syllabic (melody)
melismatic (melody)
strophic
organum (organa)
measured rhythm
motet

through-composed
virtuoso
madrigal
word painting
chanson
lied (lieder)
transcription
ricercar (fantasia)

PART III SUGGESTED LISTENING

Musical Organizations

Capella antiqua (Munich). Directed by Konrad Ruhland, this group employs original instruments of the Renaissance or modern copies. Its performances are attempts at reconstructing the original musical practices of the times. (Telefunken Records, *Das Alte Werk series.*)

The Early Music Quartet (Munich). This vocal and instrumental ensemble of three Americans and one German specializes chiefly in medieval song literature. (Telefunken Records, *Das Alte Werk* series.)

New York Pro Musica Antiqua. Founded in 1952 by Noah Greenberg, this group (now, sadly, defunct) was for a number of years the most prominent of American early music groups. (Decca Records.)

The Waverly Consort (New York). This ensemble of ten men and women, directed by Michael Jaffe, is now the leading American group specializing in the performance of medieval and Renaissance music. (Vanguard and Columbia Records.)

Choir of the Monks of the Abbey of Saint Pierre de Solesmes (Solesmes, France). The performances of chant by this Benedictine Order are considered by many scholars to be among the best, historically as well as musically. (Deutsche Grammophon Gesellschaft, DGG, Archive series,)

Medieval Secular Music

John Dunstable, *O Rosa bella.* Though Dunstable was an English composer, he spent much of his life on the Continent; some of his vocal works employ French or Italian texts.

Medieval Sacred Music

Guillaume de Machaut, *Messe de Nostre Dame* (*Mass of Our Lady*). One of the earliest and best-known polyphonic settings of the Ordinary of the Mass. The five interrelated movements demonstrate most of the important compositional techniques of the late medieval period.

Renaissance Secular Music

Roland de Lassus, *Matona, mia cara* (*Matona, Lovely Maiden*). One of the best-known of Renaissance satirical pieces, this madrigal for four voices makes fun of the German soldiers occupying much of sixteenth-century Italy by—among other things—mocking their pronunciation of Italian ("Matona" for "Madonna").

Orlando Gibbons, *The Silver Swan.* One of the loveliest vocal compositions ever written, this melancholy work is an outstanding example of English madrigal style.

Thomas Morley, *My Bonnie Lass She Smileth.* Using both homophonic and polyphonic textures, swift changes from the major to minor, and a *"fa la la"* section, this song is typical of Morley's balletts.

Renaissance Sacred Music

Guillaume Dufay, *Missa Se la face ay pale* (*Mass on "If My Face Is Pale"*). A classic example of early Renaissance polyphonic style, this four-voice setting of the Ordinary takes its rather odd name from the title of the chanson melody upon which it is based.

Josquin des Prez, *Missa Pange lingua* (*Mass on "Sing, My Tongue"*). One of the great masterpieces of the Renaissance, this work is based on the plainsong hymn for the Feast of Corpus Christi.

Giovanni Pierluigi da Palestrina, *Sicut cervus desiderat* (*Like as the Hart Desireth*). One of Palestrina's most expressive and technically perfect works, this motet, its text taken from Psalm 42, is a classic example of Palestrina-style harmonic and melodic construction.

ALEXANDER,
AN
OPERA,
Compos'd by Mr. Handel.

Engrav'd, Printed and Sold by J. Cluer in Bow-Church-Yard, London

IV

MUSIC OF THE BAROQUE ERA

Title page of Handel's *Alexander*,
published by Cluer in 1726.

CHAPTER 7 | BAROQUE VOCAL MUSIC

THE BAROQUE ERA, SPANNING THE CENTURY AND A HALF BETWEEN the performance of the first opera in 1600 and the death of Johann Sebastian Bach in 1750, was a period of vast significance in the history of Western music. Stylistically, the *early* Baroque era was characterized by a change from the many-voiced polyphony of the Renaissance to chordal homophony, in which a single melodic line predominated. New forms of composition emerged, including the opera, the cantata, and the oratorio in vocal music, and the concerto, the concerto grosso, and the sonata in instrumental music. Instrumental music rose to hold a place of equal importance with the vocal idiom, developing a literature of its own apart from vocal music. The new interest in chordal homophony led to one of the most important changes in music history—a shift from the medieval church modes to the major-minor system which was to dominate Western music for the next three hundred years.

THE NEW MUSIC

Around 1600 in Italy a group of composers called the Camerata reacted against the elaborate polyphonic texture of the Renaissance. They wanted music to intensify the expressiveness of the text rather than obscure it by elaborate decoration. During the sixteenth century, composers had focused their attention on the simultaneous musical lines and the interplay between voice parts. Often, various parts sang different words at the same time, with the result that no words could be heard distinctly. And in a single part a word frequently was stretched out over so many tones that its identity and meaning were lost.

The poets and musicians in the Camerata sought to resurrect the spirit of ancient Greek drama as they envisioned it. An important member of this group was Giulio Caccini (1546–1618), whose compositions provided the basis for a new musical style.

THE MAJOR-MINOR SYSTEM

One of the most important aspects of the "new music" was that Baroque composers began to think vertically instead of horizontally. They were concerned with the harmonic organization of music. Gradually they evolved a system of harmony based on the idea of a *tonal center,* or *tonic,* using chords beneath the melodic line to establish a tonal center.

The tonic note established the key of the piece, and all other notes were ranked according to how closely they related to the tonic. The closest were the fifth note of the scale, the *dominant,* and the fourth, the *subdominant.* The dominant, or active, chord (V) tends to resolve to the tonic, or rest, chord (I). Without this resolution the music sounds incomplete; the inherent tension of the dominant-tonic relationship gives special impulse to harmonic progression.

This important dominant-tonic relationship enabled composers to establish a firm home base in the tonic key. Tension could be created by using a chord sequence that moves away from the tonic key. This tension could be eased by returning to the tonic. Modulations from the tonic to the dominant and back to the tonic opened up a new way of organizing musical time-flow. It permitted the development of larger structures, for the expectation of eventual return to the tonic key could support a fairly long excursion away from it. Most pieces leave their original tonics and establish one or more secondary tonics in the middle of the work—the new keys providing variety and making the return to the original key more significant. Baroque composers used this procedure in their vocal as well as in their instrumental music.

With the new emphasis on harmony, *modes,* the basic organizing force of melodically oriented music, lost their importance. The number of modes in common use decreased from the eight or ten of the Renaissance to just two: *major* and *minor.*

The evolution of chordal homophony and its subsequent effects took hold gradually through the early Baroque. And though we may be more familiar with the profound changes through instrumental music, the changes began in vocal music.

BASSO CONTINUO

The "new music" was founded on the premise that the music should serve the text, both in its pattern of accents and its emotional quality. It was the function of the music to reflect, enforce, and enhance the meaning of the words.

Out of this concept grew a new style, called the **monodic style,** in which the vocal line was predominant. Essentially, the composer wrote a two-part structure consisting of a melodic line for the voice and a simple bass. The bass part required two instruments: a harpsichord or organ and a bass instrument such as the viola da gamba or cello. The bass line was supplied by the latter instrument and by the left-hand part of the harpsichord or organ. Above the bass line the harpsichordist or organist improvised harmonies with the right hand. This combination of instruments and its accompanimental function are called **basso continuo,** or simply **continuo.** Since the harmonies were filled in by the keyboard player and not written out, they had to be deduced from symbols in the notation.

Numbers written below the bass line indicated which harmonies were to be filled in (Example 7.1).

Example 7.1

The numbers referred only to basic chords, not to the way they should be played. Thus, the player was given considerable expressive freedom. The notational symbols constituted an ingenious shorthand called **figured bass** or **thorough-bass.**

While the basso continuo originated in the vocal music of the early Baroque, it came to be applied to virtually all music in the period, both vocal and instrumental. So prevalent was the continuo practice that the Baroque was later nicknamed the "continuo period."

BAROQUE VOCAL STYLES

The monodic style, with its emphasis on the importance of the words, consisted of essentially two different types of vocal expression, the *recitative* and the *arioso*.

RECITATIVE

The **recitative** is a kind of singing speech in which the rhythm is dictated by the natural inflection of the words. In contrast to the Renaissance idea of an even flow of music, the recitative is sung in free, flexible rhythm with continuo accompaniment. The tempo is slowed down or speeded up according to the performer's interpretation of the text.

Within Baroque opera and oratorio, the recitative primarily served to heighten dramatic impact or to further the action of the story. As it evolved through the Baroque, the recitative acquired greater dramatic importance. The recitative with only continuo accompaniment, known as **secco recitative,** usually introduced an aria or appeared in the less dramatic moments of a piece. The **accompanied recitative,** in which the voice is accompanied by instruments in addition to continuo, produced a more powerful effect. Both types of recitatives gradually acquired stock endings. In one, the voice part dropped down a fourth, and in the other the voice part ended on a descending scale. In both endings, after the voices had concluded their parts, the instruments sounded two final punctuating chords: a dominant chord, followed by a tonic chord.

ARIOSO AND ARIA

More lyrical and expressive than the recitative, the **arioso** tends to dwell on one aspect of the action or develops the feelings or state of mind of a character. The rhythm of the arioso is determined by musical as well as textual considerations. Thus, its tempo is less flexible than that of the recitative and is maintained steadily throughout.

The lyrical arioso was expanded gradually into the **aria.** In its most common form the aria has a three-part structure known as **da capo,** consisting of two sections followed by a repetition of the first in an ABA sequence.

The first section (A) of the da capo aria was followed by a contrasting section (B). The conclusion of the B section was marked by the words "da capo," which instructed the performers to return to the beginning and repeat section A. This closed form made the aria even more dramatically static than the arioso. Although it was not suitable for swift action, it was superbly structured for lyrical expression.

As performed in the Baroque period, the repeated A section differed considerably the second time around. Performers decorated, ornamented, and otherwise altered the music to display their vocal techniques and to further intensify the spirit of the words. This style of singing became an inherent part of the opera and the oratorio of the later Baroque period. Solo performers, raised to new prominence by the monodic style, added intricate runs and trills to dress up the music. In fact, virtuosity was sometimes exaggerated to the point of overshadowing the music and drama.

Out of the monodic style, with its emphasis on the solo voice, continuo accompaniment, and lyrical projection of the text, came some of the principal ingredients for the three important forms of Baroque vocal music—the opera, the oratorio, and the cantata.

The early Baroque **opera** was a dramatic form based on secular themes and written in Italian. Sung primarily by solo voices, operas were fully staged with costuming, scenery, acting, and instrumental or orchestral accompaniment.

The early **oratorio** was a dramatic work for chorus, solo voices, and orchestra. Unlike opera, it did not include scenery, costuming, or stage action. Texts were usually taken from the Old Testament and sung in Latin. A narrator helped to explain the dramatic action, which unfolded in a series of arias, recitatives, ensemble numbers, and choruses.

The **cantata** was shorter and used fewer performers than the opera and oratorio. Either sacred or secular, it was usually written in Italian rather than Latin and emphasized solo voices in recitative style.

EARLY OPERA

The earliest surviving opera was written by a member of the Camerata named Jacopo Peri (1561–1633), whose *Eurydice* dates from the year 1600. Based on the Greek legend of Orpheus and Eurydice, it consists almost entirely of recitative with continuo accompaniment. In accordance with the principles of the Camerata, Peri wrote in the foreword to his opera that its style was intended to "imitate speech in song."

CLAUDIO MONTEVERDI

It was another Italian, however, who introduced to opera the full resources of music and the theater. His name was Claudio Monteverdi (1567–1643), and his treatment of the Orpheus legend, *La favola d'Orfeo,* marks the real beginning of opera. First performed in Mantua in 1607, *Orfeo* had elaborate costuming, staging, and lighting effects, an instrumental ensemble of forty players, and a chorus of singers and dancers. Another important innovation in *Orfeo* was the operatic overture. This type of orchestral introduction, known as a *sinfonia,* became standard in later operas.

In addition to *Orfeo,* Monteverdi wrote several other operas. Among the most successful were *Il ritorno di Ulisse in patria (The Return of Ulysses to His Homeland,* 1641) and *L'Incoronazione di Poppea (The Coronation of Poppea,* 1642). Like those of his contemporaries, Monteverdi's operas were written in Italian. They drew mainly upon Greek and Roman legends for their plots, which were adapted by poets into **libretti,** or operatic texts.

Originally performed for aristocratic gatherings, opera became a popular form of entertainment among the middle classes. Public opera houses were built in major Italian cities, and composers and librettists adapted their art to a wider and more varied audience. During the Baroque period, Italian opera spread throughout Europe, reaching its heights in the Italian operas of Handel in England. The Italian style had less influence in France, where the composer Jean-Baptiste Lully (1632–1687), ironically an Italian, headed the group that created and supported French opera.

The history of opera is discussed further in Chapter 10.

THE ORATORIO

In the early Baroque era the oratorio took two forms—the *Latin oratorio* and the *oratorio volgare,* which used Italian texts. The Latin oratorio reached its peak in the works of the Roman composer Giaccomo Carissimi (1605–1674). The finest of his fifteen oratorios, *Jepthe* (ca. 1649), was based on an Old Testament story from the Book of Judges.

Carissimi's pupil Alessandro Scarlatti (1660–1725) was one of the principal composers of the *oratorio volgare.* In the hands of Scarlatti, the oratorio became musically indistinct from opera. While the themes were still religious, the texts were in Italian, the role of the narrator was eliminated, and the chorus was abandoned. Actually, the oratorio was little more than a substitution for opera, theatrical performances of which were banned by the church during Lent.

The oratorio spread from Italy to the other countries of Europe. Henrich Schütz (1585–1672), who studied in Italy, introduced the oratorio to Germany, and Marc-Antoine Charpentier (1634–1704), a pupil of Carissimi, was the principal oratorio composer in France. But the oratorio rose to its height in England in the monumental works of George Frederick Handel.

HANDEL (1685-1759)

George Frederick Handel was born in Halle, a trading center some eighty miles southwest of Berlin, the son of a prosperous barber-surgeon attached to the court of the duke of Saxony. His father had in mind a legal career for the boy but did allow him to begin music study at age eight with the organist of the town's principal Lutheran church. Aside from learning to play the organ, harpsichord, violin, and oboe, young Handel also studied composition, writing church cantatas and numerous small-scale instrumental works.

Out of respect for his father's wish, Handel enrolled at the University of Halle in 1702. At the end of his first year, however, he withdrew from the university and went to Hamburg to pursue his interest in music.

Musical activity in Hamburg, as in most cosmopolitan cities of the time, centered around the opera house, where Italian opera thrived. Soon after Handel arrived in Hamburg in 1703, he obtained a position as violinist in the theater orchestra and industriously set about learning the craft of opera composition. His first opera, *Almira* (1704), reflected the curious mixture of native German and imported Italian musical styles then prevalent in Hamburg: the recitatives were set in German, the arias in Italian. The work was a popular success and three other operas soon followed. In 1706, feeling that he had learned all that Hamburg had to offer, Handel decided to go to Italy.

His three-year stay in Italy was amazingly successful. Traveling back and forth between Florence, Venice, Rome, and Naples, he met many of Italy's greatest composers and was the frequent guest of cardinals, princes, and ambassadors. Much of his popularity stemmed from the success of his operas *Rodrigo* (Florence, 1708) and *Agrippina* (Venice, 1709).

Through one of the friends he met in Italy, Handel obtained the position of musical director to the Electoral Court of Hanover,

Fig. 7.1 An engraving of Handel, after a painting by Thomas Hudson. The composer is shown wearing English court dress.

Germany. He had just taken up his duties in 1710, however, when he asked permission from Elector Georg Ludwig to visit London. Italian opera was then in great vogue with the English aristocracy, and the success of his opera *Rinaldo* (1711) led Handel to ask permission for another leave of absence the following year. Though promising to return "within a reasonable time," Handel stretched out his second London visit indefinitely.

In 1714 Queen Anne died, and Elector Georg Ludwig of Hanover ascended to the throne as George I of England. How Handel settled the embarrassing problem of his long-neglected contract with the Electoral Court is unknown. But the annual pension Queen Anne had given him was continued and even increased by George I, and within several years he was in high favor at the royal court.

During his years in England (he became a subject in 1726) Handel was involved in no less than four operatic enterprises. The most significant of these, the Royal Academy of Music, was organized by British nobility under the sponsorship of the king. During its eight-year existence (1720–1728), Handel's career as an opera composer reached its highest point.

Despite Handel's many personal successes, each of his four opera companies collapsed. A major reason for their collapse was the declining taste of the English for Italian opera. The enormously successful production, in 1728, of John Gay's *The Beggar's Opera* undoubtedly hastened the extinction of Italian opera in England. A parody of Italian style, *The Beggar's Opera* was widely imitated and a new form of light, popular musical entertainment was created in English.

Though Handel continued to compose Italian operas for more than a decade after the appearance of *The Beggar's Opera,* he turned increasingly to the oratorio.

His first English oratorio, *Haman and Mordecai* (later revised and renamed *Esther*), was composed in 1720. Others followed during the 1730s, but it was not until 1739, with the completion of *Saul* and *Israel in Egypt,* that he seemed to sense the full musical and dramatic possibilities of this form. Neither of these works was an immediate success, but others that followed were. In 1742, *Messiah* received high critical praise after its first performance in Dublin. By 1746, with the performance of *Judas Maccabaeus,* Handel had found a new public in the growing English middle class.

In his last years Handel was universally recognized as England's greatest composer. His popularity with all segments of English society steadily grew, and the royal patronage of George I was followed by that of George II. Despite declining health and the eventual loss of his eyesight, Handel continued to maintain a heavy schedule of oratorio performances, which he conducted himself from the keyboard. While attending a performance of *Messiah* on March 30, 1759, he suddenly grew faint and had to be taken home. He died two weeks later and was buried with state honors in Westminster Abbey. His will revealed that he had accumulated a substantial private fortune, which was dispersed—along with his music manuscripts—among friends.

HANDEL'S WORK

Handel's fame today rests largely on the half-dozen oratorios—particularly *Messiah*—still in concert repertory, several *concerti grossi* (see Chapter 8), some organ concertos, and two orchestral suites, *Water Music* and *Royal Fireworks Music*. These amount to only a fraction of his total work, which fills one hundred volumes in the collected edition of his music.

Opera With few exceptions, Handel's operas followed the pattern laid down by Italian composers of the seventeenth century. Their plots, drawn from classical mythology, were developed through a series of paired recitatives and arias. Although Handel's operas are seldom performed today, they were considerably better than those composed by his contemporaries. His gifts for melody and his imaginative, resourceful orchestration were acclaimed in his own time, and his ability to dramatize in music the psychological and emotional states of his characters was perhaps unexcelled.

Oratorio The bulk of Handel's oratorios are dramatic, with specific characters and plots. Although most of them, including *Samson, Saul, Solomon, Belshazzar,* and *Jeptha,* are based on stories drawn from the Old Testament, they were not written as church music. Instead, they were intended to be performed for the public in music halls and auditoriums.

Handel's two nondramatic oratorios are *Israel in Egypt* and *Messiah.* In *Israel in Egypt* the chorus almost completely dominates, narrating and describing the events. The solo voices do not represent specific characters as they would in a dramatic oratorio. Instead, they complement and act as a foil for the chorus. The orchestra is used brilliantly to depict the plagues that were inflicted upon Egypt, particularly in the sections representing the buzzing of the flies, and the fire and hailstones.

MESSIAH Handel's other nondramatic oratorio, *Messiah,* is based on the life of Christ. In *Messiah* the solo voices do not represent specific characters (with the exception of the passage in which the angel appears to the shepherds) nor is the orchestra used for pictorial narration. Although we might expect that the text for this oratorio would come from the Gospels of the New Testament, where the life of Christ is recorded, the bulk of the libretto consists of prophetic passages from the Old Testament. As a result, the events in Christ's life and his role as Redeemer are suggested symbolically.

Messiah was composed in only twenty-four days. It was a success in Handel's lifetime and has become one of the most loved and popular pieces of music in the history of Western civilization. At its first London performance in 1743, King George II was so moved by the opening of the "Hallelujah" chorus that he stood during its performance, a precedent that most audiences follow still.

Altogether, *Messiah* represents about three hours of music for four solo voices (SATB), chorus (SATB), and orchestra. The oratorio is in three parts comprising fifty-three movements. (A **movement** is an independent section of a larger composition.) The movements include arias, recitatives, choruses, and orchestral movements. Part I deals with the prophecy of the coming of the Messiah and his birth. Part II treats the sacrifice of Jesus and the salvation of humanity through his suffering and death; Part III, the certainty of eternal life through faith in the risen Christ.

Arias The aria received ingenious treatment in the oratories of Handel. He modifies the standard **da capo** form (ABA) in a variety of ways, very often avoiding the mechanical and expected return to and literal repetition of the first section. In *Messiah* the arias are rich in emotional expression and marvelously varied in mood. Among the many vocal gems are the aria for bass "But who may abide," with its dramatic change to "For He is like a refiner's fire"; the expressive contralto aria "O thou that tellest good tidings to Zion," followed immediately by a choral version of the same musical material; the stirring aria for bass "The trumpet shall sound"; and the exquisitely moving aria shared by contralto and soprano, "He shall feed His flock."

Recitatives In some respects, the recitatives in *Messiah* are less important than those of Handel's dramatic oratorios. Secco recitatives, for example, function almost entirely as short introductions to arias. However, such recitatives as "Thus saith the Lord," "For behold darkness shall cover the earth," and the opening piece for tenor and orchestra, "Comfort ye," are as important musically and expressively as the more lyrical and lengthy arias.

Choruses In Handel's time the *Messiah* chorus was rather small, consisting of only twenty singers. Later it became traditional in England to present *Messiah* with huge choral and orchestral forces. Recent research in Baroque music has enabled modern listeners to hear the work performed with smaller forces, more or less as Handel intended.

A primary factor that stamps Handel's oratorios as historically unique is the use of the chorus as a major element in the dramatic and musical structure. The choruses in *Messiah* function in several ways. First, as we shall see (p. 121), they are sometimes the climactic element in a three-part complex consisting of a recitative, an aria, and a chorus. A second use of the chorus is as a structural "frame" beginning and ending a large section. Part II of *Messiah,* for example, begins with the restrained and sorrowful "Behold the Lamb of God" and concludes with the joyous and triumphant "Hallelujah." These two choruses constitute a frame for the entire section. Handel also joins one chorus to another, so that each chorus depends upon the one immediately preceding or following it. Thus, each chorus is a unit in a larger complex of several choruses.

In addition to their functional importance, many of the choral movements have extraordinary emotional impact and musical appeal on their own. Such well-known choral movements as "And the glory of the Lord," "For unto us a Child is born," and the magnificent "Hallelujah" help account for the tremendous popularity of the work.

Orchestra Because of the limited orchestral resources available to him in Dublin, where *Messiah* had its premiere, Handel employed a modest instrumental ensemble consisting of only oboes, bassoons, trumpets, timpani, strings, and continuo. Today, the orchestral forces vary from relatively modest to as large as a hundred.

In *Messiah,* there are only two movements for orchestra alone—the French overture that begins the work, and the short, eloquent "Pastorale" in Part I.

Organization Part of the genius of *Messiah* derives from Handel's ability to achieve coherence and unity among the elements of a complex musical structure consisting of numerous individual movements. Frequently he employed the pattern recitative-aria-chorus to organize a long stretch of music. The recitative introduces the aria, which progresses to a culminating choral movement. Each movement possesses its own internal organization and interest but also contributes to the larger structure. This organizational procedure dominates the first part of *Messiah* and is well illustrated by the movements that immediately follow the introductory overture:

RECORD 1/SIDE 1

Overture	Recitative	Aria	Chorus
	Comfort ye	*Every valley*	*And the glory of the Lord*

The first movement (recitative) displays Handel's masterful handling of Baroque techniques. The text is divided into two parts.

Isaiah 40:1–3   Comfort ye, comfort ye my people, saith your God; speak ye comfortably to Jerusalem, and cry unto her, that her warfare is accomplish'd, that her iniquity is pardon'd.

The voice of him that crieth in the wilderness, Prepare ye the way of the Lord, make straight in the desert a highway for our God.

Part A, in the key of E major, is very much like an arioso in that it is quite lyrical and its tempo is steady. Both the orchestra and the melodic material sung by the tenor voice convey the feelings inherent in the words. This is evident from the tenor's opening motive:

Com - fort   ye   *Example 7.2*

which not only matches the rhythmic inflection of the text but also conveys the overall feeling of serenity that characterizes the first part of the movement.

Another example of musical treatment of words to reflect and intensify their expressive quality is shown in the phrase:

and   cry   un - to   her   *Example 7.3*

The large upward leap from "and" to "cry" and the relatively long note on "cry" reinforce the drama of the joyful announcement to Israel.

This part of the movement is also characterized by considerable musical unity, which is provided by the statement and reappearance of material played by the orchestra:

Example 7.4

The first portion of this material (sometimes only the first five notes) re-appears several times, either giving way to the tenor voice:

Tenor

Speak   ye   com   *Example 7.5*

or coming in "on top" of it:

that her war - fare, her war - - -

Example 7.6

The last appearance of the material is a full statement which, after the various fragment versions, imparts a feeling of completion and concludes the first part of the movement.

In the second part of the movement the decisive emotional change in the text is reflected in the musical structure The lyricism and serenity of the "comfort" section give way to a feeling of dramatic assertiveness in the B section. The voice executes short, clipped phrases while the orchestra punctuates with short, isolated chords:

the voice of him that crieth in the wil - der-ness pre - pare

Example 7.7

This procedure is typical of the recitative style, as is the ending, with its downward motion of the voice followed by two concluding chords from the orchestra:

for our God

Example 7.8

Thus Handel uses both arioso and recitative in one movement to exploit the contrasting character of the two sections of text. In addition, the recitative portion not only brings the movement to a close, but leads naturally into the next movement, the aria "Every valley."

Isaiah 40: 4   Every valley shall be exalted and every mountain and hill made low, the crooked straight, and the rough places plain.

Probably the most immediately striking aspect of this aria is its use of word painting, a device we encountered earlier in our discussion of Renaissance secular music. The word "exalted" is set to a long ascending sixteenth-note melisma which gives a feeling of rising:

shall be _____ ex - alt   -   -   -   -   -   -

Example 7.9

-   -   -   -   -   -   -   - ed.

The words "crooked" and "plain" (meaning "level") also receive musical treatment which reflects their meaning and spirit:

the crook - ed straight, the crook - ed straight and rough pla-ces plain _____

Example 7.10

The angular figure on "crooked" contrasts sharply with the static, simple melody on "plain."

Word painting is used again in the setting of the phrase "and every mountain and hill made low," in which the melody rises to a peak on "mountain" and then descends to a tone an octave below on "low":

and ev -'ry moun-tain and hill ____ made low.

Example 7.11

The use of individualized musical figures and technical devices to reflect the emotional feeling or physical characteristics of a word or phrase was common in the Baroque period and, indeed, is found in music of virtually every composer of the period. Extended melismas and highly ornamented figures provided the perfect vehicle for virtuoso soloists to display their remarkable vocal skills.

"Every valley" is followed immediately by the allegro choral movement in A major, "And the glory of the Lord."

Isaiah 40: 5   And the glory of the Lord shall be revealed, and all flesh shall see it together, for the mouth of the Lord hath spoken it.

This choral movement is based upon four melodic ideas, each with its own set of words:

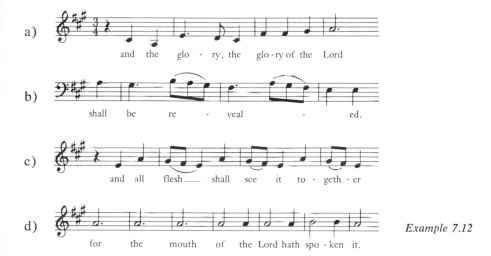

Example 7.12

Handel contrasts these ideas in a variety of ways, perhaps the most striking of which is the use of both polyphonic and homophonic textures. The first polyphonic section of the movement is based upon "a" and a combination of "a" and "b."

Example 7.13

Here the texture is very thin, with no more than two voice parts singing at the same time and with the orchestra reduced to continuo only. This thin polyphonic texture is maintained until the climactic point when all four parts of the chorus and the full orchestra join in a *homophonic* phrase, which brings the first section of the movement to a close (Example 7.14). The change from thin texture to full chorus and orchestra and the sudden switch from polyphony to homophony provide a powerful climax.

Example 7.14

The rest of the movement consists of several sections organized in roughly the same manner. Each is characterized by imaginative and flexible use of the four melodic ideas and their combinations. And each involves the same alternation between polyphonic imitation and strong homophonic endings, each more powerful than the one before. The movement culminates in a passage of almost breathtaking force:

Example 7.15

Just before the final statement of "hath spoken it," Handel brings the music to a sudden and surprising halt, followed by silence, creating a feeling of excitement and suspense. This suspense is resolved by a prolonged cadence on "hath spoken it," as all parts of the chorus and the full orchestra combine to provide a stirring conclusion to the entire three-movement complex.

Of course, we have discussed only a small portion of this work. The rest of *Messiah* is full of equally glorious music, masterfully crafted. Certainly, it is no wonder that *Messiah* is one of the world's most beloved pieces of music.

THE PASSION

One of the most important forms of religious music in Lutheran Germany was the Passion, a choral setting of the story of the suffering and death of Christ.

The Passion was particularly important during Holy Week, especially on Good Friday. Settings of the Passion made full use of the aria, the recitative, the chorus, and the orchestra—the full dramatic range of the "new music." Consequently, the Baroque Passion is often referred to as the *oratorio* Passion.

Prior to the Baroque period, settings of the Passion had relied almost exclusively on the four Gospels for their texts. In the eighteenth century, particularly in Germany, it became the practice to treat the Gospel text freely and to add nonbiblical text. The *Passion According to Saint Matthew* by Johann Sebastian Bach (whose biography is given in Chapter 8) is probably the finest example of the Baroque oratorio Passion. Indeed, this work joins *Messiah* in representing the culmination of Baroque vocal music.

THE CHORALE

The German *chorale* grew out of the reforms that began the Protestant movement. Martin Luther (1483–1546) believed that people should participate in the act of worship. To this end, he inaugurated religious services in the native language and composed "German psalms" or **chorales** for the congregation to sing.

The chorale melodies came from a variety of sources. Some were adapted from Gregorian chants, others came from secular tunes popular at the time, and many were newly composed. Usually in four-part harmony with a simple rhythmic structure, they were characterized by a clear melody in the soprano that could be sung by the musically untrained. Luther's famous *"Ein' Feste Burg ist Unser Gott"* ("A Mighty Fortress Is Our God") typifies the strength and solidity of the chorale.

In the Baroque era, chorale melodies provided a rich body of sturdy materials from which larger musical structures could be built. Thus, they functioned in much the same way in the Lutheran church as the Gregorian chant had functioned in the Roman Catholic church during the Renaissance.

THE CANTATA

The simplicity of the chorale as a unifying theme was especially suited to the *cantata*. In Germany, the cantata developed into a religious form that served as an integral part of the Lutheran service. Like the opera and oratorio, the cantata went through considerable transformation during the Baroque era, reaching its height in the works of Dietrich Buxtehude (ca. 1637–1707) and Johann Sebastian Bach. By Bach's time (1685–1750), the cantata often combined the standard Baroque elements of aria, recitative, chorus, and instrumental accompaniment. Frequently, cantatas were built upon a simple chorale tune.

Cantata texts related to specific feast days of the church year. For church musicians such as Bach, the writing of cantatas was a professional obligation. Between 1704 and 1740, with but a few brief interruptions, Bach produced cantatas on a regular basis for the churches he served. He is believed to have written

(*Continued on page 132.*)

THE TRIUMPH
OF THE BAROQUE STYLE

Baroque is a word that eludes easy definition. It refers to a special approach to the arts that dominated all of the European continent in the seventeenth and eighteenth centuries—an approach that sought consciously to move the emotions and arouse the feelings of an audience through spectacular displays of sight and sound.

The early Baroque is grounded in Italian art and reflects the recovery of the Roman Catholic church after the Protestant challenge of the sixteenth century. In 1517, Martin Luther had openly defied the authority of the Pope and the legitimacy of Church doctrine. He and his followers wanted to reform and "purify" the Christian religion; in doing so they set into motion a religious controversy that shattered European stability for more than a century. In the 1500s, large blocs of anti-Romanists threatened to bring about the utter collapse of Catholicism.

The Catholic response to the Protestant heresy is called the Counter-Reformation. It included a far-reaching "housecleaning" within the Church to stamp out clerical abuses and to shore up the faith where it was crumbling. Between 1545 and 1563 church leaders at the Council of Trent drew up a broad program that included tighter discipline for the clergy and a strong denial of the individual's right and ability to interpret the Bible. The Church reexamined its rituals. The Jesuit Order was established as an international force for teaching, missionary work, reconversion, and protection of the faith. By the seventeenth century the Counter-Reformation had paid its dividends: most of Europe remained bound to Catholicism and Rome.

After 1600, the arts were used by the Italians to celebrate the power and glory of the Church. The Italian artist became a narrator of the Christian spectacle. All over the peninsula painters and sculptors reworked ceilings and chapels. Architects built new churches and palaces, and craftsmen decorated them with rich gilding and ornament. The energy of Italian design was imitated throughout the continent, and Rome became an unparalleled cultural center where artists from many different countries came to admire the classical ruins and modern wonders of the city. Pilgrims and noblemen returned to their lands with marvelous tales of "the first city of the world."

The Baroque style grew out of Renaissance forms that were employed in dynamic and grand ways to trumpet churchly prestige. The "look" was sparkling, exciting, and new: it is not surprising that the new Roman style was immediately and immensely popular, that it rapidly spread to the north and became an international style.

In the case of painting, the most radical of early Baroque artists in Italy was Caravaggio, whose striking contrasts of light and shadow and whose vigorous

*realism in figures and settings redirected the course of all European painting
(Plate 14). But the two greatest Baroque painters who followed him were Rubens,
who was Flemish, and Poussin, who was French. In different ways these artists
both depended on Italian sources. Rubens traveled in Italy as a young man and
was influenced by Michelangelo's powerful figures and Venetian color as well as
by Caravaggio. Poussin lived more than forty years in Rome.*

*The differences between Rubens and Poussin reveal the breadth of the
Baroque style in painting during the seventeenth century. Rubens's complicated
compositions, full of rich color and straining movement, packed with gesturing
figures and dramatic emotions, are one kind of Baroque (Plate 13). Poussin, who
had tremendous impact on French contemporaries, was much more reserved,
crisp, and logical in his design. He was deeply affected by classical sculpture and
anxious to achieve a Baroque that was more balanced and elegant in its drama
(Plate 10).*

Plate 10. Nicholas Poussin's *Rape of the Sabine Women* (1636–1637) exemplifies the classical style of the
most influential of seventeenth-century French artists. While Poussin exploited the drama of his subject, he
presented it with balance and restraint, with figures based on Roman statuary rather than on Rubens's fleshy
nudes. (Courtesy The Metropolitan Museum of Art; Harris Brisbane Dick Fund, 1946.)

Plate 11. Despite its diminutive size, Borromini's San Carlo alle Quattro Fontane (1662–1667) is highly Baroque in its undulating, sculptural facade, which engages the passer-by with its complicated architectural detail. (Courtesy Alinari/Art Reference Bureau.)

Plate 12. Rembrandt's *The Blinding of Samson,* done in 1636, indicates the impact outside Italy of Caravaggio's modeling through light and shadow. Likewise, its passionate energy and violence are unmistakably Rubenesque. Later in his career Rembrandt developed a more individual style. (Courtesy The Staedel Institute, Frankfurt.)

Bernini, another of the great Baroque artists, was aided by a large group of assistants. He produced, over a very long career, an extraordinary amount of sculpture whose appearance set the style of work in stone and metal in the seventeenth century. His most famous work was the exquisite Ecstasy of St. Theresa *(Plate 16). To present this radiant moment Bernini showed the instant when the saint was pierced by an angel's golden arrow. His cutting of the marble is so delicate and fluid, the drapery sweeping in such magnificent folds, that the saint appears to float in absolute exaltation in the clouds of heaven itself. The drama of the scene makes apathy or detachment on the part of the observer unlikely. Like so much Baroque work, Bernini's sculpture meant to force the onlooker into active participation with the image.*

Bernini was also a great architect. He finished the great basilica of St. Peter's, begun 150 years earlier, and gave it his masterful colonnade in front of the facade, a monumental pair of arms that reach out toward the faithful and almost compel them to move toward the church itself. The most inventive of Baroque architects, however, was Borromini, a designer whose work was the culmination of Baroque ingenuity. The most radical of his buildings was San Carlo alle Quattro Fontane. Full of weirdly undulating surfaces, the walls of the church protrude and recede, creating a wavelike effect, and the contrasting planes of stone produce sculptural patterns of light and shade. The church seems built not of stone but of some pliable material (Plate 11).

Plate 13. *The Rape of the Daughters of Leucippus* (ca. 1618), by Peter Paul Rubens. Rubens created a highly charged style full of color, energy, voluptuous and powerful figures, and complex, dynamic composition. (Courtesy Alte Pinakothek, Munich.)

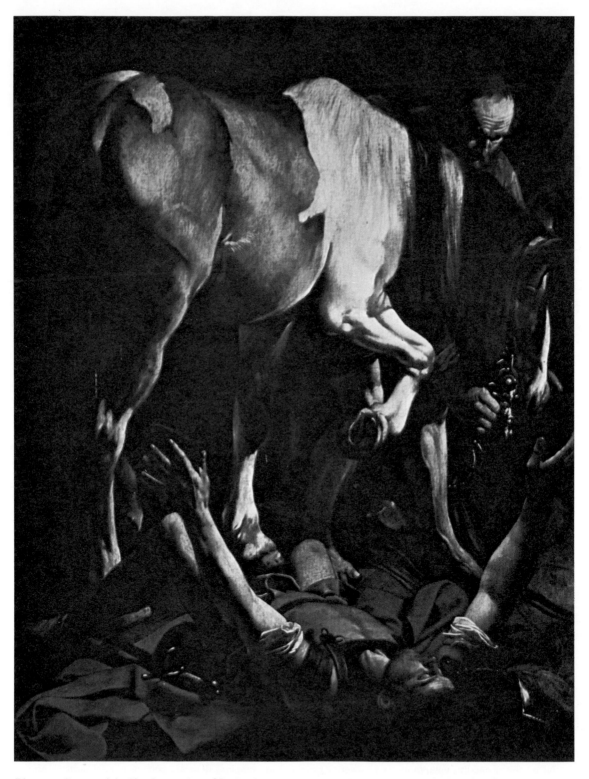

Plate 14. Caravaggio's *The Conversion of St. Paul* (1600–1601) not only demonstrates the theatrical lighting for which he is famous but also shows his rejection of the idealism of the High Renaissance. Caravaggio declared early in his career that nature—not tradition—would be his teacher. (Courtesy Scala/Editorial Photocolor Archives.)

Plate 15. Baroque opera achieved a synthesis of many different arts in one grand spectacle to thrill its audience. The opera at Versailles was built for Louis XIV (1638–1715), the most grandiose of the French kings and one of the chief patrons of the new art form. (Courtesy Scala/Editorial Photocolor Archives.)

Plate 16. Bernini's *Ecstasy of St. Theresa* (1646) demonstrates the Baroque attempt to involve the spectator in art through highly dramatic, emotional presentations. Here, the fluid interaction of space and stone belie the marble's hardness. (Courtesy Alinari/Art Reference Bureau.)

Borromini had great influence on the building of the late Baroque churches of Germany and Austria (a more delicate eighteenth-century style usually called Rococo). The Baroque fondness for ornate decoration reached its greatest emotional extremes here in gilded altars with carved scrolls and garlands, and in gold and white walls with pastel-painted ceilings—all calculated to awe and delight. Critics of these beautiful churches too easily disregard their sincerity and dismiss them unfairly as "gaudy" and "vulgar" interiors with "false fronts." To their builders they were magical syntheses of painting, sculpture, and architecture that mirrored the magnificence of the Roman Catholic church.

Music played an important role in the life of the churches. Sound, perhaps more than the visual arts, could move, elevate, and involve a congregation and thus intensify the spiritual experience. While Protestants were skeptical of visual displays and the veneration of images, they warmed to the use of music in church services. In the seventeenth century, major churches began to form orchestras and choirs and to hire organists, soloists, and music masters. The greatest of Baroque church musicians was Johann Sebastian Bach, who spent a major part of his career at Leipzig, leaving a vast treasure of sacred music, vocal and instrumental, at the time of his death in 1750.

It is wrong, however, to think of the Baroque arts as exclusively religious. In France they were used to enhance the position of Louis XIV and his court. The efforts of architects, stonemasons, sculptors, painters, furniture makers, and gardeners were carefully coordinated to remake the royal palace at Versailles in the latter half of the seventeenth century. By 1700, the visitor to Paris would have been overwhelmed by French monuments to the power of the Crown, in a style codified and taught by a Royal Academy, a style increasingly fashionable throughout the continent. In the eighteenth century, Paris replaced Rome as the leader in European culture and design.

Because the seventeenth century was fascinated with the natural world, Baroque art could also celebrate the ordinary and commonplace. In Dutch painting a brilliant artist like Rembrandt might craft biblical scenes (Plate 12) but the predominant taste in Baroque Holland sought paintings of the familiar world of town and country. Walls were decorated with landscapes, still lifes, and scenes from everyday life. There was a rage for portraiture among bankers and businessmen, prominent civic leaders, and well-heeled families. Citizens, soldiers, and peasants, their daily occupations and amusements, their gardens and taverns, all became the subjects of works of art. This naturalism reminds us of the scientific investigation of the century, when basic laws of the physical and biological sciences were uncovered. In 1702 a primitive steam engine was developed.

The best example of the worldly side of the Baroque spirit is perhaps in opera, a medium developed to entertain royalty and aristocrats of highly discriminating taste (Plate 15). This kind of theater integrated scene painting, costuming, dancing and choreography, and vocal and instrumental music. Opera thus achieved the synthesis of many different arts in one grandiose spectacle to thrill its audience. It is this elevating exploitation of the senses that is the hallmark of the Baroque style.

Versus V

Hier ist das rechte Osterlamm,
Davon hat Gott geboten,
Das ist hoch an des Kreuzes Stamm
In heisser Lieb gebraten,
Das Blut zeichnet unser Tür,
Das hält der Glaub dem Tode für,
Der Würger kann uns nicht mehr
    schaden.
Halleluja!

Verse V

Here is the true Easter lamb
That God has offered us,
Which high on the stem of the cross
Is roasted in burning love;
His blood marks our door,
Faith holds this up to death,
The destroyer can no longer
    harm us.
Hallelujah!

Versus VI

So feiern wir das hohe Fest
Mit Herzensfreud und Wonne,
Das uns der Herre scheinen lässt,
Er ist selber die Sonne,
Der durch seiner Gnade Glanz
Erleuchtet unsre Herzen ganz,
Der Sünden Nacht ist verschwunden.
Halleluja!

Verse VI

Therefore we celebrate the high feast
With joyous heart and rapture,
Which the Lord lets shine for us;
He is himself the sun,
Who through the splendor of his grace
Fully illumines our hearts,
The night of sin has disappeared.
Hallelujah!

Versus VII

Wir essen und leben wohl
In rechten Osterfladen,
Der alte Sauerteig nicht soll
Sein bei dem Wort der Gnaden,
Christus will die Koste sein
Und speisen die Seel allein,
Der Glaub will keins andern Leben.
Halleluja!

Verse VII

We eat and live well
By the true Passover bread,
The old leaven shall not endure
Beside the word of grace;
Christ will be the feast
And he alone will feed the soul,
Faith is sustained through no other.
Hallelujah!

—Martin Luther

Although the chorale melody (Example 7.16) is the unifying element, each movement uses it in a different way. Throughout most of Verse I, the sopranos of the chorus state the melody in long, sustained tones, while the other voice parts sound more active contrapuntal material. Each new phrase in the soprano is preceded by several statements of the same phrase by the other voice parts in imitation, using short note values. At times the orchestra doubles the voice parts, but most of the time it has active contrapuntal material of its own.

At the word "Hallelujah," there is an abrupt change in tempo, while the four parts of the chorus have short, imitative entrances of the Hallelujah phrase of the chorale tune. The increase in the tempo gives the movement an ending of excitement and joy.

Example 7.16

Verse II employs a rhythmic **basso ostinato**—a musical phrase repeated persistently in the bass voice—against which the soprano and alto sing a variation of the chorale tune. This time the Hallelujah takes on the sorrowful quality that has characterized the rest of the movement.

In contrast, Verse III is joyous, reflecting the text. The violins have a rapidly moving pattern of sixteenth notes.

Example 7.17

The bass again has an ostinato figure against the violins.

Example 7.18

The tenor states the chorale tune in its original form until the Hallelujah, where the chorale tune is decorated so as to give it the sixteenth-note character of the violin figure. The constant driving motion of this movement is abruptly suspended to dramatize the text (death's image), after which the rigorous texture is resumed, for "death has lost its sting."

Example 7.19

In Verse IV the chorale tune is sung by the alto, while the other voice parts sing snatches of the chorale tune in shorter note values as part of the counterpoint against the alto.

Verse V pits the entire instrumental ensemble against the solo bass voice. The movement is in triple meter, and the chorale tune takes on a more lyrical quality. For most of the movement the solo bass alternates with the first violin

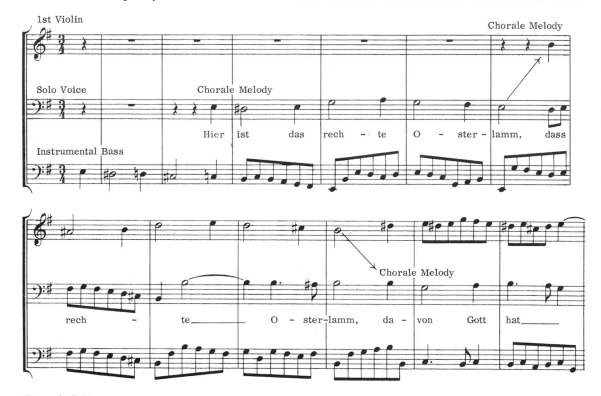

Example 7.20

in stating the phrases of the chorale tune, while the rest of the strings and continuo provide harmony (see Example 7.20). The verse displays word painting as *"Kreuzes"* ("cross") is emphasized by a lengthening and decoration of the note of the chorale tune on which the word occurs.

Example 7.21

And of special interest is the setting of the words "dem Todefür," with its emphasis on *Tode* (death).

Example 7.22

Verse VI is scored for soprano and tenor duet with continuo accompaniment and displays yet another variation of the chorale melody, in which each phrase is decorated and extended by a triplet figure.

Verse VII is a straightforward statement of the chorale tune in the soprano, the rest of the chorus providing a simple harmonic support doubled by instruments.

Example 7.23

In comparison to the elaborate settings in the previous movements, the final verse is considerably less complex, allowing the congregation to join the choir in singing the last verse of the cantata. This participation provides the religious and spiritual fulfillment of the experience as a whole.

With the sparsest of means—the chorale melody and its text—Bach has created a multimovement work, unified by the presence of the melody in each movement, yet highly diversified by the variety of treatments the chorale tune receives.

SUMMARY

The Baroque era, which began in Italy around 1600, was a period of significant development in the history of music. Perhaps the greatest musical innovation during this era was the movement away from melodically oriented music and toward a new emphasis on harmonic organization. The major-minor system, which employed chordal relationships built around a clear tonal center, gradually came to replace the medieval modes as the basic organizing device.

Although the changes brought by the major-minor system are more familiar in instrumental music, they began in vocal music. A basic principle of Baroque vocal music was that the music should support and enhance the vocal line. Out of this concept grew the monodic style, which was facilitated by the device known as basso continuo. The monodic style consisted of essentially two different types of vocal expression, the recitative and the arioso (which was gradually expanded into the aria). These vocal styles were employed extensively in Baroque operas, oratorios, and cantatas—the three important forms of Baroque vocal music.

The beginnings of modern opera date from the early seventeenth century, when *Orfeo*, by Claudio Monteverdi, was performed in Italy. The oratorio rose to its height in England, in *Messiah* and other monumental works of George Frederick Handel. The cantata is best exemplified in the many works that Johann Sebastian Bach organized around German chorale tunes.

NEW TERMS

monodic style

basso continuo

figured bass (thorough-bass)

recitative

secco recitative

accompanied recitative

arioso

aria (da capo aria)

opera

oratorio

cantata

movement

libretto (libretti)

chorale

basso ostinato

CHAPTER 8 | BAROQUE INSTRUMENTAL MUSIC

THE BAROQUE ERA WAS NOT ONLY A PERIOD OF MAGNIFICENT achievement in vocal composition. It also saw the gradual development of the first significant body of instrumental music. The Baroque was the age of the great violin makers, among them the members of the Stradivari family. Improvements were made in the construction of virtually every wind and brass instrument, and the organ and the harpsichord became the basic keyboard instruments. By the end of the Baroque era, instrumental music had gradually equalled and surpassed vocal music in importance, and the style of vocal music itself was very much influenced by the instrumental idiom.

Fig. 8.1 Vast technical improvements in wind, brass, and keyboard instruments and the development of the violin encouraged the growth of instrumental music during the Baroque era. Pictured here is an imaginary instrument-maker's workshop.

EQUAL TEMPERAMENT

Fundamental to the development of instrumental music (particularly that written for keyboard instruments) was the need to devise a system of tuning so that the keyboard instruments could play equally in tune in all keys without having to be retuned. Before 1700, all attempts to develop such a system had achieved only partial success. The problem was that, according to the logical system of frequency ratios that was applied, the size of a half step varied slightly, depending on its position in relation to the first note of the scale. It was left for Baroque composers and music theorists to construct a completely satisfactory method of tuning that would facilitate frequent modulation to distant keys. This method of tuning is called **equal temperament.**

In the system of equal temperament, instruments are tuned so that all half steps within an octave are exactly the same size. As a result, each of these half steps is minutely larger or smaller than the "pure" half step that results from strict application of frequency ratios. Indeed, with the exception of the octave and the unison, all intervals are proportionally "out of tune." But the imperfections are so slight that the ear accepts the intervals as being in tune. The application of this method of tuning made it possible for keyboard instruments to play equally well in every key without retuning.

Although modern listeners have become completely adjusted to the tempered scale, musicians in the eighteenth century had to be convinced that the gains in flexibility were worth the loss of perfectly tuned intervals. Bach's *Das Wohltemperierte Klavier (The Well-Tempered Clavier),* which consisted of two sets of preludes and fugues in all possible keys, was designed in part to demonstrate the advantages of the new system.

KEYBOARD MUSIC

A large body of keyboard music, especially for organ and harpsichord, was produced during the Baroque period. These pieces appeared with various titles —fantasia, capriccio, prelude, toccata—that were carryovers from the names given to lute music in the sixteenth century. The terms described the style and character of a piece rather than its form, for all the pieces bearing these titles were cast in "free form," with no standard formal design.

The **fantasia** was an improvised piece, characterized by displays of virtuosity in composition and performance.

The **prelude** was also an improvised piece that customarily introduced another piece or group of pieces. Bach used it in combination with the fugue in *Das Wohltemperierte Klavier.* The two styles represented the extremes of formal procedure: the prelude, in free form, contrasted with the highly organized and controlled formal structure of the fugue (see below).

The term **toccata** derives from the Italian verb *toccare* ("to touch") and describes a piece full of scale passages, rapid runs and trills, and massive chords.

All these keyboard styles often served as introductory pieces to the **fugue,** one of the great intellectual musical structures of the Baroque era.

THE FUGUE

A fugue is a statement and polyphonic development of a short melodic idea called a **subject.** The precise formal outline varies greatly from work to work. However, the initial introduction and restatements of the fugue subject are more or less standard. The first section of a fugue is called the **exposition.** In it the fugue subject is introduced by different melodic lines or "voices" in turn.

First, a single voice part states the fugue subject in the tonic key. This statement of the subject is imitated by the second voice part, which restates the subject in the key of the dominant. This restatement in the dominant is referred to as the **answer.** While the second voice part states the answer, the first voice part continues with new, contrasting melodic material called the **countersubject.** After a modulation back to the tonic key, a third voice part states the subject again in the tonic, exactly as it was stated by the first voice. As the fugue progresses, each voice part enters with the subject or its answer until all voice parts have come into play. When all the voices have been presented, the exposition section of the fugue is concluded. The number of voice parts varies from fugue to fugue—two-voice fugue, three-voice fugue, etc. However, not many fugues go beyond five voices. What does *not* vary is the tonic-dominant relationship between the fugue subject (tonic) and its answer (dominant).

After the exposition, the piece continues (without pause) with a number of sections in which the subject, the countersubject, and in some works new melodic material are developed. Presentations of the subject alternate with transitional passages called **episodes,** which can be derived from the subject or based on entirely new material. Episodes relieve the steady presentation of the subject and thus make its reappearance more interesting.

A number of different techniques may be used in fugue. Modulation through many different keys (with a return to the tonic at the end of the piece) is typical. Also, any number of contrapuntal devices may be employed to vary the manner in which the subject is treated. For example, the subject can be played in longer time values, a procedure called **augmentation;** or it can be played faster in shorter note values **(diminution).** It can be turned upside down **(inversion),** with ascending intervals replacing descending intervals and vice versa. Frequently that portion of the piece just before the conclusion employs the device known as **stretto**—before one voice completes the subject, another voice begins the subject. This overlapping of statements of the subject creates the impression of increased momentum and leads to a climactic conclusion of the fugue. Another characteristic procedure is **pedal point,** in which a long-held tone, usually in the bass, is sounded through changing harmonies in other parts.

In listening to a fugue, the primary interest lies in following what happens to the subject in the course of the piece. It must be remembered that no two fugues are exactly alike. The only procedures they hold in common are the general method of introducing a melodic idea (embodied in the exposition) and the subsequent alternation between subject and episodes.

Although the fugue originated in the Baroque period, it has held a place (sometimes very important) in all musical eras after the Baroque, up to and including the present time. The unchallenged master of the Baroque fugue was Johann Sebastian Bach.

BACH (1685–1750)

Johann Sebastian Bach was the most distinguished member of a family of musicians that reached back four generations before him and was carried forward by three of his sons. His father, Johann Ambrosius, was a musician in service to the town council of Eisenach, a small community in Thuringia—now part of East Germany. Little is known about Bach's early life, but it seems that his father, an excellent violinist, taught him to play stringed instruments, and another relative, the organist of Eisenach's leading church, began instructing him at the organ.

Orphaned when he was only ten, Bach was sent to live with his eldest brother, Johann Christoph, an organist at the nearby town of Ohrdruf. He remained there five years, taking organ and harpsichord lessons from his brother, earning some money as a boy soprano, and studying at the town's famed grammar school. He did so well at the school that he was offered a scholarship at St. Michael's, a secondary school in Luneburg, a city in northern Germany.

In 1703 Bach obtained his first musical position, as violinist in the small chamber orchestra of the ducal court of Weimar, but when a post as church organist became available in Arnstadt in August of 1703, he accepted the position. Dissatisfied with working conditions in Arnstadt and the poor state of the church choir, Bach left in 1707 to become organist at the church of St. Blasius in the Free Imperial City of Muhlhausen. In that same year he married a cousin, Maria Barbara Bach.

Soon entangled in a feud between factions within the Lutheran church, he left Muhlhausen in 1708 to become court organist, and later concertmaster, in the ducal chapel of Weimar. His nine years in Weimar constitute his first major creative period. Here he composed a number of cantatas and many of his greatest organ works, and he worked inten-

Fig. 8.2 Bach at the age of thirty.

sively with singers and instrumentalists as a conductor.

Because of his evident talent as a composer, performer, and conductor, Bach expected to be offered the top position of *Kapellmeister* (chapelmaster) at Weimar when it became available in 1716. However, he was passed over in favor of another. The following year he accepted the position of court conductor to the small principality of Anhalt-Cöthen.

Bach had enjoyed a growing reputation as an organist and composer of church cantatas and had made annual performing tours to important centers such as Kassel, Leipzig, and Dresden. His duties at Cöthen, as conductor and composer for the eighteen-member court orchestra, led to a shift in emphasis toward instrumental music. Much of his finest orchestral music dates from this period, including the six Brandenburg Concertos.

The happy and productive years at Cöthen were marred by the death of his wife in 1720. Bach soon remarried, however, and his new wife, Anna Magdalena, proved to be a hard-working, cheerful companion who raised Bach's four children by Maria Barbara along with her own. She gave birth to thirteen children in all, six of whom survived.

In 1723 Bach was offered the position of cantor (director of music) at St. Thomas Church in Leipzig, one of the most important musical posts in Protestant Germany. However, it was not a completely auspicious beginning for Bach, as the city council turned to him only after it had received refusals from two other composers. His duties included composing cantatas for St. Nicholas Church as well as St. Thomas Church, supervising the musical programs in all the municipal churches, and teaching Latin in the St. Thomas choir school.

Despite the irksome nature of some of his duties and his uneasy relationship with his superiors, the Leipzig town council, Bach remained in Leipzig for the rest of his life. He personally supervised the musical education of his most gifted sons, Wilhelm Friedemann, Carl Philipp Emanuel, and Johann Christian, and saw them embark on promising musical careers. Though, like Handel, he went blind in old age, his creative powers remained undimmed. His last composition, dictated to a son-in-law a few days before his death, was a chorale prelude, "Before Thy Throne, My God, I Stand."

BACH'S WORK

Bach's profound genius extended to nearly every form of musical composition prevalent in the Baroque period. His vocal music is best represented by his B minor Mass, his Passions, and his many chorales and cantatas. In his instrumental music he was equally prolific and far-ranging in style. His consummate

Fig. 8.3 Bach's organ in St. Thomas Church, Leipzig. This superb instrument stimulated Bach's musical genius for more than a quarter of a century.

skill with contrapuntal technique is clearly seen in the Fugue in G Minor (ca. 1709), subtitled "The Little" to distinguish it from his longer fugue in the same key.

**FUGUE IN
G MINOR
("THE LITTLE")**
RECORD 1/SIDE 2

The Fugue in G Minor is a four-voice fugue based upon the following subject:

Example 8.1

Voice I (in this case the highest, or soprano voice) states the subject in the tonic key of G minor. This is followed immediately by the answer in the dominant key of D minor from Voice II while Voice I continues with the countersubject:

Example 8.2

After the completion of the answer and the countersubject, there is a brief modulation back to G minor, whereupon Voice III enters with the subject, again in G minor. This time Voice II states the countersubject while Voice I is silent. Continuing the previous pattern, Voice IV (the lowest, or bass) enters with the answer in the key of the dominant, pitted against the countersubject in Voice III; meanwhile, Voice I enters with melodic material derived from the countersubject, bringing the exposition to a close.

Note that this musical organization is heavily dependent upon the device known as *imitation*—Voice II imitates Voice I, and each voice in turn imitates the one before it. It is also interesting to observe that at no point in the exposition do all four voices sound at the same time. This use of thin texture is typical of the Baroque fugal style, in which the use of all voices at the same time is usually reserved for climactic cadences.

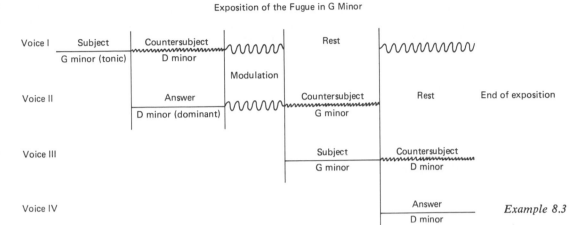

Example 8.3

After the exposition there follow several sections, each characterized by a modulatory episode that is based on material taken from part of the subject or countersubject and leads to a new statement of the subject (see Example 8.4).

There is no pause after the exposition; rather the first episode proceeds in very much the same fashion as the exposition except for the absence of the fugue subject itself. After a modulation back to G minor there appears to be an entry of the subject in Voice III. However, after the first few notes, Voice III continues not with the subject but the countersubject, while Voice I steals the subject and goes on with a full statement. Aside from this "false entry," the piece consists of a number of approaches to statements of the subject in various keys and voice parts, ending with a final statement in the bass voice in the tonic of *G minor.*

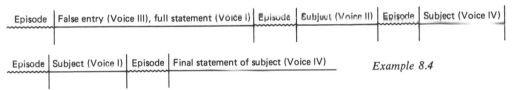

Example 8.4

A significant part of the interest in listening to a piece of this kind is the sense of discovery of what is happening to the material with which we have become familiar in the exposition.

Aside from the structural fugal procedures, this little piece illustrates two important stylistic features of much Baroque music—namely, a single mood, and an unbroken, uninterrupted, steady flow of music from the first note to the last chord. Quite unlike later styles, in which sections of music are separated by pauses, the polyphonic instrumental style of the Baroque is characterized by continuous motion and progression from beginning to end.

WORKS BASED ON A GIVEN MELODY

As a prologue to the singing of the chorale, which occupied a central place in Lutheran church music, church organists would frequently improvise pieces using the chorale melody as a point of departure. From this practice grew the chorale prelude, chorale partita, and chorale fantasia. In the *chorale prelude* the chorale melody is placed in a contrapuntal texture that may or may not be based on motives derived from the chorale melody. The *chorale partita* is a set of variations on the chorale melody. In the *chorale fantasia,* the melody is treated much more freely, being embellished with highly ornamental figurations. The chorale fantasia was designed to display the virtuosity of the performer.

PASSACAGLIA AND CHACONNE

Two other keyboard forms that employed given melodic material were the *passacaglia* and the *chaconne.* Both made use of *basso ostinato,* one of the most important unifying devices of Baroque music.

The distinctions between passacaglia and chaconne have occasionally been obscured because composers have used the terms interchangeably. Strictly speaking, however, in the **passacaglia** the basso ostinato is a melodic phrase of usually four or eight measures, while in the **chaconne** the ostinato element is a series of harmonies that are repeated over and over again.

THE SUITE

A favorite form of keyboard music of many Baroque composers was the suite. The **suite** is a series of movements, each based on a particular dance rhythm. Usually it consisted of the German *allemande,* the French *courante,* the Spanish *saraband,* and the English and Irish *gigue* (jig). The series of separate dance movements of a suite was designed to offer interesting contrasts in meter, rhythm, tempo, and texture. The first movement, the *allemande,* followed a rather stately duple meter that began with a short upbeat and frequently employed running figures in eighth and sixteenth notes. Contrast was provided by the *courante,* a quick dance in triple meter, in which the melodic interest shifted from voice to voice. The *saraband* following the *courante* was in a slow, dignified triple meter. The concluding *gigue* was a rapid dance in either 6/8 or 6/4 that employed the fugal procedure. Its melody, usually based on wide leaps, made considerable use of dotted rhythms. Although other multimovement forms used contrasting keys, the suite retained the same key throughout.

The dance movements of the suite were not intended to accompany actual dancing. Composers simply borrowed the rhythms of the dances, turning them into fine compositions meant for listening. Bach wrote three sets of suites: two for keyboard—the so-called French and English Suites—and one for orchestra. He also wrote four other orchestral suites, but called them *overtures* because their first movements, the overtures, were the longest and musically most significant.

It has not been definitely established whether the orchestral suites were written while Bach was at Cöthen or Leipzig, but they nonetheless follow a uniform procedure. All open in **French overture** style, in which a stately largo section with dotted rhythms is followed by a brisk, fugal allegro. The succeeding movements are based on dance forms, specifically the *bourrée, gavotte,* and *minuet.*

Bach's third orchestra suite, in D major, is the best known of the set, principally because of its lovely second movement, which has come to be known as the *Air on the G String*. The work is scored for two oboes, three trumpets, timpani, and strings.

The first movement, the overture, employs all the instruments. It alternates a slow, stately section using dotted rhythm with one that is rhythmically lively, fast in tempo, and polyphonic throughout. Frequently the first violin section is treated as a solo "instrument," with the rest of the orchestra providing light accompaniment. The form of the movement is:

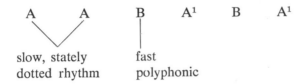

$$A \quad A \quad B \quad A^1 \quad B \quad A^1$$

slow, stately   fast
dotted rhythm   polyphonic

The second movement is a beautifully lyrical *air* (a term derived from the operatic *aria*) with a long melody spun out in the first violin section. It is slow in tempo, quiet in dynamics, and it uses only strings and continuo. It uses the binary form AABB.

The third movement is a lively *gavotte* in which the full ensemble alternates with passages scored only for strings and oboes. It is in da capo form, with all sections repeated: AA BB AA.

The fourth and fifth movements are also lighthearted dance forms: the *bourrée,* in duple meter and binary form (AB); and the *gigue,* in a lilting triple meter and also in binary form.

The dance forms played an important part in Baroque instrumental and vocal music. In the hands of Bach and his contemporaries, they provided individual movements for stylized concert pieces.

CONCERTO GROSSO

The **concerto grosso** is a multimovement work for instruments in which a solo group called the *concertino* and a full ensemble called the *ripieno* (Italian for "full") are pitted against each other. In the early concerto grosso the concertino generally consisted of two violins and continuo (cello and harpsichord). The ripieno was usually a small string orchestra with its own continuo. Through contrasts in tone color, texture, melodic line and relative complexity of musical material, the solo and ensemble groups compete with each other for the listener's attention. These contrasts are the very essence of the concerto grosso.

The first important examples of the concerto grosso appeared in the works of the Italian composer Arcangelo Corelli (1653–1713). Corelli's concertos had no fixed number of movements and no set plan of contrast between the movements. He made very little distinction between the material given to the solo group and that given to the ripieno; the contrast was essentially one of weight—two violins and continuo against the full string ensemble.

Another Italian, Antonio Vivaldi (1669–1741), was the first great master of the genre. Vivaldi systematized the structure of the concerto grosso by standardizing a three-movement form. Vivaldi was a prolific composer of instrumental music, and over 450 of his concertos have been preserved. His concertos are consistently in three movements: the first is fast and long, played by the full instrumental ensemble; the second is slow and short, played by a reduced ensemble; and the third like the first, is fast, long, and written for the full ensemble. Vivaldi made a greater distinction between the solo and ensemble groups both in timbre and in complexity of musical material than did his predecssors.

Vivaldi's concertos strongly influenced Bach, who often transcribed for keyboard the works, especially the concertos, of Italian composers. Between 1714 and 1717, Bach transcribed six Vivaldi concertos for solo organ or harpsichord and orchestra. In his own concerti grossi, Bach achieved an even stronger contrast between the concertino and the ripieno in instrumental color and the degree of complexity of the music for each group.

In 1721 Bach completed six concertos for orchestra. He dedicated them to Christian Ludwig, the Margrave of Brandenburg, who had requested Bach to write some pieces for the court orchestra at Brandenburg. Although Bach referred to these works as "concertos for several instruments," they have come to be known as the *Brandenburg Concertos*. Three of them (Nos. 2, 4, and 5) follow in the tradition of Vivaldi in that they are concerti grossi that contrast a group of solo instruments (concertino) against a full ensemble (ripieno).

BRANDENBURG CONCERTO NO. 5 IN D MAJOR *RECORD 1/SIDE 2*

The Brandenburg Concerto No. 5 is scored for a concertino consisting of flute, violin, and harpsichord. This solo group is contrasted with a ripieno of violins, violas, celli, and continuo. The concerto is laid out in the three-movement format standardized by Vivaldi.

First Movement The first movement, in D major, is characteristically in a fast tempo and employs the full complement of instruments ("tutti"). Also characteristically, it is cast in **ritornello** form, the usual plan for the first movement of a concerto grosso. In ritornello form (from the Italian word meaning "return"), the thematic material given to the ripieno returns between passages played by the solo group of instruments—an example of alternation (see p. 28). In broad outline, this form follows the pattern outlined below:

A	B	A	C	A	
ritornello	concertino	ritornello	concertino	ritornello	etc.

In this particular concerto, the ritornello statements *within* the movement are often fragmentary, consisting of only part of the original material. Nevertheless, these returns of the theme perform the same organizing function as a full statement and give the movement a great sense of unity. The *final* ritornello is complete and is an exact repeat of the opening section.

The first movement and the two that follow it are highly typical of Baroque instrumental music in that they proceed in what has been called **unflagging**

rhythm—a constant spinning out of music with no stopping points, which gives a relentless rhythmic drive to the piece. Also, there is a constancy of tempo within a movement or section. Once a tempo has been established, it is almost always maintained throughout the movement. Baroque composers did create contrasts by varying dynamic levels. The music tends to shift from loud to soft, soft to loud, seldom progressing gradually from one level to the other. This shifting dynamic level, sometimes called **terraced dynamics,** is an important element in the concerto grosso, where it is intensified by the opposing small and large groups of instruments.

While the first movement of the Concerto No. 5 exemplifies the above features, it is unusual in several respects:

1. Much of the material played by the solo instruments is derived from the ripieno:

Example 8.5 (Ripieno)

Solo Materials:

Example 8.6 (Augmented version of a small motive)

Example 8.7 (Augmented and decorated version of same motive)

Example 8.8 (*Simplified version of part of the ripieno theme*)

2. As the movement progresses, the equality among the three solo instruments gradually gives way to the almost total predominance of the harpsichord. In fact, in several long sections, particularly toward the end of the movement, both the violin and the flute of the concertino and the ripieno cease altogether and the harpsichord is heard as a solo instrument in passages that require great virtuosity on the part of the harpsichordist.

Example 8.9

Still, the rhythmic momentum never lags and the final entance of the entire ensemble comes as a wonderful climax to the solo harpsichord passage.

Second Movement The second movement, quite typically, is slower than the first, is in a contrasting key, and is reduced to just the three solo instruments that make up the concertino plus continuo. It is based on two contrasting rhythmic motives:

   *Example 8.10*   *Example 8.11*

which take on varying melodic shapes.

Third Movement The very light texture and slow tempo of the second movement is in marked contrast not only to the first movement but also to the third movement, which is very lively and employs the full ensemble, both concertino and ripieno. The third movement is in the spirit of a *gigue* and features the solo instruments, with the ripieno confined to light accompanying support except in a few places where it rivals the concertino. It constitutes a joyous conclusion to one of Bach's most interesting and enjoyable concerti grossi.

The *Brandenburg Concertos* represent the culmination of this fascinating form. Unlike the solo concerto, which thrived during subsequent stylistic periods, the concerto grosso ceased to occupy the attention of composers to any appreciable extent after Bach.

SOLO CONCERTO

In all respects except one, the solo concerto is the same as the concerto grosso. It is cast in three movements, fast-slow-fast. Its first and last movements are often in ritornello form. It emphasizes contrast between concertino and tutti. In the solo concerto, however, the concertino consists of only one instrument, which in the Baroque period was most often the violin. Vivaldi, whose contribution to the solo concerto was as important as his development of the concerto grosso, wrote hundreds of solo concertos. His works in this genre became the models for later Baroque composers, notably Handel and Bach.

Of all Vivaldi's concertos, the group called *Le Quattro Stagione* (*The Four Seasons*) is perhaps the most interesting because of the extramusical basis of its inspiration. Vivaldi was one of the first to try to depict by musical means the feelings and sounds of the changing seasons. His four concertos are an early form of Baroque descriptive or *program music,* and the music for the solo violin, which calls for virtuoso playing, demonstrates Vivaldi's skill at writing for the instrument.

THE FOUR SEASONS
RECORD 2/SIDE 1

Each of the four concertos bears the title of one of the seasons—spring, summer, winter, fall—and each is preceded by a sonnet describing that particular season. For instance, the concerto entitled *Spring* has the following introduction:

Spring has come, and the birds greet it with joyous songs, and at the same time the streams run softly murmuring to the breathing of gentle breezes . . .

The song of the birds, the murmuring streams, and the gentle breezes all are vividly represented by the solo violin and the full ensemble. But all of this takes place within the three movements of the basic concerto structure. And the ritornello structure of the first and last movements is also maintained.

Program music has attracted composers of every age. We have already mentioned the program chansons of Jannequin in the Renaissance, and an entire chapter (Chapter 13) is devoted to program music in the Romantic period.

THE BAROQUE SONATA

In the Baroque era, the name *sonata* was given to pieces that varied widely in structure, character, and medium of performance. Scored for one or more instruments, the sonata opened with a fast fugal movement, was followed by a slower, homophonic movement of a dancelike nature, and closed with a final movement that resembled the first. Additional movements, however, were frequently included.

CHARACTERISTICS OF BAROQUE MUSIC

Texture	Chordal homophony and polyphony (contrapuntal technique) both extensively employed
Tonality	Major-minor system
Rhythm	Unflagging, relentless rhythmic drive; also, free-type rhythm used in preludes, toccatas, and other keyboard styles
Melody	Ornamentation used
Harmony	Systematized harmonic system characterized by firm home base in tonic key with modulations to new keys; figured bass
Mood	Emphasis on expressing a single mood throughout a work or movement of a work
Dynamics	Terraced (abrupt dynamic changes) in instrumental music
Small Works	Instrumental: fantasia, capriccio, prelude, toccata, fugue, passacaglia, chaconne Vocal: chorale
Large Works	Instrumental: suite, concerto grosso, sonata, solo concerto Vocal: opera, oratorio, Passion, cantata
Vocal Styles	Monodic style—emphasized that the function of the music is to serve the text Recitative—follows natural inflection of words, furthers dramatic action Aria—is lyrical and expressive Virtuoso solo singing in late Baroque opera and oratorio
New Musical Devices	Equal temperament method of tuning instruments Basso ostinato as unifying device Use of dance forms for individual movements of concert pieces Ritornello form for first movement of concerto grosso; basso continuo Figured bass (thorough-bass) Da capo aria (ABA) Ornamentation, especially in keyboard music
Instruments and Ensembles	Vast improvements in all families of instruments; harpsichord, organ, concertino, ripieno; development of independent instrumental style based upon idomatic characteristics of the instruments

The early sonata existed in two forms: the *sonata da camera* (the chamber sonata) and the *sonata da chiesa* (the church sonata). Originally these sonatas differed only in the place of performance, but later the two terms indicated formal distinctions. The sonata da camera became a suite with an introduction and three or four dance movements, and the sonata da chiesa, a four-movement work in which the movements alternated: slow-fast-slow-fast.

The later Baroque sonata could be divided according to the medium of performance into four categories: those written for one part, those for two, those for three, and those for four or more. The most remarkable of the sonatas for one part were the unaccompanied violin and cello sonatas by Bach. The sonatas for two parts usually required three players, one to play the solo instrument and two, usually playing the cello and the keyboard, for the continuo. The sonata for three parts, the *trio sonata,* was the most important type of Baroque chamber music. It required four instruments: two violins for the upper parts, and a cello and a keyboard instrument for the continuo. The great English composer Henry Purcell (1659–1695), Corelli, Handel, Vivaldi, and Bach all contributed to the trio sonata literature.

Sonatas for four or more parts were intended for small orchestral ensembles. These were often called *sinfonie,* and often acted as overtures to or interludes within larger works such as operas or oratorios.

SUMMARY

Baroque composers generally tailored their works to fit a specific need. Thus, Handel wrote for the stage and concert hall, while Bach wrote primarily for the churches or aristocrats he served.

The Baroque era was a period of great progress in instrumental music. Instruments were improved technically. Keyboard instruments in particular enjoyed greater versatility after the development of equal temperament enabled them to perform equally well in every key. The most important keyboard instruments during the period were the harpsichord and the organ.

A large body of keyboard music was produced during the Baroque period. The fantasia, capriccio, prelude, and toccata were carryovers from styles originally developed for the lute, the most popular instrument during the Renaissance. The prelude and toccata often served as preliminaries to the fugue, a musical procedure that attained its greatest heights in the works of Bach.

Another form of keyboard music, the suite, was based on dance music. Usually the four movements of a suite consisted of an allemande, a courante, a saraband, and a gigue.

The concerto grosso was a multimovement work that pitted a small group, called the concertino, against a full ensemble, called a ripieno. A solo concerto differed from the concerto grosso only by the fact that the concertino was reduced to a single instrument. The concerto's three-movement pattern (fast-slow-fast) became standardized during the Baroque period and influenced the development of musical forms of the Classical era.

NEW TERMS

equal temperament	inversion
fantasia	stretto
prelude	pedal point
toccata	passacaglia
fugue	chaconne
subject	suite
answer	French overture
voice	concerto grosso
episode	ritornello
countersubject	unflagging rhythm
augmentation	terraced dynamics
diminution	

PART IV SUGGESTED LISTENING

Bach, Johann Sebastian

Magnificat in D. Composed shortly after he settled in Leipzig, this concise setting of the Latin canticle of the Virgin Mary is one of Bach's finest and most melodious works; it is scored for five-part chorus, four soloists, and orchestra.

Mass in B Minor. Actually a compilation of separate movements, this immense composition encompasses all of the major choral and vocal techniques developed over the preceding century and a half.

Organ Works: Toccata in D Minor; Passacaglia in C Minor; Fantasia and Fugue in G Minor; Prelude and Fugue in E-Flat Major (St. Anne). This quartet of works, spanning Bach's most active period of organ composition, demonstrates the major Baroque techniques of keyboard writing.

Musikalisches Opfer (A Musical Offering). In 1747, Bach visited Frederick the Great of Prussia and improvised at the keyboard upon a theme proposed by the king; after returning to Leipzig, he revised and wrote his improvisations. It is a cycle of canons, two ricercari, and a trio sonata for flute, violin, and continuo.

Corelli, Arcangelo

Concerto Grosso in G Minor, Op. 6, No. 8 (Christmas Concerto). This concerto was written for performance at Midnight Mass on Christmas Eve. The final movement (Pastorale) is an evocation of the angels hovering over Bethlehem.

Handel, George Frederick

Israel in Egypt. An oratorio in three sections. Unlike most of Handel's oratorios, the solo voices complement the more dominant chorus in this work. Of particular interest is the description of the plagues.

Orchestral Suites: Water Music; Fireworks Music. The *Water Music,* actually a compilation of three individual suites, was first performed at a royal boating party. The *Fireworks Music,* a much shorter work, originally scored for a large wind band and later revised to include strings, was composed to celebrate the Peace of Aix-la-Chapelle.

Monteverdi, Claudio

L'Orfeo. Monteverdi composed this opera in the new monodic style, in which the prime importance of the music was to support and dramatize the story. To intensify the drama of the recitatives, Monteverdi broke many rules of harmony "for the sake of the truth."

Purcell, Henry

Dido and Aeneas. Purcell wrote this opera to be performed by a school for young gentlewomen—all but one of the roles are for female voices. The music is faithful to the mood of the libretto; for example, it mixes major and minor modes to heighten emotional tension and creates the sounds of laughter and echoes.

Schütz, Heinrich

Historia von der Geburt Jesu Christi (*The Christmas Story*). One of the earliest masterpieces of Baroque oratorio, this work is divided into eight parts, with an introductory and concluding chorus.

Vivaldi, Antonio

Concerto in D Major for Flute, Op. 10, No. 3 (*Il gardellino*). One of Vivaldi's thirty solo concertos for flute, *Il gardellino* (*The Goldfinch*) shows his ability to use an instrument's potential to full advantage.

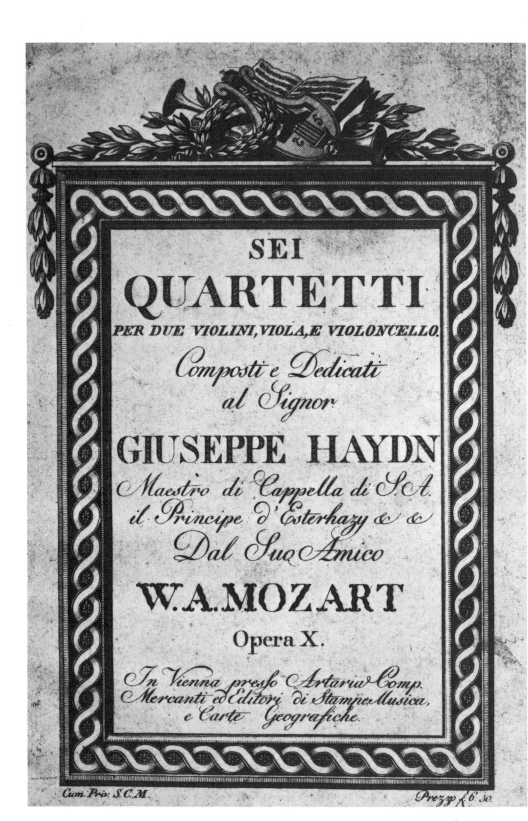

SEI
QUARTETTI
PER DUE VIOLINI, VIOLA, E VIOLONCELLO.
Composti e Dedicati
al Signor

GIUSEPPE HAYDN
Maestro di Cappella di S. A.
il Principe d'Esterhazy & &
Dal Suo Amico

W. A. MOZART
Opera X.

In Vienna presso Artaria e Comp.
Mercanti ed Editori di Stampe Musica,
e Carte Geografiche.

Cum. Priv. S. C. M.

Prezzo f 6. 30.

MUSIC OF THE CLASSICAL ERA

Title page of string quartets by Mozart that
he dedicated to Joseph Haydn.

9 | MOZART AND HAYDN

THE TERM "CLASSICAL" IS APPLIED TO MUSIC IN SEVERAL DIFFERENT ways. In one sense, we speak of a "classic" as any work of lasting value. "Classical" sometimes designates so-called *serious* or concert music, as opposed to *popular* music. In this case the term is applied without regard to historical or stylistic factors, so that composers of different style periods—Bach, Beethoven, and Tchaikovsky, for example—may all be considered "classical" composers. In a narrower and more accurate sense, the term is applied to music in either of two meanings: First, it describes those periods in music history when style emphasized formal clarity, balance and structure, lucid design, objectivity, and traditionalism, as opposed to the romantic qualities of sentimentalism, exaggerated emotionalism, subjectivism, and experimentation. (Seen in this light, the late Renaissance and late Baroque periods, when the art of polyphony was brought to its greatest heights, were periods of classicism.) Second, it designates the music of the Viennese classic school (that is, the music of Haydn, Mozart, and to an extent, Beethoven and Schubert) from about 1770 to 1830. It is the second meaning that is intended when we capitalize the term, referring to the "Classical era."

THE CLASSICAL SONATA

The meaning of the word "sonata" varies from age to age in music history. Originally a sonata meant something to be *played,* as opposed to a cantata, something to be *sung.* The term had various applications throughout the Baroque period, but in the Classical era it took on very specific and important meaning.

The Classical **sonata** is a multimovement work in one of two schemes:

Three-Movement Plan

First movement	Second movement	Third movement
Fast tempo	Slow tempo	Fast tempo
Key of tonic	Contrasting key	Key of tonic

Four-Movement Plan

First movement	Second movement	Third movement	Fourth movement
Fast tempo	Slow tempo	Minuet and trio	Fast tempo
Key of tonic	Contrasting key	Key of tonic	Key of tonic

FIRST-MOVEMENT FORM (SONATA-ALLEGRO)

In both plans, the first movement is invariably cast in what has become known as **sonata-allegro form.** Sonata-allegro form (sometimes referred to simply as **sonata form**) consists of three sections: (1) the *exposition,* (2) the *development,* (3) the *recapitulation.*

Exposition The **exposition** introduces the thematic material that will be used throughout the movement. It consists of two contrasting themes or groups of themes connected by a bridge. The first theme is usually strong and energetic; the second is almost always more lyrical and relaxed. The first theme establishes the overall tonality for the movement as a whole; the second theme is always in a different key. If the first theme is in a major key, the second will nearly always be in its dominant key, a fifth higher; for example, if the first theme is in C major, the second will be in G major. If, on the other hand, the first theme is written in a minor key, the second will usually appear in its relative major, a step and a half higher in pitch. Thus, if the original theme is in C minor, the second will be in E-flat major.

The **bridge,** which is usually less distinctive melodically than either of the two themes, serves primarily the function of modulating from the key of the first theme to the key of the second theme. Frequently, a short section called a **codetta** is employed to conclude the exposition. (The codetta is sometimes called the **closing theme**.)

The exposition is immediately repeated so that it may adequately establish the basic melodic ideas in the listener's mind. Thus, the listener will be able to follow the use of the melodic ideas in the development section.

Development The **development** concentrates upon some of the materials of the exposition and reworks them in a variety of ways. Themes may be fragmented, small motives expanded, or counterpoint added. Changes in timbre, rhythm, and dynamics are among the devices that may be employed. No two development sections are the same; however, what is common to all of them is the process of modulation. In the development section frequent and extreme modulation is the rule. But no matter how far afield the modulations may go, they must eventually return to prepare for the key of the tonic, which arrives at the beginning of the recapitulation.

Recapitulation The **recapitulation** is a restatement of the whole exposition with one important change—the second theme appears in the *tonic,* rather than in a contrasting key as in the exposition. This reaffirmation of the tonic key in addition to the return of the melodic material in its original form lends great unity to

Fig. 9.1 Sonata-allegro form.

Exposition	Development	Recapitulation
Theme I (tonic)	Transformation of exposi-	Theme I (tonic)
Bridge (modulates to	tional material	Bridge (extended)
new key)	Rapid modulations	
Theme II (new key)		Theme II (tonic)
Codetta to cadence		Codetta
		Coda
		Intensification of thematic material
		Final cadence (tonic)

this formal structure. In some pieces a short concluding section, the **coda** ("tail") is added as a kind of extended conclusion.

OTHER MOVEMENTS OF SONATAS

The second movement of the sonata is slower and more lyrical than the first. It always contrasts in key with the first movement. Theme and variations or an alternating form such as ABA or ABACA is commonly used, although sonata-allegro form is occasionally employed.

In the four-movement plan, the third movement is usually a **minuet and trio** in the key of the first movement. It is in a stately triple meter and cast in ternary form:

A	B	A
minuet	trio	minuet

The minuet developed from a form of dance music popular between 1670 and 1790. The middle section is called a trio because it was originally a contrapuntal section using three voice parts. In the Classical sonata, it rarely is a three-voice piece, but does use a smaller instrumental grouping than the minuet.

The minuet-and-trio plan described above is typical of works by Haydn and Mozart, and of early works by Beethoven. However, Beethoven experimented with this movement a great deal and eventually adopted, in place of the minuet, a much faster type of piece known as a **scherzo,** which is Italian for "joke." As we shall see, the scherzo and trio became a movement of great power and drama in the works of Beethoven.

The last movement of the sonata (third or fourth) returns to the general quality of the first movement. It is fast and in the key of the first movement. It is often a **rondo.** The rondo is an extended alternating form in fast tempo, usually ABACA or ABACABA. It is generally spirited and playful. Occasionally the last movement of a sonata employed the sonata-allegro form or a combination of the two.

Fig. 9.2 The complete classical sonata.

First movement	Second movement	Third movement	Fourth movement
Sonata-allegro form Fast tempo Dramatic	Theme and variations, alternating form, or sonata-allegro form Slow tempo Lyrical Key contrasts with first movement	Minuet and trio or scherzo and trio Triple meter (minuet) Fast tempo (scherzo) Light, cheerful Key of first movement	Rondo or sonata-allegro Fast tempo Spirited, playful Key of first movement

The sonata principle outlined above was an all-pervasive concept that served as a procedure for the composition of thousands of works of music during the Classical and Romantic periods. The four-movement plan became the basis for the **symphony** (sonata for orchestra) and the **string quartet** (sonata for four stringed instruments). The three-movement scheme omitting minuet and trio was typical of works for solo piano (piano sonata), for solo instruments and the piano (e.g., sonata for piano and violin), and for the **concerto** (sonata for solo instrument and orchestra.

THE CLASSICAL ORCHESTRA

In the Baroque era instrumental music had become an independent idiom, and a vast literature for instrumental ensembles was produced. But the Baroque orchestra, aside from the usual complement of strings, had no fixed makeup.

In the Classical era the makeup of the orchestra became standardized to a great extent. Its development was largely the work of Johann Stamitz (1717–1757), a violinist, composer, and conductor of the orchestra at the German city of Mannheim. Under his direction it became the most celebrated musical ensemble in Europe. The excellence of its playing was praised by the leading composers of the day, Mozart among them.

By Baroque standards the Mannheim orchestra was of rather large dimensions. In 1756 it consisted of twenty violins, four violas, four cellos, and four basses. The wind section included four horns in addition to flutes, oboes, clarinets, and bassoons. Trumpets and timpani were also used.

The Mannheim orchestra was capable of achieving a great variety of startling effects. Chief among these were the Mannheim "rocket" (a rapidly rising arpeggio), crescendo, the string tremolo, and a forte of shattering impact. The German poet and musician D. F. D. Schubert (1739–1791) recorded his impressions of the orchestra in his *Essay on Musical Esthetics:*

No orchestra in the world ever equalled the Mannheimers' execution. Its forte is like thunder, its crescendo like a mighty waterfall, its diminuendo a gentle river disappearing into the distance, its piano is a breath of spring. The wind instruments could not be used to better advantage; they lift and carry, they reinforce and give life to the storm for violins.

While the technical improvement of the instruments during the Baroque period contributed to the creation of a significant body of solo and chamber music, the development of this collective instrument, the orchestra, enabled the growth of a vast body of symphonic compositions. Symphonic composition centered in the cities of Berlin, Mannheim, and Vienna. The Berlin or North German composers, of whom C. P. E. Bach was the leading figure, retained the more conservative three-movement structure and preserved elements of the contrapuntal style. The Mannheim group, under the leadership of Stamitz, employed the four-movement structure. The Viennese symphonists also favored the four-movement form. One of the greatest of the Viennese symphonic composers was Wolfgang Amadeus Mozart.

MOZART (1756–1791)

Born in Salzburg, Austria, Wolfgang Amadeus Mozart began his musical career as one of the most celebrated child prodigies in eighteenth-century Europe. His father, Leopold, a highly respected composer and violinist, recognized his son's extraordinary talent and carefully supervised his musical education. Mozart began harpsichord lessons when he was four and wrote his first compositions when he was five. At the age of six he and his older sister, Maria Anna ("Nannerl"), were taken by their father on a concert tour of Munich and Vienna.

From this first public performance until he was fifteen, Mozart was almost constantly on tour, playing prepared works and improvising. While the harpsichord and later the piano remained Mozart's principal instruments, he also mastered the violin and the organ. In addition to keyboard pieces, he wrote church works, symphonies, string quartets, and operas. In 1769, on a long trip to Italy, Mozart composed his first major opera, *Mitridate,* which was performed in Milan in 1770. His success in Italy, as triumphant as Handel's had been some sixty years earlier, brought him a number of commissions for operas.

Fig. 9.3 This portrait of Mozart at the clavier shows the young prodigy in his early teens.

His father, court composer and vice chapelmaster to the Archbishop of Salzburg, obtained a position for his son as concertmaster in the Archbishop's orchestra. But the new Archbishop of Salzburg, installed in 1772, failed to appreciate Mozart's genius. Relations between the haughty churchman and the high-spirited young composer steadily deteriorated until, in 1781, despite his father's objections, Mozart quit his position and settled in Vienna.

The first years in Vienna were fairly prosperous. Mozart was in great demand as a teacher; he gave numerous concerts, and his German **Singspiel**—a German comic opera with spoken dialogue—*Die Entführung aus dem Serail* (*The Abduction from the Harem;* 1782), was a success. He married Constanze Weber, a woman he had met several years earlier on a concert tour, and looked forward to a happy family life. But Constanze was a careless housekeeper, and Mozart was a poor manager of finances. Intrigues at the Viennese court kept him from obtaining a permanent post. Public taste changed and his teaching began to fall off. Except for occasional successes —his opera *Le Nozze di Figaro* (*The Marriage of Figaro,* 1786) and the *Singspiel, Die Zauberflöte* (*The Magic Flute,* 1791)—the last ten years of his life were spent, for the most part, in poverty.

In 1788 he gave up public performances, relying on a meager income from teaching and loans from various friends to sustain himself and his family. In spite of these troubles he continued to compose, but his health began to decline. When he died in 1791 at the age of thirty-five, he was buried in an unmarked grave in a part of the cemetery reserved for the poor.

MOZART'S WORK

Unlike the meticulous Haydn, who kept a chronological list of all his compositions, Mozart never bothered to organize his musical papers in any fully consistent fashion. In the nineteenth century, Ludwig von Köchel compiled a roughly chronological listing of Mozart's music (numbering up to 626). This catalogue, along with substantial revisions and additions by later musicologists, remains in use today.

The most recent edition of Köchel's catalogue, in which the number of each piece is preceded by the initial "K," includes twenty-one stage works, twenty-seven concert arias, fifteen Masses, over fifty symphonies, twenty-five piano concertos, twelve violin concertos, some fourteen concertos for other instruments, twenty-six string quartets, seventeen piano sonatas, forty-two violin sonatas, and numerous works for miscellaneous chamber-sized ensembles.

Religious music Mozart composed almost all of his church music at the beginning of his career, when he was working in Salzburg. His two greatest choral works, unfortunately, were left incomplete. The first of these was the gigantic Mass in C Minor (1782), intended as an offering of thanks for his marriage to Constanze. The second is also his last work, the Requiem in D Minor. In 1791 Mozart accepted a commission to write this work on behalf of a nobleman who wished to remain anonymous. Mozart died before the work was finished. On his deathbed Mozart extracted a promise from his wife that Franz Süssmayr, his favorite pupil, would be selected to finish the piece. Süssmayr did so, making some additions of his own.

Opera Mozart's operas are the only eighteenth-century works in this genre to have remained consistently in general repertory. For the most part, they fall into one of three categories: (1) Italian *opera seria,* based on serious plots, including *Mitridate* (1770), *Idomeneo* (1781), and *The Clemency of Titus* (1791); (2) comic Italian opera, including *The Marriage of Figaro* and *Cosi Fan Tutte* (1790); and (3) German *Singspiel,* including *The Abduction from the Harem.* Two of Mozart's most popular and significant operas resist such classification. *Don Giovanni* (1787), subtitled "humorous drama," vacillates between high comedy and genuine tragedy in following the career of the legendary Don Juan. *The Magic Flute,* though cast in the form of a *Singspiel* with intermittent spoken dialogue, might better be considered a morality play bound up in a fairy-tale setting. In many ways *Don Giovanni* may be regarded as the greatest of the eighteenth-century Italian operas; *The Magic Flute* may be considered the first German opera and one of the greatest. We will discuss the ever-popular opera *The Marriage of Figaro* in the next chapter.

Instrumental music The amazing fluency with which Mozart composed his operas is also evident in his instrumental music. He was able to carry around finished compositions in his head, once remarking that "the committing to paper is done quickly enough. For everything is already finished, and it rarely differs on paper from what it was in my imagination."

Many of the twenty-five piano concertos were composed for Mozart's own use in his public performances. These concertos demonstrate many of Mozart's most progressive ideas. His string quartets, at first influenced by Haydn's, also reveal Mozart's mastery of musical forms.

His final three symphonies—Nos. 39, 40, and 41 (the *Jupiter Symphony*)—were composed during the summer of 1788, three years before his death. Little is known about the circumstances of their composition, but these three works stand among Mozart's finest contributions to instrumental music.

Mozart's G-minor symphony follows the four-movement plan outlined earlier: fast-slow-medium-fast. It is scored for an orchestra consisting of flute, two oboes, two clarinets, two bassoons, two horns, and strings.

**SYMPHONY
NO. 40
IN G MINOR**
RECORD 2/SIDE 1

FIRST MOVEMENT: SONATA-ALLEGRO FORM

Exposition The opening theme of Mozart's Symphony No. 40 is strongly symmetrical:

Example 9.1

The two phrases are the same length and have the same durational pattern. They differ in *melodic contour* and *melodic activity.* Phrase 1 is melodically static for most of its life, dwelling on the two notes Eb and D. It suddenly becomes active as it leaps upward at the end. Phrase 2, on the other hand, is melodically active at the beginning, based on a descending scale passage, and becomes melodically static in its last two notes, which are the same pitch.

These paired phrases and elements drawn from them—especially the rhythmic motive♪♪ ♩—are crucial to the life and structure of the entire movement. As the theme begins, they are sounded softly by the first and second violins, with the second violins played an octave lower than the first. The violas, cellos, and basses play an accompaniment, and the woodwinds are silent. Consequently our attention is riveted on the pair of phrases in the violins.

Both phrases are repeated one step lower. By this time we have come to expect repetitions of the rhythmic structure, melodic contour, and length of the two phrases, but now Mozart introduces a new phrase. This new phrase begins like Phrase 1 but continues in a different melodic contour and rhythmic pattern. It does maintain the same phrase *length,* thus satisfying our expectation to a degree.

Example 9.2

Phrase 3 is repeated, but this time it is extended, an alteration in *phrase length.* The woodwinds then enter and introduce a new melodic element, while the strings preserve the familiar rhythmic motive.

Example 9.3

The new melodic element leads to a cadence in the dominant key of D. After this interruption in the flow of the melody, there is a return to the original paired phrases, which are played twice. Just as we become convinced that we are going to hear them repeated as they were before, there is an abrupt change of dynamics from piano to forte and the sudden entrance of new material—the bridge—played by the entire orchestra.

Example 9.4

The bridge is an extended modulation closing with a strong cadence on the dominant chord of the key in which the second theme will be stated (B-flat major). A pronounced pause follows, which clearly separates Theme 1 and the bridge from Theme 2. This marked differentiation of themes is typical of both Haydn and Mozart.

Theme 2, played between the strings and woodwinds, appears in the relative key of B-flat major. It is a lyrical, expressive melody composed of phrases of unequal length and different contours. The second theme acts mainly as a foil to the agitated first theme.

Example 9.5

In the last section of Theme 2, before the closing material, Mozart utilizes elements of the first theme, notably the figure ♫ ♩ ♫ ♩, with both the original rhythmic and melodic patterns found at the beginning of Phase 1. This last section is presented in dialogue fashion between the clarinet and the bassoon, then finally is stated and expanded in the high first violins, accompanied by a sudden change in dynamics from soft to loud. By this means of referring back to material that was so noticeable in Theme 1, Mozart adds a unity to this exposition over and above that contained in the procedure of sonata-allegro form. Indeed, the entire exposition is unified by the basic motive ♫ ♩.

The exposition is immediately repeated, providing the listener with the opportunity to become more familiar with the themes so that their destinies may be followed in the drama of the development section.

Development As the development section begins, the violins present the paired phrases of the first theme in a variety of keys and at a variety of pitch levels. The material is restated in the course of modulation to new keys. The changes that occur in the melodic structure are the result of modulation.

Just as the third statement of the two phrases is finishing, Mozart adds a new developmental technique. Suddenly the phrases are stated not in the violins, but in the lower strings. They are then passed back and forth between the lower and upper strings. The upper strings provide contrapuntal material to the theme when it appears in the lower strings, and the lower strings play the same contrapuntal material when the theme passes back to the upper strings. The beginning of this passing back and forth technique is accompanied by a sudden and unexpected change from piano to forte (Example 9.6).

This passing back and forth from high to low strings continues, and the listener becomes accustomed to it and expects it to continue. Then, after the second statement of the phrases in the lower strings, the violins take up the phrases and a remarkable change takes place. After Phrase 1, Phrase 2 is begun.

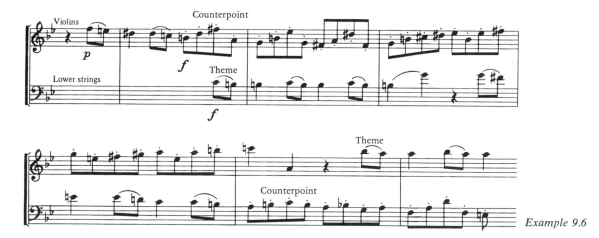

Example 9.6

But instead of Phrase 2's static ending, there appears the sudden leap that ends Phrase 1. In other words, Mozart has combined the melodically active elements of each phrase into one new phrase:

Example 9.7

This is a new developmental technique, a *reduction* of the basic material from the exposition. The new phrase, a composite of the two original phrases, states material from both phrases in the same length of time formerly required to state the material of just *one* of the phrases.

After the combination of phrases is stated three times, it is followed by still another change. The polyphonic texture that began when the paired phrases were passed back and forth between the upper and lower strings and continued through the three statements of the composite phrase gives way to a return to a homophonic texture, in which the upper strings have a new version of the two phrases. This new version combines the *static* elements of the two phrases.

Example 9.8

It represents a further reduction of the melodic material, but this time the reduction is not only one length, but also of *melodic activity*.

The rest of the developmental section continues systematically to break down the material. Before the violins have concluded the second composite phrase, the flute and clarinets state a shortened version of it.

Example 9.9

After this is stated several times, the woodwinds answer with a further shortening of the phrase.

Example 9.10

This figure is the shortest form of the material, and the rest of the development section exploits it by passing it back and forth between high and low strings. Finally, the flute and clarinets alternately state the figure, using it as a springboard to reintroduce gently the entire first theme as the violins begin the recapitulation.

Thus the "drama" of the development section ends as the melodic material, having been reduced to its smallest component, reappears in its original form.

Recapitulation The recapitulation opens with a statement of the first theme as it was heard in the exposition. A bridge passage, similar to but even longer than the bridge in the exposition, leads to the second theme, again after a pause for the entire orchestra. The second theme appears in the tonic key of G minor.

Coda A brief coda, based on the first phrase of the first theme, brings the movement to a close in the original key of G minor. Here again the appearance of Phrase 1 adds additional unity and structural solidity to the movement.

SECOND MOVEMENT: ANDANTE

In accordance with the four-movement plan of the sonata, the second movement is in a key (E-flat major) that contrasts with the key of the first movement (G minor); it is slower in tempo and, to some extent, quieter and more lyrical than the first movement.

Exposition The first theme consists of three parts (A, B, and C). Part A begins with imitative entrances—first in the violas, then in the second violins, and finally in the first violins, which end part A. The melodic material of B consists of short fragments separated by rests. These fragments are stated by the first and second violins duplicating each other an octave apart.

Both A and B are then repeated, with changes and additions. The repeat of A begins in the cellos and basses, moves to the violas, and is then finished by the second violins, while the first violins play a new, added melody. When B is restated, the first violins continue to play new material, while the B melody, originally played by the upper strings, is now played by the lower strings (Example 9.11). The last measure of B is replaced by the beginning of C. It is built on a small figure (so small it is barely noticed) from the B part of the first theme: . As the movement continues, this small figure becomes more important.

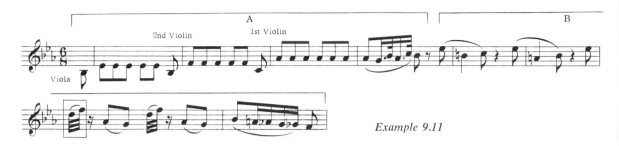

Example 9.11

The orchestra is brought to a full cadence and pause before the bridge is introduced. The bridge begins with a downward octave leap in which the higher note is played loudly (*forte*), the lower note is played softly (*piano*), and the rhythm is somewhat syncopated. But as it unfolds, the figure ♪♪ becomes the predominant element, stated by the string, answered by the woodwinds, and cast into scalelike passages. This fragment "takes over" and is continued throughout the remaining part of the bridge by the woodwinds, while the strings play an expanded version of the imitative opening of the first theme.

The second theme begins with new and contrasting material, but soon the familiar figure is integrated into it (at the places marked with an "x" in the following notation).

Example 9.12

The figure is also present in the closing material of Theme 2. Indeed it is included in every part of this exposition—sometimes barely noticeable, sometimes dominating the material—tying together the entire exposition. Here again, Mozart has bound together the contrasting themes by carrying a common element through them all. The unity of the exposition becomes even more apparent when it is repeated.

Development The development section is based on the opening rhythmic pattern of the first theme ♪ ♫♫ and the figure that played such a prominent part in the thematic material of the exposition ♫. These two ideas are presented consecutively first and then in combination, one played in the strings and the other in the woodwinds, and vice versa.

Recapitulation In the recapitulation, Mozart again finds ingenious ways to intrigue the listener. Parts A and B of the first theme are presented normally. When the theme is repeated, however, the end of part A is changed somewhat and is immediately followed not by part B, but by the beginning of the bridge. After this "premature" entrance of the bridge, part B appears. The bridge resumes and leads to the second theme, which is stated in the principal key of E♭. A closing section, based on the ♫ ♫ figure, ends the recapitulation. Mozart indicates that the entire development and recapitulation is to be repeated, resulting in the overall scheme: exposition, exposition, development, recapitulation, development, recapitulation.

This movement is evidence of the flexibility with which the forms of the Classical period were treated.

THIRD MOVEMENT: MINUET AND TRIO

This relatively simple movement provides a contrast to the structural complexities of the other movements. It is cast in ABA form, with minuet (A), trio (B), repeat of minuet (A). There are also internal repeats within the large sections. The overall structure of the minuet and trio can be diagrammed as:

A	B	A
Minuet	Trio	Minuet
a a b b	c c d d	a b
G minor	G major	G minor

Again, Mozart adds unity by including a suggestion of "a" in the "b" section and a full statement of "c" as part of the "d" section. Note that when the minuet reappears after the trio, the internal repeats are not observed.

FOURTH MOVEMENT: SONATA-ALLEGRO FORM

Exposition The first theme consists of two melodic ideas: the triad of G minor played in a rapidly rising "rocket" figure, which is played *piano*, and a contrasting figure, which is played *forte*.

Example 9.13

After the theme is repeated several times, a new element adds dynamic contrast, moving from loud to soft. A bridge leads to a cadence and pause, and the second theme begins, played by reduced orchestra, first only the strings and then only the woodwinds. A closing, based on the bridge material, leads to a repetition of the exposition.

Development and Recapitulation The "rocket" motive of Theme 1 and an extensive modulation are the basis of the short development section. Passed from one section of the orchestra to another, the motive is treated polyphonically with overlapping entrances. Gradually it leads to a pronounced pause that separates the development from the recapitulation. Mozart intended that the entire development, recapitulation, and coda be repeated.

SUMMARY

The G-minor symphony not only provides a superb example of Mozart's craft, but also illustrates general characteristics of the Classical style and the Classical symphony.

1. The four-movement plan of the sonata (fast-slow-medium-fast) is followed, the first movement being cast in sonata-allegro form.

2. There is *no thematic relationship* among the movements; each movement is self-contained and none of the materials of one movement appears in any other movement.

3. Structurally, the main unifying force is *key;* movements 1, 3, and 4 are in the common key of G minor, creating *tonal unity*.

4. Within individual movements, clarity and balance are probably the most pronounced stylistic features. Contrasting materials and sections are for the most part clearly and carefully set off from each other—often with the help of such musical devices as changes in dynamics, cadences, and pauses—without the blurring of relationships we will encounter in later periods of music.

Mozart's symphony demonstrates the organizing power and wonderful flexibility of sonata-allegro form. Three of the work's four movements are organized by this formal procedure, all of them solid in design, yet completely different from each other in their expressive qualities.

CHAMBER MUSIC

Even after the orchestra had emerged, music for smaller ensembles continued to thrive as wealthy patrons commissioned works to be performed in their salons for private audiences.

The multimovement sonata structure that we encountered in the symphony was also used in chamber music for a wide variety of instrumental combinations. The string quartet, consisting of a first and second violin, a viola, and a cello, became, in the Classical era, the most important chamber music medium. Its popularity continued well into the twentieth century in the works of Bartók, Hindemith, and others.

Franz Joseph Haydn was the first great master of string quartet composition, which occupied him throughout most of his long and creative life.

HAYDN (1732–1809)

Franz Joseph Haydn was born in Rohrau, a small Austrian village located near the Hungarian border southeast of Vienna. His parents, both of peasant stock, seemed to have encouraged their son's musical ability and entrusted his earliest musical training to a relative, Johann Franck, a schoolteacher and choirmaster in the nearby town of Hainburg. At age six, Haydn was already singing in Franck's church choir and had begun playing the *clavier* (an early keyboard instrument) and violin.

In 1740, the composer and choirmaster at St. Stephen's Cathedral in Vienna stopped in Hainburg to recruit singers for his choir. Impressed with Haydn's voice, he arranged to take the young boy back with him to Vienna.

For the next nine years Haydn immersed himself in the routine of a Catholic choirboy. He received a smattering of elementary education at St. Stephen's choir school and continued with violin and voice lessons, but his training in composition and theory was erratic and largely self-taught. In 1749, when his voice began to mature, Haydn was abruptly dismissed and turned out into the street.

The following years were hard ones. At first Haydn made his living teaching clavier by day and playing in street bands and serenading parties by night. His reputation as a teacher and vocal accompanist, however, gradually spread, and he started serious composition. In 1759 he was appointed *Kapellmeister* and chamber composer to a Bohemian nobleman, Count Morzin. He composed his first symphonies for the count's small orchestra.

In 1760 Haydn married Maria Anna Keller, but the marriage, which lasted forty years, was a tragic mistake. They were incompatible in temperament and finally separated.

The unhappy marriage was offset by his appointment in 1761 as assistant music director to Prince Paul Anton Esterhazy, head of one of the most powerful and wealthy Hungarian noble families. Haydn's contract stipulated that he was to compose whatever music was required of him (which would become the property of his patron), to keep the musical instruments in good repair, to train singers, and to supervise the conduct of all of the musicians.

Despite the rigid and burdensome requirements of his contract, Haydn enjoyed his work and was to say later, "My prince was pleased with all my work, I was commended, and as conductor of an orchestra I could make experiments, observe what strengthened and what weakened an effect and thereupon improve, substitute, omit, and try new things; I was cut

Fig. 9.4 Portrait of Haydn, after a wax bust by Adolf Neumann; probably done in 1790.

off from the world, there was no one around to mislead and harass me, and so I was forced to become original."

Haydn remained in the employ of the Esterhazy family for almost thirty years, serving first Prince Paul Anton and then his brother, Prince Nikolaus. Despite his isolation at their country estate, his fame gradually spread throughout Europe. He was able to fulfill commissions from other individuals and from publishers all over the Continent. When Prince Nikolaus died in 1790, Haydn was retained as nominal *Kapellmeister* for the Esterhazy family, but he was now independent. Moving to Vienna, he resumed his friendship with Mozart, whose talent he had admired since their first meeting in 1781. Haydn also gave lessons to a young, rising composer named Ludwig van Beethoven. He made two successful trips to London (1791–1792, 1794–1795), where he conducted a number of his own symphonies, written on commission for the well-known impresario Johann Salomon. After his second London visit, he ceased writing symphonies, turning instead to the composition of Masses and oratorios. After 1800 his health began to fail, and he lived in secluded retirement. He died in 1809 at the age of seventy-seven.

HAYDN'S WORK

The great majority of Haydn's work was composed during his service to the Esterhazy princes. The biweekly concerts and opera performances at Esterhaz, Prince Nikolaus's country estate, engendered a prodigious flow of instrumental and vocal music. Most of Haydn's 104 symphonies were written for the small but excellent Esterhazy orchestra.

Symphonies The symphonies form a remarkably complete record of Haydn's development as a composer, ranging in unbroken continuity from his earliest, somewhat crude efforts to the rich and masterful works of the 1780s and 1790s. Many of the more popular symphonies bear identifying nicknames: the *Horn Signal* (No. 31, 1765), the *Farewell* (No. 45, 1772), the *Surprise* (No. 94, 1791), and the *Drumroll* (No. 103, 1795) are but a few. His greatest works in this genre are the last twelve symphonies, called the *London* symphonies, which were written for his two London visits.

Fig. 9.5 Haydn, shown here directing the rehearsal of a string quartet, spent many of his most productive years composing for and conducting the orchestra of the Esterhazy princes.

Chamber Music While many of Haydn's experiments with musical form were carried out in the symphonies, his chamber music, particularly the string quartets, was equally significant in his development as a composer. In his eighty-three quartets, Haydn laid down many of the fundamental principles that were taken up by younger composers such as Mozart and Beethoven. The six works making up Opus 20* (the *Sun Quartets,* 1772) are among his masterworks in this genre. The later sets of Opus 33 (*The Scherzos* or *Russian Quartets,* 1781) and Opus 50 (1787) represent still further advances in Haydn's musical development.

Among Haydn's other chamber works are more than twenty *divertimenti.* As their title suggests, these were light "diversionary" pieces written in a simple, popular style. Other chamber music included a multitude of trios and sonatas for various instruments. Of some sixty sonatas written for piano, fifty-two survive.

Though he was a good string player, Haydn did not consider himself a virtuoso performer. Consequently his solo concertos are few. A good many concertos have been lost, and still others attributed to Haydn have not yet been authenticated as coming from his hand.

Operas Opera was a highly important part of musical activity at the Esterhazy palace, and Haydn was for a long time quite proud of his more than twenty stage works. The Austrian Empress, Maria Theresa, reputedly said, "If I want to hear a good opera, I go to Esterhaz." When Haydn became familiar with Mozart's incomparable genius for opera composing, however, he realized that his own works were of lesser quality. Today they are all but forgotten.

Masses and Oratorios Haydn's Masses and oratorios present a different story. The last six of his twelve Masses, composed between 1796 and 1802, are his crowning achievement as a church composer—works of old age demonstrating a mastery of form and technique accumulated over more than fifty years of composing. Several of them—*Missa in Tempore Belli* (*Mass in Time of War,* 1796), the *Missa in Angustiis* (*Nelson Mass,* 1798), and the *Harmoniemesse* ("Wind-band" Mass, 1802)—rank among Haydn's masterworks. Stimulated by Handel's oratorios, some of which he had heard during his London visits, Haydn produced two of his own. Titled *The Creation* (1796–1798) and *The Seasons* (1798–1801), they have remained in concert repertoire to this day. Contemporary with these major vocal works was Haydn's gift to the Austrian people, the national anthem, *Gott erhalte Franze den Kaiser* (*God Save the Emperor, Franz,* better known as the *Austrian Hymn*). He wrote it on his own initiative as a patriotic gesture when Napoleon's armies invaded Austrian territory in 1796. During the French bombardment of Vienna in 1809, he played it to comfort himself. It was the last music he heard before he died.

---

* The term opus refers to a musical composition numbered to show its place in the composer's published work.

**STRING QUARTET
OPUS 33, NO. 3
(THE BIRD)**
RECORD 2/SIDE 2

Haydn developed the string quartet from the eighteenth-century *divertimento,* giving more substance to the light, popular form and scoring it for two violins, a viola, and a cello. His eighty-three quartets, written over the course of his creative lifetime, evolved slowly into a sophisticated form. Together they constitute one of the most important bodies of chamber music literature.

The quartets of Haydn's Opus 33 are collectively known as *Gli Scherzi* (*The Scherzos*) because Haydn uses the more rapid scherzo rather than the minuet and trio. Number 3 of this set became known as *The Bird,* owing to the birdlike trills and ornaments in the first, second, and fourth movements.

"Bird" motive

Example 9.14

FIRST MOVEMENT

Exposition The clarity and balance that we encountered in the music of Mozart are again evident here in the clearly separated, repeated phrases, the sudden contrast and extension of one phrase, and the use of dynamics to reinforce structure.

The "bird" ornaments heard in the first theme provide a unifying element among the contrasting sections of the movement.

The first theme begins with soft, short, repeated notes in the second violin and viola. Against this background, the first violin enters with the main melodic material. Characteristically, the bridge between Themes 1 and 2 uses elements from Theme 1. The second theme makes abundant use of the ornamental ("bird") element of the first theme. The exposition closes with material derived from the very end of the bridge. The entire exposition is then repeated.

Development Although relatively short, the development section draws from all three stages of the exposition. It begins with a statement of the A phrase of Theme 1. Then elements of Theme 2 and the bridge are combined, after which Theme 2 is stated first in the high strings, then in the low strings. Elements from Theme 1 and the closing material are briefly combined and lead into successive statements of the ornamental notes at rising pitch levels. The rising feeling is helped along by a crescendo leading to two long chords that create a sense of suspense. The suspense is quieted by an apparent return to Theme 1, but the return turns out to be false. Instead, the passage leads to a development of the bridge, which then leads to genuine recapitulation.

Recapitulation The recapitulation is rather standard except that the second part of Theme 1 is omitted. After the entire development and recapitulation are repeated, there is a coda consisting of (1) an exploitation of the "bird" ornament, (2) a fragment of the closing material, (3) a crescendo and cadence, and (4) a complete statement of the A phrase of Theme 1. The movement ends in the original key of C major.

SECOND MOVEMENT

The six quartets of Opus 33 depart from sonata structure in two respects. First, the minuet and trio movement is replaced by the scherzo and trio. Second, the positions of the second and third movements are reversed: the scherzo and trio is second and the slow, lyrical movement is third.

This scherzo movement is a wonderful example of Haydn's ability to use instrumental range, color, articulation and musical texture, dynamics, and form for expressive purposes. The movement has a three-part scherzo-trio-scherzo structure, with the sections set off from each other by obvious cadences and pauses. The contrast between them is marked. The scherzo employs all four instruments in a low register and homophonic texture. It is dark, smooth, sustained, and thick. The trio is reduced to two violins playing in the higher part of their ranges, within a polyphonic texture using staccato articulation. It is light, bright, thin, and brittle, employing ornamental trills reminiscent of the first movement.

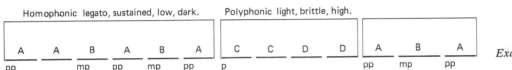

Example 9.15

THIRD MOVEMENT

The slow third movement is a theme and variations. The first violin, which spins out the long theme, is clearly prominent. The theme is lyrical, almost aria-like in its melodic arches and contours. In the two variations the shape of the melody is altered. Those sections that are preserved are extensively varied, mostly through the addition of decorative notes, creating a much more florid melodic line. Throughout the entire movement the first violin is a solo instrument and the other three strings provide accompaniment.

FOURTH MOVEMENT

The last movement of the quartet is an intriguing example of Haydn's sense of humor in music. The melodies are jocular, the tempo is very fast, and the texture is light. A series of tricks and surprises fascinate the listener up to the concluding measures.

Technically the movement combines the rondo principle of alternating themes with the development and recapitulation of sonata-allegro procedures. It starts with a gay, bouncy two-part theme in C major; the second part combines materials of the first part with the "bird" figure of the first movement. After both parts are repeated, Theme A ends with a pause. Theme B begins without a bridge passage. This theme, also in two parts, is in A minor. The first part is repeated, and the second part develops material from the first part. Toward the end of the section the rhythmic material that began Theme A is passed back and forth among the instruments. The intent of this is to suggest the return of Theme A, but the listener is kept in suspense as to *when* it will return. The suspense increases when the rhythmic figure is shortened to a two-note version, the dynamic level changes suddenly from forte to piano, and a dominant chord is outlined which cries for resolution to the tonic. At this point, when it appears that the music will plunge into the A theme, there is instead a sudden, unexpected pause, after which the A theme enters at last (Example 9.16).

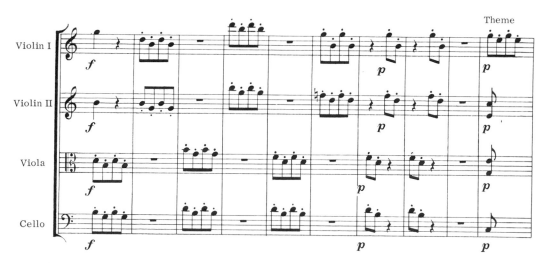

Example 9.16

This "trickery," involving the reappearance of Theme A, is again evident later in the movement. After the restatement of Themes A and B, another developmental section occurs that leads back to A. This presentation of the theme ends in a cadence and a pause. But after this convincing ending, Haydn launches into a coda beginning with the two-note "bird" motive and moving to the more active rhythmic material from Theme A. A feeling of conclusion is created by the increase of activity as all four instruments play the rhythmic material. The crescendo pushes forward, but instead of ending, Haydn stops not on the expected C major chord but on a chord in a different key. The chord is full of suspense and implies anything but a conclusion. After a pause, which intensifies the suspense, there is a drive to a forceful cadence in the tonic C major, and, apparently, the long-delayed ending. But this is followed by yet another section, played very softly, to give us an extra unexpected ending, a kind of final chuckle from the composer.

THE CLASSICAL CONCERTO

During the Baroque era, the term "concerto" referred to both the concerto grosso and the concerto for solo instrument. Bach's Brandenburg Concerto No. 5 and Vivaldi's *The Four Seasons* are examples of the two types.

In the Classical era, composers continued to develop the solo concerto while the concerto grosso fell into virtual disuse. The violin and piano were the favored solo instruments, but concertos were also written for other instruments such as the cello, trumpet, French horn, and clarinet.

Although it conforms to the sonata principle, the Classical concerto differs from the symphony and the string quartet in several respects. Unlike the others, which have four movements, the concerto consists of *three* movements, almost always in a fast-slow-fast sequence. The minuet and trio is omitted.

Other differences result from the fact that the concerto features a solo instrument that is heard in relationship to the orchestra. For instance, sonata-allegro movements are structured to exploit the interplay between the solo instrument and the orchestra. Instead of the literal repetition of an exposition, there is a **double exposition.** In the first exposition the thematic material is set forth by the orchestra alone. In the second exposition it is presented by the solo instrument and the orchestra. Thus the exposition takes the following form:

First Exposition	Second Exposition
A bridge B	A bridge B
orchestra alone	solo instrument and orchestra

The development section involves both the solo instrument and the orchestra, and the movement ends with a recapitulation based upon the *second* exposition.

The first and last movements of the Classical concerto (and occasionally the middle movement) include an additional section called the **cadenza.** Played by the solo instrument without accompaniment, the cadenza offers the perfect vehicle for the virtuoso soloist. It has the quality of an improvised performance; even if in fact it is written out or at least well planned in advance, it is supposed to sound as if it were being made up by the performer "on the spot." The exact placement of the cadenza in the sonata-allegro movement varies, but it always occurs toward the end of the movement, usually after the recapitulation, and is followed by closing material:

Recapitulation
A   bridge   B   cadenza   closing material

The two main musical ingredients of the cadenza are fragments of the thematic material from the movement proper and the free use of the instrument. Rapid scale passages, brilliant arpeggios, trills, and other technical feats contribute to the dazzling display. The tempo is erratic, the beat is often obscured, and modulation occurs. Both the fermata ($\frown$) and silence help to heighten the drama and rivet attention on the solo performer. Typically, the cadenza increases in intensity, ending with a trill followed by a chord which coincides with the return of the orchestra. Thus, the balance between solo instrument and orchestra is restored.

It was Mozart who, in his more than fifty concertos, established the general form and style of the Classical concerto. His concertos for piano are among the most enduring works of the Classical period; many of them are frequently performed today.

Mozart's piano concertos span virtually his whole productive life. The Concerto in B-Flat Major, written in his last year, is his final contribution to the form.

The piece is in three movements and is scored for flute, oboes, bassoons, French horns, strings, and solo piano.

PIANO CONCERTO NO. 27 IN B-FLAT MAJOR (K. 595)

FIRST MOVEMENT

The first movement is in sonata-allegro form with a double exposition as outlined above. Its tempo is fast (allegro) and it is set in the tonic key of B-flat major. The first theme is stated by the violins and answered by the winds. When the solo piano enters, beginning the second exposition, it plays a slightly decorated version of the first theme (Example 9.17).

Example 9.17

With the entrance of the piano the orchestra drops out altogether until the strings take over the answering function first performed by the winds.

The alternation between piano and orchestra, in which one is silent while the other is active, is a device favored by Mozart and typifies this particular movement. In the example above we saw how the orchestra and piano alternate in rather large blocks of music; in other parts of the movement they often "share" a phrase:

Example 9.18

Example 9.19

In Example 9.18 the piano begins a phrase which is completed by the flute; in Example 9.19 the reverse is true: the orchestra initiates the phrase, which is finished by the solo piano.

In this movement the solo instrument and the orchestra rarely work together for any appreciable length of time. When they do, the solo instrument is almost always dominant. The most obvious place where the solo piano "shines" is the cadenza, which occurs after the recapitulation and leads into the closing material. The cadenza that is usually played is one written by Mozart himself. It exhibits all the qualities outlined earlier and provides a convincing and exciting conclusion to the first movement.

CHARACTERISTICS OF CLASSICAL MUSIC

Texture	Largely homophonic, but flexible, with shifts to polyphony
Tonality	Major/minor system with frequent modulations to related keys; heavy dependence on tonic-dominant relationship
Rhythm	Variety of rhythmic patterns within a work
Melody	Composed of short, balanced phrases; melodic phrases often contrasted with each other Melodies often lyrical and expressive; less ornamentation of notes
Mood	Expression of variety of moods within a work and sudden changes of mood
Dynamics	Gradual dynamic changes
Large Works	Sonata, symphony, concerto, string quartet, Mass, oratorio, opera
Instruments	Piano and violin favored for solo concerto; makeup of orchestra becomes standardized; development of orchestra favors growth of symphonic works
Formal Structures	Sonata principle (multimovement structure for long pieces); sonata-allegro form (first-movement form); rondo; minuet and trio; scherzo and trio; theme and variations; cadenza and double exposition used in concertos
Symphonic Style	Follows four-movement plan, with first movement in sonata-allegro form Each movement self-contained Key is main unifying device Clarity and balance are major stylistic features

SECOND MOVEMENT

The second movement is a glorious example of Mozart's lyrical use of the piano as a "singing" instrument. The movement is slow in tempo (larghetto) and in the contrasting key of E-flat major. Its structure is a large ABA form with each section containing a rich variety of melodic materials.

The B section features the solo instrument, supported throughout by unobtrusive orchestral accompaniment. The A section that frames the movement is more elaborate, both in the variety of its materials and in the relationship between the orchestra and the piano. As in the first movement, the solo instrument and orchestra tend to alternate rather than work together.

The most important thematic material is the simple melody played by the solo piano at the beginning of the movement (Example 9.20). The flowing beauty of this short melody sets the mood for the entire movement.

Example 9.20

THIRD MOVEMENT

The third movement returns to the key of B-flat major and is fast (allegro), thus conforming to the three-movement fast-slow-fast pattern of the Classical concerto. Its brisk tempo is emphasized by jocular 6/8 meter, giving the piece a particularly lively quality. It is based upon the principal theme:

Allegro

Example 9.21   The movement is essentially a rondo but includes developmental sections which impart to sections of the piece the flavor of the sonata-allegro. Of particular interest is the fact that the movement includes two cadenzas, both of which function to reintroduce the principal theme after contrasting material or development. The movement conveys a feeling of gaiety and good cheer.

Taken as a whole, Mozart's last piano concerto is one of his most serene and sublime works, well deserving of its honored place in the piano repertoire.

SUMMARY

Instrumental music arrived at a new level of maturity during the Classical period. The ranges and technical capabilities of many instruments were improved greatly and composers began to score their works for standard groupings. Larger groups evolved into the orchestra, which included an increased number and variety of instruments. Because of the social customs of the day, chamber music also flourished and encouraged sophisticated compositions in which each player performed an individual part.

Sonata-allegro form and the multimovement structure became the main basis for music composed in the early classical period. The two great masters of the Classical era—Haydn and Mozart—developed and refined sontata-allegro form in their symphonies, string quartets, and concertos.

NEW TERMS

sonata	development	symphony
sonata-allegro form (sonata form)	recapitulation	string quartet
	coda	*Singspiel*
exposition	minuet and trio	concerto
bridge	scherzo	double exposition
codetta (closing theme)	rondo	cadenza

CHAPTER 10 | CLASSICAL VOCAL MUSIC

THE CLASSICAL ERA WAS ESSENTIALLY A PERIOD OF INSTRUMENTAL music. The new instrumental style and forms became the area of greatest concentration for the major composers of the time. Vocal music occupied a position of lesser importance. The lieder (songs) written by Haydn, Mozart, and Beethoven are considered a relatively secondary part of their compositional efforts. The operas composed by Haydn to entertain the guests at Esterhazy have vanished into history, and Beethoven wrote only one opera, *Fidelio.* However, the age was not without significant and lasting achievements in the area of vocal music. Specifically, some of the large choral works of Mozart, Haydn, and Beethoven and many of Mozart's operas made lasting contributions to the body of vocal literature.

CHORAL MUSIC OF HAYDN

Of the three giants of the Classical era, Haydn contributed the largest number of compositions to the choral music repertoire. Two of his oratorios, *The Creation* and *The Seasons,* are still widely performed; together with his Masses, they constitute his most important contribution to vocal music.

Haydn's *Missa in Angustiis* (*Mass in Time of Peril*) is one of the choral masterpieces of the Classical period. Better known as the *Nelson Mass,* it was written in 1789 during the naval Battle of the Nile. When Lord Nelson visited Eisenstadt Castle in 1800, this Mass was among the works performed in his honor.

   The orchestration of Haydn's Masses varied from work to work according to the instruments and players available to him at the time. The *Nelson Mass* is scored for a comparatively small orchestra consisting of three trumpets, timpani, organ, and strings, together with four solo voices (SATB) and four-part chorus (SATB). The organ is used alternately as a continuo instrument, merely filling in

MISSA IN ANGUSTIIS (NELSON MASS)

chords—a carryover from Baroque practice—and as an ensemble or solo instrument.

The text is divided into six main sections and five subdivisions, constituting eleven movements in all:

Kyrie	*Credo*	*Benedictus*
Gloria	*Et incarnatus*	*Agnus Dei*
Qui tollis	*Et resurrexit*	*Dona nobis*
Quoniam tu solus	*Sanctus*	

KYRIE

The prevalence of sonata-allegro procedure in instrumental music has been well established in the previous chapter, but its organizing force was by no means confined to instrumental music. The first movement of the *Nelson Mass* is an example of how the sonata-allegro principle was applied to choral composition.

The first theme, in D minor, is characterized by short, emphatic pronouncements by the chorus on the text *"Kyrie eleison"* ("Lord have mercy"). The trumpets and timpani sound a prominent figure (♪♪♪♪♪♪|♩), which alternates with sharp chords in the strings. The organ, meanwhile, plays sustained continuo chords. The second theme is dominated by the soprano solo voice, singing elaborate virtuoso passages, quite instrumental in character.

Chri – ste e – lei – son, e - lei – son

Example 10.1

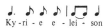
Ky -ri - e e - lei - son

The light texture, the *piano* dynamic level, the key change (to the relative F major), and the concentration on the individual voice are in marked contrast to the driving force of the first theme.

The prominent elements of the development are sung by the chorus. The solo part from the second theme is now played by the violins. Imitative entrances in the chorus lead to a climax where all four parts come together. The drive that results from these insistent overlapping entrances of the voices is enhanced by constant modulation.

The key returns to D minor for the recapitulation. Here the second theme resembles the original theme in texture, dynamics, and the relationship of the solo soprano voice to the orchestra, but new melodic material is involved.

The coda ends with the entire orchestra hammering out the rhythmic figure (♪♪♪♪♪♪|♩) on which the movement began.

GLORIA, QUI TOLLIS, AND QUONIAM TU SOLUS

RECORD 3/SIDE 1 Although the second, third, and fourth movements each appear to be self-contained, they are actually parts of one three-movement complex.

The driving tension and restlessness that characterized the *Kyrie* are immediately dispelled at the striking beginning of the *Gloria*. The important thematic material of the A section, on the text *"Gloria in excelsis deo"* ("Glory to God in the highest"), is introduced in dialogue fashion between the soprano soloist and the chorus.

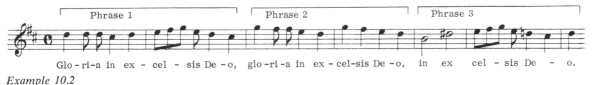

Glo - ri-a in ex - cel - sis De - o, glo -ri -a in ex - cel-sis De - o,   in   ex   cel - sis De - o.

Example 10.2

The dynamic level drops to *piano* for the contrasting B section, *"et in terra pax hominibus"* ("and on earth peace to men"). The emphasis is on the solo tenor and bass parts, whose imitative entrances grow into a moving, expressive duet.

The chorus enters in octaves in the C section, loudly proclaiming in short, clipped statements *"laudamus te"* ("we praise Thee"), *"adoramus te"* ("we adore Thee"), and the section builds to an ending on an extended setting of *"glorifi-camus te"* ("we glorify Thee").

A kind of development begins with successive statements of the A melody, utilizing new words and modulating into different keys. It opens with the solo alto, who is answered by the soprano, and then, more fully, by the chorus. After expanded statements of B by the solo voices, the chorus brings the movement to a rather abrupt close, without the expected return of the A theme.

The slow, quiet *Qui tollis* movement is, structurally, a straightforward example of alternating themes. The solo bass has the dominant part, often paired with the first violins. Frequently the bass voice and first violins answer each other back and forth. The organ is used as a solo instrument in conjunction with the choral entrances, and while the choral entrances are expressive in themselves, they also constitute a considerable "surprise" element in the movement. It is impossible to anticipate either when they will occur or whether they will occur softly in unison or loudly in full harmony on statements of *"miserere nobis"* ("have mercy on us") and *"deprecationem nostram"* ("our prayer").

The *Qui tollis* has no real conclusion, but ends instead on a chord of suspense, the dominant. Its resolution comes in the opening measures of the *Quoniam tu solus* movement, which, in addition, returns to the melody from the *Gloria.* Thus the lack of conclusion in the preceding movement, coupled with the reappearance of the original theme of the *Gloria,* acts as a powerful unifying element in the three-movement complex.

Solo Soprano

Quo - ni-am tu so - lus,   so - lus sanc-tus.

Example 10.3

After the solo and choral statements of the A theme, a quiet transition section on the words *"cum sancto spiritu"* ("with the holy spirit"), leads to a long, vigorous fugue. The coda, which uses material from the *Gloria* movement, creates further unity and builds to one of Haydn's brilliant and exhilarating endings on

A- men   A - men!

CREDO

The *Credo* is divided into three parts, which constitute the fifth, sixth, and seventh movements. The fifth movement, which begins with *Credo in unum Deum* ("I believe in one God"), is a two-part canon. The sopranos and tenors sing the first part against the altos and basses on the second. The tempo is fast, and there is a driving rhythm throughout, with much activity in the orchestra.

In contrast to the fifth movement, the sixth, *Et incarnatus* "and was incarnate"), is slow and quiet. An atmosphere of lyricism and melodic grace pervades. The first theme is stated in turn by the orchestra, the solo soprano, and the chorus. A concluding coda adds weight to the movement's mood of loss.

The seventh movement, *Et resurrexit tertia dia* ("and on the third day He arose"), bursts forth *forte,* in a fast tempo, and with great musical activity to convey the atmosphere of triumph and resurrection. This movement is particularly interesting for the abundance of technical devices employed to organize it: imitative entrances are used to build momentum; homophonic texture and choral declamation set off the meaning of the text, and striking differences in dynamics and pitch contrast the *vivos* ("living") with the *mortuos* ("dead"). The movement ends with a brilliant "Amen."

SANCTUS AND BENEDICTUS

The eighth and ninth movements consist of five subsections:

8			9	
1	2	3	4	5
Sanctus (slow, short, and piano)	*Pleni sunt* (fast and loud)	*Osanna* (fast and loud)	*Benedictus* (slow and long with fluctuating dynamics)	*Osanna* (repeat of section 3)

The *Sanctus* is a slow introductory section. The *Pleni sunt* is an allegro choral section with an active orchestral background. This section merges without a break into the *Osanna.*

The *Benedictus,* which follows, is very much like the sonata-allegro movement of a concerto. It consists of a double exposition (the first in the orchestra, the second in the solo soprano and chorus), a short development section, a genuine recapitulation, and a dramatic coda. The *Benedictus* stops on a dominant chord, followed by a pause. The resulting suspense is dispelled when the *Osanna* returns, bringing the entire complex to a stirring ending.

AGNUS DEI AND DONA NOBIS

The quietest section of the entire Mass, the *Agnus Dei,* is the only movement that does not include the chorus, trumpets, or timpani. Adagio in tempo and lyrical in expression, it is the perfect foil for the loud and buoyant finale.

The *Dona nobis* is a fast, loud, choral fugue set against intense orchestral activity. The imitative entrances of the soprano, alto, tenor, and bass are followed by a jocular, homophonic section in the chorus, while the violins play a kind of chirp in the background. This lightheartedness turns into gaiety near the end, when there is a sudden and unexpected halt, followed by a pause, then a resumption of the very quiet statements of *"Dona nobis pacem"* ("grant us Thy peace") by the chorus with interjections of the chirping figure by violins.

Example 10.4

Finally, there is an energetic push to a brilliant ending.

THE HISTORY OF OPERA

Music and drama have been closely associated ever since the beginning of civilization. Ancient Greek drama included music, as did the liturgical plays of the Middle Ages. In the sixteenth century, actors began to perform musical interludes between the acts of plays. These *intermezzi* led to the development of a new form which combined music and dramatics.

The first operas were composed around 1600 in Florence, Italy, and consisted mostly of simple melodies and harmonies. The book, or *libretto,* usually centered on a mythological or historical subject. Occasionally, comic characters were included. The great Baroque composer Claudio Monteverdi used more expressive melodies, richer harmonies, and fuller orchestras in his operas. In *Orfeo* (1607) he introduced a variety of innovative elements, including solos, choruses, and orchestrally accompanied dances.

In 1637, when the first public opera house opened in Venice, the center of operatic activity moved there. Venetian-style operas were popular throughout Europe (except in France, which had its own type of opera, based on earlier court ballets and dramatic tragedies).

During the late Baroque, songlike arias and duets provided contrast to the recitatives. The recitatives served to move the action along; during the arias the action stopped while the singer expressed a character's feeling or reactions to a situation.

Like comedy and tragedy, opera evolved in two forms. While **opera seria** were based on serious plots, lighter versions, called **opera buffa,** were developed around comic plots. During the eighteenth century, opera buffa rose in importance, and some of its elements began to penetrate the mainstream of operatic convention. The most important of these was the ensemble finale, in which all the characters were on stage and singing at the end. Opera buffa was also the first genre to exploit the bass voice, particularly in comic roles. Gradually, the plots and characters of the two operatic styles began to merge, with even the lightest operas containing some serious or even tragic episodes.

As opera developed, its established practices became more rigid. The dramatic elements, for example, became secondary in importance to the virtuosity of the singers, who demanded extra arias which they could ornament in elaborate and dazzling displays of vocal technique. Recitatives were strictly alternated with arias in da capo (ABA) outline. These vocal pyrotechnics finally proved excessive, and Christoph W. Gluck (1714–1787), a German pre-Classical composer who had studied in Italy, led a reform movement to restore simplicity and natural expression to opera. In his operas, including *Alceste* (1767), *Iphigenie en Aulide* (1774), and *Iphigenie en Tauride* (1779), the purely musical elements were more closely integrated with other aspects of the work to serve the overall dramatic unity.

Although they show some influences of the work of Gluck, Mozart's operas reveal a basic difference. For him, the drama did not dominate, but rather served the supreme element, the music. Mozart's broad training and outlook made him equally comfortable with Italian opera seria and opera buffa and with their German counterpart, the *Singspiel*.

LE NOZZE DI FIGARO (THE MARRIAGE OF FIGARO)

Mozart's first opera buffa, with its lively, amusing libretto and delightful solo and ensemble music, is the epitome of the genre. Mozart read over one hundred librettos before he found his collaborator, Lorenzo da Ponte, who was willing to translate Beaumarchais's play from the French into Italian and adapt the story to the specifications of the composer. The choice of the language was important since, even in German-speaking countries, audiences preferred to see operas performed in Italian. *The Marriage of Figaro* was first produced at the Burgtheater in Vienna in 1786.

Beaumarchais's original play was a political satire, but da Ponte removed the political references, leaving a very human and natural comedy. The plot is complex, involving several pairs of lovers, intrigues between servants and their masters, a case of mistaken identity, and a few unlikely coincidences. The plot revolves around the efforts of a servant (Figaro) to outwit his master (Count Almaviva). This theme was a favorite convention of the period, and Mozart applies it with humor and skill. (Since there are several complications and subplots, it is important to have a libretto in hand while listening to the music.)

THE PLOT

Figaro, a valet to Count Almaviva, is preparing to marry Susanna, the countess's chambermaid. Figaro has borrowed a large sum from Marcellina, the old castle housekeeper, promising to repay the money by a certain date or marry her if he defaults. The count has designs on Susanna and tries to seduce her, but she tells Figaro and the countess, and together they scheme to frustrate the count's plans.

Since Susanna will not yield to him, the count decides to take Marcellina's side in the financial dispute and force Figaro to marry her. This plot is foiled by the discovery that Marcellina and her advocate, Dr. Bartolo, are actually Figaro's long-lost parents, from whom he was kidnapped as an infant.

Meanwhile, Susanna and the countess have been conniving; their trick involves a case of mistaken identity. Susanna promises to meet the count in the garden that night, but it is the countess, disguised as Susanna, who actually keeps

Fig. 10.1 Count Almaviva (William Justus) rages furiously at his wife the countess (Johanna Meier) in a recent production of *The Marriage of Figaro.*

the appointment. Figaro learns of the meeting and thinks that Susanna is deceiving him. The count is caught red-handed by his wife, confesses his attempted infidelity, and begs forgiveness, which she laughingly grants. It all ends happily when Figaro marries Susanna.

THE MUSIC

The Marriage of Figaro stands out from the usual opera buffa because both the music and the libretto create characters who are not simply stereotypes but rather exhibit the emotions of multidimensional people. This is accomplished both in the solo arias and in the ensemble numbers as well. In an operatic ensemble (which involves three or more singers) it is possible to have each character singing different words and displaying different emotions while singing with the others; in other words, everyone can think and react simultaneously, without waiting to take turns, as is necessary in spoken drama. This is often done in the finale, which brings all the events to a resolution.

In Classical opera the orchestra was subordinate to the voices; nevertheless, it had its own elaborate and lively idiom. Mozart made full use of the opportunity to develop motives in the traditional symphonic manner. The opera orchestra also helps with characterization, particularly in accompanied recitatives, where the moods are dramatic and change quickly. The orchestra can be used to hint at action that is supposedly taking place offstage and can contradict a character's words and expose his or her true feelings.

RECORD 3/SIDE 1   By examining one scene of *The Marriage of Figaro,* we will be able to see Mozart's use of musical devices to further the dramatic action and the characterization. At the beginning of Act III, Susanna and the Countess arrange for Susanna to meet the count that night. Their dialogue, and the subsequent conversation between the count and Susanna, are in secco recitative. In the duet that follows, the count rejoices at Susanna's agreement to meet him, while she (in an aside to the audience) asks forgiveness for her lie. Each one has distinctive music, so that it is quite clear that they are singing about two different things.

The next recitative ends with Susanna mentioning to Figaro, as they leave, that he has won his case. The count overhears her remark and sings a recitative expressing his fury and plotting to force Figaro to marry Marcellina. This recitative is accompanied by the full orchestra and includes many sudden changes of key, tempo, and dynamics. It leads to an aria by the count in which he explains how jealous he is of his happy servant Figaro, how he will get revenge, and how happy the thought of revenge makes him. The aria is in two large sections; the second section is faster than the first and is repeated with an extended and ornamented cadence. The style of the accompaniment changes frequently, to reflect the count's different thoughts.

As the count finishes, he meets the judge, Don Curzio, who has just upheld Marcellina's right to repayment or marriage. Figaro mentions that he cannot get married without his parents' consent, and he has not been able to locate them, since he was kidnapped as a child. He describes the circumstances, and Marcellina and Dr. Bartolo realize that he is their child. This dramatic action is covered quickly in recitative, and then a large ensemble begins: the reunited family rejoices together ("beloved son," "beloved parents").

Susanna enters, sees Figaro embracing Marcellina, and misunderstands the situation. During the next section, a sextet, Susanna and the count both rage furiously, with a jagged, dotted musical line,

Fre –mo,Sma–nio dal fu – ro – re

Example 10.5

("I fret, I rave with fury"), while Figaro and his parents calmly note that Susanna's jealousy is a sure sign of her love. The judge joins the count, making the balance in the sextet even—three against three. Finally Susanna listens to their explanation that Marcellina is Figaro's mother. Scarcely believing it, she questions each one of them in turn: *"Sua madre?"* Each one answers *"Sua madre!"* and the pitch level rises with each statement. The same device is used when Dr. Bartolo is introduced as Figaro's father.

The sextet ends with all characters singing, but the balance has changed from three and three to four and two, since Susanna has changed sides and is no longer angry. The two groups have almost identical texts:

SUSANNA, MARCELLINA, BARTOLO, FIGARO:

Al dolce contento	*To the sweet content*
di questo momento	*of this moment*
quest' anima appena	*my mind can*
resister or sà.	*hardly resist.*

COUNT, DON CURZIO

Al fiero tormento	*To the fierce torment*
di questo momento	*of this moment*
quest' anima appena	*my mind can*
resister or sà.	*hardly resist.*

The musical setting makes their different feelings perfectly clear. The happy four sing smoothly and lyrically, with Susanna (the highest soprano) expressing her joy with an ornamented musical line. The count and the judge sing another jagged, dotted line to express their anger. At the end, where both groups have identical words, the different meanings are expressed by the speed of the notes: the angry men sing much faster than the others.

Example 10.6

SUMMARY

Although the main area of concentration for most Classical composers was instrumental music the age did produce lasting achievements in vocal music as well.

Haydn's *Nelson Mass* well represents the Classical treatment of the Mass. In the six main sections, comprising eleven movements, the listener is carried from themes of driving force to adagio passages of light texture, from exhilarating and dynamic movements to slow and expressive sections. Considered a masterpiece, this work is a favorite in contemporary choral repertoires.

The Classical era brought significant changes to the opera form. Baroque opera had pushed the role of the virtuoso singer to its limits; the pre-Classical composer Christoph Gluck sought to restore simplicity and natural expression to the genre, integrating the purely musical elements closely with other aspects in order to better serve the dramatic unity.

Although Mozart was influenced by Gluck, the supreme element in his operas was the music. His first comic opera, *The Marriage of Figaro,* stands out among opera buffa for its realistic characters, amusing libretto, delightful solo and ensemble music, and skillful use of orchestral devices to enhance the characterization.

NEW TERMS

opera seria
opera buffa

INTERLUDE | THE CLASSICAL ERA: REASON AND REVOLUTION

The Classical Era in the arts lasted from about 1750 to the end of the first quarter of the nineteenth century. These turbulent generations witnessed the breakdown of the Baroque style and the return to classically inspired forms in building, statuary, and painting. The upheaval of the late eighteenth century was highlighted by the American and French Revolutions; at the same time the application of the steam engine to industrial production and transportation was transforming the nature of European life. In this seventy-five-year period every quarter of the continent breathed change.

European intellectuals of the eighteenth century were the first to consider themselves fully emancipated from the Middle Ages. They spoke of themselves as living in Enlightenment and an Age of Reason. They were confident believers in human control over a reasonable world, in the marvelous machine of a universe they thought they understood, where God was not so much the awesome Father and Judge as the cosmic Watchmaker. But the discord and irrationality in France in the 1790s made reason a questionable proposition. In the early nineteenth century many intellectuals dismissed those who had absolute faith in reason as naive at best and hypocritical at worst.

BEFORE THE FRENCH REVOLUTION (1750–1789)

In the eighteenth century towns grew, interregional trade quickened, fortunes were made, and the bourgeoisie (the middle class) enjoyed more economic power than ever before. Towns like London and Amsterdam bustled with high finance, warehouses, trading marts, and ship movements. Taste, however, was determined in France, the country that had become the leading cultural center of the continent. Fashion, in dress, design, and ideas, radiated from Paris and Versailles. It was the aristocracy rather than the busy entrepreneurs of the middle class that had the money and time for the cultivation and refinement of life.

It is wrong, however, to imagine the members of the upper class as wicked pleasure-seekers. In townhouse and palace, they strove for worldly perfection in art and thought as well as in manners. In fact, the eighteenth century was a period of vigorous intellectual activity. Scientific advance continued with even greater velocity; more important, the century was energized by the active philosophical debate over the nature of reform and progress.

Some thinkers believed that the human race could attain perfection through the application of common sense to social problems, a viewpoint eloquently championed by the German mathematician Leibnitz and brutally satirized by Voltaire in Candide. Diderot and other brilliant French philosophes undertook the Encyclopedia, a massive enterprise of twenty-four volumes that tried to *codify accumulated knowledge from the past and current ideas in the present. Rousseau, a harbinger of nineteenth-century Romanticism, challenged the ultra-refined world around him. He believed that human beings enjoyed a god-like character that had been corrupted and deadened by civilization. He wanted to abandon the cerebral world of logic and analysis and return to the more natural, instinctual, primitive world of the aborigine. All these different points of view appear contradictory on the surface; they all assumed, however, that the human condition could be improved or perfected. The eighteenth century glorified the power of the individual to control and order the world, a viewpoint that nurtured both economic growth and the notion that governments should reflect the will and interests of the people.*

For much of this period the visual arts, dominated by the late Baroque style called Rococo, did not mirror the rising tide of reason and simplicity. The Rococo style emphasized elegance rather than clarity, delicacy rather than strength, softness rather than severity, and playfulness rather than solemnity. French interiors were decorated with beautiful gold-and-white curved woods, crystal chandeliers, and gilt ceilings (Plate 20). The French painters Boucher and Fragonard, who idealized the joy and sweetness of aristocratic life, were deluged with commissions (Plate 19).

Rococo art, though, became less popular in the last decades of the eighteenth century. Cream colors and rich velvet grew less fashionable. The "new taste" of the 1770s and later, called Neoclassicism, borrowed from the seventeenth-century French artist Poussin (Plate 10) as well as from Greek temples and

Plate 17. Thomas Jefferson's Monticello (1770–1784; 1796–1806) was modeled after Palladio's Villa Rotunda (see Plate 7) in brick and painted wood. It is an excellent example of the impact of European Neoclassicism on architecture in the American colonies and new United States. (Courtesy Virginia State Library.)

Plate 18. Sir Joshua Reynolds, the most powerful and respected English painter of the eighteenth century, portrayed a distinguished actress of the time in *Mrs. Siddons as the Tragic Muse* (1784). His *Discourses* on an academic approach to art had immense impact on English and American students. (Courtesy Henry E. Huntington Library and Art Gallery.)

Plate 19. *Venus Consoling Love,* by François Boucher (1751). Boucher was the most popular painter at the court of Versailles in the middle of the eighteenth century. His style is consummately Rococo—light, delicate, playful, and colorful. Its innocence and sensuality were dismissed by later generations as frivolous and trivial. (Courtesy The National Gallery of Art, Washington; gift of Chester Dale.)

Plate 20. This reconstruction of an eighteenth-century French interior is a magnificent example of the elegant decoration of the Rococo. Tapestries, mirrors, chandeliers, curved woods, and gilt all contributed to the luxury of the Parisian townhouses. (Courtesy The Philadelphia Museum of Art; bequest of Mrs. Alexander Hamilton Rice.)

Plate 21. Jacques Louis David's *The Death of Socrates* (1787) was exhibited in Paris just two years before the French Revolution broke out. It exemplifies the Neoclassical style in its classical subject matter, sculptured figures, and emphasis on form instead of color. It was also a political statement, memorializing the heroism of a great man who died for ideas that an oppressive state could not accept. (Courtesy The Metropolitan Museum of Art; Wolfe Fund, 1931.)

Roman statuary. In short, the last quarter of the eighteenth century rejected Baroque design and began to work from "more noble" classical models.

Music, with all its evocative powers, held a high position in the ancien régime ("the old order," a phrase later used to summarize the elegance and grandeur of France before 1789). The two greatest composers of the late eighteenth century were both Austrian—Wolfgang Amadeus Mozart (1756–1791) and Franz Joseph Haydn (1732–1809). Both depended on commissions in their early careers, Mozart as a concertmaster to the Archbishop of Salzburg and Haydn as a music director for a Hungarian prince.

Both Mozart and Haydn ended their careers in Vienna. This eastern city, the seat of the Hapsburgs and the capital city of the Holy Roman Empire, was a magnet for first rate musicians, since the Hapsburg court and the Viennese townspeople placed a very high premium on musical achievement and excellence. The prestige of the composer, musician, and performer—from whatever back-ground—was high. The demand for new composition, frequent concerts, and the competition between the private orchestras of the nobility made it the first city of European music by the end of the eighteenth century.

THE FRENCH REVOLUTION AND ITS AFTERMATH (1789–1825)

In the first half of the eighteenth century royal governments were able to exercise tremendous power over their subjects. In 1776, however, leaders in England's North American colonies, convinced that London no longer represented their economic interests and infuriated that it was trying to extinguish their local political rights, declared their independence from George III and his Parliament. Thirteen years later, the French bourgeoisie acted to wrest law-making power from Louis XVI. This was the beginning of a political struggle that in the 1790s reduced France to a state of anarchy and made for war throughout Europe.

The progress of the French Revolution is confusing and (like most revolutionary periods) often irrational. In the first stage the bourgeoisie established a limited monarchy; later, after Louis XVI tried to escape to the company of royalists and fight against the rebels, the monarchy was abolished and the king was executed for "treason." In the 1790s revolutionaries argued among themselves while they tried to stamp out aristocratic and peasant opposition to their programs: the result was a busy guillotine and political chaos.

At the same time, a revolutionary French army battled the armies of a more conservative European continent. From these contests there emerged a new French hero and leader—Napoleon Bonaparte. Napoleon's mind was tenacious and perfectly ordered; his spirit was dazzling. By 1799, he had enough power to take over the French government. In the next fifteen years he came to control almost all of Europe.

In the last quarter of the eighteenth century the visual arts underwent as radical a change as European politics. The Rococo faded entirely, to be replaced by that Neoclassicism which idealized ancient Athens and Rome and attempted to recreate a heroic world based on Antiquity. In the 1790s Napoleon's counterpart in the arts was Jacques-Louis David (1748–1825), a painter who became a *kind of art dictator during the Revolution and whose style was undisputed before the 1820s. David avoided the "capricious ornament" of earlier art. Instead, he built solemn scenes of noble sacrifice and great historical moments in a clear, balanced, linear style (Plate 21). To David and his fellow revolutionaries, the excellence of Antiquity was a guide to the perfection of the human race: in politics and art the French Revolution was a culmination of the spirit of reform of the generations that preceded them.*

In some respects the use of the term "classical" to describe the milieu of the late 1700s and early 1800s is misleading. Classical suggests clarity, harmony, evenness, and tranquility—all qualities for which this period is not known. It was an age of ferment, of differing values, of change. Nevertheless, the music of the Classical period attaches great importance to balance and clarity of structure. The symphonic form reached its zenith and became a kind of music that later composers could only elaborate on or reject.

No musician of the nineteenth century could ignore the impact of Beethoven (1770–1827), who came to Vienna as a young man to play under Mozart and study under Haydn. It was Beethoven who brought the Classical musical style to completion; moreover, for many musicians and critics of the nineteenth century, he served as a model and a beacon of musical perfection.

Plate 22. Jean Antoine Houdon was the most renowned of late eighteenth-century French sculptors. He was commissioned to produce this sculpture (1788–1792) of George Washington, first President of the United States and a model of the republican hero to many French revolutionaries. (Courtesy Virginia State Library.)

CHAPTER 11 | THE MUSIC OF BEETHOVEN

PROBABLY NO SINGLE COMPOSER HAS INFLUENCED THE COURSE OF musical events more than Ludwig van Beethoven. His evolving style had a profound effect on the musicians of his time, and the music he left to the world has continued to influence musicians and to have great public appeal. In 1970, concert halls around the world presented programs of his music to commemorate the 200th anniversary of his birth in 1770. Although he is considered a representative of the Classical era, Beethoven in many ways was a precursor of Romanticism. His life bridged two centuries almost equally, and his spirit seemed more in tune with the upheaval that followed the French Revolution than with the relative stability of the Age of Reason. While he injected a new freedom into the Classical forms, Beethoven continued to adhere to them. His great contribution was to carry forward the tradition of Mozart and Haydn, building on the structures they had developed and elevating them to new heights of power and expressiveness.

BEETHOVEN (1770–1827)

Ludwig van Beethoven was born in the Rhineland city of Bonn, the son of a singer in the Electoral Court chapel. His musical education was taken over by his father, who hoped to make his boy into a child prodigy like Mozart. Though never fulfilling his father's hope, young Beethoven did learn piano and violin quickly. He received instruction from several musicians at the court, and by the age of twelve he was substituting at the chapel organ. In 1784 he was appointed to a permanent position as assistant organist and had already begun to make his mark because of his virtuoso improvisations at the piano. After his mother died in 1787, his father's alcoholism grew worse, and Beethoven's home life became increasingly unbearable.

The year 1790 marked a turning point in the young composer's career. Haydn, passing through Bonn on his way to London, urged the

Fig. 11.1 Beethoven's music encompasses both the Classical love of form and the fiery passion of Romanticism. The force and intensity of his stormy personality are evident in this engraving.

Elector to send Beethoven to Vienna for further study. Two years later, at the age of twenty-two, Beethoven moved to Vienna, where he remained the rest of his life. At first he studied composition with Haydn; but, unsatisfied with the older man's methods, he turned to other composers for instruction. Though he was a frequent performer at musical evenings held by prominent Viennese nobility, Beethoven did not play in public until 1795, when he performed one of his early piano concertos.

Unlike Mozart, he always retained his popularity with both the general public and the aristocracy of Vienna; and unlike Haydn, he never had to endure the rigors of the eighteenth-century system of musical patron-

age. Though he may have yearned at times for the prestige and security of a court position, he remained proudly and fiercely independent throughout his life. During most of his career he was able to count on annual stipends from a small circle of aristocratic friends and admirers. He seemed to enjoy moving about in the upper echelons of Viennese society, remarking that "it is good to mingle with aristocrats, but one must know how to impress them." He was one of the first composers to demand and obtain an equal footing with this aristocracy solely on the basis of his genius. It was his fortune to come upon the world in a time of rapidly changing values and increasing social mobility. The emerging middle-class audience and the growth of public concerts provided ample opportunities for performance of his music. The rising demand for his works enabled him to live off the sale of his music to publishers.

During the first years of the nineteenth century, when Beethoven seemed to be approaching the height of his career, he became aware that he was growing deaf. He became deeply depressed when he realized that his career as a performer would end. In a moving letter to his two brothers, written from the small town of Heiligenstadt outside Vienna and intended to be read after his death, Beethoven confessed:

My misfortune pains me doubly, in as much as it leads to my being misjudged. For me there can be no relaxation in human society, no refined conversations, no mutual confidences: I must live quite alone and may creep into society only as often as sheer necessity demands; I must live like an outcast. If I appear

in company I am overcome by a burning anxiety, a fear that I am running the risk of letting people notice my condition. . . . Such experiences almost made me despair, and I was on the point of putting an end to my life—The only thing that held me back was my art. For indeed it seemed to me impossible to leave this world before I had produced all the works that I felt the urge to compose, and thus I have dragged on this miserable existence.*

After his affliction became painfully obvious, he gave up conducting and playing in public. His principal means of communication became a notebook in which his few visitors were invited to write their remarks. As he withdrew into his art, his works became more complex, more abstract, and more incomprehensible to his fellow musicians. He never married, and when total deafness set in after 1820, he became almost a recluse. Beethoven died in 1827 at the age of fifty-seven.

*   Emily Anderson (ed. and transl.), *The Letters of Beethoven,* 3 vols. (New York: St. Martin's, 1961), Vol. 3, p. 1352.

BEETHOVEN'S WORK

In comparison to the production of Mozart and Haydn, Beethoven's works seem surprisingly few. This is partly due to his method of composing. Mozart never lacked musical inspiration, and ideas flowed from his pen with miraculous ease; Haydn confessed to the necessity of resorting to prayer at difficult moments, but he kept to a regular schedule of composition. Beethoven, however, had to struggle. Ideas did not come easily, and he filled innumerable pages with slowly evolving sketches. Even his finished compositions were continually rewritten and revised (see Fig. 11.2). The second reason for limited production was his attitude toward composition. He regarded music, above all, as art, and he generally took on only those commissions that he personally wished to fulfill.

If his works took longer to write than was usual at the time, they were also more substantial, both in content and length. His works include nine symphonies; nine concert overtures; five piano concertos; one violin concerto; sixteen string quartets; ten sonatas for violin and piano; five sonatas for cello and piano; thirty-two sonatas for solo piano; twenty-one sets of variations for piano; one opera, *Fidelio;* an oratorio, *Christus am Ölberg, (Christ on the Mount of Olives); Choral Fantasia* for piano, chorus, and orchestra; and two Masses, one in C major, the other, entitled the *Missa Solemnis,* in D major.

Fig. 11.2 The manuscript for *Egmont* shows signs of the struggle and painstaking reworking that marked Beethoven's composing sessions.

Most musical scholars divide Beethoven's career into three periods: the first extending to about 1802, the second extending to 1814, and the last ending with his death in 1827. The first period was a time of assimilation of the Classical tradition of Mozart and Haydn and includes the string quartets of Opus 18 (1798–1800), the First Symphony (1799), and his first three piano sonatas.

The second period was perhaps the happiest of his life; it was certainly the most productive. During it he wrote masterpiece after masterpiece: seven more symphonies, including the gigantic *Eroica* (No. 3, 1803) and the Fifth (1805); the *Rasoumovsky Quartets* of Opus 59 (1806); his opera *Fidelio* (with no fewer than three versions appearing from 1805 through 1814); and the *Waldstein* and *Appassionata* piano sonatas of 1804.

His last creative period, a time of great personal troubles including his deafness, was less productive, but in many ways it was the most important of the three. It culminated in his monumental Ninth Symphony (1823), the equally immense *Missa Solemnis* (completed in 1824), and increasingly abstract late quartets and piano sonatas. In these works he developed many of the musical ideas that influenced the coming Romantic movement. The innovations they contained in form and harmonic structure were not fully understood or appreciated until almost half a century after his death.

ELEMENTS OF HIS STYLE

Beethoven's music reveals several original stylistic characteristics. One that is immediately apparent is size. His works tend to be much longer than those of Haydn or Mozart.

Another striking characteristic is the prevalence of the developmental process. Beethoven lengthened the development section of sonata-allegro form, giving it a weight equal to that of the exposition and recapitulation, and used development in other parts of the movement, especially in the coda. In many of his works the coda is not a short, tacked-on ending but is extended into a second development section, sometimes followed by a second coda that acts as a genuine coda, i.e., a short, concluding section.

In general, Beethoven adhered to the schemes of separate, self-contained movements, unrelated thematically. But there are exceptions: the Sixth Symphony (the *Pastoral*) has five movements, and there is no break between the last two. And the Fifth Symphony, which we shall analyze below, was a striking departure from the principle of thematic independence among the movements.

Within the four-movement scheme, he radically transformed the *third* movement. The short, stately minuet and trio was replaced by a scherzo and trio movement of an entirely different character. Swift of tempo, and fully proportioned in their length, Beethoven's scherzos are the equal of the other movements, performing an important structural and expressive role in the overall scheme of the work.

His music is characterized by an intense, dramatic use of fluctuating dynamics. Frequently he used special dynamic effects, such as a crescendo that is not allowed to climax, but is aborted by a sudden change to pianissimo. He also used long crescendos for structural and expressive purposes. A crescendo slowly builds momentum and energy culminating in the appearance of an important event, such as the beginning of the recapitulation. Under these circumstances, the beginning of the recapitulation would also serve as a climactic ending of the development section.

Beethoven was ingenious in the use of *silence*. In his music, silence functions both as a structural element, separating sections, and as an expressive element, building suspense.

The qualities that we have outlined here are characteristic of Beethoven's work in general. Other, more specific, qualities can be seen in his orchestral works.

ORCHESTRAL STYLE

Beethoven's orchestral sound is more powerful and dramatic than that of Mozart or Haydn. This increased intensity was the result of both larger orchestra and a change in the ways in which the instruments were used. More players were added to the string section, and two horns (sometimes four), two trumpets, and timpani were included as standard parts of the orchestral ensemble. The normal woodwind section comprised two flutes, two oboes, two clarinets, and two bassoons. For extra color and power, Beethoven occasionally added piccolo, contrabassoon, and three trombones. The trumpets, horns, and trombones assumed a greater role than they had previously and the timpani, which formerly merely reinforced the trumpets, were used independently, even as solo instruments.

Working with this expanded orchestra, Beethoven made important contributions to the craft of **orchestration**—writing and arranging music for orchestra to achieve the most effective overall combinations. In this area he greatly influenced later composers in the Romantic era for whom orchestration became a major component of musical composition.

The increased dimensions, extended use of development, advanced exploitation of dynamics, employment of suspense-building devices, and powerful use of an expanded orchestra are among the most important stylistic features of Beethoven's symphonies. Beginning with the Third and culminating in the Ninth, they revolutionized orchestral writing and playing.

SYMPHONY NO. 5 IN C MINOR
RECORD 3/SIDE 2

Beethoven's Fifth Symphony, which he began in 1804, was first performed in Vienna in December, 1808. It is probably the most popular of Beethoven's symphonies, not only for its terse and memorable themes, but also for its unity.

FIRST MOVEMENT

The first movement of the symphony is an excellent example of Beethoven's skill at building a large structure out of a small motive, in this case the famous ♪♪♪ 𝅗𝅥 .

Its stark and forceful announcement, played fortissimo by all strings and clarinets, stands at the beginning of the movement.

Example 11.1

After these two statements, there is a change to *piano* as the motive is used to create the initial phrase of the first theme, in the principal key of C minor.

Example 11.2

The theme is soon abruptly driven to a dramatic halt by a crescendo, leading to three loud, separated chords. The last chord lingers on a long-held note in the first violin, creating a feeling of suspense that is dispelled when the full orchestra, fortissimo, hammers out the motive. This dramatic and isolated statement of the motive draws attention to it, interrupting the flow of the theme. With another extreme change, from full orchestra playing fortissimo to strings playing piano, the theme is resumed, building on the motive.

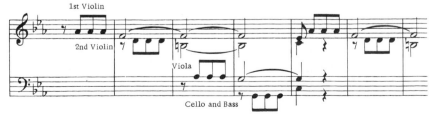

Example 11.3

Shortly after the resumption of the theme, several important features of Beethoven's style appear. The intensity increases, underlined by the gradual addition of instruments, stepped-up rhythmic activity, and climbing pitch level, all combining in a mighty crescendo that envelops the bridge and culminates in two sharp chords separated by silence and followed by silence, dramatically setting off the appearance of the second theme.

The second theme, in E-flat major, is launched by the four-note motive announced by the horns.

Example 11.4

The second theme continues with a lyrical legato melody in the first violins and the woodwinds. The basic motive is still present as a kind of punctuation in the lower strings.

Example 11.5

As the rhythmic activity of the theme increases, the basic motive reasserts itself, commanding full attention in the closing material ending the exposition, which is then repeated.

Example 11.6

The first phase of the development concentrates on the basic motive, in a manner similar to Theme 1, gradually leading to the winds and strings answering each other.

The second phase of development begins with the opening phrase of Theme 2 and turns it into one of the most intense examples of suspense building in the history of musical composition. After the violins state the phrase twice, each time followed by rhythmic punctuations in the winds and lower strings, the phrase is transferred to the winds, where it is played fortissimo in a shortened form. The strings answer with the two long notes of the phrase, and the winds and strings continue to alternate this two-note pattern.

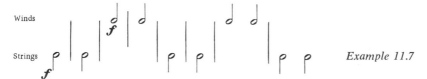

Example 11.7

This stretch of music creates the atmosphere of suspense and expectation that is intensified when the dynamic level is progressively lowered through a diminuendo (>) and the musical material is reduced to one chord.

Winds

Strings

Example 11.8

There is no "theme," no "motive," only the seemingly endless answering back and forth on this barest of fragments. Finally there is a jolting, forte entrance of

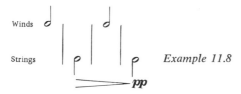

and it would appear that all the suspense is ended, but the music immediately reverts to softly alternating winds and strings. Again the suspense returns, finally ·to be ended with another entrance of the basic motive that now crescendos to a climactic

Here Beethoven shows complete mastery of form and structure—the simple four-note motive acquires an awesome impact as he develops it. Its reappearance constitutes the climactic ending of this development and at the same time the beginning of the recapitulation.

The recapitulation is quite straightforward, with the addition of a short oboe solo and minor changes in orchestration. But the closing material does not end the movement. Instead, there is a long coda, which is actually a new development section treating the basic motive, followed by the lyrical first phrase of the second theme. This becomes the new driving element which builds to yet another climatic statement of the opening figure in Example 11.8. There is then a short second coda based on the first theme and a crescendo to a final appearance of the basic motive.

SECOND MOVEMENT

Superficially, the second movement follows the Classical style: it is in a contrasting key (A-flat major) and meter (3/8); it is slower in tempo (andante con moto) and, at least in the beginning, establishes a lyrical, relaxed atmosphere in relation to the first movement.

It is a theme and variations, with a two-part theme containing several distinctive contrasting elements. The first part begins with a lyrical, flowing melody played by violas and cellos, followed by a contrasting phrase initiated by the woodwinds. The second half of the theme is dominated by a loud phrase, played by horns and trumpets in C major. It is followed by a soft, suspenseful ending that leads into the first variation.

In the first variation, only the viola-cello melody is varied. With minor changes in the accompaniment, the rest of the theme is merely repeated in its original form. The second variation begins with an intensification of the first variation of the viola-cello melody.

Example 11.9

At this point the movement appears to consist of a clear theme and variations. But after the beginning of the second "variation," the theme never again appears intact, either in varied or original form. Only parts of it are used.

The music that follows is more characteristic of development than of variation. Fragments as well as whole phrases of the theme are manipulated in a variety of ways. Modulation, change of tempo, fluctuating dynamics, crescendos climaxing in the dramatic appearance of part of the theme are all used in building the movement. The movement closes with a return to the "woodwind" phrase followed by a coda based on the viola-cello theme.

THIRD MOVEMENT

As we pointed out earlier, the third movements of Beethoven's symphonies utilize scherzo and trio rather than the minuet and trio found in the symphonies of Haydn and Mozart. In this symphony Beethoven employs a most unusual technique for his time—he links the third movement with the first by reintroducing the famous motive from the first movement (♪♪♪ 𝅗𝅥). This technique of bringing back the same thematic material in succeeding movements is referred to as **cyclical treatment** (we shall consider another example of cyclical treatment, Dvořák's Symphony No. 9, in Chapter 15). Another distinguishing feature of this movement is that it is not self-contained, but leads directly into the last movement without a break. Further, it is a fascinating example of how dynamics and orchestration influence musical structure.

The literal meaning of the word "scherzo" is "joke," and the early pieces (for instance those by Haydn) had a frolicsome character. Many of Beethoven's scherzos also reflect a playful, often whimsical atmosphere. However, the scherzo of the Fifth Symphony has a brooding, almost ominous quality.

Like the minuet and trio, the scherzo and trio has a three-part structure: scherzo-trio-scherzo. It too, is in the key of the first movement, but the similarities end there.

The first scherzo alternates two contrasting ideas: a quiet, brooding, mysterious section (A) with a faltering, "stop-and-go" quality is followed by the loud, vigorous, driving thrust of the second theme (B), which is based on the familiar motive:

Example 11.10

The trio shifts to C major and begins with a short section that is immediately repeated. After the two false beginnings,

Example 11.11

the second section of the trio continues with imitative entrance material in the strings that is eventually taken up by the entire orchestra, culminating in forte pronouncements of the motive (see B above).

The section is repeated, beginning forte, but as it continues it becomes not louder but softer. Instead of the gradual accumulation of instruments and crescendo, there is a diminuendo and a thinning of orchestral sound until only cellos and basses are left for the quiet return to the scherzo (A).

In the repeat of the scherzo, the themes no longer contrast dynamically; both are now pianissimo. The ♪♪♪ │ ♩ motive, originally so loud and bold as played by the horns, is now subdued as it is shared by the clarinet and pizzicato first violins. By reducing the dynamic level and subduing the orchestration throughout the entire repeat of the scherzo, Beethoven has profoundly changed the character of the music and created an atmosphere of almost excruciating restraint and expectation.

The scherzo does not "end" but turns into one of those suspense-ridden stretches of music of which Beethoven was a master. Here he uses the technique called *pedal point,* in which a long tone is maintained in the bass against changing harmonies in other parts. In this case, the timpani continually plays the note C. Over this pedal point, a long melodic arch gradually unfolds, played by the first violins, first in fragments, and then as a continuous rising line pulling against the timpani roll. Higher and higher this line pulls, eventually joined by the rest of the orchestra on a long dominant chord and a crescendo that climaxes with breathtaking force in the triumphant and stirring C major melody that begins the last movement. The third and fourth movements are thus united with dramatic effect.

Example 11.12

FOURTH MOVEMENT

The last movement is fast and is in the key of C major rather than making the expected return to C minor. Beethoven tended to end large works brilliantly in major keys. To provide greater color and strength to the movement, he added a piccolo, contrabassoon, and three trombones to the orchestration.

It is a sonata-allegro movement with three themes. Two of them draw upon the basic motive of the first movement for part of their material. In Theme 1 the motive is "hidden" within the theme,

Example 11.13

but in Theme 2 the motive constitutes the primary melodic and rhythmic substance.

Example 11.14

The motive is not used in Theme 3, although later in the movement the material from this theme is used in association with the motive.

Example 11.15

The bridge between Themes 1 and 2 is exceptionally long, and its melodic importance rivals that of the themes themselves.

Example 11.16

It modulates from C to G major, ending with repetitions of the motive as it leads to the second theme.

After the repeat of the exposition (many conductors do not make this repetition), the closing section flows directly into the development section—indeed, there is almost no indication of where one ends and the other begins.

The development section makes forceful use of the orchestra, with emphasis on winds and brasses, extended use of dynamics and modulation. Toward the end of the development section a loud, fanfare-like section leads to a remarkable phase of development. There is a direct quote of the end of the *third* movement. Using this quote the development builds through a long crescendo to the recapitulation. Again, as in the beginning of the fourth movement, because of the way it is approached, the first theme produces a "victorious" effect.

The piece does not end with the conclusion of the recapitulation. Instead, there is a long coda which is actually a new development section. It is characterized by an exhilarating increase in tempo leading to what is without question one of the longest and most emphatic endings in music history—bringing to a close one of the most remarkable compositions of all time.

COMPOSITIONS FOR PIANO

Another portion of Beethoven's major work was his compositions for the piano. Two of his greatest sonatas, the *Waldstein* (Opus 53) and the *Appassionata* (Opus 57), were both written in 1804, the year he began work on his Fifth Symphony. Both were works for solo piano, but unlike Classical chamber compositions, they were not intended for performance before a few listeners in a small room. Rather they are "symphonic" in proportion and suitable for the concert hall.

The capabilities of the piano had developed considerably since the time of Mozart. Improvements were due primarily to the addition of metal braces to the frame, permitting thicker strings to be stretched under greater tension. The result was to give the piano a much greater dynamic range and brilliance.

PIANO SONATA, OPUS 57 (APPASSIONATA)

In the *Appassionata Sonata* Beethoven masterfully exploited the effects that could be obtained from this improved instrument. He fully understood how rich and powerful the sound of the piano could become in the hands of a skilled performer.

The sonata maintained the three-movement plan—fast, slow, fast—without the characteristic break between the second and third movements.

FIRST MOVEMENT

The first movement, in the key of F minor, is in sonata-allegro form. Here Beethoven makes use of the pitch range of the keyboard from very low to very high. The utilization of these extremes of pitch was one of the ways in which Beethoven expanded the style of keyboard music.

Example 11.17

Example 11.18

Example 11.19

Two stretches of music in this movement are very much like cadenzas. One ends the development and introduces the recapitulation, and the second ends the recapitulation and introduces the allegro finale. The closing coda is a tour de force for the virtuoso pianist, as it races at breakneck speed and with fortissimo dynamics. The theme is doubled in octaves and sounded in the most brilliant register of the piano. In a gesture typical of Beethoven, it then progresses from its point of climax to one of repose. In the last measures, the dynamic level drops from fortissimo to pianissimo to triple piano. The theme is sent soaring to the heights of the keyboard, then plummeting to a final whispered cadence five octaves below.

SECOND MOVEMENT

The second movement is a lyrical theme and variations in D-flat major. In this movement Beethoven exploits the lower range of the piano and creates striking effects by juxtaposing high and low sections. The initial somber theme is stated in the rich and sonorous lower register of the keyboard. The theme is in two parts, each of which is repeated.

The first variation preserves the theme's contour but alters the rhythm. The right hand transforms the legato articulation into short, detached notes. The left hand, meanwhile, syncopates the rhythm of the theme, so that notes now appear slightly after the beat.

The second variation returns to the smooth legato of the opening, with the right hand playing chordal figures while the left hand retains the original bass line with slight rhythmic alterations. The material in both hands has been transposed one octave higher than in the original, thus creating a lighter, less massive texture.

In the first two variations the repetition structure of the theme is retained, but in the final variation this is no longer the case. Beethoven uses a motive based on the opening of the theme as a superstructure around which he weaves rapid chordal and scale figurations; here again we witness his exploration of development possibilities.

The magic that sometimes results from the juxtaposition of high and low registers emanates from the last simple statement of the theme at the close of the movement. The first three chords of the phrase are low, the next high, and this continued alternation gives the theme a new dimension. The movement does not end, but after a final statement of thematic material, merges directly into the third movement.

THIRD MOVEMENT

The last movement is in sonata-allegro form. But here the distribution among the various thematic elements is obscured. Indeed the three major sections of the form—the exposition, development, and recapitulation—are not clearly set off from each other.

After a brief introductory section, an arching sixteenth-note passage enters.

Allegro

pp

Example 11.20   This passage, or some variant of it, seems omnipresent throughout the entire movement. The movement sounds like a continuous development of this material, with other thematic elements embedded within or grafted onto it. The movement ends with a presto finale in a climax of overwhelming brilliance and excitement.

CONCERTO NO. 3 IN C MINOR

The capabilities of the piano so forcefully evident in the *Appassionata Sonata* were also utilized in Beethoven's five piano concertos. In them he combined the virtuoso aspects of the solo instrument with the dynamic and expressive capabilities of the symphony orchestra. The first three, composed during his early years in Vienna, were written for his own needs as a concert pianist.

Sketches for Beethoven's Concerto No. 3 in C Minor have been found dating back to 1797. The work was finished in December of 1800, and first performed, with the composer at the piano, in Vienna in April of 1803. It has a three-movement structure of fast-slow-fast, and is scored for the standard Beethoven orchestra.

FIRST MOVEMENT

The opening movement, in the key of C minor, makes use of the sonata-allegro scheme with a double exposition.

Marked *allegro con brio* (fast with vigor), the movement contains the brilliant piano writing we have seen in the sonata—fast scale and trill passages, sweeps throughout the range of the keyboard, and extreme pitch registers. For a good part of the movement, particularly in the development, the orchestra states the important thematic ideas while the piano plays cadenza-like material. The cadenza, which divides the two sections of the coda, takes on added importance and weight as it rhapsodically improvises on and develops the themes. The orchestra joins the piano as it rises to the flourishes of the fortissimo ending.

SECOND MOVEMENT

Again illustrating his willingness to use unusual key combinations, Beethoven cast the second movement in the distant key of E major. The structure takes the form of a theme and variations. The theme is typical of Beethoven—rhapsodic, expressive, and highly ornamented. The variations that follow assume the character of freely invented improvisations. The orchestra has been reduced to flutes, bassoons, horns, and muted strings, and the dynamic level rarely rises above piano.

THIRD MOVEMENT

The third movement is a spirited rondo, with the orchestra restored to its original strength. The rondo theme is announced first by the piano alone and then taken up by the orchestra. Between statements of the main thematic material, the piano plays brilliant improvisations, sometimes developing elements of the theme, sometimes freely invented figurations. The rondo theme returns following the first cadenza and is again interrupted by brilliant passages from the soloist. After the second solo cadenza, Beethoven dramatically introduces the surprise elements characteristic of the closing moments of a rondo: the meter shifts from 2/4 to 6/8, the tempo from *allegro* (fast) to *presto* (very fast), the key from C minor to C major, and the thematic material changes to a rhythmically and melodically altered version of the initial rondo.

In the final measures, the solo and tutti sections alternate in abrupt changes of dynamics, and the movement ends in a fortissimo burst by the full orchestra.

SUMMARY

In his symphonies, sonatas, and concertos, Ludwig van Beethoven expanded nearly every aspect of Classical composition. He lengthened the coda, development, and bridge sections; increased the size and volume of the orchestra; replaced the minuet with the scherzo; and introduced a variety of surprise elements to suit his expressive purposes.

With the piano's new concert hall proportions, Beethoven made wide use of the instrument's lyric and virtuoso capabilities. His melodic themes alternated with brilliant improvisations utilizing the full range of the keyboard.

The grace, sophistication, and lucidity of Mozart and the good-natured humor of Haydn were succeeded by music of extraordinary intensity and power. Beethoven shook the earth and music was never the same again. In the next chapters we will see how his musical innovations directly affected the composers of the Romantic era.

NEW TERMS

orchestration
cyclical treatment

PART V SUGGESTED LISTENING

Beethoven, Ludwig van

Symphony No. 3 in E-Flat, Op. 55 (Eroica). Initially titled "Bonaparte" (Beethoven withdrew the title in anger at Napoleon's self-proclamation as Emperor), this was the first of Beethoven's truly revolutionary works. In place of the usual slow movement it has a funeral march with contrasting major and minor sections; the minuet is replaced by one of the composer's earliest orchestral scherzo movements; and the finale is a complex set of variations.

Symphony No. 9 in D Minor, Op. 125. Perhaps the greatest symphony ever composed, this work remained a source of inspiration to subsequent composers throughout the nineteenth century. Its most striking innovation is the choral finale on Schiller's *Ode to Joy;* the three preceding movements are on an equally grand scale: the second is an immense scherzo built around a single rhythmic motif, and the third is a set of variations on a double theme.

Egmont Overture. This is part of the incidental music Beethoven wrote for Goethe's play *Egmont,* the story of a hero's struggle against tyranny. Enforcing Goethe's theme, Beethoven has written a strong musical statement for freedom and brotherhood. Although the play ends in tragedy, part of the overture is then repeated as a "Victory Symphony."

Violin Concerto in D. Often called Beethoven's most serene work, this was the longest and most symphonically organized concerto that had yet been written. The entire first movement grows from the first, simple motive: five taps of the timpani.

Piano Sonata in G Major, Op. 14, No. 2. The flowing first theme of this sonata is rhythmically ambiguous—the accent seems to fall not on the first beat, but on the first offbeat. This uncertainty plays off the rythmic regularity of the other themes.

Haydn, Franz Joseph

Symphony No. 45 in F-Sharp Minor (Farewell). One of Haydn's most dramatic and unorthodox symphonies, this work illustrates his style at its most romantic and imaginative. The opening movement introduces, by way of experiment, an extended new theme in place of the regular development; and in the final movement, the tempo suddenly changes from presto to adagio and the instruments drop out one by one, leaving only two violins to conclude the work.

The Creation. Through words and music, this oratorio paints the creation of the world. Haydn was able to capture musically every nuance of the Biblical story: the Chaos, the first triumphant light, the sounds of the first animals.

Symphony No. 94 in G Major ("Surprise"). The "Surprise Symphony" is the most famous example of Haydn's delight in musical jokes. A simple first theme is stated softly and suddenly interrupted by an explosive chord. The theme moves softly on, as though nothing has happened.

Mozart, Wolfgang Amadeus

Die Zauberflöte (The Magic Flute). If *The Marriage of Figaro* may be considered the culmination of eighteenth-century Italian comic opera, *The Magic Flute* stands as the first masterpiece of German Romantic opera.

Symphony No. 41 in C Major, K. 551 (Jupiter). The "Jupiter" is particularly famous for its closing movement, in which several thematic ideas are used as subjects for short fugal sections and then are combined together in the coda.

Eine Kleine Nachtmusik (A Little Night Music). This serenade for strings was written as outdoor evening entertainment for some festive occasion. Its tone is light, its structure and instrumentation compact and simple.

Lieder
für die
Jugend
von
Robert Schumann.
Op 79

VI
MUSIC OF
THE ROMANTIC ERA

Title page by Ludwig Richter for Robert
Schumann's *Songs for the Young*.

③ main topics of romantic music

1) characteristics — *a) importance of classical form (the way it is made up)
*emotional depth
one of most impt. char.

b) blurring of formal lines of classical form)
enlarged the key signatures

2) art song

3) piano music

c) classical form was abandoned all
together by some composers

* d) changes in harmoney
- became more chromatic
(away from the tonic key)

e) chords more complicated (arpeggio)
+ more expressive

* f) more interest in tone color, (timbre)
more use of solo instruments
Bee. emphasizes violin + chorus as solos
+ oboe

g) greatly inc size of the orch.

h) found great inspiration in lit.
+ visual arts + nature

II. Art Song
- came to be called the Lied — formal pattern
- 1st lied is call strophic — where one sings same tune to each verse w/ diff words
- thrucomposed — diff music for diff sections of the text
- most impt romantic composer was Schubert
- piano was impt universal instrument of the romantic era.
parlor type settings

III   2 types of compositions for piano
a) short, intimate, lyrical, song like, many moods
or
b) great brilliant exhibition like pieces to display virtuosity.
Beethoven greatly developed this.
(period of great virtuosity) esp for violin + piano

2 or 3 impt. composers
1) Schumann — small lyric like char. pieces. Expressing a single mood.
abrupt changes in mood
2) Chopin — outstanding romantic piano composer
short, lyric, variety of moods, tremendous restraint.

3) Liszt — greatest virtuoso pianist of the time.
expanded technique of piano.

adapt.

CHAPTER 12 | SONG AND PIANO MUSIC

THE ROMANTIC PERIOD IN MUSIC ROUGHLY COINCIDES WITH THE nineteenth century. In some respects it was a logical extension of the principles established during the Classical era. In other respects, however, it represented a fundamental departure from those principles. Even within the outlines of the basic musical structures of the Classical period—the sonata-allegro form, theme and variations—formal balance and clarity of structure gave way to spontaneity, to emotional depth and richness, qualities foreshadowed in the works of Beethoven. In addition, the Romantic era saw the Classical forms abandoned altogether by some composers. Instead, there was a heavy reliance on literature, nature, visual images, and the supernatural as sources for musical inspiration and as frameworks for musical forms.

SOME ROMANTIC INNOVATIONS

Romantic composers made some of their most remarkable achievements in harmony and tone color, and the harmonic vocabulary became increasingly rich during the nineteenth century. Chromatic harmonies, modulations to distant keys, complicated chords, all tended to blur the outlines of the tonal system of major and minor keys. Harmony became more a means of expression than an element of musical structure.

The Romantic interest in tone color is shown by the phenomenal growth of the orchestra during this period. For the first time, instrumental color was regarded as an important element of music, on a par with melody, harmony, and rhythm. Instruments were improved, new ones were invented, new combinations were discovered, and the art of orchestration became a prime preoccupation for many composers of the age.

The Romantic period is often described as the age of the art song and the short piano piece, since these two genres constitute some of the most interesting musical literature of the nineteenth century. This fascination with the smaller forms is one of the two major aspects of the Romantic spirit; the other aspect centered upon the larger forms, which offered greater scope in which to expand and develop. (We will discuss the larger forms in succeeding chapters of this unit.) These small pieces had an intimate quality, as though the composer were speaking directly to a small group of friends. The media that seemed most suitable to them were the piano and the solo voice.

ART SONG

The **art song** is a musical setting of a poem for solo voice and piano. The German words **lied** and **lieder** (plural)—which we previously encountered in Chapter 6—became the standard terms for this type of song. The lied became an important musical genre in the work of major composers early in the nineteenth century.

In the mid-eighteenth century the lied had been a simple song with keyboard accompaniment. The musical setting used **strophic form,** with the same melody repeated for every stanza (or strophe) of the poem. The text was treated syllabically (one note for each syllable) and the accompaniment served merely to support the singing voice.

Toward the end of the eighteenth century, the **ballad**—a narrative poem set to music—became popular in Germany. The ballad was long, emphasized dramatic situations, and alternated in structure between narration and dialogue. These characteristics required greater musical resources than the strophic procedure offered. Hence the ballads were **through-composed;** that is, each section of the text had new music that was different from the music preceding and following.

Fig. 12.1 The short piano piece was tremendously popular during the Romantic period. The social intimacy created by this smaller musical form is well illustrated by this romanticized painting entitled "A Schubert Evening in a Viennese Home."

Both the strophic and through-composed procedures were used in the nineteenth-century lied, which became exceptionally popular in the early Romantic period. The earliest and, in many respects, the most important of lieder composers was Franz Schubert.

SCHUBERT (1797-1828)

In many ways the circumstances of Franz Peter Schubert's life were the very essence of the romantic's view of an artist's condition. During his brief and troubled lifetime, Schubert lived in poverty and was unrecognized, except by a small circle of friends; only after his death was his genius more widely acknowledged. He was born in a suburb northwest of Vienna, the fourth surviving son of an industrious and pious schoolmaster. His formal musical training, never very systematic, began with violin lessons from his father and piano instruction from an older brother.

In 1808, at the age of eleven, Schubert obtained a place in the choir of the Imperial Court Chapel and was thereby privileged to attend the *Stadt-Konvict* (City Seminary), one of Vienna's most prestigious boarding schools. In addition to his regular studies and music lessons, he became a violinist in the school orchestra, later assuming the duties of conductor on various occasions. The numerous works he composed during these years at the *Konvict* include songs, overtures, religious works, an operetta (light opera), and six string quartets. His first symphony was written in 1813, the year in which he left the *Konvict,* and his first Mass was successfully performed in 1814.

After leaving the *Konvict* Schubert returned home to live, first attending a training college for primary school teachers and then teaching at his father's school. The regimen of the classroom was not suited to his temperament, and he applied for the musical directorship of the new State Normal School at Laibach (now Ljubljana in Yugoslavia) in 1816, but

Fig. 12.2 Schubert's lieder exemplify the spontaneity and lyricism of the Romantic movement.

was turned down. Unable to find any other permanent employment at that time, he resolved to earn his living by taking music students, selling his compositions, and writing for the theater. In 1817 he moved to Vienna.

During the early 1820s, performances of Schubert's solo songs and vocal quartets for male voices aroused considerable public interest, and his name became widely known throughout Vienna. Two of his operettas were produced with moderate success, and a number of songs and piano works were published. These successes were offset by his continuing

Beethoven recognized genius of Schubert

wrote over 600 songs (over 1000 works)

inability to obtain a salaried position. In 1822, a serious illness, probably syphilis, necessitated a stay in the hospital and a prolonged period of recuperation. The following year, *Rosamunde,* a play with incidental music by Schubert, failed dismally, closing after only two performances. It was his last work for the theater.

The last four years of his life were a continual battle against ill health and poverty. Though his music, particularly the songs, continued to draw high praise from fellow musicians, including Beethoven, it was not until 1828 that a public concert of his works was given. He was unable to live on the pitifully small income from his music publications, but he continued to compose at a feverish pace. Despite his weakening health, he seemed at the height of his creative power. In the fall of 1828 he became ill with what was diagnosed as typhoid fever and died on November 19, at the age of thirty-one. His last wish, to be buried near Beethoven, was granted, and on his tombstone was written: "The art of music here entombed a rich possession but even far fairer hopes."

SCHUBERT'S WORK

During the seventeen years between 1811, when he was fourteen, and 1828, the year of his death, Schubert composed about one thousand works. They include nine symphonies, fifty chamber works and piano sonatas, a large number of short piano pieces, several operas and operettas, six Masses and about twenty-five other religious works, nearly one hundred choral compositions, and more than six hundred songs.

Schubert's symphonic style displays a Romantic gift for lyric melody and a love of interesting patches of color and harmony. Nevertheless, his symphonies were written in the Classical forms. His famous Symphony No. 8 in B Minor was written in 1822, when the composer was twenty-five years old, but he never chose to extend it beyond the original two movements. Nicknamed "The Unfinished," the work was not performed until 1865, 43 years after his death.

Schubert is best known, however, for his abundant body of lieder. He set to music the poetry of the great literary figures of his time, Goethe and Schiller among them. In addition to settings of individual poems, Schubert wrote two **song cycles** (a series of art songs that tell a story), *Die schöne Müllerin* (*The Maid of the Mill,* 1823), and *Die Winterreise* (*Winter Journey,* 1827).

Schubert employed both the strophic (which he used with considerable flexibility) and through-composed forms with great imgination. His songs also reflected the supremacy of the poem as the generating force. The shape and quality of the melodic line, the choice of harmonic progressions, the rhythmic character of the work, and the entire structure were fashioned to serve the poem. And the piano accompaniment, now no longer a mere harmonic background for the voice, joined with the voice, virtually as a full partner, bringing to musical life the essence of the poem.

GRETCHEN AM SPINNRADE (1814)   One of the finest examples of the use of the piano is found in *Gretchen am Spinnrade* (*Gretchen at the Spinning Wheel*). Gretchen, who in Goethe's play has fallen in love with Faust, sings as she sits at her spinning wheel.

GRETCHEN AM SPINNRADE

Meine Ruh ist hin,
Mein Herz ist schwer;
Ich finde sie nimmer
Und nimmermehr.

Wo ich ihn nicht hab;
Ist mir das Grab,
Die ganze Welt
Ist mir vergällt.

Mein armer Kopf
Ist mir verrückt,
Mein armer Sinn
Ist mir zerstückt.

Meine Ruh ist hin,
Mein Herz ist schwer,
Ich finde sie nimmer
Und nimmermehr.

Nach ihm nur schau' ich
Zum Fenster hinaus,
Nach ihm nur geh' ich
Aus dem Haus.

Sein hoher Gang,
Sein' edle Gestalt,
Seines Mundes Lächeln,
Seiner Augen Gewalt,

Und seiner Rede
Zauberfluss.
Sein Händedruck,
Und ach, sein Kuss!

Meine Ruh ist hin,
Mein Herz ist schwer,
Ich finde sie nimmer
Und nimmermehr.

Mein Busen drängt
Sich nach ihm hin!
Ach dürft' ich fassen
Und halten ihn,

Und küssen ihn,
So wie ich wollt',
An seinen Küssen
Vergehen sollt'!

Meine Ruh ist hin,
Mein Herz ist schwer . . .

GRETCHEN AT THE SPINNING WHEEL *

My peace is gone,
my heart is heavy;
never, never again
Will I find rest.

Where I am not with him
I am in my grave,
the whole world
turns to bitter gall.

My poor head
is in a whirl,
my poor thoughts
are all distracted.

My peace is gone,
my heart is heavy;
never, never again
Will I find rest.

I seek only him when I look
out of the window,
I seek only him when I leave
the house.

His noble gait,
his fine stature,
the smile of his lips,
the power of his eyes,

and the magic flow
of his speech,
the pressure of his hand,
and oh, his kiss!

My peace is gone,
my heart is heavy;
never, never again
Will I find rest.

My bosom yearns
towards him.
If only I could seize him
and hold him

and kiss him
to my heart's content—
under his kisses
I should die!

My peace is gone.
My heart is heavy. . . .

* S. S. Prawer, ed. and transl., *The Penguin Book of Lieder* (Middlesex, England: Penguin Books Ltd., 1964), pp. 33–34.

The piano accompaniment, which represents the spinning wheel, mirrors her growing agitation. As Gretchen conjures up her lover, a running sixteenth-note figure (the sound of the wheel) intensifies and gradually accelerates. As the voice rises higher and higher, the sound of the whirling wheel crescendos, stops, and Gretchen cries out *"und ach, sein Kuss!"* ("and oh, his kiss"). Gretchen sits transfixed by her passion, as does the listener.

It is not the voice but the piano that tells us that Gretchen returns to her senses. The spinning motive in the piano (pianissimo) makes two false starts; then with the third, the song is in motion again, with the spinning reintroducing the voice on *"Meine Ruh ist hin"* ("My peace is gone").

The words *Meine Ruh ist hin* and their melody begin each verse and act as a unifying element throughout the song, which is strophic in form. Gretchen repeats these words once more at the end of the song in a sigh of resignation. As the sound of her voice fades away, the whirring of the piano's spinning motive closes the piece as it began it.

DIE FORELLE (1817)

The Romantic love of nature is evident in *Die Forelle (The Trout)*, one of Schubert's shorter lieder. The poem concerns the struggle between a fish and a fisherman; typically the Romantic poet's sympathy lies with the fish.

DIE FORELLE

In einem Bächlein helle,
Da schoss in froher Eil'
Die launische Forelle
Vorüber wie ein Pfeil.
Ich stand an dem Gestade
Und sah in süsser Ruh
Des muntern Fischleins Bade
Im klaren Bächlein zu.

Ein Fischer mit der Rute
Wohl an dem Ufer stand,
Und sah's mit kaltem Blute,
Wie sich das Fischlein wand.
So lang' dem Wasser Helle,
So dacht ich, nicht gebricht,
So fängt er die Forelle
Mit seiner Angel nicht.

Doch endlich ward dem Diebe
Die Zeit zu lang. Er macht'
Das Bächlein tückisch trübe,
Und eh' ich es gedacht,
So zuckte seine Rute,
Das Fischlein zappelt' d'ran,
Und ich mit regem Blute
Sah die Betrogne an.

THE TROUT *

In a bright little stream,
in joyous haste,
a playful trout
flashed past me like an arrow.
I stood by the shore
and in sweet contentment I watched
the little fish bathing
in the clear stream.

A fisherman with his rod
stood on the bank
and coldly watched
the trout's windings.
So long as the water
—I thought—remains clear,
he will not catch the trout
with his line.

But at last the thief
grew impatient. He
treacherously dulled the clear stream,
and before I could think it
his rod quivered
and the fish was struggling on his hook.
I felt the blood stir within me
as I looked at the cheated trout.

* S. S. Prawer, ed. and transl., *The Penguin Book of Lieder* (Middlesex, England: Penguin Books Ltd., 1964), pp. 37–38.

In form *Die Forelle* is almost strophic. The first two verses have identical music: a simple melody with a very simple harmonic background. The accompaniment makes use of a short, rising figure that seems to sparkle and babble like a brook, conveying a mood of cheerful calm.

The third verse of the poem is much more excited, as the fish is caught. Schubert echoes this change of mood by putting aside the strophic form. The new melody is backed by a more agitated, more chromatic accompaniment. For the last two lines of the song, however, Schubert returns to the original melody and accompaniment. Although the text of the poem does not repeat the opening lines, the reappearance of the first melody rounds out the form of the song. In 1819 Schubert used this song as a basis for a set of variations in the Quintet in A Major (Op. 114), the famous "Trout" Quintet for string quartet and string bass.

ERLKÖNIG
(1815)
RECORD 4/SIDE 1

While two of the Romantic period's favorite themes, nature and painful love, occupy *Die Forelle* and *Gretchen am Spinnrade,* the supernatural is involved in Schubert's setting of *Erlkönig (King of the Elves).* The poem, a ballad by Goethe, tells the story of a father riding through a storm on horseback carrying his sick child in his arms. As they hurry through the stormy night, the delirious boy imagines that the Erlkönig (who symbolizes death) appears and tries to entice him away with promises of fine games and pleasures. When the father and son finally arrive home, the boy is dead in his arms.

Fig. 12.3 Illustration of Goethe's poem "Erlkönig."

The poem has four separate characters, all sung by one voice with piano accompaniment: the narrator, who introduces and closes the song, the frightened child, the frantic father, and the sinister Erlkönig.

ERLKÖNIG (GOETHE)	KING OF THE ELVES *
Narrator	
Wer reitet so spät durch Nacht und Wind?	*Who rides so late through the night and the wind?*
Es ist der Vater mit seinem Kind;	*It is the father with his child.*
Er hat den Knaben wohl in dem Arm	*He holds the boy in his arm, grasps*
Er fasst ihn sicher, er hält ihn warm.	*him securely, keeps him warm.*
Father	
"Mein Sohn, was birgst du so bang dein Gesicht?"	*"My son, why do you hide your face so anxiously?"*
Son	
"Siehst, Vater, du den Erlkönig nicht?	*"Father, do you not see the Elf-King?*
Den Erlenkönig mit Kron' und Schweif?"	*The Elf-King with his crown and train?"*
Father	
"Mein Sohn, es ist ein Nebelstreif."	*"My son, it is only a streak of mist."*
Elf King	
"Du liebes Kind, komm, geh' mit mir!	*"Darling child, come away with me!*
Gar schöne Spiele spiel' ich mit dir;	*I will play fine games with you.*
Manch' bunte Blumen sind an dem Strand,	*Many gay flowers grow by the shore:*
Meine Mutter hat manch' gülden Gewand."	*my mother has many golden robes."*
Son	
"Mein Vater, mein Vater, und hörest du nicht,	*"Father, father, do you not hear*
Was Erlenkönig mir leise verspricht?"	*what the Elf-King softly promises me?"*
Father	
"Sei ruhig, bleibe ruhig, mein Kind:	*"Be calm, dear child, be calm—*
In dürren Blättern säuselt der Wind."	*the wind is rustling in the dry leaves."*
Elf King	
"Willst, feiner Knabe, du mit mir gehn?	*"You beautiful boy, will you come with me?*
Meine Töchter sollen dich warten schön;	*My daughters will wait upon you.*

* S. S. Prawer, ed. and transl., *The Penguin Book of Lieder* (Middlesex, England: Penguin Books Ltd., 1964), pp. 34–35.

Meine Töchter führen den nächtlichen Reihn'	*My daughters will lead the nightly round,*
Und wiegen und tanzen und singen dich ein."	*they will rock you, dance to you, sing you to sleep."*

Son

"Mein Vater, mein Vater, und siehst du nicht dort	*"Father, father, do you not see the Elf-King's daughters there, in*
Erlkönigs Töchter am düstern Ort?"	*that dark place?"*

Father

"Mein Sohn, mein Sohn, ich seh' es genau:	*"My son, my son, I see it clearly:*
Es scheinen die alten Weiden so grau."	*it is the grey gleam of the old willow-trees."*

Elf King

"Ich liebe dich, mich reizt deine schöne Gestalt;	*"I love you, your beauty allures me,*
Und bist du nicht willig, so brauch' ich Gewalt."	*and if you do not come willingly, I shall use force."*

Son

"Mein Vater, mein Vater, jetzt fasst er mich an!	*"Father, father, now he is seizing me!*
Erlkönig hat mir ein Leids gethan!"—	*The Elf-King has hurt me!"—*

Narrator

Dem Vater grauset's, er reitet geschwind	*Fear grips the father, he rides swiftly,*
Er hält in den Armen das ächzende Kind,	*holding the moaning child in his arms;*
Erreicht den Hof mit Müh' und Not;	*with effort and toil he reaches the house—*
In seinen Armen das Kind—	*the child in his arms—*
war tot.	*was dead.*

In form *Erlkönig* is through-composed. As in *Gretchen am Spinnrade,* the piano is a crucial element. It sets the atmosphere at the beginning: the wild wind, the galloping horse, and the anxiety of the father.

Example 12.1

The triplet figure in the right hand occurs in various forms throughout, sustaining the highly charged atmosphere until the final moments of the song. The figure in the left hand appears periodically to indicate the running horse and to unify the piece musically.

Schubert portrays the characters and sets them off from each other by a number of devices, particularly by manipulating the piano accompaniment. Whenever the *Erlkönig* enters, for example, the dynamic level drops to pianissimo, the accompaniment changes, the vocal line becomes smooth and alluring.

Schubert reflects the son's mounting terror by repeating the same melodic material at successively higher pitch levels each time he cries out to his father. An upward leap on *"Mein Sohn"* and *"Sei ruhig"* marks the father's utterances that act as modulatory bridges linking the passages of child and *Erlkönig*.

The father's final statement ends with the strong drop of the interval of a fifth doubled by the left hand of the piano. The same figure recurs as the *Erlkönig* utters his last words as he seizes the boy,

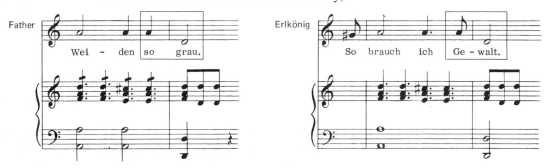

Example 12.2

and is repeated once more in the boy's cry as he is taken in death.

Example 12.3

The last verse shows Schubert's sense of drama and the manipulation of the song's elements to heighten the emotional impact. The piano is silent as the narrator sings "the child in his arms," a single chord sounds, increasing the feeling of suspense, and the narrator concludes "was dead."

PIANO MUSIC

The favorite instrument of the Romantic age, the piano, ideally suited the dual personality of the period: the intimate, delicate side as well as the brilliant, flashy one. The popularity and importance of the piano stemmed indirectly from Beethoven, who had written a great deal of excellent and demanding music for it. During the nineteenth century the piano became a universal instrument.

The huge and varied literature for piano produced during the Romantic period falls into two broad categories; one consists of short, intimate, lyric pieces, similar in scope and feeling to lieder, while the other includes the larger, more brilliant exhibition pieces written for virtuoso performers. As one might expect, the outstanding lieder composer, Franz Schubert, was also a master of the small lyric piano piece. These little pieces, which he called either *impromptus* or *moments musicaux,* are miniature gems. Each is characterized by its distinctive mood, with Schubert's matchless correlation of form and musical content. These works became models for many later composers.

The other aspect of Romantic music—the grandiose, flashy, exhibitionist side—became an increasingly important element of the rapidly growing literature for the piano. Virtuosity impressed the Romantic audience and dozens of second-rate (and worse) composers began pouring out compositions for this market. Much of this music was shallow and meaningless, offering only a display of technical prowess.

However, three important composers—Robert Schumann, Frederic Chopin, and Franz Liszt—realized the piano was capable of much more. Although each man responded in his own way, they all shared a common belief in the potential of the instrument. The pieces they wrote are so well tailored to the piano that it is virtually impossible to arrange them satisfactorily for any other medium.

Robert Schumann spent his early years composing primarily for the piano. Alternating between visionary dreams, moodiness, and exultation, his music expresses the contradictions and tensions inherent in Romanticism.

SCHUMANN (1810–1856)

Robert Schumann was born in Germany in the Saxon town of Zwickau. His father, a bookseller, recognized his son's talent and arranged for piano lessons when the boy was seven. Schumann began to compose soon after, but his interest in music was paralleled by a fascination with literature. With his father's encouragement, he read widely, particularly Goethe and Byron, and wrote poetry and a novel.

The year 1826 was a doubly tragic one: his elder sister committed suicide at the age of nineteen, and shortly afterward his father died. Schumann's mother persuaded him to take up law, and to please her he enrolled at the University of Leipzig. But "chilly jurisprudence, with its ice-cold definitions" repelled Schumann, who gained his mother's permission to devote himself to music.

By 1830 he was taking lessons from Leipzig's well-known pianist Friedrich Wieck, with whom he also boarded. His dreams of becoming a piano virtuoso, however, were cut short by a permanent injury to his right hand caused by a gadget he had rigged in hopes of improving his fingering technique. Accepting the disaster with philosophical detachment, he threw all his energies into composition and the writing of music criticism.

During the decade of the 1830s, Schumann developed steadily as a composer and critic. His compositions, primarily for piano, received favorable attention and a number of them were published. In 1834, with a small group of friends, he founded the highly influential *Neue Zeitschrift für Musik (New Journal for Music)*. As editor from 1835 to 1844, he strongly supported progressive music, attacking with great fervor the shallow *salon* music and insipid Italianate stage productions then in vogue. Through his many articles and essays, often signed with fanciful pseudonyms, Schumann helped shape the taste of the nineteenth century. He was among the first to acknowledge the genius of both Chopin and Brahms.

In 1835 he fell in love with Clara Wieck, the daughter of his former piano teacher, who was then sixteen. Their marriage was opposed by her father, who wanted her to marry someone wealthy enough to support her own career as a concert pianist. They finally married, without her father's consent, in 1840. The years immediately following the marriage were among Schumann's happiest, and his joy was reflected in his composition. It was Clara who was the first interpreter of his piano works. In 1840 he devoted himself almost exclusively to composing more than 130 songs; in the next year he completed his first two symphonies; and in 1842 he turned to writing chamber music.

In 1843 he joined the faculty of Mendelssohn's newly founded conservatory at Leipzig, but his career, up to now so promising, was threatened by periods of depression and with-

Fig. 12.4   Robert and Clara Schumann.

drawal. He resigned from the conservatory, moving first to Dresden and then to Düsseldorf. There his mental condition became worse; he threw himself into the Rhine, and after being saved from drowning, was confined to an asylum near Bonn. He died there, at the age of forty-six, leaving behind his wife and seven children.

SCHUMANN'S WORK

Along with Chopin and Liszt, Schumann was one of the creators of modern piano technique. Almost all of his most popular and greatest works for piano date from his early years as a composer, up to 1840. They range from miniature **character pieces** (pieces portraying a single mood, emotion, or idea) whose titles establish them as wholly Romantic—*Papillons (Butterflies), Carnaval, Kinderscenen (Scenes from Childhood)*—to large, Classically oriented works such as the three piano sonatas, the Fantasy in C Minor, the Symphonic Études, and the Piano Concerto in A Minor.

As a symphonist, Schumann is frequently criticized for his weakness in orchestration and his failure to unify large-scale compositions. However, of his four symphonies, the Symphony No. 1 in B-Flat Major (*Spring,* 1840) achieves a spontaneity that perhaps outweighs any structural defects.

Schumann's lyric gifts and his poetic imagination show themselves to best advantage in his songs. His great cycles of 1840—*Myrthen (Myrtle), Frauenliebe und Leben (Woman's Love and Life),* and *Dichterliebe (Poet's Love)*—rank with those of Schubert as the greatest of nineteenth-century song cycles.

His chamber music, much of which was written in 1842 after he had thoroughly studied the quartets of Haydn and Mozart, includes three string quartets, three trios, a piano quartet, and a piano quintet. Of the choral music, most of which is neglected today, *Das Paradies und die Peri (Paradise and the Peri,)* 1843) and *Scenes from Goethe's Faust* (1849–1853) are his most important compositions.

Schumann was well aware of the conflicts between the introspective and outgoing aspects of Romanticism, and the same conflicts were reflected in his own personality. He often wrote about imaginary characters who represented the two sides of his nature: Florestan, the impulsive revolutionary, and Eusebius, the moody, introspective dreamer. In his writings these two characters often engage in spirited debates, and in his music it is often possible to weigh the influence of these two outlooks.

Much of Schumann's music was inspired by poetry; the titles of his songs and collections of piano pieces are often derived from extramusical sources. Schumann's style is very free and flexible, almost kaleidoscopic, with rapid alternations between the Romantic extremes of intimacy and brilliance. There is never any attempt to overwhelm the listener with virtuoso displays; the technical difficulties in the music serve the poetic inspiration.

FANTASIESTÜCKE (FANTASY PIECES), OPUS 12

Schumann considered the *Fantasiestücke* to be among his best compositions. This set of eight short character pieces represents a constant interchange between the two mythological characters, Florestan and Eusebius; for the first four pieces, they alternate, while the last four include elements of both within each piece. The first, second, seventh, and eighth pieces from the *Fantasiestücke* illustrate Schumann's freedom of content, form, and style.

Des Abends (The Evening) This piece embodies the reflective character of Eusebius, with the picture of a peaceful, undisturbed evening, and illustrates a single mood with great economy of means. The work is in six sections, each of which begins with a descending melodic line:

Example 12.4

The same accompaniment is used throughout the piece. The sections are quite similar, even though the piece modulates several times. The dynamic level remains soft throughout.

Aufschwung (Soaring) In sharp contrast to the opening piece, this one is fast, loud, and enthusiastic, mirroring the character of the youthful Florestan. The work is in ternary form (ABA), with each A section further subdivided into an aba form of its own (Schumann was very partial to ternary form). The "a" section alternates between hammering chords with a melody beneath them and a smoother descending theme. The "b" section, which follows, is quieter, longer, and far more lyric. The "a" theme then returns briefly. The B section has no such distinct formal outlines; it modulates freely, with many changes of dynamics and tempo. A long crescendo leads to the return of the A section.

Traumes Wirren (Dream Visions) This short and lively piece is monopolized by lighthearted Florestan; the moody Eusebius emerges only in the short B part of the ternary (ABA) form. The A section is light and fast, requiring considerable pianistic technique. The B section is slower, sustained, chromatic, and lower in pitch.

Ende vom Lied (End of the Song) In a letter to his intended bride, Clara Wieck, Schumann explained that this piece pictured a wedding (probably theirs), with all the good spirits that usually attend such an event. The piece is again in ternary (ABA) form, and the exuberant Florestan predominates. But in the coda, Eusebius takes over, as the composer's happy thoughts change to despair at his fear of losing his beloved. The A section is marchlike, while the B portion is livelier, with more dancelike rhythms and more dynamic contrasts; the return of the A section is somewhat abbreviated. The coda utilizes some melodic material from the A section, and this poignant concluding section is soft, low in pitch, and sustained.

CHOPIN (1810–1849) ·Polish

Frederic Chopin (Sho-pan′) was one of the most creative and original composers in the history of music. Almost none of his mature works relies on traditional devices or forms; he created an entirely new musical idiom. His style is unique and easy to identify; every phrase is characteristically his. Chopin's art is inescapably linked to the sonority of the piano, the only possible means of expression for him. Chopin suffered neither the privation and neglect that Schubert experienced nor the corroding mental illness that tormented Schumann. But although his life was marked by fame and the friendship of some of the greatest artists of the time, it ended in a mortal illness and an early death. When he died at the age of thirty-nine, he left behind him a literature for the piano unequaled before or since, and his critics, borrowing a character from Shakespeare's *The Tempest,* dubbed him the "Ariel of the piano." He followed no national school of Romanticism, and one can be no more specific than to call him a European composer.

Chopin was born near Warsaw on February 22, 1810, of a French father and a Polish mother. His father, Nicolas, had come to Poland to teach French to the sons of the Polish nobility, and it was in these surroundings that Young Frederic received his formal education. He studied piano at the Warsaw School of Music, showing an early talent for the instrument. He gave his first public concert at the age of seven. By the age of fifteen, he had already published some compositions, and by nineteen he had achieved eminence in both composition and performance. He traveled widely through Europe and was received enthusiastically wherever he played. So cordial was the reception at Chopin's first concert in Paris, in 1831, that he decided to make that city his home and never again returned to Poland.

The public and his peers immediately recognized his genius, and he was in constant demand as a teacher and performer. He played frequently in Parisian salons, which had become the meeting places of the artists, musicians, and writers devoted to Romanticism. His circle of friends included the writers Victor Hugo, Honoré de Balzac, and Alexandre Dumas, the composers Liszt, Berlioz, and Schumann, and the painter Delacroix. Reviewing some of Chopin's works, Schumann wrote of him that he was the "boldest and proudest poetic spirit of the time." His admirers were legion and he was the recipient of almost fanatical acclaim.

Among the influential members of Parisian society was a woman novelist, Mme. Aurore Dudevant, who wrote under the name of George Sand. Through Liszt, Chopin met George Sand in 1837, when he was twenty-eight and she was thirty-four. It was a relationship that was to have a profound effect on his life, and though happy at first, their relationship became increasingly bitter. By the time Chopin developed tuberculosis in 1847, their once deep affection had deteriorated completely.

Fig. 12.5 Portrait of Chopin by his friend, the Romantic painter Delacroix.

In 1848, with the full knowledge that he was in failing health, Chopin traveled to England and Scotland, where he stayed for seven months. There his concerts and strenuous activities sapped his fast-ebbing strength. Heartbroken over the bitterness that accompanied the conclusion of his relationship with George Sand, his energies exhausted, he returned to Paris, where he spent his remaining months. The funeral following his death on October 17, 1849, was attended by the elite of Paris society, artists as well as aristocrats; only Mme. Sand was absent from among the mourners. As a final gesture to his homeland, he wished his heart to be returned to Poland, while his body was buried in Père Lachaise Cemetery in Paris.

CHOPIN'S WORK

Chopin wrote almost exclusively for the piano. His only major works that include orchestra are the Piano Concertos in F Minor and E Minor (Warsaw, 1830), written when he was twenty. These works still appear in the concert repertory.

The bulk of Chopin's music falls into one of three categories. The first consists of technical studies or **études.** Each of the études is built upon a single technical problem and usually develops a single musical motive. In many ways they summarize Chopin's conception of the technical possibilities of the piano. But they are more than mere exercises; they are also a series of miniature, abstract tone poems.

The second category consists of works composed in small, intimate forms, including preludes, waltzes, polonaises, and mazurkas. The influence of Polish melodies and rhythms on Chopin's style is most clearly demonstrated in the **polonaises** and **mazurkas.** These are Polish national dances in triple meter, with Slavic rhythmic patterns and folklike melodies. The simple dance forms are frequently expanded into fantasies and tone poems. Chopin's most intimate pieces are the **nocturnes** (night pieces). These were character pieces of melancholy mood with expressive melodies sounding over an arpeggiated accompaniment.

The third category consists of works written in relatively large, free form. It includes scherzos, ballades, and fantasies. The ballades and scherzos demonstrate Chopin's ability to work within large-scale forms. He was apparently the first to employ the term *ballade* for an instrumental piece. All of his ballades are in 6/4 or 6/8 meter, and Chopin borrowed freely from the existing sonata-allegro, rondo, and song forms to create this new and epic genre. Good examples of these large-form works are the Ballade No. 1 in G Minor (Opus 23, 1831) and the Ballade No. 2 in F Major (Opus 38, 1836–1839). Chopin adopted the scherzo, a piece in 3/4 meter moving at a rapid tempo, from Beethoven.

Two other pieces stand in a category by themselves: the Fantaisie in F Minor (Opus 49, 1840–1841) and the *Polonaise fantaisie* (Opus 61, 1845–1846). These two pieces are among Chopin's most monumental works.

It is significant that, contrary to the prevailing fashion of the time, none of Chopin's pieces bears a fanciful, romantic title. Chopin, a master at creating expressive atmosphere and mood, resisted using programmatic elements in his pieces.

There are no real precedents for Chopin's works. His compositions depend on no large standard forms. His music is whimsical, elegant, and enchanting. In the large compositions, beautiful melodies and sparkling harmonies weave arbitrary, free-flowing forms. In both the smaller and larger works there is considerable repetition, often with just a touch of ornamentation to add interest to the repeat. Chopin's pieces give the illusion of being improvised (something every Romantic composer longed to be able to do), but actually they are carefully and consciously constructed.

Chopin's music expresses sentiments ranging from melancholy to exultation, but he avoids empty virtuosity. The subtle qualities of his music are enhanced by the use of the performance technique called **rubato,** in which the melody is permitted to forge ahead or lag behind very slightly, while the accompaniment maintains a steady beat.

This ballade is one of Chopin's larger works. The repetition of three themes forms the structure of the ballade. Chopin deliberately obscures the form by interspersing beautiful and lengthy episodes, transitions, and a coda between the repetitions of themes. The emphasis on nonstructural material, as well as the absence of pauses between the sections, reinforces the sense of continuity and the apparently free-flowing and evolving character of the work.

BALLADE NO. 1 IN G MINOR (OPUS 23)
RECORD 4/SIDE 1

The piece opens with a short, improvisatory introduction; the subsequent first theme is a waltzlike melody in a minor key.

Example 12.5

A long transition section builds to a climax, and then subsides to a quiet imitation of horn calls. Theme 2, in a major key, is soft and lyrical, with an accompaniment of slowly arpeggiated chords in the left hand.

Example 12.6

Theme 3 follows immediately, still very soft but in somewhat faster note values and with a triplet figure in the melody.

Example 12.7

Theme 1 returns, this time over a pedal point, and is stated much more dramatically; there are several sudden changes of dynamics. Eventually it builds up to a *forte* restatement of Theme 2, with full chords in both hands. A very long episode follows, with brilliant passage work* and modulations; a long descending scale leads into another restatement of Theme 2, still *forte,* and with a faster-moving accompaniment than before. Theme 3 follows again, this time *forte,* but

---

*   Passage work refers to rapidly moving melodies using many notes.

grows quieter and introduces the final and abbreviated return of Theme 1, again over a pedal point. The coda is long, fast, and full of scales and arpeggios, utilizing the full range of the piano.

PIANO MUSIC OF LISZT

The third of the major Romantic composers who focused on compositions for the piano was Franz Liszt (1811–1886). An important and innovative composer of descriptive orchestral music, he was also a significant force in the creation of a new style for the piano.

Almost all of Liszt's compositions for the piano come from his early compositional years, until about 1840. During this period he not only wrote original works for the piano, but also transcribed operas and symphonies for the instrument. In so doing he attempted to find piano sonorities that could create the impression of the tone colors of an entire orchestra. His innovations in the area of sonority revealed possibilities in the instrument that no composer before him had imagined.

Liszt made important contributions to piano style as well as sonority. He acknowledged the originality of Chopin's style, but saw that it would not serve as the basis for a new general approach; it was too personal and intimate to be adopted by other composers. Instead, he created a grander, more dramatic style that exploited the orchestral possibilities of the instrument and demanded enormous technical skill on the part of the performer. (Indeed, the technical feats required to play Liszt's piano works make them very easy to identify.) But this virtuosity was not the empty showmanship that characterized much of the lesser music of the time; it was intimately bound up with the content and structure of his works.

We will discuss the music of Franz Liszt further in the next chapter.

SUMMARY

The Romantic movement sought a fusion of all art forms and a union of humankind with nature. In music, the Romantic style was characterized by a concentration on the lyrical and melodic aspects of a work. The carefully constructed forms of the Classical period were freely manipulated by Romantic composers.

The German lied became exceptionally popular in the early Romantic period and attracted the greatest composers of the time. In many ways the most important composer in this genre was Franz Schubert, who wrote more than six hundred songs in his brief lifetime.

The piano, which was ideally suited to both the intimate and brilliant aspects of Romanticism, was the favorite instrument of the period. The literature produced for the piano consisted of two main types: short, lyric pieces, similar in scope and feeling to the lieder, and larger exhibition pieces written for virtuoso performers. Three composers in particular realized the capabilities of the piano and developed a new type of literature for it.

Robert Schumann wrote works ranging from miniature character pieces to large, classically oriented sonatas and concertos. His style was free and flexible, alternating between the Romantic extremes of intimacy and brilliance.

Frederic Chopin wrote almost exclusively for the piano. His work falls into three main categories consisting of études, intimate forms, and large, free forms. With their rhapsodic melodies, his pieces often give the illusion of being improvised, but were actually very carefully constructed.

Franz Liszt, who transcribed a large number of operas and symphonies for the piano, discovered new ways of exploiting the orchestral possibilities of the instrument. In his compositions he replaced the empty showmanship of inferior Romantic music with a complex technique that was a structural element of his works.

NEW TERMS

art song

strophic

ballad (vocal)

through-composed

song cycle

character piece

étude

polonaise

mazurka

rubato

CHAPTER 13 | PROGRAM MUSIC

THE ROMANTIC ERA SAW THE RISE OF FASCINATING NEW FORMS OF instrumental music. Radical innovators such as Hector Berlioz and Franz Liszt were not content to stay within the confines of Classical forms, which they found limiting and not well suited to their melodically oriented music. Their chief problem was to find a means of making their longer instrumental pieces coherent without inhibiting the free flow of musical inspiration.

The solution that appealed to Berlioz, Liszt, and other composers who were committed to the Romantic ideal of unifying the arts was to use a nonmusical idea as the inspiration for the musical organization. Poems, visual objects, and natural phenomena not only provided the general suggestive impulses but, to varying extents, became the dominating ideas of particular pieces of music, determining shape and form. The use of the nonmusical idea thus became a primary force in the development of Romantic music. Frequently the composer had a detailed plan, often a story, in mind, and the music was correlated with it as closely as possible. Works of this kind are known as **program music.**

THE AGE OF PROGRAM MUSIC

Neither the principle nor the techniques of program and descriptive music were invented during the Romantic period. In fact, they extend far back into the medieval and Renaissance eras. We have already mentioned Clément Jannequin's *Chant des oiseaux* in which the singers imitate bird calls. In the Baroque period, Antonio Vivaldi depicted the scenes and activities of each season of the year in his violin concerto *The Four Seasons.* Johann Sebastian Bach contributed to the genre of program music with his *Capriccio on the Departure of a Beloved Brother* (1704), a set of descriptive movements for solo harpsichord. Beethoven's Sixth Symphony, the *Pastoral Symphony,* has descriptive titles attached to each of the five movements. They depict country scenes: "Merrymaking of the Peasants,"

"Storm," "Thankful Feelings after the Storm," and so forth. Certain natural effects, like bird calls and thunderstorms, are portrayed very clearly.

With all these early examples of programmatic techniques, why is the Romantic period always singled out as the age of program music? There is a very good reason: Romantic composers substituted the device of the nonmusical **program** (which contained the composer's explanation and comments) for the traditional methods of musical organization. The earlier composers, by contrast, had used programmatic technique in conjunction with their usual formal patterns. Beethoven's Sixth Symphony is essentially Classical in outline, with sonata-allegro movements, a scherzo—all the usual forms. The programmatic elements are subordinate to these forms. In fact, Beethoven warned that the descriptive titles were not to be taken too literally; the music was to be an "expression of feeling rather than a depiction of events."

Some Romantic composers, particularly those more oriented toward Classical forms, continued to use the techniques of program music in this subordinate way. Mendelssohn (whose work will be discussed in Chapter 14) is a prime example; several of his symphonies are descriptive, but they are still constructed along Classical lines. His *Italian Symphony* (1833) and *Scottish Symphony* (1842) are generalized landscape paintings. The former includes images of the sunny, vibrant south, with peasant dances and chanting pilgrims; the latter depicts the gray and somber north, using the heroic ballads of the area and the swirl of bagpipes. Here the relation of music to the extramusical element is general.

The more radical Romantic composers used programmatic techniques in a very direct and dramatic way. Among the most radical was Hector Berlioz, whose compositions centered on the grand forms of opera, oratorio, the symphony, and the Mass.

BERLIOZ (1803-1869)

Hector Berlioz (Behr'-lee-ohz) grew up in a small town near Grenoble, France. Hector was expected to follow his father's profession and was sent to medical school in Paris. However, by his own inclinations he was drawn to the opera and the music library. When he appeared in class, he would annoy his fellow students by humming at the dissecting table. Finally, to the fury of his father, he quit the study of medicine to become a composer.

At twenty-three Berlioz began what he called "the great drama of my life." At a performance of *Hamlet* he was overwhelmed, both by "the lightning-flash" of Shakespeare's genius and "the dramatic genius" of Harriet Smithson, who played Ophelia. Berlioz tried to meet the actress, but his wild letters convinced her that he was a lunatic.

In 1830, on his fifth attempt, Berlioz won the Prix de Rome—a composition prize offered at the Paris Conservatory. In that year he also wrote the *Symphonie fantastique,* the outpouring of his passion for Harriet Smithson. When the composition was performed in Paris two years later, Harriet Smithson was in the audience. Realizing that the music was about her, she felt (according to Berlioz) "as if the room reeled." They were married a year later, but the romantic dream faded and several years later they separated.

Although he had become successful, Berlioz had difficulty getting his work performed. His music soon ceased to appeal to most of "the frivolous and fickle public." Both to support his family and to promote an understanding of the kind of music he advocated, Berlioz wrote musical criticism. He also wrote a fascinating prose autobiography. In it he emerges as a Romantic hero, falling in love, scheming murder, talking politics, passionately composing. He conducted performances of his own works throughout most of Europe, but in Paris he was ignored for various honors and conducting posts. Increasingly bitter, his energies spent, he did not compose during the last seven years of his life.

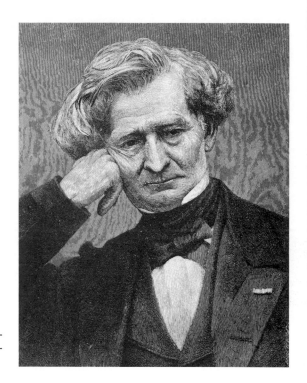

Fig. 13.1 In his passionate emotionalism, daring experimentation, and rich imagination, Berlioz epitomized the nineteenth-century Romantic spirit.

BERLIOZ'S WORK

Perhaps Berlioz's greatest contribution to music was in the art of orchestration. In his music, tone color was as prominent an element as melody or harmony. He experimented extensively with individual instruments and devised many unusual blends, combining bells with brasses and directing violinists to strike the strings with their bow sticks. In 1844 he wrote his treatise on orchestration, the first comprehensive text on the subject and a work that is still in use today.

Berlioz's ideas were grandiose, and he wanted to carry them out on a grandiose scale. The first performance of *Symphonie fantastique* was thwarted because there were not enough chairs and music stands for the performers. At a time when orchestras usually numbered sixty players, Berlioz's ideal (never realized) was an orchestra of two hundred and forty strings, thirty harps, thirty grand pianos, and wind and percussion to scale!

Berlioz's major works are immense and dramatic. He usually composed from a literary text, favoring plays, epic poems, and novels. Works inspired by Shakespeare include the "dramatic symphony" *Romeo and Juliet* (1839), the *King Lear* overture (1831), and the opera *Béatrice et Bénédict* (1860–1862). The *Waverly* and *Rob Roy* overtures (c. 1827 and 1832) are based on the novels of Sir Walter Scott, and *Harold in Italy* (1834), a program symphony, on the poem by Byron. Berlioz also composed massive choral works as well as choral pieces of modest proportion. These are covered briefly in Chapter 16.

The *Symphonie fantastique* is a powerful musical drama in five movements. It is based on the following program, drawn from Berlioz's own experience:

SYMPHONIE FANTASTIQUE
RECORD 4/SIDE 2

Introduction

A young musician of extraordinary sensibility and abundant imagination, in the depths of despair because of hopeless love, has poisoned himself with opium. The drug is too feeble to kill him but plunges him into a heavy sleep accompanied by weird visions. His sensations, emotions, and memories, as they pass through his affected mind, are transformed into musical images and ideas. The beloved one herself becomes to him a melody, a recurrent theme (idée fixe) *which haunts him continually.*

I. Reveries. Passions

First he remembers that weariness of the soul, that indefinable longing, that somber melancholia, and those objectless joys which he experienced before meeting his beloved. Then, the volcanic love with which she at once inspired him, his delirious suffering, his return to tenderness, his religious consolations.

II. A Ball

At a ball, in the midst of a noisy, brilliant fête, he finds his beloved again.

III. In the Country

On a summer evening in the country, he hears two herders calling each other with their shepherd melodies. The pastoral duet in such surroundings, the gentle rustle of the trees softly swayed by the wind, some reasons for hope which had come to his knowledge recently—all unite to fill his heart with a rare tranquility and lend brighter colors to his fancies. But his beloved appears anew, spasms contract his heart, and he is filled with dark premonition. What if she proves faithless? Only one of the shepherds resumes his rustic tune. The sun sets. Far away there is rumbling thunder—solitude—silence.

IV. March to the Scaffold

He dreams he has killed his loved one, that he is condemned to death and led to his execution. A march, now gloomy and ferocious, now solemn and brilliant, accompanies the procession. Noisy outbursts are followed without pause by the heavy sound of measured footsteps. Finally, like a last thought of love, the idée fixe *appears for a moment, to be cut off by the fall of the axe.*

V. Dream of a Witches' Sabbath

*He sees himself at a Witches' Sabbath surrounded by a fearful crowd of specters, sorcerers, and monsters of every kind, united for his burial. Unearthly sounds, groans, shrieks of laughter, distant cries, to which others seem to respond! The melody of his beloved is heard, but it has lost its character of nobility and reserve. Instead, it is now an ignoble dance tune, trivial and grotesque. It is she who comes to the Sabbath! A shout of joy greets her arrival. She joins the diabolical orgy. The funeral knell, burlesque of the Dies Irae. Dance of the Witches. The dance and the Die Irae combined.**

* Translation from Hector Berlioz, *Symphonie Fantastique* (New York: Edition Eulenburg, Inc.), p. iii.

Berlioz felt that the audience did not have to be aware of this program; he intended the musical work to be self-sufficient. However, the program does serve to introduce the music and explains the situation that inspired each movement.

The *Symphonie fantastique* was revolutionary in its use of a single melody to link the five movements. This musical *idée fixe* ("fixed idea") represents the hero's image of his beloved and recurs in various transformations throughout the piece. In the second movement it becomes a waltz tune; in the fourth, it reappears fleetingly just before the fall of the axe; and in the fifth, it becomes a grotesque witches' dance. Here is the *idée fixe* in some of its various guises:

Example 13.1

Berlioz's rich Romantic imagination and inventiveness are evident in practically every measure of the *Symphonie fantastique*. These qualities, as well as his daring experimentations in orchestration, greatly influenced later composers such as Debussy and Stravinsky.

LISZT (1811-1886)

Franz Liszt was another important composer of Romantic program music. He considered the music and its program as parallel works of art, evoking the same feelings in different media.

Next to his good friend and admirer, Hector Berlioz, Liszt stands as the supreme Romantic of the nineteenth century. As a virtuoso pianist, a renowned lover, and a friend and supporter of almost all the great composers of his time, Liszt embodied what subsequent generations have come to consider as the Romantic ideal.

Born in Hungary, the son of a steward of the Esterhazy family, he began his instruction on the piano at the age of six. Following a number of successful concert appearances as a boy, a group of Hungarian nobles offered an annual stipend over a six-year period to further his musical training. In 1821 his family moved to Vienna, where Liszt took lessons from the famous teacher Carl Czerny and studied theory with Antonio Salieri. His public appearances were so successful that his father took him to Paris. There he continued to develop his piano technique on his own, studied composition under Anton Reicha, and began a series of extended concert tours. After the death of his father in 1827, Liszt settled permanently in Paris. In 1831, after attending a recital by the virtuoso Italian violinist Niccolò Paganini, he determined to adapt Paganini's extraordinary technical feats to the piano. From Paganini, more than anyone else, he derived his style of showmanship.

Though Liszt was flamboyant in personality and performance, his mannerisms never outshone his musicianship. As a pianist he held firmly to the idea that the interpreter's duty was to reveal the innermost intention of the composer, and his understanding of Beethoven's piano works was no less intimate than it was of Chopin's compositions.

During the 1830s he carried on a love affair with the Countess Marie d'Agoult and

Fig. 13.2 Liszt, a virtuoso artist of great physical attractiveness and personal charm, enthralled audiences of the nineteenth century much as a movie or rock star does those of today.

settled with her in Switzerland. (One of the three children born to them, Cosima, later married Richard Wagner.) In 1848 he found a firm position, as court music director at Weimar, from which to promote the "new music" of such composers as Berlioz and Wagner. At Weimar he continued his second great love affair, with the Princess Carolyne von Sayn-Wittgenstein, whom he had met during a concert tour of Russia. In 1859, feeling a call to the priesthood, he settled in Rome and took minor orders, and in 1866 Pope Pius IX conferred on him the title of Abbé. After 1870 he divided his time among Rome, Weimar, and Budapest, surrounded always by a throng of friends, students, and admirers. He died in Bayreuth during the Wagner festival of 1886.

LISZT'S WORK

Liszt's greatest achievement as an orchestral composer was his development of the **symphonic poem** or **tone poem,** a single-movement programmatic work, relatively long, and very free in form. Liszt's tone poems have descriptive titles, but they derive their basic unity from purely musical elements rather than from non-musical ideas. In this sense Liszt's concept of program music is closer to Beethoven's than to Berlioz's. His tone poems are unified by a single theme or melody which he continuously transforms through changes in tempo, dynamics, and orchestration. In *Les préludes* (1854), discussed below, a three-note motive is used to construct a variety of themes: in one section it is used to suggest love; in another it becomes a pastoral theme; in still another it takes on a martial character. This technique (which was not unique to Liszt) is called **theme transformation.** Liszt composed thirteen tone poems, mostly at Weimar; but only one, *Les préludes,* remains in the concert repertory today.

Liszt's other important works for orchestra include a symphony based on Dante's *Divina Commedia* (1867) and the very popular *Mephisto Waltzes* (the first in 1860, the second in 1880). For piano and orchestra Liszt wrote two concertos (No. 1 in 1849, revised in 1853; No. 2 in 1848, revised 1856–1861) and the *Totentanz* (*Dance of Death,* 1849; revised 1853–1859), which is a symphonic paraphrase of the medieval funeral chant, the *Dies Irae.*

The vocal works include three large-scale Masses for chorus and orchestra, a Requiem, a number of psalm settings, and three oratorios.

Liszt's piano music includes an enormous variety of forms and styles: variations on well-known symphonic and operatic themes, brilliant showpieces, technical studies, and impressionistic tone poems. The *Hungarian Rhapsodies* and *Liebestraum* (*Love Dream,* c. 1850), are among his best-known piano pieces. One of his most significant large-scale piano works is the one-movement Sonata in B Minor (1853), in which four themes are worked out and transformed in a free, rhapsodic manner.

In addition to his original compositions, Liszt transcribed a large number of orchestral and operatic works for piano and performed his transcriptions on his concert tours. In an age that lacked radio, television, and recording mechanisms, Liszt's concerts brought otherwise unavailable music to large segments of the public. His transcriptions included selections from all of Wagner's major operas, Weber's *Der Freischütz,* Verdi's *Rigoletto* and *Aida,* complete versions of all of Beethoven's symphonies, Berlioz's *Symphonie fantastique* and *Harold in Italy,* overtures by Weber, Rossini, and Berlioz, and his own orchestral tone poems.

LES PRÉLUDES
RECORD 4/SIDE 2

The best known of Liszt's symphonic poems, *Les préludes* was originally written as the orchestral overture to a choral work but Liszt later decided to publish it separately. Looking for a suitable program, he was struck by the parallel construction of one of Alphonse de Lamartine's *Méditations poétiques.* He translated it freely and adopted it as the program for his composition.

Préludes

What is our life but a series of Preludes to that unknown song, the first solemn note of which is sounded by Death? The enchanted dawn of every existence is heralded by Love, yet in whose destiny are not the first throbs of happiness interrupted by storms whose violent blasts dissipate his fond illusions, consuming his altar with fatal fire? And where is to be found the cruelly bruised soul, that having become the sport of one of these tempests does not seek oblivion in the sweet quiet of rural life? Nevertheless, man seldom resigns himself to the beneficent calm which at first chained him to Nature's bosom. No sooner does the trumpet sound the alarm, than he runs to the post of danger, be the war what it may that summons him to its ranks. For there he will find again in the struggle complete self-realization and the full possession of his forces.

Liszt composed *Les préludes* for a full Romantic orchestra—flutes, oboes, clarinets, bassoons, four horns, trumpets, trombones, tuba, timpani (three drums), harp, and strings. For the finale (the section analogous to the call to battle), a side drum, cymbals, and a bass drum are added. The manner in which the orchestra is used is also typically Romantic: the winds are often used as solo instruments; the French horn, a favorite Romantic instrument, is particularly prominent; fluctuations in tempo and dynamics occur frequently.

Fig. 13.3 Franz Liszt at the piano. At his feet, Marie d'Agoult; in the armchair, dressed as a man, George Sand; near her, Alexandre Dumas; behind them, Victor Hugo; in the background, Paganini and Rossini. Painting by J. Danhauser, 1840.

The stages of life mentioned in the poem correspond to the sections of Liszt's piece. It opens with a brief introduction, built on a three-note motive

Example 13.2

that will later be used in the construction of most of the themes in the composition. The opening is slow and tentative. The motive gradually expands by enlarging its second interval

Example 13.3

and eventually leads to the first theme. It is an expansive and majestic melody, vaguely related to the opening motive. The accompanying figure includes a direct statement of the motive.

Example 13.4

The next section, which reflects the mention of love in the poem, contains two themes. The first,

Example 13.5

is introduced by the low strings and then is treated as a horn solo in another key. The opening motive is quite prominent in this theme. The second theme (played by the four horns, and the violas divided into four sections) has the notes of the motive spaced out, with other material in between.

Example 13.6

x indicates the notes of the basic motive.

Eventually these two themes are used simultaneously.

In the section of the piece corresponding to the storm, rushing chromatic patterns are interlaced with brief statements of the basic motive. Frequent changes of tempo increase the sense of agitation. As the storm subsides, the first love theme returns and leads to a section corresponding to the "sweet calm of rural life." The beginning of this lovely section, with its pastoral theme,

Example 13.7

features the woodwinds. Soon the strings join in and the second love theme is added to the pastoral tune.

A gradual increase in tempo, dynamics, and intensity leads to the climactic finale, the call to battle. The final section opens with a transformation of the first love theme into a march sounded by the horns and trumpets.

Example 13.8

A bridge leads to a marchlike variation of the second love theme, with drums and cymbals added to the rest of the orchestra. Eventually the section returns to the majestic first theme, accompanied by the basic motive, and the piece comes to a vigorous conclusion.

RICHARD STRAUSS

Although the life of the late Romantic composer Richard Strauss (1864–1949) extended nearly halfway through the twentieth century, the bulk of his tone poems were written in the nineteenth century. These works exhibit the influences of both the detailed descriptions of Berlioz and the less specific descriptions of Liszt. Thus, *Tod und Verklärung* (*Death and Transfiguration,* 1889) and *Also sprach Zarathustra* (*Thus Spake Zarathustra,* 1896) have general, philosophical programs, while the comic *Till Eulenspiegels lustige Streiche* (*Till Eulenspiegel's Merry Pranks,* 1895) and *Don Quixote* (1897) have more specific programs.

Strauss was a skilled composer, a virtuoso at writing effectively for large orchestra. Although his thematic inventions were rarely profound, they were always fresh and uninhibited. A practical musician, Strauss realized that he was not innovative enough to follow in Liszt's steps, with essentially programless tone poems. He therefore chose to continue the detailed programs of Berlioz, but incorporated some of the supreme musicianship that marks Liszt's works.

A knowledge of the program is essential to the understanding of a Strauss tone poem. The explanations and comments are an integral part of the work and help give it coherence.

The program of Richard Strauss's tone poem *Don Quixote* (1897) is taken from the great Spanish satirical novel of the same title, written in the early seventeenth century by Miguel de Cervantes. Don Quixote is a gentle, dignified, and rather simpleminded old man who becomes slightly addled by reading about the Age of Chivalry. He decides that he must become a knight, seeking adventure and revenging wrongs.

DON QUIXOTE (OPUS 35)

Fig. 13.4 Strauss was not the only one to be attracted to Cervantes's foolish but invincible character Don Quixote. The addle-pated knight was also a favorite subject of the painter and lithographer Honoré Daumier, who depicts him riding forth toward another imagined adventure.

Strauss selected a series of episodes from Cervantes's tale and depicted them in a set of ten freely constructed variations on two themes, which represent Don Quixote and his squire, Sancho Panza. These musical characterizations are enhanced by assigning particular instruments to each man. A solo cello portrays Quixote, described as "The Knight of the Sorrowful Countenance"; Sancho Panza is depicted by a solo viola, with occasional help from the bass clarinet and tenor tuba.

The variations on these two themes are freer than those encountered in earlier music; no attempt is made to preserve the structure or the harmonic pattern of the themes. In fact, it might be more accurate to consider these "fantastic variations" (as Strauss himself subtitled them) as short episodes or rhapsodies on the themes, transformed to suit the particular adventures the composer selected.

Here is a brief summary of the program:

VARIATION I. Don Quixote mistakes a windmill for a giant and attacks it; he is dumped from his horse.

VARIATION II. Mistaking a herd of sheep for an enemy army, Quixote manages to kill several before the shepherd stones him.

VARIATION III. Quixote's sentimentality and Panza's practical nature are contrasted in conversation between the knight and his squire.

VARIATION IV. Quixote encounters a procession of pilgrims, attacks them, and is routed; they continue on their way.

VARIATION V. Standing watch by his weapons at night, Quixote dreams of his lady love, Dulcinea.

VARIATION VI. Quixote and Panza meet three village girls; Panza tries to persuade his knight that one of them is Dulcinea, but Quixote is not fooled.

VARIATION VII. The adventurers imagine a ride through the air as they sit blindfolded on a wooden horse.

VARIATION VIII. Finding an oarless boat, they embark and capsize.

VARIATION IX. Mistaking two Benedictine monks for evil magicians, Quixote puts them to flight.

VARIATION X. Quixote is defeated in a duel with another knight, and returns home in humiliation.

EPILOGUE. Don Quixote's mind clears, and he meditates over his imagined adventures; death comes, and he faces it in a noble and dignified manner.

SUMMARY

Because they chose to abandon the Classical forms, some Romantic composers were forced to find new ways of unifying their larger instrumental works. A favorite method was to correlate the music with a nonmusical idea, frequently a story. Such music is known as program music.

Although Beethoven used programmatic elements in his music, he cautioned his listeners that the music was to be "an expression of feelings rather than a depiction." The more traditional Romantic composers followed his lead in subordinating the nonmusical idea. Mendelssohn, in particular, wrote symphinies that were called descriptive but that were clearly unified within the Classical structure.

The more radical Romantic composers used the programmatic technique more directly. Hector Berlioz supplied detailed programs with several of his larger works. These works derive their unity from the occurrence of versions of the same musical theme in each movement (*idée fixe*) and from the unity of the narratives they present.

Franz Liszt wrote single-movement works in a new and relatively free form which he devised, called the symphonic or tone poem. Each piece was unified by a single theme or melody which Liszt continuously transformed through changes in tempo, dynamics, and orcestration. This technique, called theme transformation, was also employed by other Romantic composers.

Richard Strauss combined influences from both Berlioz and Liszt in the tone poems he wrote near the turn of the century. Unlike Liszt, however, Strauss depended heavily on the text to unify his works. The explanations and comments are integral parts of his tone poems, helping to give them coherence.

NEW TERMS

program music   **symphonic poem (tone poem)**
program   **theme transformation**
idée fixe

14 | **THE ROMANTIC TRADITIONALISTS**

AS WE SAW IN CHAPTER 13, SOME OF THE MORE RADICAL ROMANTIC composers abandoned the Classical forms altogether, turning instead to nonmusical sources for inspiration and as frameworks for organizing new musical forms. At the same time, a stream of Classical tradition continued to flow through the Romantic period, as a number of composers cultivated and expanded the traditional forms in both orchestral and chamber music. In so doing, they utilized elements from two periods of music history. Though essentially Classical in broad design, their works were richly endowed with Romantic harmonies, color, dynamics, theme constructions, and orchestration. The leading composers in this group were Franz Schubert, Felix Mendelssohn, Johannes Brahms, and the Russian Peter Ilyich Tchaikovsky.

THE ROMANTIC SYMPHONY

The Romantic symphony grew in the shadow of Beethoven's symphonic writing. Virtually all the early Romantic composers were affected by Beethoven's music, some by his use of the orchestra, others by his expansion of form.

Early in the Romantic period, the symphonic writing of Franz Schubert was influenced first by Haydn and Mozart and finally by Beethoven. Schubert's last two symphonies, the *Unfinished Symphony* (1822) and the big C Major (1828), take their place along with those of Beethoven in the repertoire.

If Schubert was the outstanding symphonist of the beginning of the Romantic period, Johannes Brahms deserves that honor for the latter part of the century. Brahms occupies a unique place in the history of the Romantic movement. Although he was much admired by his contemporaries, he had no wish to seek new forms of musical expression and new sources of musical inspiration. He disagreed with the popular Romantic notion—championed by more radical composers such as Berlioz and Wagner—that literature, the visual arts, and philosophy should be united with music. In a period of experimentation and change, he looked back to Beethoven and the Classical era, finding in traditional forms new and worthwhile ideas to express.

Schubert
Mendelssohn
Brahms
mahler
Bruckner

THE ROMANTIC TRADITIONALISTS   **253**

BRAHMS (1833–1897)

Born and raised in Hamburg, Johannes Brahms received his earliest musical training from his father, a double-bass player. The family was not wealthy and at an early age Brahms had to contribute to the family income by playing the piano in local taverns. At the age of twenty he met the famed Hungarian violinist Eduard Reményi and toured Germany as Reményi's accompanist. On one of his tours, his first attempts at composition were heard by Joseph Joachim, the foremost violin virtuoso of the time. Through Joachim, Brahms was introduced to Franz Liszt and Robert Schumann, who were both greatly impressed by the young composer. Schumann, always eager to do what he could to advance the career of young, promising composers, wrote a laudatory article heralding Brahms as the coming genius of German music.

Fig. 14.1 Brahms at the age of thirty-four.

Schumann and his wife, Clara, welcomed Brahms into their home. After Schumann suffered his mental collapse, the devoted friendship of Brahms enabled Clara to survive the tragedy of her husband's illness. Their friendship grew to love even though she was fourteen years Brahms's senior. When Schumann died in a Bonn asylum, Brahms was at Clara's side. After Schumann's death, however, the passion subsided into a lifelong friendship and Brahms never married Clara Schumann.

In his thirties, Brahms took several posts in various German towns, conducting and organizing choral groups and music societies. He spent much of his time in Vienna, finally settling there in 1878. His reputation as a composer grew to international proportions, and in 1878 Cambridge University offered him the degree of Doctor of Music. He declined, being reluctant to make the long journey, but he accepted a similar honor from the University of Breslau, acknowledging it by writing the celebrated *Academic Festival Overture,* which is based in large part on popular German student songs.

Brahms was not a controversial figure, as so many of his contemporaries were, and he had no enemies. Yet in his dealings with others his characteristic charm could give way to the most acerbic sarcasm. To one musician who was trying to maneuver Brahms into paying him a compliment, he said, "Yes, you have talent, but very little." But when the daughter of Johann Strauss (the "Waltz King" of Vienna) presented him with her fan so that he might autograph it, he wrote on it the first few measures of Strauss's *Blue Danube Waltz* and signed it, "Not, alas, by Johannes Brahms."

Brahms remained a bachelor all his life, living simply and composing methodically. He enjoyed the respect and admiration of his peers, inspiring the noted conductor Hans von Bülow to coin his famous phrase, "the Three B's of Music," which placed Brahms on the same level of genius as Bach and Beethoven. After his death, his fame grew as many societies were founded to publish and perform his works. In the concert repertoire, Brahms's symphonies occupy a place second only to that of his acknowledged master, Beethoven.

BRAHMS'S WORK

With few exceptions Brahms composed in all the familiar instrumental and choral idioms of the nineteenth century. He was a careful and disciplined composer who frequently revised his earlier works.

Brahms did not attempt to compose symphonies until quite late in his life. His first symphony (in C minor) took him twenty-one years to write and was not finished until 1876. Three others followed during the next nine years: No. 2 (in D major, 1877), No. 3 (in F major, 1883) and No. 4 (in E minor, 1884–1885). These works remain as some of the most frequently performed symphonies in modern times.

Brahms's masterful symphonic style was developed through the composition of serenades, concertos, and overtures. His first orchestral composition was a Serenade in D Major (1857–1858), followed by his first piano concerto (in D minor, 1858). His other concertos include the renowned Violin Concerto in D Major (1878), the second piano concerto (in B-flat major, 1878–1881), and the Double Concerto in A Minor for violin and cello (1887). His overtures include the *Academic Festival Overture* (1880) and the *Tragic Overture* (1880–1881). Falling into none of these categories is the very popular *Variations on a Theme by Haydn* (1873).

Choral music, both sacred and secular, attracted Brahms throughout his career. His *Ein Deutsches Requiem* (*A German Requiem,* 1857–1868), analyzed in Chapter 16, ranks as one of the choral masterpieces of the nineteenth century.

Brahms's contributions to chamber music repertory were the most substantial of those made by any nineteenth-century composer after Beethoven. Among them are duos, trios, quartets, and quintets for a variety of instrumental combinations. His piano works reveal a mastery of contrapuntal texture and require virtuoso performance technique. They include variations on themes by Schumann, Paganini, and Handel, three sonatas, and a number of short lyric pieces including ballades, rhapsodies, fantasies, and intermezzi.

HIS SYMPHONIC STYLE

Brahms retained the traditional four-movement structure of the late Classical symphony: fast, slow, scherzo-like, fast. In many ways his style is a direct outgrowth of the symphonic style of Beethoven: he continued to expand sonata-allegro form, enlarge the orchestra, and use dynamics and sonorities as structural elements.

Brahms's use of sonata-allegro form involves some changes, primarily in the treatment of the bridge section and the coda. The bridge becomes much more important; its material often sounds like a genuine theme, and it is often difficult to distinguish between the bridge and second theme on first hearing. The first and second themes are still contrasted in the Classical manner, but there is often no noticeable separation (such as a rest) between them.

The beginning of the recapitulation is sometimes obscure because Brahms tends to lead into it unobtrusively; frequently the exposition material reappears with different instrumentation, a device Beethoven used. The coda is extended, as in Beethoven's works, and used as a second development section. In contrast to Beethoven, however, Brahms often ends movements very quietly.

One of Brahms's favorite structural devices is to build new themes out of short motives taken from earlier material. This brings an additional element of unity to a movement, beyond that provided by sonata-allegro form. Brahms often incorporates the motive into themes in a subtle way, and it appears in many rhythmic variations.

Brahms uses a slightly larger orchestra than Beethoven, with still more important roles given to the lower strings, winds, and brasses. Lyrical themes are often assigned to the violas and cellos, a choice that contributes to the warm, dark tone colors that characterize much of his symphonic music. Brahms's orchestra includes four French horns, which are given important parts. Trombones continue to be part of the orchestra, and a tuba is added. The timpani are often treated independently, and even have solo passages. Although Brahms's orchestra is large by Classical standards, it is conservative in comparison with the huge ensembles used by more radical Romantic composers such as Berlioz and Wagner.

Brahms's Symphony No. 2 well illustrates the composer's manipulation and expansion of Classical forms.

SYMPHONY NO. 2 IN D MAJOR

FIRST MOVEMENT: *ALLEGRO NON TROPPO*
(SONATA-ALLEGRO FORM)

Exposition Theme 1 is divided between two groups of instruments. It begins with a three-note motive in the cellos and basses, and continues with additional material, first in the horns and bassoons and then in the upper winds.

Example 14.1

It is typical of Brahms to disperse a theme among several instruments or instrumental groups. Their instrumental colors become part of the theme, and thus the theme can be effectively varied by changing its instrumentation. In the bridge the basic motive is incorporated into a melodic phrase which is heard first in the violins. Later the time values of the motive are cut in half (the technique known as diminution)

Example 14.2

and a modulatory section leads to Theme 2.

Theme 2 has two distinct components, arranged in ABA form. The A section is a long, lyrical melody, introduced by the lower strings. The B part of the theme begins with a loud, jagged, syncopated idea, followed by another rhythmic variation of the basic motive. After this lengthy variation the A section is restated by the strings with a highly decorative flute accompaniment. A short closing section completes the exposition. Although Brahms intended the exposition to be repeated, most conductors today ignore his intentions.

Development The development section opens with the basic three-note motive in the low strings and the remainder of Theme 1 in the horns, as was done in the exposition. The motive is answered by a new phrase from the oboe. This new idea is taken from the horn part, and it is the inversion (upside-down version) of the basic motive. Soon the original second half of Theme 1 is brought into play, as it was in the exposition, and builds to a fortissimo climax. The trombones interrupt with overlapping statements of the basic motive, which is taken up by other instruments. After another Beethovenian climax, the melodic bridge material returns in the winds, and is answered by yet another new idea from the oboe, again using the basic motive. For a period of time, all these themes are interwoven. Then, with a change of dynamics from fortissimo to piano, a false recapitulation begins, followed immediately by the bridge material. This builds to another climax, which leads into the true recapitulation.

Recapitulation In the recapitulation Theme 1 returns in the oboes instead of the horns, accompanied by the bridge material in the viola. Theme 2 is introduced by a series of descending arpeggios, a timpani roll, and a short pause. Again Theme 2 appears in ABA form; the first A section has flutes and clarinets added above it. The B section of the theme, with its jagged, syncopated pattern, followed by a version of the basic motive, is restated quite literally. Following the return of the A section, a series of descending scales and a deceptive cadence lead to the coda.

Coda The coda of this movement includes two new themes, both built from earlier material. The first new theme is a long solo for the French horn (one of the favorite instruments of the Romantic period), built from the inversion of the basic motive. The violins introduce the second new theme, which is related to the first, while the cellos and basses play the basic motive. This builds to a climax and subsides to a quiet version of the basic motive at double speed. A rapid crescendo leads to the final climax, and then the movement gradually subsides. After isolated statements of thematic fragments and the basic motive, getting softer and softer, the winds sustain a final chord.

SECOND MOVEMENT: *ADAGIO NON TROPPO*

This movement combines features of several formal procedures, without strictly adhering to any of them. Basically, the movement consists of a number of themes, some of which are developed, most of which are recapitulated.

The movement opens with Theme A, a slow, lyric melody played by the cellos and partially restated by the flutes and violins. The horn begins Theme B, which is treated contrapuntally, with entrances heard in the oboe, flute, and cello parts. The following C section, with a prevailing off-beat triplet pattern, is remotely related to the first part of A.

The rising triplet theme of the D section is introduced by the strings, and then taken up by the winds:

Example 14.3

This is the most steadily driving section of the movement. The section builds to a loud climax, which is followed by several soft statements of the opening triplet figure of the D material. After another climactic build-up, and more isolated thematic fragments, there begins what seems to be a recapitulation but proves to be only a further development of Theme A.

The real recapitulation of A is carefully disguised; only the last section of the theme is presented in its original, undecorated form. The recapitulation of the B section has the theme in the flutes and horns, and is then somewhat altered in the lower strings. The C section never appears in the recapitulation. The D theme is stated once, after a false beginning, and then becomes fragmented. The short coda returns to the A material, with triplets in the horns and timpani. The movement ends quietly.

THIRD MOVEMENT: *ALLEGRETTO GRAZIOSO—PRESTO MA NON ASSAI*

With this movement Brahms has written a cross between the minuet and trio of the earlier Classical symphony and the Beethovenian scherzo that developed from it. This is a light, graceful movement, basically in triple meter, and very sectionalized. It is organized into a five-part alternating form ABACA, and the large sections are clearly distinguished by changes in meter and tempo. Several of the individual sections can also be divided into aba subsections. Almost all the musical material is derived from the opening theme.

FOURTH MOVEMENT: *ALLEGRO CON SPIRITO* (SONATA-ALLEGRO FORM)

The final movement of the Second Symphony is one of the most confident and jubilant movements Brahms ever wrote. The usual sonata-allegro form is followed, and the contrast between the two themes is particularly notable. The first, although quiet, is brisk and sparkling, while the second theme is a lyrical, expressive melody, played at a slower tempo. Though they sound quite different, both themes are based on the original three-note motive that opened the symphony. By relating the first and last movements of the symphony in this way, Brahms provided an uncommon degree of unity to the entire work. This desire to make a four-movement structure into a single entity is typical of much Romantic music.

The statement of Theme 1 is followed by a very long bridge leading to Theme 2. The closing section of the exposition is also very developmental, with many sudden changes of dynamics.

The development section opens with a restatement of Theme 1, and most of the development is based on this theme. Several changes of tempo occur, and the section ends slowly and softly. The recapitulation begins with a sudden resumption of the original tempo and proceeds through abbreviated versions of the first theme and bridge. The second theme is louder and more emphatic than it had been originally. A long coda ends with a great crashing finale, at the climax of which the trumpets and trombones play a stirring, marchlike version of the once-lyrical second theme.

OTHER ROMANTIC SYMPHONISTS

ANTON BRUCKNER

Anton Bruckner (1824–1896), an Austrian composer and organist, joined Brahms in the effort to retain Classical forms within an expanded harmonic and structural framework. Bruckner was a simple and very religious man, deeply involved with Catholic mysticism. Symphonic in technique, his three Masses are of sufficient caliber to rank Bruckner as the most important church composer of the late nineteenth century.

Bruckner's nine symphonies show his kinship to Classical tradition in their formal design, but their exceptional length and weighty orchestration mark them as Romantic works. Wagner was one of Bruckner's idols, and Bruckner's emphasis on chromatic tones and shifting tonalities shows Wagner's influence. (We shall consider Wagner in detail in Chapter 17.) Bruckner, in turn, influenced later composers in his native Vienna, particularly Mahler and Schoenberg.

GUSTAV MAHLER

The Austrian Gustav Mahler (1860–1911) was a conductor as well as a symphonic composer. His nine completed symphonies are immense and complex, and encompass a vast emotional range. Although the symphonies follow the Classical outline and have separate movements, their style incorporates many elements from vocal music, including opera. His symphonies contain long, lyrical melodies, often treated contrapuntally; four of them have parts for voices as well as instruments. Mahler's works span the spectrum of emotions, from ecstasy to despair. He tried to make each symphony a complete world in itself, with all types of themes and techniques. These large-scale works are unified, to some extent, by the use of recurring themes and motives.

Mahler is also famous for his songs and song cycles; the *Kindertotenlieder* (*Songs on the Death of Children,* 1902) and *Das Lied von der Erde* (*The Song of the Earth,* 1908) are particularly outstanding. Themes from the songs are often quoted in the symphonic works. Mahler's last works—the Ninth Symphony, the unfinished Tenth, and *Das Lied von der Erde*—are in a more contrapuntal style than his earlier compositions. They also show a weaker sense of tonality and thus point toward the important developments in atonal music in the early twentieth century.

THE ROMANTIC CONCERTO ✓

As we pointed out in Chapter 12, Romantic audiences were dazzled by exhibitions of virtuosity. All through the Romantic era there was a steady growth of virtuoso technique, particularly on the piano and the violin. The trend was begun by Beethoven, whose works were considerably more difficult to play than Mozart's. It was spurred on in 1820 by the arrival on the European concert stage of Niccolò Paganini (1782–1840); this phenomenal Italian violinist astounded and enchanted all who heard him by the incredible speed and brilliance of his playing.

element of virtuosity solo becomes difficult

The concerto for solo instrument and orchestra, with the improvised quality of its cadenza section, lent itself especially well to displays of technical skill. Composers wrote very difficult solo parts in their concertos. Unfortunately, many second-rate Romantic composers mistook virtuosity for substance; thus, the majority of Romantic concertos were either pleasant pieces or bombastic tirades, full of technical acrobatics but essentially meaningless.

cadenza for solo instrument at end of 1st movement become complicated

The master composers of the period, however, joined virtuoso technique to lyric and expressive writing. Robert Schumann, Johannes Brahms, Felix Mendelssohn, and Peter Ilyich Tchaikovsky all wrote outstanding concertos. *Liszt*

Fig. 14.2 Niccolò Paganini's unusual appearance—he was tall, pencil-thin, and habitually dressed in black—combined with his unearthly virtuosity gave rise to rumors that his violin was the devil's consort and that the phenomenal Italian violinist was the devil himself. The German poet Heine called him "a vampire with a violin."

MENDELSSOHN (1809–1847)

Unlike most of the great composers of his generation, Felix Mendelssohn not only achieved artistic success but also lived a life of relative ease and financial security. Born into a wealthy and cultured Jewish family—his father was a banker, his grandfather, Moses Mendelssohn, a distinguished philosopher—he and his brother and two sisters were brought up as Christians. His precocious talent was quickly recognized, and his mother began teaching him piano when he was very young. After the family moved to Berlin in 1812, his formal training was entrusted to Carl Zelter, an eminent composer, teacher, and head of the famous *Singakademie*.

Mendelssohn's parents both loved music, and chamber ensembles frequently performed in their home. The young boy's earliest compositions were played by these instrumentalists, and by 1821 he had composed trios, quartets, sonatas, and operettas. His debut as a concert pianist had been made even earlier—at the age of nine—and he mastered both violin and viola while still in his teens. The first striking demonstration of his genius as a composer was the overture to Shakespeare's *A Midsummer Night's Dream,* written in 1826 when he was seventeen. Three years later he made his mark as a conductor when he revived J. S. Bach's *St. Matthew Passion.* This performance of the Passion, a great triumph for Mendelssohn, was the first given since Bach's death almost eighty years earlier and began a wide-scale revival of Bach's music.

Early in the 1830s, Mendelssohn traveled extensively throughout Europe. He conducted his concert overture *Fingal's Cave* (*The Hebrides*) in London and met Hector Berlioz in Italy. Returning to Berlin in 1833, Mendelssohn decided to seek a permanent post and applied for the directorship of the *Singakademie*. He was turned down—one of his few failures—but in the same year he was asked to become town musical director conductor at Düsseldorf. Two years later he accepted an

Fig. 14.3 A child prodigy, Mendelssohn made his debut as a concert pianist at the age of nine. His magical concert overture *A Midsummer Night's Dream* was written when he was seventeen. (Courtesy The Metropolitan Museum of Art; The Crosby Brown Collection of Musical Instruments, 1901.)

offer to become conductor of the famous *Gewandhaus* Orchestra in Leipzig.

In 1837 Mendelssohn married Cécile Jeanrenaud, the daughter of a French Protestant clergyman. In 1841 they moved to Berlin where, at the request of Kaiser Friedrich Wilhelm IV, Mendelssohn took charge of the music division of the newly established Academy of Arts. The position did not require close supervision and he was able to develop his plans for a conservatory at Leipzig. In 1843 the conservatory opened with a distinguished faculty in residence, and several years later Mendelssohn moved his family back to Leipzig.

Though his health began to deteriorate after 1846, Mendelssohn continued to immerse himself in his work. The death of his elder sister, to whom he was deeply attached, was a major shock. Falling into a severe depression, he soon became bedridden and died in Leipzig at the age of thirty-eight.

MENDELSSOHN'S WORK

Despite his relatively short life, Mendelssohn produced many works, ranging from large-scale symphonies and oratorios to intimate chamber works and lieder. His first published symphony (in C minor, 1824) was actually the thirteenth he had written. Of the four symphonies that still remain, one—apparently influenced by Beethoven's Ninth—is for chorus and orchestra, entitled *Lobgesang* (*Hymn of Praise,* 1840). The others are descriptive: No. 3 (*Scottish,* 1830–1842), No. 4 (*Italian,* 1833), and No. 5 (*Reformation,* 1830–1842). His imaginative and original *concert overtures* (see page 272) include *A Midsummer Night's Dream* (1826), *Calm Sea and Prosperous Voyage* (1830–1832), *Fingal's Cave* (*The Hebrides,* 1830–1832), and the overture to Victor Hugo's play *Ruy Blas* (1839).

Along with these major orchestral works, Mendelssohn composed many chamber pieces, the octet for strings (Opus 20, 1825) being one of his most original and delightful works.

Mendelssohn's long-standing appreciation of Bach's music shows up in his several collections of preludes and fugues for piano. The bulk of his piano music, however, consists of short character pieces in a highly Romantic vein. The most popular of these are the eight collections of *Songs Without Words,* published between 1829 and 1845. His finest large-scale work for piano is the *Variations sérieuses* (Opus 54, 1841).

Though he composed a great many church choruses and an equally substantial number of art songs, Mendelssohn's reputation as a vocal composer rests on his two oratorios, *St. Paul* (1836) and *Elijah* (1846). In them, Mendelssohn incorporated elements of Bach's Passion style and of Handelian oratorio form. They are generally considered the most successful nineteenth-century works of their kind.

Many of Mendelssohn's later works, composed in the 1840s, appear to be somewhat uninspired. In one work, however, he fully recaptured the magical verve of the *Midsummer Night's Dream* overture: The incidental music he wrote for the same play in 1842, including the famous "Wedding March," stands as a fitting companion to his youthful masterpiece. And one of his greatest concertos is the Violin Concerto in E Minor (Opus 64, 1844), discussed below.

Mendelssohn's violin concerto retains the three-movement structure of the Classical concerto, with two minor departures: there is no definite break between the first and second movements, and the first movement lacks a double exposition. The work is scored for solo violin and an orchestra composed of two each of flutes, oboes, clarinets, bassoons, horns, trumpets, and timpani, and the usual string sections.

VIOLIN CONCERTO IN E MINOR (OPUS 64)
RECORD 5/SIDE 1

FIRST MOVEMENT: *ALLEGRO MOLTO APPASSIONATO* (SONATA-ALLEGRO FORM)

Exposition As stated above, this movement lacks the double exposition common to most Classical concertos. Instead, the solo violin enters at the beginning, and makes the first statement of Theme 1. The opening measures of the

(*Continued on page 270.*)

THE ARTS OF
THE ROMANTIC ERA

Voltaire, the preeminent essayist of eighteenth-century France, held that feelings and passions were not significant in the discussion of existence and experience. He maintained that the world was intelligible only through reasoned, clear analysis. The Romantics, led first by Rousseau, disagreed. Like the Spanish artist Francisco Goya, whose early nineteenth-century etching shows a sleeping man haunted by bats, owls, and other nocturnal apparitions, they were often preoccupied with the irrational side of human nature. For them, "the sleep of reason produces monsters" (Plate 24).

The term "Romanticism" describes a school of thought that infused much of the philosophy, literature, and visual arts of the early nineteenth century.* The Romantics were particularly drawn to "the exception to the rule." They were excited by the turbulence that followed the French Revolution in European politics. They were fascinated by the power of the individual, especially the man or woman of feelings, who dwelt in a private world of emotions and solitary dreams, and the hero, who represented the grandest possibilities of the individual. They searched for the exotic, the mysterious, and the unfamiliar. They were adventurers drawn to experience that affected their senses and stimulated their passions.

The Romantics mused over landscape and nature. Great doubts about progress, civilization, and industrialization moved them from the "salon to the field and hillside," where the delights of refined society were replaced by "private reverie, melancholy introspection, and contemplation of the overwhelming heart." Landscape painting, which had been merely decorative backdrop to eighteenth-century portraits and aristocratic idylls, became independent and respectable subject matter. Writers sought inspiration in nature and found in its changes metaphors for their own moods and emotions. For some Romantics, like the poet Wordsworth, nature was elevated into a religion. Rejecting absolutely the Age of Reason, Wordsworth wrote:

> *One impulse from a vernal wood*
> *May teach you more of man,*
> *Of moral evil and of good,*
> *Than all the sages can.*
>
> *Sweet is the lore which Nature brings;*
> *Our middling intellect*
> *Misshapes the beauteous forms of things:*
> *We murder to dissect.*

---

*   Musical Romanticism had a longer lifespan, extending across the entire century.

Plate 23. Horace Walpole built Strawberry Hill (1748–1772) in the Gothic style, a design favored by Romantics because of their fascination with the mystery and heroism of the Middle Ages. The Gothic Revival, especially in church building, continued into the twentieth century. (Courtesy A. F. Kersting/Art Reference Bureau.)

Plate 24. Francisco Goya's etching *The Sleep of Reason Creates Monsters* (1797–1798) reflects the Romantic preoccupation with dreams, fantasies, and hallucinations. The Romantics were interested in the "exceptional" rather than the "reasonable" side of human nature. (Courtesy Prints Division, New York Public Library; Lenox and Tilden Foundations.)

Plate 25. Eugene Delacroix (1798–1863), the leader of the French Romantics, rejected the Neoclassical style of David and instead used the bright colors and forms of Rubens as his models. He was especially attracted by action-packed scenes in exotic, foreign locales, as shown in this late example, *The Lion Hunt* (1861). (Courtesy Art Institute of Chicago; Potter Palmer Collection.)

Plate 26. William Turner's painting of a Swiss avalanche (*The Fall of an Avalanche in the Grisons,* 1810) is typical of his explosive, highly abstracted scenes that reflected the power of nature. His practice of painting light and atmosphere in patches of pure color anticipated the Impressionists by about 40 years. (Courtesy The Tate Gallery, London.)

This Romantic point of view has gained new currency in our own genera-tion. For many, particularly those born after World War II, the Romantic drive toward a harmonic reconnection of humankind and nature has fresh appeal in a world where the individual seems progressively devalued.

The two greatest landscape painters of the early nineteenth century were John Constable (1776–1837) and J. M. W. Turner (1775–1851), both of whom were Englishmen unconstrained by the powerful influence of the Neoclassical painter David. Constable was a realist who believed that accurate representa-tion of nature was "scientific as well as poetic." Unlike painters who drew their inspiration, color schemes, and compositions from old masters, Constable went to the countryside, where he made sketches of meadows, trees, and clouds that he later reworked in his studio.

Turner was a very different kind of landscapist. His paintings celebrated the Sublime—the elemental force of nature that overpowers man in the cosmos. His work—full of storms, wind, water, and fire, dramatically veiling concrete reality —is sometimes breathtaking in its dazzling color and advanced abstraction (Plate 26).

The most radical painter in early nineteenth-century France was Eugène Delacroix (1799–1862), who rejected the Neoclassical principles by which the artist was enjoined to imitate classical models and to subordinate color and brushstroke to composition and line. Delacroix painted in a free and colorful manner that sometimes makes his work indistinguishable from that of Rubens, whom Delacroix revered (Plate 25). Accordingly, some art historians have called the Romantic style in French painting and sculpture a Neobaroque movement.

Romantic writers, fascinated by the macabre and fantastical, depicted a world of the supernatural in works like Poe's The Masque of the Red Death *and Walpole's* The Castle of Otranto. *These authors were especially drawn to out-standing individuals—it was an age that made Napoleon and Beethoven divine! In literature, a significant character type was the Byronic hero, who towered above ordinary human beings in his unique abilities and his capacity for feeling, especially suffering. The Byronic hero was driven by violent passions that were ultimately fatal to himself and others; nonetheless, mortals could not resist his powerful personality. Lord Byron himself introduced this figure in poems such as* Childe Harold's Pilgrimage *and* Don Juan. *In Emily Brontë's* Wuthering Heights *he is personified in the brooding, tormented Heathcliff.*

Romantic music displayed the features of the movement in special ways. As the couplets of Alexander Pope gave way to the musings of Keats and Shelley, the formal structures of Classical music gave way to new emotionalism. Berlioz experimented with the different possibilities of musical instruments and greatly expanded the size of the orchestra. In his Symphonie fantastique *a young musi-cian dreams that he is at a witches' sabbath attended by fearful monsters and grotesques, all awaiting his burial. In the Romantic era musical virtuosos like Franz Liszt and Niccolò Paganini became international celebrities who attracted huge audiences by their extraordinary technical showmanship.*

During the nineteenth century there was a close relationship among all the arts. The Romantic poetry of Byron and Goethe inspired the art of Delacroix, who likewise painted his friend, Chopin. Franz Schubert was enchanted by the

Plate 27. The Arc de Triomphe (1833–1836) was a huge monument to the victories of Napoleon, modeled after the imperial arches of ancient Rome. Here, the sculpture on the Arc demonstrates the movement toward exciting, dramatic sculpture in the Romantic era. (Courtesy Bulloz/Art Reference Bureau.)

poetry of Schiller and created many beautiful songs from the texts of his lyric poems. Romanticism gave new life to opera, and the great German composer Richard Wagner envisioned opera as a fusion of all the arts.

Romanticism as a general movement was countered in the middle of the nineteenth century by the fashion of Realism. Realism discarded the earlier movements of Neoclassicism and Romanticism on the grounds that both invented a world rather than reflecting the world in which people live. To the Realists, the vulgar and commonplace were legitimate subjects for high art and literature; they despised what they called the sentimentality and mock-heroism of earlier nineteenth-century art.

The high priest of Realism in French art was Gustave Courbet (1819–1877), who, to the disgust or discomfort of the critical establishment in Paris, chose provocative subjects of peasants and common laborers. Charles Dickens and Emile Zola wrote about the brutal lives of the working class; Georges Bizet's opera Carmen *tells the story of a girl who works in a cigarette factory.*

Where Romanticism had imagined a grander, more mysterious world beyond, Realism sought factual truth. Realism presaged the material objectivity of the modern world, a world that has been liberated by the technological wonders of the applied sciences and engineering, but a world curiously uneasy in its wealth. Because the Realist viewpoint is practical, it has had tremendous influence on the thinking of industrial society. Because Romanticism has more feeling, it still has appeal to those who remain convinced that "the heart is the proper guide."

(Continued from page 261.)   theme contain two contrasting ideas, the first built of leaps from one chord tone to the next and the second a smooth descending figure:

Example 14.4

A series of short virtuoso passages for the soloist, some of them unaccompanied, leads to the orchestral statement of Theme 1, and then to the bridge. The bridge material—an angular and chromatic descending line—is stated first by the orchestral violins and oboes, and then, an octave higher, by the soloist.

Theme 2, in G major, is played by clarinets and flutes, while the solo violin sustains a long, low pedal point. Then the roles are reversed—the violin takes the melody and the winds accompany the violin. This kind of interchange between soloist and orchestra is typical of the whole piece.

Development   In the development section the first theme and the bridge material are exploited fully, while the second theme is completely ignored.

The cadenza for this movement, written out by Mendelssohn, forms an integral part of the work. It serves as a transition to the recapitulation—an example of the Romantic urge to remove the formal distinction between sections. The violinist plays a series of arpeggios, ending with a long one that rises to a high note; this happens three times, with the last note higher each time. After a series of trills on fragments that recall Theme 1, the violin performs a long series of fast arpeggios, at the end of which the orchestra quietly enters, playing Theme 1.

Recapitulation   The orchestra performs the entire recapitulation of the first theme while the violinist continues to perform cadenzalike arpeggios. The soloist stops when the bridge material is introduced by the orchestra, and enters again with a descending passage that modulates from E minor to E major. The second theme is recapitulated in this key, again with a reduced orchestration. The section ends with the violin's extension of Theme 2 into a long lyric melody.

Coda   This movement has an extensive coda, containing more development of the first theme, and then a Beethovenian rush to the end, combining bridge material and fragments of the first theme. The movement ends with a loud orchestral cadence; with almost no break, a long note in the bassoon links the first and second movements.

SECOND MOVEMENT: *ANDANTE*

The slow movement is in alternating form, ABA, with a coda; its key is C major.

The solo violin is totally dominant in the A section, singing a long, sustained melody in a very high register, with string accompaniment.

The B section opens with a theme stated by the orchestral violins, cellos, and oboes. The second violins and violas play an accompaniment figure that alternates rapidly between two notes.

Example 14.5

After this orchestral statement of the theme, the soloist enters and plays both the theme and the accompaniment simultaneously. Soon the orchestra takes over the accompaniment figure, and the soloist plays the theme in octaves. Eventually the thematic material is reduced to short fragments, and a descending chromatic solo passage leads to the return of the A section. The coda consists of a series of sequential passages by the solo violin, accompanied only by winds, almost to the cadence.

THIRD MOVEMENT: *ALLEGRETTO NON TROPPO—* *ALLEGRO MOLTO VIVACE* (INTRODUCTION AND SONATA-ALLEGRO FORM)

Introduction The use of a short, slow section to introduce a movement in sonata form was a frequent occurrence in the Classical period, and Mendelssohn uses it in this concerto. The allegretto non troppo section, for solo violin and strings, also serves the purpose of modulating from the C major cadence of the second movement to the key of E major.

Exposition The brasses, bassoons, and timpani start the exposition with emphatic rhythmic statements, which are answered by the soloist with fast-rising arpeggios. Then the violinist quietly introduces the first theme, a fast, scherzo-like motive with a very light accompaniment.

Example 14.6

The bridge material is derived directly from Theme 1.

Theme 2 has two distinct halves, clearly separated by a sharp change in dynamics (a Beethovenian technique). The first phrase is a bouncy figure, played loudly (ff); the second phrase is piano and is almost identical with Theme 1.

Example 14.7

Development The development section begins with orchestral exploitation of the first half of Theme 2, modulating through several keys while the soloist embellishes it with rapid scales and arpeggios. Soon the violin introduces Theme 1, in its entirety—but it is a false recapitulation, for the theme is in the key of G major. The orchestra elaborates on this theme, and the violin joins in, gradually developing the idea into cadenza-like material, although the accompaniment never drops out. A long scale passage by the soloist introduces the recapitulation.

Recapitulation The recapitulation is somewhat abbreviated. It moves quickly from the first theme to the second, with its alternation of orchestra and soloist and its sharp dynamic contrasts. A closing section elaborates on the material of the first half of the second theme, while the violinist plays excited arpeggios and chords. A big orchestral climax leads to the coda, which builds in intensity to a grand conclusion.

CONCERT OVERTURE

Prior to the nineteenth century, the overture had been an instrumental piece that functioned as an introduction to a longer musical work (such as an opera or oratorio) or, in some instances as "incidental music" to spoken drama. Although this type of overture continued to be written during the nineteenth century, the Romantic period gave rise to a new type of overture, one that was not an introduction to something else. The **concert overture** was a one-movement, self-contained musical work intended for performance in the concert hall. As such, it took its place alongside the symphony and the concerto as one of the major symphonic forms of the period.

Some concert overtures were written for specific festive occasions. Beethoven's *Consecration of the House* is one such work. Others, such as Mendelssohn's *Hebrides Overture,* attempted to evoke some aspect of nature. And still others, including Brahms's *Tragic Overture,* expressed a generalized mood or human condition.

Many concert overtures have programmatic and descriptive elements and in some respects resemble the symphonic poem. But unlike the symphonic poem, the concert overture retains the strong musical organization embodied in sonata-allegro form. In this respect the concert overture is much like the first movement of a symphony, except that it is complete in itself.

One of the most popular concert overtures written during the Romantic era, *Romeo and Juliet,* was composed by the Russian Peter Ilyich Tchaikovsky.

During the Romantic period there were two schools of musical thought in Russia. The nationalists (who will be discussed in Chapter 15) attempted to create a music that was totally Russian in character and style. The cosmopolitans, on the other hand, looked to the Western European tradition for their inspiration and composed in the general Romantic style. Tchaikovsky was the outstanding composer of the cosmopolitan school and the first Russian composer to gain an international reputation.

[handwritten margin note: Symphonic movement played by an opera or oratorio.]

TCHAIKOVSKY (1840–1893)

Born in Votkinsk, in a remote province of Russia, Peter Ilyich Tchaikovsky received his earliest musical training from a French governess. When he was ten his family moved to St. Petersburg, where he was enrolled in a school of jurisprudence. Upon graduation at the age of nineteen he became a government clerk, but soon decided to pursue a musical career. He was accepted at the age of twenty-one to the newly established St. Petersburg Conservatory, where he began serious composition under Anton Rubinstein (1829–1894), the institution's founder and an eminent pianist and composer.

He graduated in 1865, winning a gold medal for a cantata based not on a Russian subject but, significantly, on a German one— Schiller's *Hymn to Joy.* The following year he became a professor of harmony at the Moscow Conservatory, a position he was to hold for twelve years. His early works, which include overtures, string quartets, and a programmatic symphony, demonstrate little of the individual style that marked his later achievements. He widened his experience, however, through frequent trips abroad.

In 1876 Tchaikovsky acquired the support of an unusual benefactress, Nedezhda von Meck, a widow who had inherited an immense fortune. Impressed by his music and told by a third party that the composer was in financial need, she commissioned several works at large fees. She arranged to pay him a fixed annuity so that he could devote himself completely to composition. Their relationship, lasting thirteen years, was carried on entirely by letter. They agreed never to meet, and except for several accidental encounters in public places, the bargain was kept.

In 1877 Tchaikovsky married Antonia Milyukova, an unstable conservatory student who threatened suicide if he would not marry her. The marriage was a disastrous failure, for Tchaikovsky's sympathy for the girl quickly turned to repulsion. After he himself made an attempt at suicide by plunging into the Moscow River, he arranged a legal separation. With the financial help of Mme. von Meck, he then embarked on a trip to Italy, Paris, and Vienna.

Despite an increasing tendency toward depression, Tchaikovsky remained a highly productive composer. His Fourth and Fifth Symphonies (1877 and 1888) and the ballets *Swan Lake* (1876) and *The Sleeping Beauty*

Fig. 14.4 Peter Tchaikovsky wrote in the Western Romantic style, yet he often incorporated folksongs of his homeland which gave his works a Russian flavor.

(1889) were soon performed all over Europe. By the 1880s he had reached the height of his career. Suddenly, for reasons that have never been fully explained, Mme. von Meck withdrew her support and friendship. Though her action was a severe blow to his pride, Tchaikovsky was by now able to afford the financial loss, and his capacity for work remained undiminished. During 1891 and 1892, he undertook several concert tours in America, Poland, and Germany. When he went to St. Petersburg in 1893 to conduct the premiere of his Sixth Symphony, the *Pathétique,* he fell ill and died, a victim of the cholera epidemic that had been raging in the city.

TCHAIKOVSKY'S WORK

Tchaikovsky's best-known works are his last three symphonies, his three ballets, his two symphonic fantasies, his violin concerto, his concert overtures, and his first piano concerto. He composed his first three symphonies between 1866 and 1875. The fourth was completed in 1877, the fifth in 1888, and the sixth (the *Pathétique*) in 1893.

Although Tchaikovsky followed traditional procedures in his symphonies, his main efforts were directed at creating beautiful melodies and brilliantly orchestrated textures. The Fourth Symphony has an elaborate program wedged into the traditional symphonic format. Tchaikovsky's Fifth Symphony uses a single theme to link the four movements, much as Beethoven and Brahms had done in the symphonies previously studied.

His ballets—*Swan Lake, The Sleeping Beauty,* and especially *The Nutcracker* (1891–1892)—remain among the most celebrated works of their kind, and the orchestral suites drawn from them are basic items in present-day repertoire as well.

Fig. 14.5 Since its premiere in old St. Petersburg, Russia, in 1892, Tchaikovsky's ballet *The Nutcracker* has become a perennial favorite with audiences throughout the world. Pictured is a scene from the production by the renowned choreographer George Balanchine.

Of Tchaikovsky's ten works for solo instrument with orchestra, the most popular with performers and audiences alike are the Piano Concerto No. 1 in B-Flat Minor (1875) and the Violin Concerto in D (1878). Of his several operas, only *Eugene Onegin* 1877–1878) and *The Queen of Spades* (1890) continue to be performed regularly. Few of his chamber works are performed today, but *None But the Lonely Heart,* one of the more than one hundred songs written during his career, is still a favorite.

Although Tchaikovsky is best remembered for his last three symphonies, the ballet scores, and the piano and violin concertos, two of his concert overtures have also becomes an almost indispensable part of symphonic repertoire: the *1812 Overture* and the overture-fantasy *Romeo and Juliet.*

ROMEO AND JULIET
RECORD 5/SIDE 2

    Romeo and Juliet is a relatively early work (1870), composed at the suggestion (almost the insistence) of Mili Balakirev (see Chapter 15), to whom Tchaikovsky dedicated the piece. The composer revised the work in 1881 and it is this later version that is performed today.

    Despite its title, *Romeo and Juliet* is programmatic only in that it selects some of the basic elements of Shakespeare's drama for musical treatment. But the drama is not used to organize the piece. Rather, these elements are worked out in strictly musical ways within the highly organized yet flexible structure of sonata-allegro form.

    The piece begins with a long introduction whose generally "religious"-sounding texture is usually held to represent Friar Laurence. The expressive use of the full Romantic orchestra, including harp, is immediately obvious even in this early part of the piece. After several changes of tempo, the introductory section builds into the agitated first theme of the exposition, played by the full orchestra—the feud between the Montagues and Capulets:

Example 14.8

This feud theme is contrasted with the exquisite, flowing love theme of Romeo and Juliet, first stated briefly by solo English horn and muted violas.

Example 14.9

Very shortly the love theme appears again, greatly extended and lushly orchestrated. This time the French horns provide a countertheme, thus creating a love duet:

Example 14.10

The love music is closely associated with the short, atmospheric section played by muted strings:

Example 14.11

This short stretch of music separates the first two statements of the love music and is used again later in the movement.

The development focuses on the feud theme and the Friar Laurence material from the introduction. As the piece unfolds, the feelings of anger and chaos gradually dominate until, at the end of the recapitulation, a coda clearly signifies that the lovers are dead. The final few measures, with their isolated chords, are often held to represent a final union of the lovers, transfigured through death.

Tchaikovsky makes full use of the richness of the Romantic orchestra as well as other Romantic techniques: changes of tempo, sharply contrasting dynamic levels, dynamic crescendos, and long, lyrical melodies. In *Romeo and Juliet* he has created a fascinating example of the Romantic concert overture as well as a clear illustration of the Romantic sensibility.

SUMMARY

A stream of Classical thought continued to flow through the Romantic period. Although some composers discarded the Classical forms, one group cultivated and expanded them in both orchestral and chamber music settings. The leading composers in this group were Schubert, Mendelssohn, Brahms, and Tchaikovsky.

Nearly all of the early Romantic composers were influenced by Beethoven, either by his use of the orchestra or by his expansion of form. Brahms, the greatest of the late Romantic symphonists, retained the four-movement symphonic structure. He continued to expand sonata-allegro form, to enlarge the orchestra, and to define structures by means of dynamics and instrumental colors.

The interest of Romantic audiences in virtuosity encouraged composers to write concertos which contained very difficult solo parts. While many Romantic concertos were second-rate, those written by Schumann, Brahms, Mendelssohn, and Tchaikovsky were outstanding.

The Romantic era gave rise to a new type of overture, one which did not introduce a longer work but was instead a self-contained work in one movement, intended for performance in the concert hall. The concert overture, exemplified by Tchaikovsky's *Romeo and Juliet,* often had programmatic elements, but retained the sonata-allegro form of organization.

NEW TERMS

concert overture

CHAPTER 15 | NATIONALISM

DURING THE LATER PART OF THE ROMANTIC ERA, NATIONALISM became an important force in music. *Nationalism* in this context refers to any musical expression that is intended to emphasize the unique character and interests of a particular culture. There had been some stylistic differences in the music of different nations ever since the early fifteenth century. In the seventeenth century France and Italy had dominated the European musical scene. Germany became an important force by about 1750 and assumed the dominant position in music at the beginning of the nineteenth century. But the Classical style, as established by Mozart, Haydn, and Beethoven, had no distinctive national characteristics—it was international and cosmopolitan.

During the Romantic era, however, self-conscious and even aggressive nationalistic feeling flared up in both literary and musical circles. The reaction took different forms in different countries, although there were some common features. They ranged from the use of national subjects for operas and symphonic poems, and the occasional quoting of folk music material, to more general traits, such as the adoption of characteristic national idioms (in melody, harmony, rhythm, form, and tonal color) into the mainstream of Germany's Romantic musical language.

The most important and obvious effect of the nationalistic movement took place in countries that did not have strong musical traditions of their own. Before the nineteenth century, areas such as Russia, Bohemia, and the Scandinavian countries had been musically dependent on the leaders of European culture, particularly Germany and Italy. They had imported their music, and the musicians to perform it.

Many important nationalistic composers were not founders of schools of composition, but were isolated figures. The whole nationalistic movement was rather short-lived, soon joining the prevailing currents of the more strongly established European cultures. Nevertheless, nationalism enriched the central musical language with new idioms and procedures and added works of lasting value to the repertory.

RUSSIA

Russia is the classic example of a nation that was suddenly exposed to Western civilization and became culturally dependent before first having a chance to find its own national voice. Prior to the reign of Peter the Great (1672–1725), Russia had been isolated from the West; Peter forced Western customs and ideas on his people and eliminated national traditions. This pressure created the beginnings of a cultural division between the liberal, Western-oriented aristocracy and the more traditional, conservative masses. The split was reflected almost immediately in Russian literature and gradually appeared in music as well.

European music was introduced to Russia late in the seventeenth century, and Italian opera was particularly popular at the Imperial Court. Music was definitely a luxury in Russia, imported for the upper classes and monopolized by foreigners. But in the nineteenth century, a new sense of national pride began to grow, demanding that there be something "Russian" about the music produced for Russian consumption. At about this time, the first significant Russian composer, Glinka, appeared.

MIKHAIL GLINKA

Although Mikhail Glinka (1804–1857) studied with German and Italian musicians, he became closely associated with the members of a nationalistic literary movement in St. Petersburg. At their urging, he wrote a "national opera," which he filled with the spirit and melody of the Russian people. His opera *A Life for the Tsar* was first performed in 1836. Russia had a vast supply of folk music and liturgical chant (for the Orthodox church), and Glinka was one of the first to draw on these resources.

THE SPLIT BETWEEN NATIONALISTS AND COSMOPOLITANS

About the time of Glinka's death the Russian musical world divided into two camps. Some Russian composers wanted to be completely independent of the West, writing Russian music addressed to Russians only. Others were convinced that Slavic culture should be abandoned for the cosmopolitan culture of Western Europe. This split was paralleled in literary circles, in which the novelist Dostoyevsky was a leading nationalist, while Turgenev represented the more conservative faction. The outstanding composer of the cosmopolitan school was Peter Ilyich Tchaikovsky, who was discussed in Chapter 14.

THE RUSSIAN "FIVE"

The leaders of the nationalistic school of composition in Russia, who professed to have no interest in the music of the West, were a strange group. Known as the "Five," they were not professional musicians, except for the leader and teacher of the others, Mili Balakirev (1837–1910). The rest were professionally employed in other fields: Alexander Borodin (1834–1887) was a chemistry professor at a medical school, César Cui (1835–1918) was a military engineer, Modest Mussorgsky (1839–1881), an army officer, and Nikolai Rimsky-Korsakov

(1844–1908), a naval officer. The most significant of these composers were Borodin, Rimsky-Korsakov, and Mussorgsky. Borodin's best works are an opera, *Prince Igor* (1890), and a symphonic sketch, *In the Steppes of Central Asia*. The music for the Broadway musical *Kismet* is taken from his work. Rimsky-Korsakov, who employed opulent and overwhelming orchestrations, is best known for his orchestral tone poem *Scheherazade* (1888) and for "Song of India" from his opera *Sadko* (1898).

MUSSORGSKY (1839–1881)

Modest Mussorgsky, the outstanding composer of the Russian nationalistic school, is often called the founder of modern musical realism. Mussorgsky was born in Pskof to an aristocratic family. His mother gave him his first piano lessons, and at thirteen, Mussorgsky studied with one of the better piano teachers in St. Petersburg. He acquired facility on the piano and became familiar with German music, but received no training in musical theory. At seventeen, Mussorgsky became an army officer, indulging in such regimental pastimes as boasting, drinking, and wenching. He soon resigned his post to devote full time to composing, but when the emancipation of the Russian serfs in 1861 left his family in financial trouble, Mussorgsky became a government clerk, a position he held almost until his death.

At twenty-one, Mussorgsky became a pupil and friend of Balakirev. However, Balakirev never completely trusted Mussorgsky's judgment—either musically or personally—and eventually the two grew apart.

Some of Mussorgsky's earliest nationalistic feelings were expressed in a letter to Balakirev on his first trip to Moscow. He was equally moved by the tombs of the Tsars and by the common people, who had, he said, "a strange demeanor, a nimbleness of motion. . . . I was a cosmopolitan; now I feel reborn, and quite close to all that is Russian." Increasingly, Mussorgsky began to base his music on Russian themes—its literature, legends, folk songs, and the memories of his own childhood.

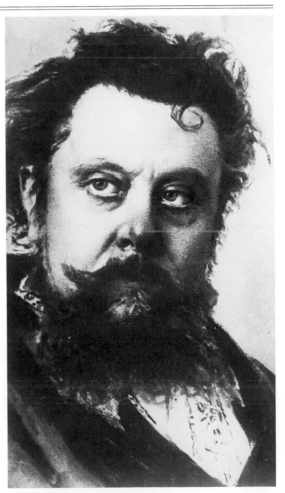

Fig. 15.1 Mussorgsky's new kind of music—based on Russian themes, full of dissonance and rhythmic variety—initially met considerable resistance from musical conservatives. But his harmonic and rhythmic innovations pointed the way for later composers.

At twenty-nine Mussorgsky began his greatest work, the opera *Boris Godunov*. He wrote the libretto himself, basing it loosely on Pushkin's drama of Boris, who became Tsar in 1598 by arranging the murder of the child heir to the throne. The opera was finally performed in 1874. It was acclaimed by the public, but panned by most critics, especially by César Cui, Mussorgsky's old friend. It was dropped from the repertory shortly after his death, but revived some years later.

Mussorgsky's life became more and more disordered. Periods of happiness and productivity alternated with periods of depression and bouts of drinking. He felt increasingly isolated from his friends, and in 1881 he died at the age of forty-two.

MUSSORGSKY'S WORK

"My music," Mussorgsky wrote, "must be an artistic reproduction of human speech in all its finest shades, that is, the sounds of human speech, as the external manifestations of thought and feeling, must, without exaggeration or violence, become true, accurate music. . . ."

This credo helps to explain Mussorgsky's disdain for the conventions of the conservatory. His music is full of strange dissonances and rhythmic innovations that seemed to his contemporaries inexplicable and crude. But with these sounds Mussorgsky attempted to evoke Russian speech, folk music, and real and imagined happenings—bells clanging for Boris's coronation, a witches' sabbath, the laughter of peasant girls.

Mussorgsky strove for complete realism in his music. His orchestral suite *Night on Bald Mountain* retells the legend of St. John's night, when witches assembled to glorify Satan and hold their sabbath. His song cycle *The Nursery* describes different aspects of the life of an aristocratic child. His program work for piano (now more familiar in its orchestral version), *Pictures at an Exhibition,* describes both particular paintings and the composer's thoughts as he looks at them. In *Boris Godunov* the realism is evident on all levels. His vocal lines follow the accents of natural speech, and his portrayal of crowd scenes is intensely real. On a deeper level, he expresses musically the deep and often unutterable sufferings and passions that rage in the human soul.

BORIS GODUNOV   Although *Boris Godunov* is now regarded as a masterpiece, it has had a strange history. As mentioned earlier, it was an immediate success with the public but was condemned by critics and most rival composers, who considered its realism vulgar, its harmonies inept, and its orchestration unorthodox and crude. After his death it was removed from the repertory and neglected for years.

Thanks to the interest and skill of Nikolai Rimsky-Korsakov, *Boris Godunov* renewed its lease on life. In the early 1890s Rimsky-Korsakov made extensive revisions of the work, "correcting" harmonies, reorchestrating the entire work, omitting some of the original music, and even adding some new music of his own. Later he made still another version, closer to Mussorgsky's conception. It is this

Fig. 15.2 Costume designs for Mussorgsky's unfinished opera *Khovanshchina* (first performed five years after his death) reflect the distinctively Russian flavor of the work.

second version by Rimsky-Korsakov that is most frequently heard today, although many opera companies are now finding Mussorgsky's unretouched original to be the most powerful version after all.

The drama, which contains a Prologue and four acts, centers on the character of Boris, his psychological disintegration and eventual death. We see Boris become Tsar after arranging for the murder of the rightful heir to the throne. We watch him from the moment of his coronation to his death, tormented by hallucination, fear, and guilt from within and political intrigue from without.

But aside from the powerful figure of Boris and the realistic dramatization of his spiritual and physical deterioration, at the heart of the opera is the other central protagonist—the Russian people. Indeed, they are the drama's real hero. In choral sections and solo arias Mussorgsky realistically depicts a variety of Russian types and sympathetically evokes the struggle and suffering of an oppressed people.

One of the opera's most powerful scenes in this regard is the brilliant *Coronation Scene,* which occurs in the Prologue to Act I. As the Prologue begins, it is clear that Boris, the son-in-law of the Tsar, has devised the murder of the child Dmitri, the rightful successor to the throne. Upon the death of Tsar Feodor, Boris pretends to withdraw into seclusion but secretly contrives for the police to arouse the people to implore him to assume the throne. Thus the stage is set for the *Coronation Scene.*

The scene opens with a clamorous orchestral introduction based on the alternation of two dissonant chords. As bells peal, the curtain rises on a courtyard of the Kremlin with the Cathedral of the Assumption and the Cathedral of the Archangels at either side. The people kneel between the great churches, and a procession of brilliantly dressed boyars (noblemen) and churchmen moves across the courtyard toward the Cathedral of the Assumption. From the cathedral porch, Prince Shuiski turns to proclaim, "Long life to Tsar Boris Feodorovich." The crowds (prodded by police) and the boyars respond by singing a hymn of praise based on a Russian folk tune. As the chorus and orchestra reach the height of a crescendo, Boris, accompanied by his two children and robed in magnificent cloth of gold, appears before the kneeling throng.

The atmosphere changes to one of quiet intensity. In an introspective monologue, Boris sings of the anguish, guilt, and fear that grip his heart. He invokes the aid of his departed father to help him rule justly and with glory. Then, singing a stronger, more resolute melody, Boris bids the people, boyar and beggar alike, to be his guests at a royal feast.

To the renewed peals of the great bells, the royal procession moves on to the Cathedral of the Assumption. The people arise and again sing in praise of Boris. The chorus and orchestra surge to a climax and the scene ends with the continued reverberation of the cathedral bells.

The *Coronation Scene* has achieved great popularity in its own right and is frequently performed in concert form (without costumes or scenery).

NATIONALISM IN OTHER COUNTRIES

The distinctive nature of Russian folk music and Slavic culture made the nationalist movement there very obvious. But Russia was not the only country in which nationalistic forces influenced the musical scene. Jean Sibelius in Finland, Edvard Grieg in Norway, Isaac Albéniz, Enrique Granados, and Manuel de Falla in Spain each drew in some way on the folk idioms of their native countries.

The forces of nationalism also influenced musical developments in Bohemia. Bohemia (an area which is now part of Czechoslovakia) had been an Austrian colony for centuries, and thus had always been in touch with the mainstream of European music. Many fine musicians were produced in this region, but until the Romantic era no distinctively Czech national style had developed. Even when a nationalist movement did arise, no extreme effort was made to avoid Western influence.

The two composers who led in the formation of a national style were Bedřich Smetana and Antonín Dvořák. Both were fully trained in traditional methods: Smetana's style was closely related to Liszt's, while Dvořák's was much closer to that of Brahms.

SMETANA (1824–1884)

Regarded as the founder of the Czech national school, Bedřich Smetana (Smet'-n-ah) was a composer dedicated to merging the spirit of Bohemian folk music with the innovations of the European musical pioneers of his day. A gifted pianist from childhood, Smetana performed the works of the Classical masters. His traditional orientation was supplanted, however, when on a visit to Prague, he had the opportunity to hear Liszt and Berlioz. Smetana came to share with these men not only a fascination with progressive musical ideas but a spirit of nationalism, to which his dream of a Bohemia free from Austrian rule responded.

The spirit of Czech nationalism was widespread in Austrian-ruled Bohemia, and rising unrest culminated in the revolution of 1848. The uprising was a failure and left in its wake a long period of repression which Smetana eventually found unbearable. In 1856 he traveled to Sweden, where he worked as a teacher and conductor. He returned to his homeland after six years, this time finding a new and dynamic liberalism in the air. Shortly after his return a Czech national theater for opera, drama, and ballet was established, and Smetana began work on an opera in the Czech language.

Over the next twenty years the composer produced ten operas, eight of them on patriotic themes. *The Bartered Bride* (1866), which told of a village romance and recounted the comic antics of local Bohemian peasants, was instrumental in establishing his reputation.

In 1874 Smetana suddenly became deaf. But, like Beethoven before him, he continued to compose until nearly the end of his life.

SMETANA'S WORK

Aside from his operas, Smetana is best known for his famous cycle of symphonic poems, *Má Vlast* (*My Country,* 1879). The six works in this cycle celebrated his country's legendary past, its splendid rivers and hillsides, and great moments in Bohemian history. One of the finest of the six is called *Vltava* (*The Moldau*). It traces musically the course of the river Moldau from its sources through central Bohemia to Prague and on to join the Elbe.

THE MOLDAU

Although *The Moldau* is just one part of a large work and has some thematic relationship to other parts of the cycle, it stands complete in its own right and has become one of the most popular works in symphonic repertoire. The piece is a reflection of the composer's love for his country and an expression of the Czech national character. In addition, it is a good example of program music.

As Smetana himself indicates in the score, the work consists of eight sections. It begins with (1) a depiction of the two sources of the river, played by the flutes,

Example 15.1

which are joined by clarinets and lower strings, gradually flowing into (2) the river itself, represented by the following melody in E minor:

Example 15.2

Beneath this flowing melody (the Moldau theme) the sixteenth-note motive that began the piece continues (Example 15.1). In fact, with two notable exceptions, this "swirling" water motive acts as a unifying element throughout the work, continuing as a background against which events of greater importance take place.

The river flows through a hunting forest (3) where the French horns and trumpets sound hunting calls above the swirling water figure.

In the course of the river's flow the forest is replaced by (4) a rustic village in which a wedding celebration is taking place. The celebration is represented by joyous, dancelike music:

Example 15.3

In this section the sixteenth-note motive that has characterized the piece thus far is absent and, as a result, there is a feeling of repose.

The simple wedding scene gives way to an even more serene, almost unearthly section (5), "moonlight and the dance of the water sprites." The sixteenth-note figure now appears in an entirely different guise—as a gently rippling accompaniment to the "moonlight" theme played by the high strings, which are muted and have a shimmering effect:

Example 15.4   In the midst of this quiet and relaxed section the horns and trombones slip in, almost without notice, repeating the "water sprites dance" motive pianissimo. The serenity and quiet intensity of this section offer the perfect foil for the excitement and drama that follow.

As the water-sprite dance section draws to a close, the "swirling" motive begins to assert itself; the strings and brass contribute to a general increase in momentum, and the "river" theme (again in E minor) appears afresh (6). Then, abruptly, the entire orchestra interrupts the serene melodic flow with a theme suggesting great turbulence. We have reached St. John Rapids (7). Here Smetana uses the full resources of the Romantic orchestra to evoke swirling rapids of chaotic and frightening proportions.

Soon, however, the rapids give way to the most beautiful and expansive part of the river (8). The "river" melody appears in its most stirring form, this time in E *major,* played forte by the full orchestra. At its broadest point the river flows past the Vysihrad, the glorious castle which symbolizes Bohemian grandeur, proclaimed in a hymnlike passage for brass. The combination of the "river" theme and the Vysihrad motive produces a stirring conclusion that elegantly expresses Smetana's love of his country and his skill as a composer of program music.

DVOŘÁK (1841–1904)

The desire to establish a distinctive Czech national school was the ambition of yet another Bohemian composer, Antonín Dvořák (D'vor'-zhak). Born in a small village near Prague, Dvořák journeyed to Prague at the age of sixteen to study music and to become a master of the German Classical tradition. Yet this man, who was one day to establish Czech prominence in the areas of symphonic and chamber music, found musical recognition elusive for many years.

The Prague public first became aware of Dvořák with the performance of his patriotic choral work *Hymnus* in 1873. This success prompted a grant from the Austrian ministry of fine arts, which supplied the composer with a small income. However, it was the patronage of Brahms, whom he met a year later, that thrust him into musical prominence. In 1878, Brahms persuaded a German music publisher to print the composer's *Moravian Duets* and *Slavonic Dances*. This accomplishment allowed Dvořák to spend the 1880s touring Europe conducting his own work, and eventually he was able to attain the position of professor of composition at the Prague Conservatory.

Dvořák's career ultimately brought him to America. Here he served from 1892 to 1895 as artistic director of the National Conservatory of Music in New York.

One of his students at the conservatory was Henry T. Burleigh, a black composer and baritone who introduced him to American Negro spirituals. Dvořák was much impressed, too, by the melodies of the American Indians. In these traditions, he believed, lay the basis of a new musical school capable of expressing the unique spirit of the American people. His own

Fig. 15.3 During his three-year stay in America, Dvořák was deeply impressed by Negro spirituals. Almost as if anticipating the emergence of jazz some decades later, he wrote, "the future music of this country must be founded upon what are called the Negro melodies."

nationalistic fervor impelled him to urge his American students toward the creation of a national style which would draw on these musical resources.

Homesick for his native country, Dvořák left the United States after three years. In 1901 he was appointed to the directorship of the Prague Conservatory. His death in 1904 at the age of sixty-three was mourned throughout his beloved Bohemia.

DVOŘÁK'S WORK

Dvořák's versatility is reflected in his legacy of concertos for violin, cello, and piano; his fourteen string quartets; his four great oratorios; his five symphonic poems; his cantata, *The Spectre's Bride* (1884); his four piano trios and two quintets; and his eleven operas and nine symphonies, among a multitude of other works.

Dvořák's greatest contribution was in the art of the symphony. The best-known of his works in this form, indeed one of the most famous in all of symphonic literature, is his Symphony No. 9 in E minor, Opus 95. The symphony, written in 1893 after Dvořák had come to the United States as director of the National Conservatory, is subtitled "From the New World."

SYMPHONY NO. 9 IN E MINOR (OPUS 95)

As we said earlier, Dvořák was very much interested in the music of American Indians and American blacks. Indeed, these elements helped shape his "American style" and gave the "New World Symphony" much of its particular flavor. In a letter written while he was composing the symphony he declared: "I should never have written the symphony like I have, if I hadn't seen America." However, the influence of American music was general rather than specific. Some of the melodies were suggested by but not quoted from American folk music. The influences of Czech and American music are also evident in the folklike character and syncopated rhythms of portions of the work.

FIRST MOVEMENT

The first movement, in E minor, begins with a slow (adagio) and dramatic introduction which foreshadows the first phrase of the initial theme of the movement proper. The main body of the movement is fast (allegro molto) and is cast in sonata-allegro form. It is based on three main themes:

The three themes are rather simple and tuneful, each employing syncopated rhythm. They are worked out in straightforward sonata-allegro fashion, complete with repeated exposition, development, recapitulation, and a coda that concentrates on the first part of Theme 1. This phrase is not only important in the first movement, it also reappears and gains in importance as the symphony progresses.

From the beginning of the work Dvořák uses the Romantic orchestra with great skill and imagination. Abrupt dynamic changes, energetic crescendos, full employment of brass and percussion, and a strong sense of orchestral color are evident throughout.

SECOND MOVEMENT

The character of the second movement differs sharply from that of the first. Although it employs internal changes of tempo and dynamic contrasts, it is slow (largo) and subdued in character. The movement consists of three sections (ABA).

A somber succession of chords in the low winds and brasses leads to the beautifully melodious theme of the first A section, featuring the English horn accompanied by muted strings:

Example 15.6

This flowing melody, which is reminiscent of the Negro spiritual "Going Home," is expanded by the strings, then returns to the English horns. Section A ends in an increasingly subdued mood with two French horns, muted, echoing the opening motive of the melody.

The B section has more rhythmic and melodic activity, and, like the first movement, employs a diversity of materials. The opening melody in the flutes and oboes (played a little faster than the A materials),

Example 15.7

contrasts with the more relaxed melody which follows in the clarinets:

Example 15.8

Both themes are in strong contrast to the last portion of the B section, which begins with the sprightly, staccato oboe theme,

Example 15.9

which is then combined with trills in the flute:

Example 15.10

These materials are repeated several times, building up in a crescendo that culminates in the sudden appearance of motives from the initial theme of the first movement combined with the beginning of the main theme of the second movement, which now assumes a livelier character:

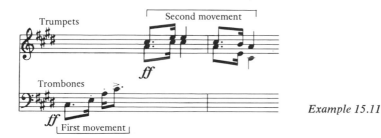

Example 15.11

This dramatic combination of motives from two movements is an example of *cyclical* treatment, a procedure we encountered earlier in our discussion of Beethoven. As in Beethoven's Fifth Symphony, cyclical technique is used here to effectively unify the two movements.

A decrescendo leads to a shortened repeat of the A section. The movement ends mournfully with a return to the somber chords that appeared at its beginning.

THIRD MOVEMENT

The third movement is a Scherzo and Trio in E minor. It is very fast (molto vivace), high-spirited, and dramatic. Its most important thematic material is the beginning of the Scherzo:

Example 15.12 Scherzo A

This driving phrase is the germ out of which the A section is built and which reappears throughout the movement. The B section is more lyrical and flowing:

Example 15.13 Scherzo B

The Trio also consists of two contrasting sections:

Example 15.14 Trio A

Strings

Example 15.15   Trio B

But instead of following the usual pattern of

Scherzo	Trio	Scherzo
ABA	ABA	ABA

Dvořák varies this structure again, using cyclical technique. Between the first Scherzo and Trio there appears a short transition, like a bridge, which employs not only the materials of the Scherzo movement but also the motive

Cello

   *Example 15.16*

pp

obviously derived from Theme 1 of the first movement.

In the coda he again features this material from the first movement in an obvious and dramatic way, combining it with the ♩ ♫ | ♩ ♩ ♩ Scherzo motive. Thus he achieves unusual unity; motives from the first movement not only permeate that movement but also lend coherence to the second and third movements.

FOURTH MOVEMENT

The fourth movement is an enormous sonata-allegro in E minor, returning to a fast tempo (allegro con fuoco—fast, with fire). A short, fiery introductory section leads to the first theme, which is strong and marchlike:

Trumpet and French Horns

Example 15.17

The contrasting second theme is tender in nature. It is stated first by the clarinet and immediately taken up by the strings, leading to a final theme straight out of a Czech village dance:

Violins and Flute

ff

Example 15.18

At first the development concentrates on the marchlike first theme, but as the section progresses, themes from *all three* previous movements are introduced in various combinations and rhythmic alterations.

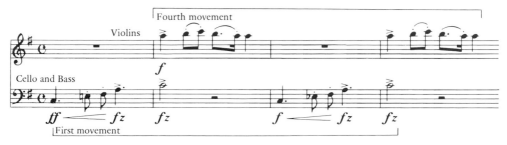

Example 15.19

Perhaps the most dramatic moments in the symphony occur in the coda, when these two ideas are combined in climactic fashion:

Example 15.20

There follows the final drive to the end which, surprisingly, fades away to the softest possible sound on the last chord.

As we have seen, the use of themes from the earlier movements in the later ones lends great unity to the work. This procedure is used most strikingly in the last movement, which includes themes from all four movements. Even more importantly, one idea—the opening phrase of Theme 1 of the first movement—is central throughout the symphony. Partly due to its original appearance, but also because of its treatment in the later movements, this motive, particularly its rhythmic structure ♩ ♪♪♩ |♩ ♪♪♩ |, is the strongest unifying factor in the work.

The "New World Symphony" was immediately popular at the time of its creation and has remained so to this day. The world of music is richer for the fact that a Czech by the name of Dvořák came to the New World.

SUMMARY

Nationalism was most evident in countries that did not have strong musical traditions of their own.

Russia began early in the nineteenth century to produce music in a unique national idiom. Mikhail Glinka drew from his country's vast supply of folk music and liturgical chant to write the opera *A Life for the Tsar,* first performed in 1836. A group of Glinka's successors formed a nationalistic school known as the "Five." The outstanding members of this group were Alexander Borodin, Nikolai Rimsky-Korsakov, and Modest Mussorgsky. Mussorgsky, composer of the opera *Boris Godunov,* is often considered to be the founder of modern musical naturalism.

The forces of nationalism were also felt in other European countries. In particular, a national style developed in Bohemia through the efforts of Bedřich Smetana and Antonín Dvořák, and nationalistic influences were felt also in Spain, Finland, and the Scandinavian countries.

CHAPTER 16 | ROMANTIC CHORAL MUSIC

VIRTUALLY EVERY MAJOR COMPOSER OF THE ROMANTIC PERIOD wrote some type of choral music. Like the instrumental music of the era, choral music expressed both the intimate and grandiose sides of Romanticism. The small, personal form was represented in fairly simple part songs (settings of poetic texts for several voices). At the other end of the scale were colossal works involving soloists, massive choruses, and immense orchestral forces. As we shall see, some of the finest of the large Romantic choral works expanded and enriched the tradition of sacred music.

SCHUBERT

Franz Schubert's most important contributions to choral music are embodied in his settings of the Mass. While still in his teens, Schubert wrote four Masses. The best of these early works is the short and modest setting in G major. The Mass in A-flat major is Schubert's choral masterpiece. Written over a period of several years (1819–1822), it is a work of major proportions, requiring approximately fifty minutes for its performance. It is scored for four soloists (SATB), chorus, and the typical Romantic orchestra. The solo parts are of secondary importance, the chorus and orchestra having the major roles. From the harmonically rich *Kyrie* through the concluding *Dona nobis pacem,* the work is one of flowing beauty.

MENDELSSOHN

In June of 1845, the Committee of the Birmingham (England) Music Festivals invited Felix Mendelssohn to conduct the Festival of 1846 and to compose a major work for the occasion. Mendelssohn declined to conduct, but he agreed to compose; the result was the oratorio *Elias* (*Elijah*), his most important choral work. Immediately popular, it assumed a place in the choral music of England ranking with Handel's *Messiah* and *The Creation* by Haydn.

Elijah is a full-fledged oratorio with a dramatic plot brought to life by a roster of soloists, an extensively employed chorus, and a full orchestra. The writing is quite dramatic, with an intensive emphasis on pictorial settings illustrating the influence of Handel's style as shown in his *Israel in Egypt*.

Today, *Elijah* is still well loved, particularly for its most memorable movements, such as the bass aria "It is enough," "If with all your hearts" for tenor, the chorus "He, watching over Israel," and the concluding "And then shall your light break forth as the morning breaketh."

BERLIOZ

In 1846, the same year that *Elijah* had its first performance, Hector Berlioz conducted the premier of his "dramatic legend" *The Damnation of Faust*. This work, along with the *Requiem* (*Grande Messe des Morts,* 1837) and the *Te Deum* (1855), are representative of the colossal Romantic choral style. The forces involved are gigantic. The *Requiem* calls for two hundred and ten voices, a large orchestra, and four brass bands positioned in various locations and representing the calls to the Last Judgment. The *Te Deum* requires two choruses of one hundred singers each, six hundred children's voices, and an orchestra of one hundred and fifty players. These and other works such as the *Funeral and Triumphal Symphony,* for symphonic band and chorus, and *Romeo and Juliet,* a dramatic symphony with choruses, are typical of Berlioz's grandiose style and similar to that found in his *Symphonie fantastique*.

Fig. 16.1 The colossal Romantic choral style is humorously depicted in this 1850 caricature of Berlioz conducting an immense chorus.

Another side of Berlioz's musical nature is found in *L'enfance du Christ* (*The Childhood of Christ,* Opus 25, 1850–1854). Quite unlike the works referred to above, this piece requires modest choral and orchestral forces and is characterized by lyricism rather than stirring bombastic power. Called a Sacred Trilogy, its three parts are entitled *Le songe d'Hérode* (*Herod's Dream*), *La fuite en Egypte* (*The Flight into Egypt*), and *L'arrivée à Saïs* (*The Arrival at Saïs*). The most effective of the three parts is the central section, which includes a lovely chorus (best known in the English translation "Thou must leave thy lowly dwelling") in which the shepherds bid farewell as the Holy Family prepares to flee from the wrath of Herod.

BRAHMS

Johannes Brahms composed some of the most enduring choral music of the Romantic period. He wrote for a wide variety of choral combinations and in diverse styles. Smaller works include a cappella choruses for various voice combinations, motets, canons, part songs, and psalm settings, many employing various types of instrumental accompaniment. One of the most popular of these works is the *Liebeslieder Walzer* (*Lovesong Waltzes,* 1868–1869) for piano, four hands, and either mixed solo quartet or chorus. Brahms composed several large works for chorus and orchestra, some with several soloists. Among these are the cantata *Rinaldo* (Opus 50); the incomparable *Schicksalslied* (*Song of Destiny,* Opus 54) for chorus and orchestra; and *Triumphlied* (*Song of Triumph,* Opus 55). The most important of his large-scale choral compositions was one of his early works, *Ein Deutsches Requiem* (*A German Requiem,* Opus 45). It was composed over a period of eleven years and was finished in 1868 when Brahms was thirty-five. It not only preceded much of his other choral writing, but was written a full eight years before his first symphony.

EIN DEUTSCHES REQUIEM (A GERMAN REQUIEM, OPUS 45)

Unlike the Requiems of Mozart, Berlioz, Verdi, and later Fauré, Brahms's setting does not employ the traditional Latin text, which is actually a Mass for the Dead (Missa pro defunctis). Rather, it is a setting of nonliturgical German texts which Brahms selected from the Lutheran Bible. A comparison of the Brahms text with the Roman Catholic liturgy shows a marked difference in intention and feeling: the Latin text prays for the soul of the dead, while Brahms's text is designed to console the living.

The opening words of the two texts confirm this:

ROMAN CATHOLIC TEXT
(Missa pro defunctis)

Requiem aeternam dona eis Domine
(Give them eternal rest, O Lord)

BRAHMS TEXT
(Ein Deutsches Requiem)

Selig sind, die da Leid tragen, denn sie sollen getröstet werden
(Blessed are they that mourn, for they shall be comforted)

Brahms's entire composition conveys this pervasive feeling of consolation in both the text and the music.

The work consists of seven movements and is scored for chorus, soprano and baritone soloists, and a large orchestra. The chorus and orchestra participate in all seven movements, although the orchestration varies somewhat from movement to movement. The role of the soloists is minimal, with the baritone appearing in the third and sixth movements and the soprano appearing only in the fifth.

FIRST MOVEMENT

Selig sind, die da Leid tragen,
    denn sie sollen getröstet werden.
	*Blessed are they that mourn,
	        for they shall be comforted.*

	MATTHEW V, 4

Die mit Tränen säen, werden mit
    Freuden ernten.
	*They that sow in tears shall reap
	        in joy.*

Sie gehen hin und weinen und
    tragen edlen Samen, und
    kommen mit Freuden und
    bringen ihre Garben.
	*They that go forth and weep,
	        bearing precious seed, shall come
	        again with rejoicing, bringing
	        their sheaves with them.*

	PSALM 126, 5–6

This movement is an excellent example of Brahms's sensitive use of the orchestra; the instruments create a dark, somber tone quality that reflects the mood of the text. Brahms achieved this effect by omitting the high, bright sound of the violins and by dividing the lower strings into several parts: violas into two sections and cellos into three.

The work begins with a short orchestral introduction in which the upper cello and viola parts enter imitatively with an expressive melodic fragment over a pedal point in the bass:

Example 16.1

This and the following choral section serve as principal unifying elements, which recur in the middle and at the end of the movement.

The contrasting section is built on the text beginning *"Die mit Tränen";* it expresses the tears *(Tränen)* with a falling melodic line, then climaxes at *"werden mit Freuden"* with a joyful rising motive and comes to a quiet conclusion at *"ernten."* The music of the opening section returns, and the chorus takes up the imitative entries with the words *"Sie gehen hin und weinen."*

After a short stretch of new material, the music set to *"werden mit Freuden"* returns, now with the text *"kommen mit Freuden."* Then the opening material is restated in its entirety, with the first two lines of text also repeated. A short coda, which decreases in intensity and volume, ends the movement.

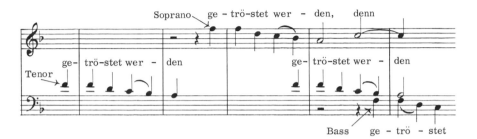

Example 16.2

This section has greater significance than might appear, since Brahms repeats it almost literally at the end of the seventh movement, thus unifying the entire Requiem.

SECOND MOVEMENT

Denn alles Fleisch ist wie Gras und
  alle Herrlichkeit des Menschen
  wie des Grases Blumen.
Das Gras ist verdorret und die
  Blume abgefallen.
I PETER I, 24

For all flesh is as grass, and
  all the glory of man
  as the flower of grass.
The grass withers, and the
  flower falls away.

So seid nun geduldig, lieben
  Brüder, bis auf die Zukunft
  des Herrn.
Siehe, ein Ackermann wartet auf
  die köstliche Frucht der Erde
  und ist geduldig darüber, bis
  er empfange den Morgenregen
  und Abendregen.
JAMES V, 7

Now therefore be patient, dear
  brethren, until the coming of
  the Lord.
Behold, the farmer waits for the
  precious fruit of the earth and is
  patient over it until it receives the
  early and the late rain.

Aber des Herrn Wort bleibet in
  Ewigkeit.
I PETER I, 25

But the word of the Lord endures
  forever.

Die Erlöseten des Herrn werden
  wieder kommen, und gen Zion
  kommen mit Jauchzen; ewige
  Freude wird über ihrem Haupt sein;
Freude und Wonne werden sie
  ergreifen und Schmerz und Saufzen
  wird weg mussen.
ISAIAH XXXV, 10

The ransomed of the Lord shall return
  and come to Zion with rejoicing,
  everlasting joy shall be upon their
  heads;
Joy and gladness shall they obtain, and
  sorrow and sighing shall flee away.

This movement calls for the full orchestra. The tempo is slow and the opening has the character of a funeral march. The upper strings are muted, maintaining the subdued tone of the first movement.

In the section based on the text *"So seid nun geduldig,"* the tempo is somewhat faster and the choral and string statement is echoed by the winds. The section ends with the same text that began it.

A sudden and startling contrast takes place at the words *"Aber des Herrn Wort,"* leading to a fast section with a fugal treatment of the text *"Die Erlöseten des Herrn."* After a contrasting section with many sudden changes of dynamics, the fugue subject returns in stretto—first in the winds, then in the chorus, strings, and brasses; it builds to a huge climax at the words *"kommen mit Jauchzen."* The coda, marked "Tranquillo," is in sharp contrast to the frenzy of the preceding section. The movement dies away, ending with a series of soft, descending scales in the orchestra.

THIRD MOVEMENT

Herr, lehre doch mich, dass ein Ende
mit mir haben muss, und mein
Leben ein Ziel hat, und ich
davon muss.

Siehe, meine Tage sind eine Hand
breit vor dir, und mein Leben ist
wie nichts vor dir.
Ach wie gar nichts sind alle
Menschen, die doch so sicher leben.
Sie gehen daher wie ein Schemen, und
machen ihnen viel vergebliche
Unruhe, sie sammeln und wissen
nicht wer es kriegen wird.
Nun Herr, wess soll ich mich
trösten? Ich hoffe auf dich.

*Lord, make me to know my end, and
what is the measure of my days, that
I may know how frail I am.*

*Behold, my days are as a handbreadth
to Thee, and my lifetime is as
nothing before Thee.
Surely, mankind walks in a vain show,
their best state is vanity.
Mankind goes about like a shadow,
and they are disquieted in vain, they
heap up riches and know not who
will gather them.
Now Lord, for what do I
wait? My hope is in Thee.*
PSALM 39, 4–7

Der Gerechten Seelen sind in Gottes
Hand und keine Qual rühret sie an.

*The righteous souls are in God's hand,
and no pain shall afflict them.*
WISDOM OF SOLOMON III, 1

This movement, which includes the first appearance of the baritone soloist, is divided into three major sections. The first two are related, both musically (they are in the same key, D minor, with common thematic material) and textually (both consider human frailty); the third section is very different, expressing confidence in God's mercy with a joyous fugue in D major on an entirely new subject. The movement ends with a huge crescendo, expressing the faith and hope evident in the text.

FOURTH MOVEMENT

Wie lieblich sind deine Wohnungen, Herr Zebaoth!	*How lovely is thy dwelling place, O Lord of Hosts!*
Meine Seele verlanget und sehnet sich nach den Vorhöfen des Herrn;	*My soul longs and faints for the courts of the Lord;*
mein Leib und Seele freuen sich in dem lebendigen Gott.	*my body and soul rejoice in the living God.*
Wohl denen, die in deinem Hause wohnen, die loben dich immerdar.	*Blessed are those who dwell in thy house, praising Thee evermore.*
	PSALM 84, 1, 2, 4

This serene and sunny movement is in obvious contrast to the exuberance of the previous one. The winds play an important role in the orchestration, often echoing the choral parts. The movement is also characterized by a frequent sense of rise and fall with melodies ascending and descending.

FIFTH MOVEMENT

Ihr habt nun Traurigkeit aber ich will euch wieder sehen und euer Herz soll sich freuen und euer Freude soll niemand von euch nehmen.	*You now have sorrow, but I will see you again and your hearts will rejoice and no one will take your joy from you.*
	JOHN VXI, 22
Sehet mich an: Ich habe eine kleine Zeit Muhe und Arbeit gehabt und habe grossen Trost funden.	*Look upon me: for a little time sorrow and labor were mine, and now I have found comfort.*
	ECCLESIASTICUS LI, 27
Ich will euch trösten, wie Einen seine Mutter tröstet.	*I will comfort you, as one whom his mother comforts.*
	ISAIAH LXVI, 13

The solo soprano plays a dominant role in this movement, the only one in which she appears. The part is full of long lyric phrases, punctuated by orchestral accompaniment and choral comment, the music for which is actually derived from the solo material. The wind instruments are particularly important, with many solo passages throughout the movement, while the strings have more of the routine accompaniment, such as the doubling of the chorus.

The text for solo is in ABA form, and the musical structure approximates an ABA outline, although the A material is not exactly the same on its return as on its first appearance.

RECORD 4/SIDE 1   SIXTH MOVEMENT

Denn wir haben hier keine bleibende Stadt, sondern die zukünftige suchen wir.	*For here we have no lasting city, but we seek that which is to come.*
	HEBREWS XIII, 14

Siehe, ich sage euch ein Geheimnis:	*Behold, I tell you a mystery:*
Wir werden nicht alle entschlafen,	*We shall not all sleep,*
wir werden aber alle verwandelt	* but we shall all be changed*
werden; und dasselbige plötzlich,	* in a moment, in the twinkling*
in einem Augenblick, zu der	* of an eye, at the time*
Zeit der letzten Posaune.	* of the last trumpet. [trombone]**
Denn es wird die Posaune schallen,	*For the trumpet shall sound,*
und die Toten werden auferstehen	* and the dead shall be raised*
unverweslich, und wir werden	* incorruptible, and we shall*
verwandelt werden.	* be changed.*
Dann wird erfüllet werden das Wort,	*Then shall come to pass the saying*
das geschrieben steht: Der Tod	* that is written: Death*
ist verschlungen in dem Sieg.	* is swallowed up in victory.*
Tod, wo ist dein Stachel?	*Death, where is thy sting?*
Hölle, wo ist dein Sieg?	*Hell, where is thy victory?*
	I CORINTHIANS XV, 51–55
Herr, du bist würdig zu nehmen	*Lord, Thou art worthy to receive*
Preis und Ehre und Kraft,	* glory and honor and power,*
den du hast alle Dinge geschaffen,	* for Thou hast made all things,*
und durch deinen Willen haben sie	* and by thy will they were given*
das Wesen und sind geschaffen.	* substance and were created.*
	REVELATIONS IV, 11

In many respects, this is the most dramatic movement of the entire work. It is characterized by extreme contrasts and driving climaxes, and its power is intensified by its position between the gentle fifth movement and the quiet, consoling seventh.

The movement consists of three large sections; the first two involve the solo baritone, while the third is a huge choral fugue. The first section is moderate in tempo (andante) and subdued in dynamics (pp); the texture is thin, with the upper strings muted and the cellos and basses playing pizzicato.

The second section begins with the solo baritone announcing *"Siehe, ich sage euch ein Geheimnis":"Wir werden nicht alle entschlafen."* The melodic activity of the last word is reduced while the winds introduce a contrasting phrase.

Example 16.3

The chorus repeats the text on static chords; the strings play the baritone's original melody, which is again answered by the winds. The alternations (between bari-

<hr>

*   In German, the "last trumpet" is a trombone (*Posaune* and not *Trompete*).

tone and chorus, strings and winds) continue during the phrase *"wir werden aber alle verwandelt werden."*

The baritone's next phrase, *"und dasselbige,"* still quiet and slow, marks the beginning of a drive to an engulfing climax at the end of the section. The momentum begins to pick up with the appearance of the original baritone melody at double speed in the violins and then flutes.

Example 16.4

A gradual crescendo in the lower strings carries it as far as the word *"Augen-blick."* After an abrupt pause, the soloist begins alone with the text *"zu der Zeit der letzten Posaune";* he is joined, appropriately enough, by the trombones and tuba. The tempo begins to accelerate, along with a gradual crescendo (*poco a poco*—little by little), and the chorus takes over from the soloist. The full orchestra joins in for a fortissimo climax on *"Po-sau– – –ne."* As the tempo continues to increase, the strings begin a rapid rising and falling tremolo figure, while the winds punctuate with short chords. This leads directly into the second large section of the movement.

The rushing string figure continues into the next section, which is marked Vivace and is in triple meter. The chorus, singing *"Denn es wird die Posaune,"* is supported by the winds, brasses, and timpani. The choral parts are a mixture of straightforward declamation, tightly woven legato lines, and sharp, stinging exclamations, all very loud.

This driving passage is interrupted by the baritone's final appearance; over a soft orchestral background, he sings *"Dann wird erfüllet,"* with melodic material reminiscent of his earlier passage, *"Siehe, ich sage euch."* His last word is engulfed by a resumption of the furious string passage work, which leads to a repetition of the material that opened the section, this time with the words *"Der Tod ist verschlungen."*

This section is extended beyond the repeat, concentrating on the contrast between the two phrases *"Tod, wo ist dein Stachel?"* with its very short, hard notes and *"Hölle, wo ist dein Sieg?"* which is very lush and legato. The accompaniment in the string section also differs for these two phrases. Gradually the emphasis shifts to the single word *"wo"*

wo----wo------wo----------
Wo ist dein Sieg?

All the forces come together to emphasize these words, and the climax leads into the final section.

Brahms ends the movement with a long and triumphant fugue in C major. In general, the fugal voices are doubled by wind instruments, while the strings play accompaniments and countersubjects. The fugue subject is a broad, majestic statement, while the countersubjects are lighter and faster-moving.

Example 16.5

As a contrast to the emphatic quality of the fugal opening, the section *"Denn du hast"* is very soft and legato; this material occurs several times during the course of the fugue. Further contrast is provided by the homophonic setting that is sometimes given to the text *"zu nehmen Preis und Ehre und Kraft."*

Perhaps more than any other, this movement demonstrates Brahms's unique ability to combine Classical design—its carefully balanced and contrasting elements—with the expressive qualities of the Romantic spirit.

SEVENTH MOVEMENT

Selig sind die Toten, die in dem
    Herrn sterben, von nun an.
Ja der Geist spricht, dass sie ruhen
    von ihrer Arbeit; denn ihre Werke
    folgen ihnen nach.

Blessed are the dead who
    die in the Lord from henceforth.
Yea, saith the Spirit, that they may
    rest from their labors; for their
    deeds do follow them.

REVELATIONS XIV, 13

The final movement of the Requiem marks a return to the spirit of the first movement, and to much of its musical material as well. Brahms has unified the entire work by linking the outer movements both textually and musically.

This movement is in ABA form with a coda; the first theme of the A section, *"Selig sind,"* is drawn almost directly from the coda of the first movement, where it was used for the words *"getröstet werden."*

Example 16.6

The B section begins with *"Ja, der Geist spricht,"* which is set for low voices singing in octaves, with trombones and horns; this leads to a tender section with the text *"dass sie ruhen,"* in which the winds play a very active part in the imitation. The material of the B section is then repeated, although in a somewhat abbreviated fashion, leading to a return of the opening material.

The opening theme is stated only once this time (by the tenor section), and the choral section is again repeated. The coda begins with a phrase in the alto and tenor sections that recalls the beginning of the return to original material from the first movement. It comes again, this time in another key, and leads directly into a literal restatement of the entire coda of the opening movement.

Ein Deutsches Requiem, like the great sacred choral works by Schütz and Bach in the Baroque period, was inspired by a deep concern for the state of the human soul; the more humanistic orientation of the Romantic age led Brahms to direct his words to the mourners rather than to the deceased. The texts of consolation and hope that he chose have an eloquent beauty of their own, and his music enhances this beauty still more.

SUMMARY

In the Romantic period, instrumental music constituted the bulk of music literature, and opera and lieder were the predominant vocal genres. Nevertheless, virtually every major composer of the period wrote choral music in some form. The large chorus, with its lush sound, was particularly well suited to the Romantic style, which concentrated on sonority and color.

Franz Schubert's most important contributions to choral music are embodied in his settings of the Mass. Felix Mendelssohn's best-known choral work is his oratorio *Elijah,* which he composed for the Birmingham (England) Music Festival of 1846. Hector Berlioz's choral compositions include a gigantic *Requiem* that calls for two hundred ten voices, a large orchestra, and four brass bands.

Some of the most enduring choral music of the Romantic period was written by Johannes Brahms. The most significant of his large-scale choral compositions is *A German Requiem,* which he composed over a period of eleven years. Its greatness rests not only on its mastery of technique, but also on its intensely personal and direct human communication.

CHAPTER 17 | ROMANTIC OPERA

OPERA WAS ONE OF THE MOST IMPORTANT MUSICAL GENRES OF THE Romantic period. In the eighteenth century each of the three leading countries of musical Europe—France, Italy, and Germany—had its own operatic style. These national styles became even more distinct during the Romantic period.

FRENCH OPERA

During the first half of the Romantic era, Paris was the operatic capital of Europe. Beginning in about 1820, with the rise of a large and influential middle class, a new type of opera developed. Called **grand opera**, it concentrated on the spectacular elements of the production: crowd scenes, ballets, choruses, and elaborate scenery. The integrity of the drama and the music was often sacrified for these special effects. Giacomo Meyerbeer (1791–1864), a German composer who had studied and worked extensively in Italy before coming to France, introduced grand opera to Paris with such operas as *Les huguenots* (1836) and *Le prophète* (1849). One of the longest grand operas of the early Romantic period was *Guillaume Tell* (*William Tell,* 1829) by an Italian, Gioacchino Rossini. The overture to *William Tell* remains popular today.

Although grand opera received the lion's share of Parisian attention, the less pretentious **opéra comique** (comic opera) continued to be popular. The distinguishing feature of opéra comique was its use of spoken dialogue rather than sung recitative. Both the music and the plot tended to be simpler than in grand opera. Despite the word "comique," many operas in this form had serious plots.

Later in the nineteenth century, a new form developed as a compromise between the overwhelming spectacle of grand opera and the lightness of opéra comique. Called **lyric opera,** it evolved from the more serious type of opéra comique. Using plots taken from Romantic drama or fantasy, these works relied primarily on the beauty of their melodies. One of the finest lyric operas of the period, Charles Gounod's *Faust* (1859), was based on the first part of Goethe's famous play.

NATURALISM

Toward the latter part of the century a new literary movement, **naturalism,** developed in France. Naturalist writers rebelled against the Romantic tendency toward escapism and emphasis on individual feeling. They sought to depict life as it is, objectively and truthfully. Often they portrayed characters from the lower classes whose lives were controlled by impersonal social forces as well as by their own passions.

Georges Bizet (1838–1875) introduced naturalism to opera in his masterpiece *Carmen* (1875). Where grand operas often portrayed historical and mythological figures, with the performers using stylized gestures to express their feelings, Bizet's main character was a gypsy girl whose fiery temper and passionate nature were dramatized realistically. Bizet's brilliant orchestration and his vital melodies and rhythms effectively complement the characterization and dramatic action.

BIZET (1838-1875)

Born and brought up in Paris, Georges Bizet (Bee-zay') entered the Paris Conservatory at the age of ten, and by seventeen had written his first symphony. His work revealed such talent and ingenuity that he was awarded the Prix de Rome, enabling him to study at the Italian capital. Unfortunately, this brilliant beginning was soon clouded by the cold reception of his audiences, who were startled and offended by the boldness of his realism and the starkness of the emotions displayed in his early operatic works.

Following his youthful compositions, Bizet created three operas: *The Pearl Fishers* (1863), *The Fair Maid of Perth* (1867), and *Djamileh* (1872). Of the three, only *The Fair Maid of Perth* was well received, but Bizet's skill in orchestration and musical structure began to build his reputation. Success came in 1872 when he composed the incidental music for *L'Arlésienne,* a piece filled with exotic harmonies and bold orchestration. This won him an offer to do an opera based on a libretto adapted from Prosper Mérimée's novel about a fiery gypsy girl.

The realism of the libretto, dealing as it did with earthy figures and driving passion, was a perfect vehicle for Bizet's imagination and love of folk melodies. He undertook the assignment, and the opera, entitled *Carmen,* was produced in 1875. The subject scandalized the audience, and the themes of desire, love, and hate proved too bold for its time. The touch of scandal that surrounded it, however, kept the opera running for several months, and Bizet was subsequently offered a contract for his next work.

But the opera's reception was a great blow to the composer, and emotionally exhausted by so many months and years of work, he was stricken by a heart attack and died. At the age of thirty-eight he had created the greatest French opera of his century and now one of the best-loved operas in the world. His inspired vocal ensembles, his use of the orchestra to comment on the action on stage, his pounding rhythms, his masterly scoring, and his eminently singable melodies assured him musical immortality. Five years after its unfavorable reception in Paris, *Carmen* returned to that city and was received with great enthusiasm.

ITALIAN OPERA

By the nineteenth century, opera was virtually the only important musical form being cultivated in Italy. The distinctions between *opera seria* and *opera buffa* were still maintained, although both were influenced by French grand opera. The orchestra began to play a more important and colorful role and the chorus was also used more effectively.

ROSSINI, DONIZETTI, AND BELLINI

The most outstanding Italian opera composer of the early part of the nineteenth century was Gioacchino Rossini (1792–1862). His sense of melody and effective staging made him an instant success. Opera buffa seemed to be a natural outlet for his talents, and *Il Barbiere di Siviglia* (*The Barber of Seville,* 1816) ranks with Mozart's *The Marriage of Figaro* as a supreme example of Italian comic opera. As with Mozart's work, the skillful treatment of ensembles and the exposition of comic situations and characters make *The Barber of Seville* an exceptional opera.

In his thirty-two operas and oratorios, Rossini sought to cultivate the aria to its highest possible level. Its function was to delight audiences with melodious and spontaneous music. This **bel canto** style, which emphasized beauty and purity of tone and an agile vocal technique, was also exemplified in the work of two of Rossini's contemporaries: Gaetano Donizetti (1797–1848), composer of some seventy operas, including *Lucia di Lammermoor* (1835); and Vincenzo Bellini (1801–1835), whose lyric and expressive style is particularly evident in his *La Sonnambula* (*The Sleepwalker,* 1831) and *Norma* (1831).

The greatest Italian opera composer of the second half of the nineteenth century was Giuseppe Verdi.

VERDI (1813-1901)

Born of a poor family in a little hamlet in Bussetto, Italy, Giuseppe Verdi (Vehr'-dee) began his musical training as the apprentice of the local church organist. His hard work and talent were rewarded with a stipend contributed by his town to enable the continuation of his studies at the Milan Conservatory. He was subsequently turned down by the examiners, but through the financial aid of a friend continued his studies by means of private lessons.

Verdi's first opera, *Oberto* (1839), written when he was 26, was an instant success. To this musical triumph he added another, with the presentation of his third opera, *Nabucco,* in 1842. It was this work that brought him not only musical recognition, but national fame. The story dealt with the plight of the Jews in Babylon, but the parallel with the Milanese crusade for freedom from Austrian rule was so striking that Verdi was exalted as a patriot and champion of the Italian cause. His name soon became linked with the cry for independence, and his evident sympathies, as they were reflected in his works, brought him under police suspicion.

After producing a number of successful works, Verdi settled on a country estate in 1849. There he continued to pursue his political activities and produced, in succession, three of his best-known works: *Rigoletto* (1851), *Il*

Trovatore (1853), and *La Traviata* (1853). These productions are regarded as the culmination of his first creative period.

Years of intensive musical productivity followed, during which such memorable works as *Un Ballo in Maschera* (*A Masked Ball,* 1859), *La Forza del Destino* (*The Force of Destiny,* 1861), and *Don Carlos* (1867) were created. In 1872, Verdi's masterpiece of spectacular grand opera, *Aida,* was written. With its cohesive dramatic structure, wealth of melodic, harmonic, and orchestral color, and subtle characterizations, this work is regarded as the height of his second creative phase.

Following this triumph, Verdi did not produce another operatic work for sixteen years. Then, in 1893, *Otello,* an opera unlike any he had previously written, was performed in Milan. Regarded by many critics as the pinnacle of Italian tragic opera, its sense of continuity surpasses that of his earlier works, while its orchestration never obscures the singing voices. Verdi's last opera, *Falstaff,* written in 1893 when the composer was nearly eighty, is one of the finest in the comic opera genre.

Fig. 17.1 Verdi was beloved not only as an operatic composer but also as a champion of the cause of Italian freedom.

VERDI'S WORK

Verdi's style is frequently contrasted with that of his German contemporary Richard Wagner. While each of these composers brought Romantic opera to its height in his native country, each did so by using quite different approaches. Wagner's plots usually involved larger-than-life, mythological characters whose activities were meant to symbolize underlying philosophical issues. Verdi's favored real people cast in dramatic, action-filled situations. Although Wagner's plots are more strictly ordered, Verdi's are notable for spontaneity and a sure sense of drama.

Verdi and Wagner disagreed on the relative importance of the singers and the orchestra. Wagner used orchestration to convey his philosophical ideas, sometimes overshadowing the singers, whose role was to move the surface action along. By contrast, Verdi's operas are dominated by the singing voice. Melody is the vehicle for expressing a vast range of emotions, and singers rarely compete with the orchestral background.

THE *VERISMO* MOVEMENT

Toward the end of the nineteenth century, a movement toward naturalism and realism took place in Italian literature, similar to the movement in France. Called **verismo** (realism), it quickly penetrated Italian opera. Bizet's *Carmen* served as a model for the three Italian composers who led the movement: Giacomo Puccini (1858–1924), Ruggiero Leoncavallo (1858–1919), and Pietro Mascagni (1863–1945). Leoncavallo is remembered for *I Pagliacci* (*The Clowns,* 1892), and Mascagni for *Cavalleria Rusticana* (*Rustic Cavalry,* 1890). Puccini, the most successful of the *verismo* composers, effectively united grand opera and realism.

PUCCINI (1858-1924)

One of the most celebrated and successful of Italian opera composers, Giacomo Puccini (Poo-chee'-nee) was descended from a line of musicians that stretched back over five generations. During most of his childhood, Puccini showed only a modest talent for music; nevertheless, his mother insisted that he continue his studies, and by the age of sixteen he was composing in earnest—chiefly organ music for church services.

In 1880, Puccini obtained a scholarship to enter the Milan Conservatory. Once graduated from the Conservatory, he entered an opera competition with *Le Villi* (*The Vampires,* 1884), a work based on a Slavonic legend. He failed to win the contest, but the opera was produced in Milan on May 31, 1884. The success of the premiere persuaded the well-known publisher Giulio Ricordi to commission a second opera by Puccini. Largely because of a poor libretto, *Edgar* (1884–1888) was not a success; however, Ricordi continued to support the composer, and both men worked over the book for the next work, *Manon Lescaut.* Its premiere on February 1, 1893, was an immense triumph.

Although *Manon Lescaut* made Puccini famous in Italy, his next opera, *La Bohème*

(*Bohemian Life,* 1893–1896), brought him worldwide fame. He completed the work in his magnificent new villa next to Lake Massaciuccoli in northern Italy.

Puccini's only serious failure was, ironically, his favorite opera, *Madame Butterfly* (1904). Despite the hisses and catcalls of the premiere, however, the work became quite popular outside Italy. His next opera, *La Fanciulla del West* (*The Girl of the Golden West,* 1910), was based on a play by David Belasco, as was *Madame Butterfly.* Its premiere at the Metropolitan Opera in New York was one of the most glittering events of 1910, with Arturo Toscanini conducting and Enrico Caruso singing the lead male role.

During World War I Puccini remained in Italy, working quietly on more operas. His last work, *Turandot,* was left incomplete at his death. In 1923 he began suffering from what turned out to be cancer of the throat, and the following year he died of a heart attack. The task of finishing the final scenes of the work was entrusted to Franco Alfano, a distinguished younger composer. The opera was produced under Arturo Toscanini at La Scala, Milan, on April 25, 1926.

PUCCINI'S WORK

Puccini's operas reflect his realistic bent and his fascination with exotic settings. *Madame Butterfly,* for example, is set in Japan and *Turandot* in China. The opera that brought him international acclaim, *La Bohème,* combines rich and sensuous Romantic melodies with realistic details of plot and characterization. '

LA
BOHEME

THE PLOT

The opera is set in the Latin Quarter of Paris (the artists' district on the Left Bank) in the 1830s. Rodolfo (a struggling young poet) and his friend Marcello (a painter) are freezing in their garret studio on Christmas Eve. Suddenly a friend enters with money, groceries, and firewood, and insists they all go out to celebrate. Rodolfo stays to finish an article he is writing but is interrupted by a knock at the door. The caller is Mimi, a neighbor, whose candle has blown out. She asks for a light, and he invites her in. She is ill and faints. When she feels strong enough to leave, they discover that her key has fallen. As they search for it on the floor, their hands meet, and they give up the search to wait for more light from the moon. Rodolfo tells Mimi about his life and hopes. She describes her life as a maker of artificial flowers and her longing for spring and sunshine. Rodolfo declares his love and Mimi responds passionately. As the act ends, they leave to join his friends at the cafe.

Fig. 17.2 Rodolfo embraces the dead Mimi just before the curtain falls on *La Bohème*.

The next act opens with a holiday crowd in the streets near the cafe. Marcello sees his old flame, Musetta, with a wealthy old codger in tow. She tries to attract Marcello's attention, embarrassing her escort and amusing the spectators. Finally she sings a provocative waltz and, having sent her escort off on a fool's errand, leaps into Marcello's eager arms.

Some months later, Rodolfo's jealousy has caused Mimi to leave him. She seeks out Marcello to ask his help and tells him of Rodolfo's unbearable behavior; Rodolfo arrives and Mimi hides. He starts to complain to Marcello of Mimi's flirting, but admits that he is actually in despair over her failing health. When Mimi's coughing reveals her presence, Rodolfo begs her to stay with him until spring, and she agrees.

Act IV is set in the garret the following fall. Rodolfo and Marcello are in the studio. Their fellow artists arrive for dinner and a hilarious evening begins. Musetta interrupts their gaiety, announcing that Mimi has collapsed on the stairs. They carry her in; all except Rodolfo leave to pawn their treasures to buy medical supplies. Rodolfo and Mimi recall their first meeting; their friends return and Mimi drifts off to sleep. She dies, and Rodolfo embraces her while the others weep.

THE MUSIC

The music of *La Bohème* follows the natural inflections of the words of the libretto. Although almost every word is sung, Puccini attempts to give the impression of normal spoken conversation in a kind of recitative style. Much of the action is delivered in short phrases, often sung on one or two notes. Characters constantly interrupt one another. Little musical ornamentation is used. Very often the orchestra has the most important melodic material and creates subtle transitions between recitative and aria, introducing new harmonies and hints of melodies to be sung.

All of this is illustrated in the last half of Act I. Mimi and Rodolfo are searching in the dark for her key. Mimi is very nervous, keeping up a steady volley of apologies and questions:

RECORD 6/SIDE 1

Mimi: Importuna è la vicina . . .	*Your neighbor is troublesome . . .*
Rodolfo: Cosa dice, ma le pare.	*What are you saying, don't mention it.*
Mimi: Cerchi?	*Would you look?*
Rodolfo: Cerco.	*I am looking.*
Mimi: Ove sarà?	*Where can it be?*
Rodolfo: Ah!	*Ah!*
(Rodolfo pockets the key)	
Mimi: L'ha trovata?	*Did you find it?*
Rodolfo: No.	*No.*
Mimi: Mi pareve . . .	*I thought . . .*
Rodolfo: In verità.	*Honestly.*
Mimi: Cerca?	*Are you looking?*
Rodolfo: Cerco!	*I am looking!*

Puccini sets each of these phrases according to its character. Mimi's apology is a plaintive melodic line, while "I am looking" and "Where can it be?" are set on only one note. Rodolfo's "Ah!" is spoken, highlighted by a sudden pizzicato from the string section. The orchestra quietly advances the tension throughout, tossing in snatches of staccato melody while the low strings keep a steady beat.

While Rodolfo is groping toward Mimi's hand, the orchestra is preparing a change of mood. The staccato phrases become legato, the short notes give way to sustained ones, and the harmony begins to modulate in preparation for Rodolfo's aria. By the time Rodolfo has captured Mimi's hand, his aria flows naturally out of the preceding music:

Example 17.1

RODOLFO Che ge - li - da ma - ni - na, se la la - sci ris - cal - dar
(What a frozen little hand, let me warm it)

Rodolfo goes on to tell Mimi about his life and hopes, and the aria builds to a climax as he is swept up in a wave of emotion:

Example 17.2

Ta - lor dal mio for - zie - re —— ru-ban tut-ti i gio-
iel - li due la - dri: gli oc - chi bel - li.

("Now and then two thieves will rob me of all the jewels from my strongbox: two beautiful eyes.")

Mimi responds with her own lovely aria, "Mi chiamano Mimi" ("They call me Mimi"). She lives by herself, she tells Rodolfo, and longs for the coming spring and the fragrant scent of rose blossoms. As Mimi ends her aria, Rodolfo's friends shout to him from the street, momentarily breaking the spell and allowing the audience a brief respite before the passionate closing duet.

As Rodolfo turns from the window he is transfixed by the sight of Mimi bathed in the glow of moonlight. He begins to sing and soon Mimi joins him in a love duet based on the climactic phrase of Rodolfo's aria (compare Example 17.3 with Example 17.2):

Example 17.3

Con anima
(Ah! love alone commands me!)
MIMI: Ah! tu sol co - man-di,a - mor
RODOLFO: Fre - mon già nel - l'a - ni - ma ——
(Trembling in my soul)

This sensuous melody becomes the love theme of the opera. The duet ends in a kiss and Act I closes as the lovers sing the word "amor."

Both thematically and musically, *La Bohème* is unified by recurring motives. The last act is in many ways the mirror image of the first. In the same garret

Rodolfo and the dying Mimi relive their first meeting. As in their first encounter, Mimi's hands are cold, but a muff is quickly bought and as she drifts into her last sleep she murmurs, "My hands are all warm. . . ."

Although in the last act they sing parts of their opening arias, Rodolfo and Mimi never again sing their love duet. Its melody is present in the orchestra, shifting with the mood of the drama. By the very end, its lilting affirmation has changed to a forbidding minor cadence:

Example 17.4

GERMAN OPERA

While the Italian *verismo* composers were influenced by the Realist movement in literature, nineteenth-century German opera drew much of its inspiration from the ideals of the Romantic movement.

The first significant composer of German Romantic opera was Carl Maria von Weber (1786–1826). A nationalist and Romanticist, he built his style on the legends and songs of the German people and on Romantic elements. His opera *Der Freischütz* (*The Freeshooter,* 1821) incorporates aspects of the supernatural, a typically Romantic fascination.

German Romantic operas, such as *Der Freischütz,* tended to stress mood and setting. Nature was represented as a wild and mysterious force, and supernatural beings mixed freely with ordinary mortals. Human characters often symbolized supernatural forces of good and evil, and the hero's victory meant salvation or redemption. Harmony and orchestral color were the primary means of dramatic expression, with the voice often relegated to a secondary role.

In the latter part of the nineteenth century, one of the most powerful personalities in the history of music emerged—Richard Wagner. In his works, German Romantic opera reached its highest point.

WAGNER (1813–1883)

Born in Leipzig, Richard Wagner (Vahg′-ner) was the son of a clerk in the city police court who died when his son was only six months old. Richard's mother soon after married Ludwig Geyer, a gifted actor, playwright, and painter. It was rumored that Geyer was the composer's real father, and Wagner himself considered this likely. Wagner was a precocious child who showed an early interest in literature, writing a tragedy in the style of Shakespeare at the age of fourteen. In his formal musical training he was among the least systematic of the great nineteenth-century composers. He began piano lessons at age twelve, but never became a first-rate performer on any instrument. Like that of Berlioz, his great French contemporary, his music brought into play the full resources of the orchestra.

Lack of adequate preparation did not prevent him from early attempts at composition.

By 1832 several of his works—including two overtures and a symphony—had been performed publicly. The following year—at age twenty—he began his professional career, becoming chorus master for the Wurzburg theater. Positions at Magdeburg, Königsberg, and Riga followed in succession, and he began composing operas.

While in Königsberg, he married the actress Minna Planer and began work on an opera based on Bulwer-Lytton's historical novel, *Rienzi, Last of the Tribunes.* The years 1839 to 1842 were spent in Paris, where he tried vainly to have the work performed. His financial situation became desperate, partly because of his increasingly spendthrift ways, and the first serious breakdown in his marriage occurred.

Rienzi was finally accepted, not in Paris but in Dresden, Germany, and Wagner returned to Germany to supervise the production. The success of both *Rienzi* (1842) and his next opera, *Der Fliegende Holländer* (*The Flying Dutchman,* 1843), led to his appointment as conductor to the King of Saxony. For the next six years Wagner busied himself producing operas and writing two more himself: *Tannhäuser* (1842–1844) and *Lohengrin* (finished in 1848). Wagner's active participation in the revolutionary uprising of 1848–1849 forced him to flee to Switzerland.

While in exile, he turned to literary activity and wrote a number of essays, the most influential of which were *Das Kunstwerk der Zukunft* (*The Art-Work of the Future,* 1850) and *Oper und Drama* (*Opera and Drama,* 1851). In these he laid the foundations for "music drama," the term he used for his unique type of opera.

During his ten years in Switzerland, Wagner began putting his artistic theories into practice. By 1852 he had completed the poems of an epic cycle of four music dramas, entitled *Der Ring des Nibelungen* (*The Ring of the Nibelung*). The music for the first two dramas—*Das Rheingold* (*The Rhine Gold*) and *Die Walküre* (*The Valkyrie*)—and for part of the third—*Siegfried*—was completed by 1857. The entire cycle was completed seventeen years

Fig. 17.3 An informal photograph of Wagner taken when he lived in Switzerland. He often posed for at-home pictures in the velvet jacket and beret.

later, in 1874, with the composition of *Die Götterdämmerung* (*The Twilight of the Gods*). These works place heavy demands on the performers, and since the individual dramas last three to five hours each, the whole tetralogy requires four separate days for its performance.

In the intervening years, Wagner wrote two other works that remain perhaps his most popular and most frequently performed: *Tristan und Isolde* (1856–1859) and *Die Meistersinger von Nürnberg* (*The Mastersingers of Nuremberg,* 1862–1867).

Although highly prolific, Wagner experienced great difficulty in arranging performances of his works. Most were formidable in scale,

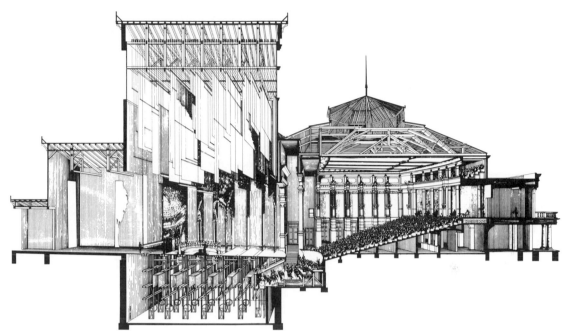

Fig. 17.4 Built in 1876, the Bayreuth Festspielhaus was designed under Wagner's direction specifically for the performance of his operas. As this transverse section shows, the orchestra pit is concealed and the audience floor is built on a rise, thus providing a clear view and a feeling of intimacy for over seventeen hundred people.

requiring theatrical and musical resources beyond the means of even the largest opera houses. As he approached the age of fifty, he became discouraged. His debts continued to pile up, and he separated from his wife and even contemplated suicide.

Then in 1864 his fortunes changed. The new king of Bavaria, Ludwig II, a devoted admirer of Wagner's music, invited the composer to Munich with the promise of financial and artistic support. At this time, Wagner fell in love with Cosima von Bülow, the daughter of Franz Liszt and wife of one of Wagner's close associates. Cosima left her husband to join Wagner, completely devoting herself to his ca-

reer. They were finally married in 1870, and together raised enough money to build an opera house devoted exclusively to producing his works. Located in the small Bavarian town of Bayreuth, the *Festspielhaus,* as it was called, was the scene of the first complete performance of the Ring cycle, in 1876 (see Fig. 17.4). One of the great artistic events of the century, this performance was the fulfillment of Wagner's lifelong dream. He completed one more work, *Parsifal* (1882), before illness forced him to travel to Italy in hope of regaining his health. He died quite suddenly, in Venice, on February 13, 1883.

WAGNER'S WORK

Although his most significant works were his operas and music dramas, Wagner also wrote some orchestral and choral music. His most important instrumental piece is the *Siegfried Idyll,* a short work composed for Cosima's birthday celebration of December 25, 1870. His most outstanding vocal work is a collection of five settings of poems by Mathilde Wesendonk, with whom Wagner had a passionate love affair in the late 1850s. Composed during 1857–1858, the collection is known today as the *Wesendonk Lieder*.

Wagner's early operas—*Die Feen* (*The Fairies,* 1833), *Das Liebesverbot* (*Love Prohibited,* 1836), and *Rienzi* (1842)—were written under the influence of Meyerbeer, Bellini, and Donizetti, the masters of grand opera whose works dominated the European opera houses of the early nineteenth century. His next three operas—*The Flying Dutchman, Tannhäuser,* and *Lohengrin*—represent a culmination of the German Romantic opera tradition that Wagner inherited from Carl Maria von Weber.

In the Ring cycle Wagner began to apply his innovative theories of operatic style and structure. The plots of the Ring cycle (all of which were his own creations, not those of a librettist) dealt with German mythology or historical legend. Underlying the surface plot were philosophical issues that he considered to be of fundamental importance: the struggles between the forces of good and evil and between the physical and spiritual, and the idea of redemption through unselfish love. In the Ring cycle Wagner attempted to symbolize the corruption of modern society through characters drawn from Teutonic mythology: giants, dwarfs, gods, and warriors.

HIS STYLE

Wagner believed that a music drama should be a *Gesamtkunstwerk* (universal artwork) combining elements from all the arts. The most important element should be drama, with the music serving to reinforce the dramatic expression. This view was directly opposed to that held by many earlier opera composers, including Mozart, who believed that the drama should serve as a framework for the music.

In Wagner's works the music is essentially continuous throughout each act, with one section moving smoothly into the next. In place of the traditional arias and recitatives, Wagner developed a musical line he called *Sprechsingen* (singing speech). This style combined the lyric quality of the aria and the speaking quality of the recitative and permitted a continuous musical flow which Wagner termed "endless melody."

The voices and orchestra each play a specific role in conveying several levels of meaning. The singers have the lesser role; through their actions and words, they explain the surface events of the drama. The orchestra is used to express the inner meaning of the events, which the characters themselves often do not understand. In addition, the orchestra serves as the major unifying force of the opera. The fabric of the orchestral music is held together by the use of the **leitmotif** (leading motive), a melodic fragment that represents a specific character, object, or idea; it is a kind of musical label that sounds every time its object appears in the drama. This technique was not original with Wagner; Verdi, Puccini, Weber, and Berlioz had used recurring themes to unify their works. But Wagner used the leitmotif much more consistently.

Apart from identifying characters or objects, leitmotivs are also used in more subtle ways. As musical phrases, they can be varied or developed in the usual symphonic fashion; with every variation and every change of context, they take on added shades of meaning. Wagner also uses them to suggest ideas to the audience. For example, the connection between two objects may be suggested by a similarity between their leitmotivs.

Although leitmotivs are woven into the orchestral fabric, they do not provide enough unification for works of such vast dimensions as Wagner's operas. Wagner therefore imposes formal structures on larger portions of the music dramas (such as whole acts), usually constructing them either in AAB or in ABA form. On such a large scale, forms are not obvious to the listener; nevertheless, they lend a feeling of balance and proportion to the work.

Another aspect of Wagner's style that deserves special mention is his use of chromatic and dissonant harmonies. Wagner continued to expand the chromatic idiom used by other Romantic composers, particularly Liszt in his symphonic poems. In *Tristan and Isolde,* discussed below, Wagner produced a new ambiguity of tonality by constantly shifting keys and by introducing dissonant chords in places where the listener would normally expect resolution to consonance. Indeed, Wagner's use of chromatic harmony represents an important step toward the development of the new, atonal systems that evolved in the twentieth century (see Chapters 19 and 20).

TRISTAN AND ISOLDE

Tristan and Isolde is an outstanding example of Wagner's mature style. In this work the complex web of leitmotivs is ever-present, but they are subordinated to a constant flow of emotions and inspired orchestral writing. The mood of tragic gloom is sustained by the highly chromatic quality of the writing.

THE PLOT

The libretto is based on a medieval legend. The opera opens on shipboard, where the knight Tristan is escorting the Irish princess Isolde to Cornwall. There she is to marry his lord and uncle, King Marke. Isolde explains to her maid Brängane that she had met Tristan before; he had come to her, unknown and wounded, and she had healed him. When she later discovered that he had been the one who killed her fiancé in combat, she became furious and tried to kill him. But when he looked in her eyes, she was unable to; she felt love instead. Isolde orders Brängane to prepare a death potion, so that she may kill Tristan and herself. They drink the potion and are condemned to a fate worse than the death she had planned, for Brängane has substituted a love potion, and their attraction becomes an irresistible passion.

The second act opens in Isolde's garden, where she and Tristan plan to meet in secret that night; King Marke and the courtiers are off on a hunt. Brängane advises caution, but Isolde signals to her lover and he comes. Their long love scene is interrupted by the return of the hunting party, which includes Melot, a jealous knight who has warned King Marke about the affair. The king, revealing that he married Isolde only to satisfy the people of his kingdom, questions Tristan. Tristan does not defend his disloyalty, but asks Isolde if she will follow him to

Fig. 17.5 A nineteenth-century engraving of Tristan and Isolde, caught up in the passion induced by their love potion. The Angel of Death hovers above, foreshadowing the tragic end of the ill-fated lovers.

the "wondrous realm of night." She agrees; Tristan pretends to attack Melot, drops his guard, and permits himself to be seriously wounded.

The final act takes place at Tristan's ancestral castle in Brittany. His squire Kurvenal has sent for Isolde; the dying and delirious Tristan recalls their love and his longing. As Isolde arrives, the dazed hero rips off his bandages and dies in her arms. King Marke, Melot, and the others arrive in a second ship, and Kurvenal and Melot kill each other. Marke forgives the unhappy lovers, and Isolde joins Tristan in death.

Such a simplified account of the plot gives no indication of the wealth of detail and symbolism with which Wagner has imbued it. The story actually represents a philosophy of life: an all-encompassing love inevitably leads to unsatisfied longing, then to death and a final transfiguration of two into one. This deeper level of meaning is symbolized by constant references to "day" and "night." Day is the world of conventional life and values, while Night is the inner world in which such a love exists. When Tristan asks Isolde to follow him to the "wondrous realm of night," he means the death in which their union can be complete.

Analysis of one scene from *Tristan und Isolde* illustrates Wagner's use of the leitmotif. In actual practice, it is difficult to label some of the motives. With slight variations, they seem to represent several different things. The opening passage of the opera is a case in point. The two motives here are often called Tristan and Isolde, or Grief and Desire. Together, they represent Yearning, or the Love Potion.

RECORD 6/SIDE 1

Example 17.5

Many basic emotions such as suffering, ecstasy, and desire are closely linked, and their motives are also related. Even the Day and Night motives are similar.

Example 17.6

In the last scene of the second act several other leitmotivs are employed. Three come from the great love duet of the preceding scene; they represent Love's Peace, Love-Death, and Ecstasy.

Example 17.7

The other two are associated with King Marke and his grief over Tristan's betrayal.

Example 17.8

The scene begins at the very climax of the love duet. As the singers reach their final notes, the orchestra plays a loud and unexpectedly dissonant chord, Brängane screams, and Kurvenal shouts to Tristan to protect himself. Marke, Melot, and the courtiers enter. The music grows quiet as the two groups study each other. The Love-Death and Ecstasy themes are heard softly in the orchestra. They are followed by the Day theme, as Tristan sings *"Der öde Tag zum letzten Mal"* (The bleak day for the last time).

Marke, shattered, tells how deeply Tristan's betrayal affects him, while the bass clarinet sounds his Grief motive. Tristan answers violently that this is all a

CHARACTERISTICS OF ROMANTIC MUSIC

Tonality	Major-minor system with less firm sense of tonal center
Texture	Largely homophonic
Rhythm	Frequent fluctuations in tempo; use of rubato
Pitch	Greatly expanded pitch range
Harmony	Use of chromatic harmonies
	Modulations to distant keys
	Complicated chords
	Harmony used as expressive element
Tone Color	Fascination and experimentation with instrumental color; color rivals other elements in importance
Melody	Lyrical, expressive, flowing; sometimes ornamented
Dynamics	Wide range of dynamics
	Frequent fluctuations in dynamic level
	Dynamics used as structural element
Small Works	Art song (lied)
	Character pieces and miniatures for piano
Large Works	Concerto, symphony, program symphony, symphonic poem (tone poem), opera, choral works, chamber works, concert overture
Instruments	Piano was favorite instrument; large orchestra; unusual instrument groupings; emphasis on orchestration and color
Performance Style	Steady growth of virtuoso technique
Formal Innovations	Carefully constructed Classical forms were freely manipulated and expanded; cyclical procedure; theme transformation; development of programmatic and descriptive music as manifested in the program symphony and tone poem; *verismo* movement in opera; development of nationalism in music.

bad dream; significantly, he calls it a day phantom, a morning vision, rather than a nightmare.

Marke, the innocent victim of fate, is a "day" person, with no control over his unhappy situation. Repeatedly he asks what he has done to deserve this. Marke can never know the answer to his question. At the same time, the orchestra answers the question for the audience by playing the Grief and Desire motive from the opening of the opera.

Tristan then asks Isolde if she will follow him; as he begins, the violins play the leitmotif associated with Love's Peace. In a lyric arioso passage he describes the dark land to which they will go. Isolde gives her assent in a similar section; he kisses her as the Ecstasy motive is heard. The infuriated Melot urges the King to defend his honor. Tristan challenges Melot, and finally lets himself be mortally wounded.

Wagner's music has been unusually influential. His harmonic style, continuous but irregular melodic writing, symphonic use of leitmotivs, and superb sense of orchestral color all influenced several later generations of composers. He attained his ideal of the *Gesamtkunstwerk,* although his music had a force that his librettos did not. Since he intended that his music should serve the drama, it is ironic that today we sometimes hear the music alone performed in concerts, while the librettos could never stand alone as plays. But despite some errors in judgment, Wagner's accomplishments were truly outstanding, expressing the universal state of ecstasy toward which all Romantic artists had been striving.

SUMMARY

During the early part of the Romantic era, Paris was the operatic capital of Europe. French opera concentrated on spectacular productions, featuring crowd scenes, ballets, choruses, and fantastic scenery. These grand operas, however, gradually gave way to lyric operas that emphasized Romantic plots and beautiful melodies. Toward the end of the century a naturalistic style developed, of which Georges Bizet's *Carmen* in a prime example.

In Italy, Gioacchino Rossini was the outstanding composer of the early part of the nineteenth century. His *Barber of Seville* is an excellent example of the Italian *opera buffa.* The dominant figure in Italian opera during the second half of the century was Giuseppe Verdi. His realistic, action-filled plots were dominated by the singing voice, which became the primary vehicle for emotional expression. Toward the end of the century a movement toward naturalism penetrated Italian opera. Called *verismo,* it is best exemplified in the works of Giacomo Puccini.

Romantic opera in Germany was strongly influenced by the Romantic movement itself. The composer who first established a genuinely Germanic style was Carl Maria von Weber. German opera reached its highest point in the works of Richard Wagner, who sought to write "music dramas" that would encompass all the arts in a unified whole. To Wagner, the most important element was the drama, with the music serving the dramatic expression. Dramatic unity was enhanced by the use of leitmotivs, or melodic fragments associated with persons, objects, or ideas. Wagner's use of chromatic harmonies represented a significant step toward the development of new tonal systems in the twentieth century.

NEW TERMS

grand opera   bel canto
opéra comique (comic opera)   verismo
lyric opera   leitmotif

PART VI SUGGESTED LISTENING

Berlioz, Hector

Harold in Italy, Op. 16. This symphony in four movements is based on Lord Byron's *Childe Harolde,* with the solo viola as the main character.

Bizet, Georges

L'Arlésienne Suite No. 2. Bizet wrote this score as incidental music for Daudet's play about doomed love.

Brahms, Johannes

Piano Quintet in F Minor, Op. 34. The four movements illustrate the juxtaposition of Brahms the lyricist with Brahms the contrapuntist.

Variations on a Theme of Haydn, Op. 56a. Originating as an Austrian pilgrim song which Haydn used and Brahms admired, the theme is the basis for a set of eight variations and a lengthy finale.

Chopin, Frederic

Etudes, Op. 25. The second set of twelve studies employing similar formal structure. Each is a study of a pianistic difficulty requiring a musical solution.

Dvořák, Antonín

Slavonic Dances, Op. 46. In versions scored both for piano (four hands) and for orchestra, this was the work that gained Dvořák an international reputation. Rather than attempting to recreate Czech folk music, the *Slavonic Dances* are a synthesis of Czech folk rhythms and an Austro-German harmonic language.

Liszt, Franz

Hungarian Rhapsody No. 2. Liszt first began to love gypsy music as a boy and later studied it exhaustively in its native surrounding. His *Hungarian Rhapsodies* combine the gypsy style with pianistic pyrotechnics.

Mendelssohn, Felix

Overture to A Midsummer Night's Dream. Mendelssohn wrote this concert overture at the age of seventeen. All the components of the play are included: the solemnity of Theseus' court, the whispering fairies, and the braying of Bottom.

Hebrides Overture (Fingal's Cave). This concert overture describes Mendelssohn's impressions of a sea journey to Fingal's Cave. The interplay of two themes—the first in a restless B minor, the second in a serene D major—evokes the play of wind and sun on water.

Mussorgsky, Modest

Pictures at an Exhibition. A series of ten pieces united by a *Promenade* which introduces the work. Composed after Mussorgsky had viewed an exhibition of Victor Hartmann's paintings, it is available in piano and orchestral versions, the latter orchestrated by Maurice Ravel.

Puccini, Giacomo

Gianni Schicchi. This very funny one-act opera, Puccini's only comic work, tells the story of the wily and wealthy peasant Gianni Schicchi, who pretends to be dying and so outwits his relatives. In the aria "O mio babbino caro," Puccini parodies his own grand opera traditions.

Rimsky-Korsakov, Nikolai

Scheherezade, Op. 35. This symphonic suite is based on the tale *A Thousand and One Nights,* in which a sultan's plan to kill each of his wives is foiled by the sultana Scheherezade, who keeps him so interested in her stories that he rescinds the death sentence. The gorgeously oriental melodies and lush orchestration have made the piece a popular favorite.

Schubert, Franz

Die Winterreise. Twenty-four songs on the theme of loneliness which are musically united through rhythmic patterns and harmonic structures.

Schumann, Robert

Carnaval, Op. 9. This work is composed of twenty small pieces, some describing a carnival (clowns, sphinxes) or one of Schumann's friends (Chopin, Clara Wieck). All the themes use the German notes A-S-C-H, spelling the name of the town in which lived a woman Schumann loved.

Strauss, Richard

Don Juan. This tone poem was inspired by the hero of Nikolaus Lenau's poem *Don Juan,* the story of a proud and sensual idealist whose life is consumed by his search for the woman who is womanhood incarnate. The music weaves together the heroic themes of Don Juan and the lyrical themes of the women.

Tchaikovsky, Peter Ilyich

Symphony No. 6 in B Minor (Pathétique). Tchaikovsky's last symphony is certainly his most masterful and the most popular today. The composer described it as a programmatic symphony, although he never revealed the program. The title *Pathétique* was suggested by the composer's brother. The most unusual formal aspect of the symphony is that it ends with a slow movement rather than with a loud and triumphant Allegro.

Verdi, Giuseppi

La Traviata. Based on a Dumas play about a beautiful, moral, and doomed courtesan, *La Traviata* was panned at its premiere as a "public presentation of prostitution." Nevertheless, it has become one of Verdi's most popular operas.

Wagner, Richard

Siegfried Idyll. Wagner composed this work as a surprise for his wife Cosima on her birthday. The piece is woven from intimate details of their life—an original lullaby, a string quartet begun for Cosima, the "orange sunrise" on the birth of their first son.

VII

MUSIC OF THE EARLY TWENTIETH CENTURY

Drawings by Hugo Valentino for the premiere of Stravinsky's *The Rite of Spring,* matched with fragments of the score. (Courtesy the André Meyer Collection, Paris, © S.P.A.D.E.M. 1978.)

CHAPTER 18 | BRIDGING THE GAP BETWEEN CENTURIES

TOWARD THE END OF THE NINETEENTH CENTURY THE CENTER OF cultural activity in Europe was Paris. Two different musical styles were current. One was the basically German-Italian late Romantic style, strongly influenced by the monumental achievements of Richard Wagner. The leaders of this pan-European style of music in Paris were César Franck (1822–1890) and his pupils. The other was the specifically French tradition, as cultivated by Camille Saint-Saëns (1835–1921), Jules Massenet (1842–1912), and Gabriel Fauré (1845–1924). The underlying spirit of the French tradition was more classical and orderly than romantic and expressive. The music was subtle and understated, full of lyric melodies and carefully wrought details.

IMPRESSIONISM AND SYMBOLISM

The musical culture of France was closely connected to the other arts, particularly painting and literature. One of the outstanding artistic movements of the turn of the century was **Impressionism,** in which artists sought to capture the visual impression, rather than the literal reality, of a subject. Though their work and methods were at first ridiculed by the critics, the Impressionists persisted in their exploration of the play of light and in their use of patches and dabs of color to build up an image. They also continued their habit of working out-of-doors and of utilizing bright afternoon light; mood and atmosphere and the richness of nature were among their major inspirations. Meanwhile, Symbolist poets were experimenting with rhythm, sound, and the clustering of images to suggest moods or emotions.

Coming slightly later than the movements in art and literature, the Impressionist movement in music was similarly characterized by experimentation and by the rejection of past viewpoints. It, too, emphasized mood and atmosphere more than structure, and it, too, adopted nature as a frequent subject. Impressionist music was recognizable by its fragile and decorative beauty, its sensuous tone colors, its subdued atmosphere, its elegance and refinement. It cast off the more pompous, heavy, and serious quality of the German tradition. Again, France produced the most important composers of this school: Claude Debussy and Maurice Ravel.

DEBUSSY (1862-1918)

Claude Debussy (Deb-you-see′) was born in St. Germain-en-Laye, near Paris, and was educated at the Paris Conservatory, where he received traditional training in the cosmopolitan late Romantic style. He absorbed it well enough to win the Prix de Rome at the age of twenty-two, but soon after he began to reject the Germanic tradition in general and Wagner's philosophy in particular.

Debussy was put off by the grand themes and ponderous quality of German Romantic music. For him the primary goal of music was to give pleasure, to appeal to the senses. An incisive critic, Debussy wrote articles on music which were published in the leading French journals. His reaction to Wagner's use of the leitmotif is characteristically witty and caustic: "Remember, [Wagnerian characters] never appear unless accompanied by their damnable leitmotiv, and there are even those who sing it! It's rather like those silly people who hand you their visiting cards and then lyrically recite key information they contain."

Opera was one of Debussy's lifelong interests, and his operatic style was very much a reaction against Wagner's influence. *Pelléas et Mélisande* (1902), which Debussy worked on over the decade of the 1890s, is taken from a Symbolist play, and the vague references and images of the text are matched by the strange harmonies and restrained colors of the music. Throughout the work the voices dominate over a continuous orchestral background. The first performance of the opera met a mixed reaction, with some critics attacking it for its lack of form and melody and its unconventional harmonies and others enchanted by its subtle,

Fig. 18.1 Debussy broke with the German Romantic style to create evocative Impressionistic music characterized by its sensuous tone colors, elusive chromatic harmonies, and freedom of form.

elusive quality. The opera caught on and established Debussy as the leader of the Impressionist movement in music.

Debussy was deeply devoted to his country, and the onset of World War I disturbed him so profoundly that for a time he felt incapable of writing music. But his sense of nationalism impelled him to return to his art and he began composing again with furious energy—an effort spurred on by the fact that he was slowly dying of cancer. His death came in March, 1918, as Paris was being bombarded by German artillery.

DEBUSSY'S WORK

Debussy's compositions for piano are among the most significant works for that instrument written during the present century. His early (non-Impressionistic) works include the *Suite bergamasque* (1893) and a suite *Pour le piano* (1901). *Clair de lune* (*Moonlight,* 1890) is perhaps his best-known work for piano. The Impressionistic style is fully evident in works published between 1903 and 1913: *Estampes* (*Engravings*), two collections of *Préludes,* and two of *Images.*

Debussy's important orchestral works are all Impressionistic, beginning with the *Prélude à l'après-midi d'un faune* (*Prelude to the Afternoon of a Faun,* 1894), and continuing with the three *Nocturnes—Nuages* (*Clouds*), *Fêtes* (*Festivals*), and *Sirènes* (*Sirens*)—and *La mer* (*The Sea,* 1905), a set of symphonic sketches. In chamber music his greatest achievement was the Quartet in G Minor for Strings (1893). The first performance of this work left its audience puzzled and critics complaining of an "orgy of modulations." A forerunner of his musical Impressionism, it came to be recognized in the twentieth century as one of the most important string quartets since those of Brahms.

Although Debussy loved opera, he completed only one of the many operatic projects he started, *Pelléas et Mélisande.* He also wrote incidental music for a play as well as art songs set to poems by Mallarmé, Villon, Verlaine, Baudelaire, and others.

HIS STYLE

The music of Claude Debussy is programmatic, but in a very general way; there is no attempt to tell a story or express specific feelings. Rather, his music creates a "mood" or atmosphere to correspond with its subject or program.

Although Debussy's style is unique, many influences can be seen to have helped form it. Most important were the Romantic pianists Chopin and Liszt and the composers in the French tradition. Paris was a center for Russian music, and Mussorgsky's idiom pointed Debussy in new directions. His interest in exotic music was stimulated by the Javanese orchestra (called a *gamelan*), which he heard at the Paris Exposition of 1889.

One of the strongest influences on Debussy's style was not musical at all, but literary; he was closely associated with a group of artists centered around Stéphane Mallarmé, the Symbolist poet. Through this connection Debussy became interested in expressing the unique sounds and rhythmic patterns of the French language in music. French generally avoids strong accents, making use of vowels of different lengths for rhythm and stress. Debussy's choice of subject matter for many of his pieces also reflects his close association with this important literary movement.

Debussy was the first European composer to break with the old system of tonality, and the new language he developed had a profound influence on almost every other composer of the twentieth century. His music is organized around sound patterns; he works with blocks of color and shifts from one to another very subtly. The harmonic basis of his music is entirely new, building on the symmetrical patterns of the whole-tone scale. Thus, instead of relying on the traditional tonic-dominant-tonic sequence of harmonies, he often uses a series of chords built on adjacent degrees of the scale. These parallel chains of chords leave the piece without any clearly defined tonal center for extended periods. Other elements of the music must therefore function as form-building devices—particularly rhythm, dynamics, texture, and instrumental timbre.

In one sense, of course, Debussy's style is clearly an offshoot of the Romantic movement; the emphasis on color and the lack of interest in traditional forms and procedures are evidence of this, as are the literary associations of most of his works. But in another sense, Debussy represents the beginning of the new and radically different music of the twentieth century. His use of atonal harmonies took music into new and uncharted areas, and his freer forms and concentration on timbre influenced almost all later composers.

PRÉLUDE À L'APRÈS-MIDI D'UN FAUNE
RECORD 6/SIDE 2

This brief work was inspired by Mallarmé's poem *L'après-midi d'un faune,* published in 1876. Debussy first intended to write an opera based on the poem but soon abandoned this project for a smaller one; he described the *Prélude* as a "very free illustration of Mallarmé's beautiful poem." The faun of the title is the sensual forest deity of pagan mythology, half man, half goat. Awakening from sleep, his mind befuddled by wine, the faun recalls two nymphs he had seen earlier in the day. Did he carry them off to his lair or was it only a fantasy? "Is it a dream that I love?" he asks. But the afternoon is warm, the effort to remember too great, so once again he drifts off to sleep. Without following the events of the poem literally, Debussy evokes a musical impression of each scene.

In the *Prélude,* which was his first orchestral work, Debussy had not completely broken with traditional ideas of form; the piece is very roughly in an AA'BA" pattern, although there is no literal repetition. However, the character and significance of the work lie, not in its formal structure, but in those elements which give it its Impressionistic quality.

The choice of instruments is in itself unusual and indicative of the nature of the piece. The winds consist of three flutes, two oboes, English horn, two clarinets, and two bassoons; there are four French horns, but the rest of the brasses (trumpets, trombones, and tuba) are omitted and the percussion is limited to a pair of tiny "antique cymbals," which produce a delicate rather than a smashing sound. Two harps and strings complete the instrumentation.

Debussy also departs from the standard orchestral practice in his *use* of these instruments. Virtually all the main melodic material is assigned to solo winds, primarily flute and oboe, with the French horn also playing an important role. The strings are often muted and divided. The use of the harps helps evoke the langorous atmosphere which is the essence of the piece.

The opening theme is a sensuous melody first played by the solo flute and heard later in various transformations throughout the work:

p doux et expressif

Example 18.1*   *(sweet and expressive)*

*   Examples 18.1 and 18.2 are used by permission of C. F. Peters Corporation, New York.

The lyric theme of the middle section is first located in the wind instruments in unison and repeated later by the strings:

p *expressif et très* ⟨ *m.f*   **p**   *cre - scen - do*   *f* ⟨
                    soutenu
        (expressive and very sustained)

Example 18.2

    In general the piece has a delicate, restrained, dreamlike quality. The dynamic level is subdued, only occasionally rising to a forte or fortissimo. There are frequent subtle changes of tempo and dynamics, a relaxed, almost vague rhythmic movement without a strong beat, and many dissonant harmonics, which provide color more than a strong sense of progression. All of these contribute to the floating, evocative nature of the work.

    Along with Debussy's later orchestral works, the *Prélude* had a profound and lasting effect on the subsequent development of orchestral music.

MAURICE RAVEL

Maurice Ravel (Rah-vell', 1875–1937) is often linked with Debussy as the other major figure who most fully realized the possibilities of musical Impressionism. But Ravel's music, especially the compositions written in his later years, combines the sonorous Impressionism of Debussy with a classical orientation toward form and balance.

    Philosophically, Ravel had much in common with Debussy. Both composers agreed that music should serve an esthetic purpose, that the creation of beautiful sound was the ultimate aim. They considered themselves rebels against German Romanticism and the Wagnerian school. They shared an attraction to the medieval modes and the novel scales employed by nationalistic composers of other countries. The rhythms of Spanish dance music also intrigued them, as did Oriental modes and colors.

    But the similarities between the two composers were limited. While Ravel made use of all the Impressionist devices, his compositional procedures were quite different in a number of ways from those of Debussy. There is less use of the whole-tone scale and sparing use of dissonance in Ravel's work. His use of orchestral color is more brilliant and dynamic than Debussy's. For musical texture, he relied on melodic lines rather than on the parallel blocks of sound which Debussy favored. Ravel also displayed a firmer sense of key and employed broader melodies, more distinct harmonic movement, and more emphatic rhythms than his predecessor.

    Ravel created many compositions for the piano. *Pavane pour une infante défunte* (*Pavane for a Dead Princess,* 1899), *Jeux d'eaux* (*Fountains,* 1901), and *Miroirs* (1905) are among the works that earned him his reputation as one of the outstanding composers of piano music of the twentieth century.

(Continued on page 340.)

THE GENESIS OF
THE MODERN ERA

Although Romanticism infused the music of the entire nineteenth century, by mid-century other art forms began to take a new direction. Rejecting emotionalism, Realist writers and artists chose to portray everyday life—and low life—as objectively and unsentimentally as possible.

Realism included an interest in portraying scenes of nature accurately and unpretentiously. What this interest led to was the awesome Impressionist departure of the 1870s. Strongly influenced by Edouard Manet (1832–1883), who played down careful perspective and abandoned the usual gradations of light and shadow in his efforts to give the illusion of three-dimensionality, the Impressionists went a step further. In their landscape painting they concentrated on producing an overall sense of what the eye sees rather than what the mind knows is there. In a way, the real subject of the Impressionists was not nature itself, but light. Leaving their studios for the out-of-doors, they carefully noted how sunlight illuminates an object and tried to duplicate that effect by applying their bright, pastel-colored pigment in tiny flecks. To give their paintings spontaneity and immediacy they consciously blurred or distorted their images. The most accomplished of the Impressionists was Claude Monet (1840–1928, Plate 28). In his later career Monet was so eager to capture the way objects change their appearance in response to changes in light and atmosphere that he undertook to paint whole series of canvasses devoted to a given subject—a cathedral, a haystack, a poplar tree—as it appeared at different times of the day.

Artists trained at the official academies and most critics in Paris were both contemptuous of and hostile toward the Impressionists, dismissing their exhibitions as the work of madmen, frauds, and incompetents. Nevertheless, though it was scorned in the 1870s, Impressionism began to achieve a measure of success and recognition in the 1880s. Meanwhile, a counterpart to Impressionism could be discerned in literature, in the movement called Symbolism. Symbolist poets, among whom were Charles Baudelaire (1821–1867) and Arthur Rimbaud (1854–1891), attempted to achieve "musical" effects by manipulating the rhythm and sounds of words. The basic idea or emotion of each poem was suggested by clusters of images and metaphors.

By the end of the nineteenth century many art collectors actively sought out Impressionist works. The academic viewpoint, which held that art should be concerned only with religious, historical, literary, and patriotic themes, had started to fade, and the Impressionist experiments of the 1870s had stimulated painters to explore a wide range of different styles. Vincent Van Gogh (1835–1890) worked with agitated, distorted shapes and brilliant color to arouse the feelings of the observer (Plate 29). Paul Gauguin (1848–1903) introduced large areas of bright, flat color, and in his scenes of primitive life in Brittany and Tahiti conveyed an overpowering sensuality. Georges Seurat (1859–1891)

Plate 28. When Claude Monet's *Impression: Sunrise* was exhibited in 1874, one critic who was appalled by its "unfinished" qualities denounced the new style and coined the term "Impressionism" in disgust. (Courtesy Musée Marmottan, Paris.)

Plate 29. In the 1880s French artists, using Impressionism as a starting point, developed far more radical design. Vincent Van Gogh's late paintings of the dazzling light and color of the Provençal countryside—as in *The Starry Night* (1889)—demonstrate the agitation and emotional power of his highly individual style. (Collection, The Museum of Modern Art, New York; acquired through the Lillie P. Bliss Bequest.)

Plate 30. Pablo Picasso's *Les Demoiselles d'Avignon,* painted in 1907, fractures and dislocates form into planes and geometrical blocks. Early critics dubbed the new style Cubism. The figures on the right reflect the influence of African sculpture. (Collection, The Museum of Modern Art, New York; acquired through the Lillie P. Bliss Bequest.)

Plate 31. *The Red Studio,* by Henri Matisse (1911). Matisse, the leader of the French Expressionists, painted through a long career in bright, decorative color. He said he wanted an art "of purity and serenity, devoid of troubling or depressing subject matter." (Collection, The Museum of Modern Art, New York; Mrs. Simon Guggenheim Fund.)

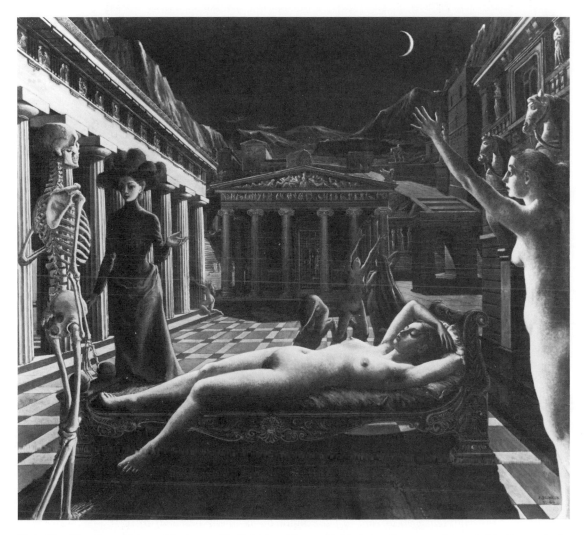

Plate 32.   The Surrealists, not in tune with Cubist or Expressionist abstraction, were interested in the mysteries and paradoxes of the unconscious and the world of dreams. Paul Delvaux's *Venus Asleep* (1944) perplexes by its polished style, classical landscape, and diverse female figures. (© S.P.A.D.E.M. 1978, courtesy The Tate Gallery, London.)

and Paul Cézanne (1839–1901), on the other hand, were more interested in new formal combinations than in the expression of feelings. Seurat, deeply influenced by the color theory of contemporary physicists, applied tiny dots of pure color to the canvas to build scenes that shimmered with light. Cézanne, whose goal was to capture on canvas the solidity of the forms found in nature, retained the color of the Impressionists but concentrated on conveying a sense of the mass of objects.

The work of the Impressionist and Post-Impressionist artists helped prepare the way for the tremendous amount of experimentation that marked all the arts of the early twentieth century. Indeed, it is fair to say that few centuries have witnessed more basic changes in the arts than the twentieth. In painting and sculp-

ture, the depiction of actual objects was abandoned for nonrepresentational abstraction. In literature, traditional narrative forms were sometimes discarded for radical new approaches such as James Joyce's stream of consciousness technique. In music, traditional harmony and tonality were redefined or rejected in favor of atonality and serialism. Indeed, it seems that the quest for innovation and new systems of expression has sometimes made newness *the most important standard of quality. Since World War II, the range of expression in all the arts has become so vast that consensus among critics and patrons has nearly disappeared.*

In the first years of the twentieth century young artists, influenced by the Impressionists and the avant-garde Post-Impressionists, exhibited styles of painting that were more daring and varied than any seen in the preceding generation. Beginning around 1905, the painters known as the Fauves ("wild beasts"), most notably Henri Matisse (1870–1954), worked in an Expressionist style, which distorted contours and colors with the intent of creating visual excitement and expressing inner feeling rather than of reproducing reality (Plate 31). One Russian-born Expressionist, who worked both in Paris and in Munich, was Wassily Kandinsky (1866–1944). In 1910, he took the drastic step of completely abandoning representational painting. Thereafter, it was recognized that the subject of the painter could be simply shapes and colors—with all the freedom and variety that this kind of abstraction implies.

A different current of twentieth-century painting developed from the experiments of Paul Cézanne, who, after a giant retrospective in Paris at the turn of the century, was now recognized as a "master." In the decade preceding World War I, Pablo Picasso (1881–1973) and others developed a style called Cubism. In this style, illustrated by the striking Les Demoiselles d'Avignon *(Plate 30), a composition was broken into angular, geometrical shapes presented from several simultaneous viewpoints. Cubism differed from Expressionism in giving primary attention to form. Instead of trying to excite the passions of the observer or reveal the inner soul of the artist, Cubism tried to reformulate the world in terms of fundamental shapes—spheres, cones, cubes, and cylinders. This concern with abstract structure held broad possibilities, and Cubism thus remained a strong influence on advanced painting throughout the first half of the century.*

The most provocative sculptor in late nineteenth-century France was Auguste Rodin (1848–1917), because he explored human form more intuitively than his contemporaries, whose sculpture was often pedantically exact and mock-heroic. By 1900, Rodin was the most renowned artist in Paris. But how different sculpture became in the next few years! Matisse designed bronzes of highly abstract human figures, and in 1909 Picasso applied the Cubist approach to a bronze head. Umberto Boccioni (1882–1916) attempted to display figures in the process of movement (Plate 33), and the Rumanian sculptor Constantin Brancusi (1876–1957) developed forms that were nearly nonrepresentational.

In architecture, designers began moving away from the historicism of the previous century, with its emphasis on the revival of earlier styles. One architectural eccentric, Antonio Gaudi of Spain (1852–1926), rejected historical building vocabularies entirely, in favor of free-flowing, almost organic forms. More influential in the development of a contemporary architecture, however,

Plate 33. *Unique Forms of Continuity in Space,* by Umberto Boccioni (1913). Boccioni tried to show the human figure in motion by suggesting several different moments of time in one sculpture. This bronze seems to have been shaped by rushing air whose currents extend beyond the fluttering shapes of the metal. (Collection, The Museum of Modern Art, New York; acquired through the Lillie P. Bliss Bequest.)

Plate 34. The Bauhaus Workshop, built by Walter Gropius in the 1920s, dramatized the principle of building a structural skeleton of steel and then giving it a floor-to-ceiling glass wall. This kind of "functional" architecture was later called the International style. (Courtesy The Museum of Modern Art, New York.)

was the Bauhaus, a German school that designed buildings and objects in a functional style that was consistent with the era of mass production and made use of industrial materials. More than any other single institution, the Bauhaus helped create the so-called International Style, an architecture of steel framing, glass, and concrete. Twentieth-century apartments, office buildings, factories, civic centers, department stores, and schools designed in this functional, anti-historical style have changed the appearance of cities all over the world.

Changes in the music of the late nineteenth and early twentieth centuries were just as substantial as those in the visual arts. Whereas the Romantic mode prevailed before 1900, the turn of the century brought new directions. Musical Impressionism was introduced in the compositions of Claude Debussy, who began to experiment with a new harmonic vocabulary and to move away from traditional forms and procedures. Later, such composers as Hindemith, Bartók, and Stravinsky redefined tonality and changed the way in which a tonal center was established. Arnold Schoenberg took an even more radical direction, rejecting tonality altogether and eventually developing a revolutionary new system of musical organization called serialism.

Between 1850 and 1950 the Industrial Revolution transformed the nature of work and the standard of living for the overwhelming majority of people in Europe and America. The great cities, railroad systems, and factories created an environment entirely different from that of the primarily agricultural world which existed before the mid-nineteenth century. It is hard for those of us who have known no other life to appreciate how complex our industrial world is. Its diversity and complexity, however, help to explain the breakdown of the Classical and Romantic styles and their replacement with a bewildering variety of movements and directions in all the arts.

(Continued from page 329.)

Songs were also a source of fascination to Ravel, and he continued their composition until the end of his life. *Schéhérazade* (1903) is a song cycle for voice and orchestra. Ravel also succeeded in combining chamber music with voice, as in the *Trois poèmes de Stéphane Mallarmé* (1913) and the sensuous *Chansons madécasses* (*Songs of Madagascar,* 1926).

Despite his popular repertoire of piano works, songs, and chamber music, Ravel is unquestionably best known for his orchestral works. His *Rapsodie espagnole* (*Spanish Rhapsody,* 1907) remains a favorite today. So, too, does his *Mother Goose Suite* (1912) for orchestra, adapted from his own piano composition. One of his most ambitious undertakings was *Daphnis et Chlöe* (1912), a ballet from which were taken two frequently performed orchestral suites. Two of his most enduring compositions are *La valse* (1920) and *Boléro* (1928). In both, the artist made use of unusual elements. *La valse* is notable for its unusual combination of traditional waltz rhythms and arresting and disturbing harmonic and textural elements. *Boléro,* drawing its inspiration from the Spanish dance of the same name, employs a gradual uninterrupted crescendo and a repetitive single melody. To this great body of work must also be added the famous Piano Concerto in G (1931) and the Concerto for the Left Hand (1931), two virtuosic masterpieces.

POST-IMPRESSIONISM

Many composers both in France and in other European countries were influenced by the musical innovations of Debussy. As we noted above, Ravel made use of all the Impressionistic devices and shared much of Debussy's musical philosophy, including his rejection of the ideas of Richard Wagner.

Another group of French composers was also strongly critical of overblown Romanticism. Erik Satie (Sah-tee′, 1866–1925) rejected the excessive earnestness of late Romantic composers by creating "unserious" works which displayed an antisentimental attitude and an ironic sense of humor. The objectivity and simplicity of his style are exemplified by the three *Gymnopédies* for piano (1888, Nos. 1 and 3, orchestrated by Debussy in 1896). Satie's experimental approach to composition attracted a group of composers who came to be known as "The Six." The most important members of this group were Arthur Honnegger (1892–1955), Francis Poulenc (1899–1963), and Darius Milhaud (Mee-yoh′, 1882–1974).

The influence of Impressionism was widespread, extending to England, Spain, Italy, and America. In America, the composer most receptive to Debussy's ideas was Charles T. Griffes, who will be discussed further in Chapter 21.

FREDERICK DELIUS

An English Impressionistic composer was Frederick Delius (Dee′-lee-us, 1862–1934), a man of German extraction who spent much of his adult life in Paris. His style is lush and chromatic, with constantly shifting harmonies. His melodies, however, are rather simple, tonal, and even reminiscent of folk songs. In England, a country which had not been a significant force in music for almost two hundred years, the twentieth century marked the beginning of a musical renaissance. A few composers early in the century, particularly Edward Elgar and Delius, had adopted the techniques and styles of the continental mainstream, but it remained for Ralph Vaughan Williams to use them in a uniquely English manner.

RALPH VAUGHAN WILLIAMS

Ralph Vaughan Williams (1872–1958) was influenced by Debussy's ambiguous tonalities and emphasis on tone color. He studied orchestration with Ravel. But his interests also extended to English folk music and to the music of the English Renaissance. Moreover, he felt that music was a democratic cultural phenomenon; it belonged to the common people and had to reflect their interests. Vaughan Williams's emphasis on choral music in his early years is a part of the centuries-old tradition of choral singing in Great Britain.

The nationalistic aspect of Vaughan Williams's music is not merely a matter of quoting folk songs; it is a philosophical position that is indirectly expressed in the music. His symphonic style involves a nontraditional approach to tonality, but a generally romantic idiom. His nine symphonies and his other large orchestral works are balanced by an extensive collection of vocal music ranging from simple folk-song settings to large operas, songs, and many choral works, including some with orchestral accompaniment. One of the finest of these is *Dona Nobis Pacem* (1936), whose text is drawn from passages in Walt Whitman, John Bright's "Angel of Death" speech, Latin liturgical prayer, and the Old and New Testaments.

MANUEL DE FALLA

A Spanish composer who was first influenced by Debussy but later displayed a more classical spirit was Manuel de Falla (day Fall'-yah, 1876–1948). His earliest works were strongly nationalistic and employed the idioms of Andalusian folk music and dance very effectively. De Falla spent his last years in South America. His best-known works are the ballet *El amor brujo* (usually translated as *Love the Magician,* 1915), which features the ritual Fire Dance, and *Noches en los jardines de España* (*Nights in the Gardens of Spain,* 1916) for piano and orchestra, which effectively blends the Impressionist style with native Spanish musical elements.

OTTORINO RESPIGHI

Impressionism also made its mark on an Italian composer, Ottorino Respighi (Reh-spee'-gee, 1879–1936), who studied with Rimsky-Korsakov in Russia before returning to his native land to teach and compose. Both instrumental and vocal music interested him; his most successful opera was *La Fiamma* (1934). He is best known today for his trilogy of nationalistically oriented symphonic poems: *Fontane di Roma* (*The Fountains of Rome,* 1917), *Pini di Roma* (*The Pines of Rome,* 1924), and *Feste Romane* (*Roman Festivals,* 1929).

SUMMARY

Around the turn of the century the musical culture of France was closely related to the other arts. Two of the dominant movements at the time were Impressionism in painting and Symbolism in literature. Both of these movements were influential in the development of Impressionism in music, a style associated primarily with Claude Debussy. Debussy's use of nontonal harmonies took music into new and uncharted areas, and his freer forms and concentration on timbre influenced almost all later composers.

Maurice Ravel, who is often linked with Debussy, incorporated many Impressionistic devices in his music, but also displayed a distinctly classical bent. Another group of French composers, associated with Erik Satie, rejected romanticism in favor of a nonsentimental, objective approach.

Debussy's innovations affected the style of composers in England, Italy, Spain, and the United States. But Impressionism per se belonged almost exclusively to him.

NEW TERMS

Impressionism

19 | TOWARD THE MODERN PERIOD

THOUGH SPECIFIC POINTS OF VIEW HAVE DOMINATED THE MUSICAL scene at various times since 1900, trends in twentieth-century music do not seem, like those of previous periods, to lead in a single direction. In fact, music since 1900 is characterized by an unprecedented diversity of styles and points of view. Different styles are displayed by composers working at the same time, styles have changed from one five-year period to the next, and differences in style are sometimes found in the musical output of a single composer. At various times, radical or conservative trends have come rapidly to the fore and then have sunk back into obscurity, only to reemerge or even to become blurred with one another. Popular music and concert music have gone their separate ways as the musical audience itself has expanded and diversified.

DISTINGUISHING FEATURES OF TWENTIETH-CENTURY MUSIC

Despite the diversity of styles to which we have just referred, it is possible to identify three characteristics that distinguish the concert music of our century from that of earlier style periods.

THE ABANDONMENT OF TONALITY

The tonal system, which had been primary to the music of previous centuries, related all notes and chords to a single note, the central or tonic note of the key. Harmonic progressions away from and then back toward the tonic implied motion and rest, expectation and arrival. Virtually all the formal structures developed during the Baroque, Classical, and Romantic periods depended on tonality as a major structural element. Fugal procedure, sonata-allegro form, and even the Romantic tone poem were all based on certain assumptions about tonality that were shared by composer and listener alike. Although much Romantic music strained the boundaries of functional tonality by the introduction of increasing numbers of chromatic notes and by more frequent modulations to distant key areas, it nevertheless retained a strongly tonal character. Many composers of the twentieth century have, by contrast, completely abandoned the assumptions on which the old tonal system was based.

Two primary paths were open to a composer who rejected the basic concepts of functional tonality. One was to avoid traditional tonality altogether, denying the importance of any one note over the others. The music of Arnold Schoenberg evolved along these lines, eventually leading to his formulation of a system called twelve-tone technique or serialism to replace tonality as a structuring force (see Chapter 20). But other important composers chose a different course; they maintained the idea of a tonal center or point of rest but significantly altered the methods by which the center was established. Composers in this category include Béla Bartók, Paul Hindemith, and Igor Stravinsky.

DISSONANCE

Before the later part of the Romantic period, consonance was considered the norm and dissonance a departure from the norm. Dissonant harmonies were expected to return to, or resolve into, consonance. To varying degrees and in differing stylistic manifestations, this convention regarding the use of dissonance was adhered to by Palestrina, Bach, Mozart, Beethoven, and Brahms, as well as all other composers from each of these eras.

The late Romantic styles of Wagner and Strauss placed more emphasis on dissonance. Dissonances became more prolonged, and frequently a series of dissonances would occur before the ultimate resolution to a consonant harmony. As composers admitted more of what were previously considered dissonant tones and chords into their vocabulary of sound, the traditional distinction between consonance and dissonance broke down. Composers found some new combinations of tones to be beautiful in their own right and delighted in their pungency and expressive power. Eventually, in the twentieth century, the use of dissonance became independent of the use of consonance. The old tendency to resolve dissonances into consonances was abandoned in what Schoenberg called the "emancipation of the dissonance."

As a logical consequence, the harmonic structure of twentieth-century music differs from that of earlier periods. From the Baroque to the post-Romantic period, chords had been built on intervals of the *third*. The tonic chord, for example, consisted of the first, third, and fifth tones of the scale, each a third apart. This formed the tonic *triad*. Other triads were constructed of the same intervals, but beginning on different tones of the scale. As interest in the possibilities of dissonance increased, new methods of chord construction were developed. Intervals other than thirds, frequently dissonant ones, became used as the basis for chord construction. The result was a greater variety of "harmonic sonorities" than had existed before and more complex combinations than had been previously possible. In fact, in much of today's music harmonic progressions take place from dissonance to dissonance. Thus, the music is heard as a series of dissonances, varying in their complexity from mild to exceedingly tense.

RHYTHMIC COMPLEXITY

The greater degree of dissonance and the use of dissonance apart from consonance in "modern music" are closely allied to the change in attitudes toward
tonality. Quite separate from these developments is the third important distinguishing feature of twentieth-century music—its increased rhythmic complexity.
In their search for freshness of expression, composers have become increasingly
interested in obliterating the *functional barline,* that vertical line which divides
one measure or bar from the next and implies an accentuation of the first beat of
each bar. Many Classical and Romantic composers were skilled at avoiding a too
monotonous regularity. By the use of syncopation, by ingenious overlapping of
phrases, or by playing unequal rhythms against each other they could "disguise"
the barline to a great extent. Nevertheless, they in general felt bound to an underlying regularity of metrical flow. Alert listeners could, if they wished, penetrate
the disguise and count out the beats in a more or less predictable fashion. More
recent composers have broken up the steadiness of the metrical flow by grouping
the beats together in measures of different lengths, or else they have avoided any
kind of recurring pulse, thus producing an impression of extreme vagueness in the
rhythmical flow. Sometimes successive single beats are divided into different numbers of equal parts, giving melodies a free, improvisatory quality. And very often,
a number of unusual rhythms are superimposed, making for a rather more complex texture than had been heard before. Thus, in much modern music it is difficult to detect regular metrical patterns, or even the actual beat. These rhythmic
features contribute significantly to the extraordinary excitement and power characteristic of the music of our century.

Rhythmic complexity, harmonic dissonance, and a less clearly defined or
nonexistent tonal center, then, are three distinguishing characteristics of much of
twentieth-century music.

NEOCLASSICISM

During the period between the two world wars a new movement in music grew up
as a reaction against Romanticism and Impressionism. Many leaders in the visual
arts had already taken a new direction, into the abstraction and formalism of
Cubism (painting and sculpture) and the International Style (architecture). Now
music, too, turned away from the emotionalism of the nineteenth century. Like
the artists of the late eighteenth century, who had embarked on a Neoclassical era
in painting after the excesses of the Baroque, composers now sought to revive the
objectivity and restraint of the Classical era in music.

Neoclassical composers often avoided the huge Romantic orchestra in favor
of smaller instrumental combinations. They preferred **absolute music,** which received its impetus from purely musical ideas, to the descriptive elements so prevalent in Romantic and Impressionistic music. They looked on musical composition
as an intellectual challenge to be approached systematically and rationally, with
irrelevant emotions held in check. The Neoclassical composers were especially
attracted to the forms of the Baroque and Classical periods. But they did not sim-

ply resurrect these old forms; they varied them to develop a new and distinctly modern idiom.

Among the most important composers whose work reflected elements of the Neoclassical outlook were Béla Bartók, Paul Hindemith, and Igor Stravinsky.

Fig. 19.1 Neoclassicism, which reinterpreted older styles to develop a new, modern idiom, was reflected in art, literature, and music. This 1906 painting by Picasso has a strong classical flavor, its figures suggestive of ancient Greek vase painting.

STRAVINSKY (1882–1971)

Igor Stravinsky is, along with Arnold Schoenberg, one of the two towering figures in twentieth-century music. His career, like that of his great Spanish contemporary Pablo Picasso, spans three generations; in their respective fields each played a dominant role in almost all significant trends of the first half of this century.

Stravinsky was born in a small Russian town on the Gulf of Finland near St. Petersburg, the third son of one of the most celebrated bass-baritone singers in the Imperial Opera. He began piano lessons at the age of nine, but his parents, though encouraging his piano studies, regarded his musical activity as a sideline and decided that he should study law at the University of St. Petersburg. At the university Stravinsky had the good fortune to make friends with the youngest son of Rimsky-Korsakov; he soon met the composer himself, then the leading figure in Russian music and one of the members of the "Five" (see Chapter 15). By 1903 Stravinsky was studying orchestration with Rimsky-Korsakov. They became close friends and the elder composer acted as best man at Stravinsky's wedding to a cousin, Catherine Gabrielle, in 1906.

After completing his university studies in 1905, Stravinsky decided on a career as a composer. His earliest serious works were written under Rimsky-Korsakov's supervision. In 1909 he met Sergei Diaghilev, the impresario of the newly formed Ballets Russes, who commissioned the young composer to write music for a ballet based on an old Slavic legend. The work, entitled *L'oiseau de feu* (*The Firebird*), had its premiere at the Paris Opera the following year. It was so successful that almost overnight Stravinsky became a celebrity.

Two more ballets quickly followed: *Petrouchka* (1910–1911) and *Le sacre du printemps* (*The Rite of Spring,* 1912–1913). The premiere of *The Rite of Spring* created an unprecedented scandal by its use of novel or-

Fig. 19.2 Igor Stravinsky, by his friend Pablo Picasso.

chestration and aggressive, "primitive" rhythms. Undeterred by what proved to be only temporary criticism, Stravinsky kept up a continuous flow of composition. Until the outbreak of World War I he divided his time among Switzerland, Russia, and France. A member of the most distinguished musical and artistic circles of Europe, he came in close contact with Debussy, Ravel, de Falla, the writer Jean Cocteau, and Picasso.

From the outbreak of World War I until 1919 Stravinsky lived in Switzerland. The difficulty in gathering together large groups of performers during this period of world conflict contributed to his evolving compositional style. He turned from his earlier penchant for huge orchestral works to compositions scored for instrumental ensembles of more modest size.

At the end of the war Stravinsky returned to Paris, where he became a French citizen (he had given up his Russian citizenship at the time of the Russian Revolution of 1917). Much of his time during the 1920s and 1930s was spent on tour through the principal cities of Europe and America. When World War II began he moved again, this time to Hollywood, California. Deciding to remain in the United States permanently, he gave up his French citizenship to become a naturalized American in 1945.

Stravinsky continued to compose well into his later years and he conducted concerts of his music all over the world into his eighties. He died in 1971 at the age of eighty-eight, leaving a musical legacy of monumental proportions.

STRAVINSKY'S WORK

Stravinsky's work constitutes a unique variety of styles, genres, musical forms, and instrumental combinations. By and large his most popular works continue to be the three early ballets, written before World War I. These works, which include Russian and Oriental elements, are characterized by exotic and colorful melodies and harmonies, glittering orchestration, and striking, often primitive-sounding rhythmic patterns.

Most of the works that he wrote between 1913 and 1923—including three ballets as well as some short piano pieces, songs, and chamber music—were scored for small instrumental ensembles of various types. One of his most popular works for stage composed during this period is *L'histoire du soldat* (*The Soldier's Tale*, 1918), "to be read, played, and danced"; it is scored for a chamber ensemble of only seven instruments.

His ballet *Pulcinella* (1919), based on music by the eighteenth-century composer Giovanni Battista Pergolesi, and the *Octet for Wind Instruments* (1923) began his Neoclassical period, which lasted until 1951. His compositions during this long creative period incorporate references to many older materials and styles, all transformed in a uniquely Stravinskian way. Many of these works demonstrate an austere style, clear—even dry—texture, and meticulous craftsmanship. Some show the influence of jazz; others make a deliberate return to Baroque or Classical models; still others represent an attempt to strip music of any subjective or emotional appeal whatever. The opera *Oedipus Rex* (1927) is based on the ancient Greek tragedy. *The Rake's Progress* (1950), titled after a series of engravings by the English artist William Hogarth and structured after the conventions of Italian opera, represents the essence of Neoclassicism.

The most important orchestral works to come out of Stravinsky's Neoclassical period include Symphonies of Wind Instruments (1920), Concerto for Piano and Wind Orchestra (1924), "Dumbarton Oaks" Concerto (Concerto in E-Flat, 1938), Symphony in C (1940), and Symphony in Three Movements (1945).

Stravinsky's first major choral work, an undisputed masterpiece, was the *Symphony of Psalms* (1930), written for chorus and orchestra. This three-movement setting of three psalms (see pp. 350–354) exhibits several innovations in tonality and rhythm. Instead of being based on traditional functions (such as the tonic-dominant relationship), the tonality is established by the frequent repetition of a particular pitch as a center of reference. An important structural technique is the simultaneous use of several different ostinato patterns (persistently repeated figures) as building blocks; these patterns overlap and produce shifting accents and conflicting rhythms.

Stravinsky's "neotonal" style was dominant in Europe between the two world wars. At the same time an "atonal" technique was being developed in Vienna by Arnold Schoenberg and his followers (Chapter 20). For many years the two approaches were considered opposites, completely irreconcilable. But after World War II almost everyone adopted some form of Schoenberg's serial procedures. Stravinsky made use of serial technique in a number of works written in the 1950s and 1960s. Among the most important are *Movements* for piano and orchestra (1958–1959); *The Flood,* a biblical allegory for actors, dancers, soloists, chorus, and orchestra (1961–1962); and *Requiem Canticles* for soloists, chorus, and orchestra (1964–1966).

During the early years of the twentieth century, many artists and intellectual leaders became fascinated with nonliterate, "primitive" cultures. Henri Matisse and Pablo Picasso incorporated into their early paintings the stylized forms of African sculpture (see Plate 30). Similarly, Stravinsky's imagination was stirred by the frenzied, irregular rhythms found in non-Western music. *The Rite of Spring,* the third in the series of ballet scores written by Stravinsky for Diaghilev's Ballets Russes, is perhaps the premier example of musical **primitivism.** Subtitled *Pictures of Pagan Russia,* it depicts the cruelty of the primitive Russian peasants' rites to celebrate the coming of spring, culminating in the sacrifice of a young virgin, who dances herself to death while the tribal elders watch.

LE SACRE DU PRINTEMPS (THE RITE OF SPRING)

The music is wild and elemental-sounding, frequently employing unconventional rhythms and dissonant chords. The first performance of the work (in Paris in 1913) provoked loud whistling and booing from the audience, which was accustomed to the graceful melodies of Romantic ballet.

The work is divided into two large parts, each of which includes several scenes; they are not really distinct movements, however, and are played without pause. The first half is called "The Adoration of the Earth"; after a slow introduction depicting the awakening of spring, the scenes are "Dance of the Adolescents," "Game of Abduction," "Round Dance," "Games of the Rival Tribes," "Procession of the Priest," "The Kiss," and "Dance to the Earth." The second part, "The Great Sacrifice," also opens with a slow introduction, followed by "Secret Mime of the Girls," "Glorification of the Victim," "Invocation of Ancestors," "Dance of the Elders," and "Sacrificial Dance."

The orchestra for which Stravinsky composed *The Rite of Spring* is unusually large, calling for two piccolos, three flutes, alto flute, four oboes, two English horns, six clarinets of various sizes, four bassoons, two contrabassoons, eight French horns, five trumpets, one bass trumpet, three trombones, four tubas, a very large percussion section, and the usual strings. Stravinsky tends to use the instruments in blocks, keeping the string, wind, and brass sections fairly distinct. There are solos for almost every instrument, many of them in extremely high or low registers. The work is full of a variety of special effects, including some raucous slides and flutters.

The aspect of *The Rite of Spring* that most shocked its first audience and that has had the greatest impact on later composers was the rhythm. Stravinsky made a break with the traditional procedure of having the accents determined largely by the melodic and harmonic structure; in this work the rhythm is very definitely a form-producing element in its own right.

The new kind of rhythm that Stravinsky introduced here, especially in the "Glorification of the Victim" and the "Sacrificial Dance," is characterized by a rapid and rather mechanical mixture of two very short note values which are scattered in an irregular way, and the irregularity is emphasized by the appearance of strong accents in unpredictable places.

Example 19.1*

The effect is one of considerable tension. This new kind of rhythm also appears in most of Stravinsky's later compositions.

The melodic material of *The Rite of Spring* is not really used thematically; it is stated without ever being developed. Most of it appears in short fragments, with relentless ostinato accompaniments that prevent it from expanding to its full length and reaching a cadence. A folksong quality is evident in much of the melodic material, although, as far as we know, only the opening bassoon solo is taken from a genuine folk song.

Example 19.2

Stravinsky followed this monumental composition with a number of works for chamber groups of instruments and voices and with another of his Russian-based works, *Les Noces,* a set of choral sketches describing a peasant wedding.

SYMPHONIE DE PSAUMES (SYMPHONY OF PSALMS)

Stravinsky's mature technique can be seen quite clearly in this work for chorus and orchestra, written in 1930 for the fiftieth anniversary of the Boston Symphony Orchestra. The orchestration is unusual in that the violins and violas are omitted and two pianos and harp are used. The text is taken from Psalms 38, 39,† and 150 and is sung in Latin. These Biblical excerpts form a sequence of prayer, testimony, and praise; the setting is divided into three corresponding parts, which are to be performed without pause.

---

*   Examples 19.1 and 19.2 are from Igor Stravinsky, *Le sacre du printemps.* Copyright 1921 by Edition Russe de Musique. Copyright assigned 1947 to Boosey & Hawkes, Inc. Reprinted by permission of Boosey & Hawkes, Inc.

†   Psalms 38 and 39 in the Vulgate are Psalms 39 and 40 in the King James Version.

PART I: Psalm 38, verses 13–14

Exaudi orationem meam, Domine et deprecationem meam; auribus percipe lacrimas meas.
Ne sileas, quoniam advena ego sum apud te,
et peregrinus, sicut omnes patres mei.
Remitte mihi, ut refrigerer, prius quam abeam et amplius non ero.

Hear my prayer, O Lord, and give ear to my cry; be not heedless of my tears.
For I am a guest with Thee,

a sojourner, as were all my fathers.
Turn from me, that I may recover, before I go and am no more.

PART II: Psalm 39, verses 2, 3, and 4

Expectans expectavi Dominum, et intendit mihi.
Et exaudivit preces meas, et eduxit me de lacu miseriae, et de luto faecis.

Et statuit super petram pedes meos,
et direxit gressus meos.
Et immisit in os meum canticum novum,
carmen Deo nostro.
Videbunt multi, et timebunt,

et sperabunt in Domino.

I hoped, I hoped in the Lord, and He stooped down to me.
And He heard my cry, and He drew me out of the pit of destruction, from the mire of the swamp.

And He set my feet upon a rock,
and made firm my steps.
And He put a new song in my mouth,

a hymn to our God.
Many shall see, and they shall be filled with awe,
and they shall hope in the Lord.

PART III: Psalm 150, complete

Alleluia.
Laudate Dominum in sanctis ejus;
Laudate eum in firmamento virtutis ejus.
Laudate eum in virtutibus ejus;

laudate eum secundum multitudinem magnitudinis ejus.
Laudate eum in sono tubae,
laudate eum in psalterio et cithara.
Laudate eum in timpano et choro;
laudate eum in cordis et organo.

Laudate eum in cymbalis benesonantibus;
laudate eum in cymbalis jubilationibus.
Omnis spiritus laudet Dominum!

Alleluia.

Alleluia.
Praise the Lord in His holy place,
Praise Him in His majestic firmament.

Praise Him because of His wonderful works;
praise Him because of His sublime majesty.
Praise Him with the sound of trumpet,
praise Him with harp and lyre.
Praise Him with drum and dancing;
praise Him with stringed instruments and pipe.
Praise Him with sonorous cymbals;

Praise Him with crashing cymbals.
Let everything that breathes praise the Lord!
Alleluia.

PART I

The first movement opens with an abrupt, widely spaced chord played by the entire orchestra. During the first part of this movement, the same chord is repeated five more times; it thus serves as an organizing force and also establishes a temporary tonality. Between the first few statements of the chord, rushing arpeggios treated as ostinato patterns are played by solo winds and then by the pianos.

Example 19.3*

The altos enter with a sustained line that alternates between two tones; the winds have much more active parts, with several different ostinato figures going simultaneously.

Example 19.4

The rest of the chorus joins in as the winds continue their patterns. After a very brief interlude, the altos and winds begin again. They are interrupted by the opening chord, and a new set of ostinatos begins, with the tenors singing *Ne sileas* on a single pitch. The section ends with a final jolt from the opening chord.

The second section opens with a familiar sound: active but repetitive parts in the winds, and slower, more lyric choral parts. The altos and basses begin at *Quoniam advena* in octaves and are soon joined by the rest of the chorus. When they reach the word *mei* the original type of orchestral background returns, as does the two-note theme, first as part of an alto-tenor duo, then in conflict between the sopranos and tenors (Example 19.5). The ostinato patterns drop out for the last few measures of the movement.

Example 19.5

PART II

The second movement begins with a long, slow woodwind fugue; the subject is   RECORD 7/SIDE 1
marked by a series of wide leaps.

Example 19.6

After a brief episode for flutes alone, a second fugue subject is introduced by the
chorus.

Example 19.7

During the exposition of this subject, fragments of the first one are still heard in
the orchestra. The choral subject is used unaccompanied and in *stretti* (close overlapping entrances) at the words *Et statuit*. The orchestra returns with a few more
fragments of the instrumental fugue subject, and then a dotted rhythm in the trombone part introduces a contrasting section.

The chorus parts are homophonic (chordal) from here to the end of the
movement, although they are rhythmically almost as active as the orchestral parts.
Fragments of the instrumental fugue subject are continued, first stated in a very
jagged dotted rhythm, then broadly stated by the lower brasses. The music builds
to a loud climax at *videbunt et timebunt;* then a sudden decrease in volume to
piano is introduced for the last words, *et sperabunt in Domino.* The chorus sings
this phrase in octaves while a muted trumpet slowly plays the fragment of fugue
theme and the cellos and basses play it twice as fast.

PART III

The last movement is considerably longer than either of the first two, and uses
the setting of the word *Alleluia* as an organizational pillar. The entire first phrase,
Alleluia laudate Dominum, is used again at the end of the movement, while the
Alleluia alone serves as a major point of punctuation in the middle of it.

The opening section, with its slow-moving choral parts and instrumental
ostinatos, is followed by a faster section for orchestra alone. It is characterized

first by a repeated-note figure, always six notes, with the accent on the first. Gradually a rising triplet figure "takes over" (Stravinsky has said that it was inspired by a vision of Elijah's horse and chariot climbing the heavens). The section ends with a loud, crashing chord.

The next section, which begins with a soprano-alto duet, is somewhat calmer and is accompanied by short ostinato figures. After building to a climax, the six-note repeated pattern is reintroduced, this time sung to the words *Laudate Dominum*. This brief and very staccato interlude is followed by another slow section, with sustained vocal parts (starting with just the basses and gradually adding the other sections) and staccato wind ostinatos. This material builds to a huge climax, which is aborted as soft chords introduce the opening *Alleluia* again.

New ostinatos begin in the orchestra as the chorus sings *Laudate Dominum* with sharp accents on each syllable. A lively pattern is introduced by the harp and piano, and soon the chorus begins to interject the staccato repeated-note *Laudate Dominum* phrase, singing in block chords.

Example 19.8

The orchestral parts grow more and more active and eventually the rising-triplet pattern from earlier in the movement returns; the chorus drops out and the orchestra continues alone. After a chordal climax the six-note pattern is heard slowly and softly for the last time.

The chorus dominates the next section, which begins with imitative entrances of a jagged, yet lyric theme.

Example 19.9

It leads into the long and slow final section, where both voices and instruments chant hypnotically repetitive phrases. The work ends quietly with a literal restatement of the opening measures of the movement, and the words *Alleluia, laudate Dominum*.

Some of Stravinsky's music has a reputation for being "dry and unexpressive"; although this is a rather strong statement, it would certainly be valid to say that he goes out of his way to avoid anything that might seem like sentimentality. This leads him to some strange, even paradoxical, contrasts between the text and the music to which it is set. For example, he saves his most moving and poignant chord progression for the joyful words "Praise Him with crashing cymbals"; and the praises of the finale are surrounded by a solemn processional and soft, awe-inspired *Alleluias*.

BARTÓK (1881–1945)

The most significant composer to emerge from Eastern Europe in the twentieth century was Béla Bartók. He was born in Hungary, the son of the director of a government argicultural school. His first piano lessons, begun at the age of five, were given by his mother. Following the death of his father in 1888, the family moved to Bratislava (now in Czechoslovakia), where Bartók began formal studies in music. While a student at Bratislava, he made his first public appearance as a composer and pianist in 1892, playing one of his own works, and formed a close friendship with Ernö Dohnányi, in later years one of Hungary's most noted pianists and composers.

In 1899, though admitted to the prestigious Vienna Conservatory, Bartók decided to follow Dohnányi to the Royal Academy of Music in Budapest. In Budapest he became strongly attracted to the music of Wagner and Richard Strauss. He also was caught up in the nationalistic movement in politics, literature, and the arts then sweeping through Hungary. His first major composition, an immense orchestral tone poem entitled *Kossuth* (1903), commemorated the nationalist leader of the unsuccesful revolution of 1848. He became friends with Zoltán Kodály (1882–1967), the third member (with Dohnányi and Bartók himself) of the great trio of modern Hungarian composers.

Both Bartók and Kodály developed a strong interest in the problem of creating a national music and began collecting and analyzing Hungarian folk music. The earliest product of their research was a joint publicacation of arrangements, *Twenty Hungarian Folksongs* (1906). Bartók's interest in folk music began to have an immediate effect on his own work; side by side with the most current devices in composition appeared folk-derived rhythms and melodic patterns.

Following his graduation in 1902 from the Royal Academy, Bartók began a series of concert tours throughout major European cities

Fig. 19.3 Béla Bartók's lifelong interest in eastern European folk music had a profound effect on his composing, especially in his approach to tonality.

which lasted for the next several years. During this period he became increasingly influenced by the French Impressionistic music of Debussy and his contemporaries. Bartók's own effort at composition, however, did not seem to get off the ground during this period, and for a while he leaned toward a career as a concert pianist rather than as a composer.

In 1907 Bartók accepted an appointment as a piano teacher at the Budapest Academy, a post that he held for nearly thirty years. In 1909 he married Márta Ziegler, one of his pupils, and settled into a routine of teaching, composing, researching folk music, and making extensive concert tours. In 1923 he was divorced and married another of his piano students, Ditta Pásztory. They often toured together, playing works for two pianos, and in 1927 they came to America for a series of solo recitals and appearances with various orchestras.

The political turmoil of the late 1930s, brought on by the expansionist policies of Nazi Germany, convinced Bartók that he had to leave Hungary. In 1940 he emigrated to the United States, where he was soon given an appointment at Columbia University. While in New York, however, he developed leukemia and his health began declining seriously. He died in September, 1945.

BARTÓK'S WORK

Bartók was primarily an instrumental composer; with a few exceptions almost all of his music falls into one of the following categories: music for solo piano, chamber music for strings (often with piano), concertos, orchestral works of various types, and stage works.

His works for piano range from technical studies and beginners' pieces to difficult recital pieces and concertos. His major contribution to piano literature is the six-volume *Mikrokosmos* (1926–1937), a collection of 153 pieces graded in order of difficulty.

Among his chamber works, the most outstanding pieces are the six string quartets. Since they span a large portion of his creative life, they offer a comprehensive picture of his development as a composer. In particular the Fifth String Quartet, written in 1934, is considered to be a pivotal point in his stylistic development, after which his music assumes qualities that make it much more accessible to the listener. The Sixth String Quartet (1939) is in many ways the culmination of Bartók's life and work; it displays the ingenuity and self-discipline which are the hallmarks of his style. Taken as a whole, Bartók's quartets rank among the finest contributions to the literature in the modern era.

His ten concertos are all major works and most of them remain essential items in twentieth-century repertory. The Second Concerto for Violin (1937–1938) is one of the finest in the modern idiom.

Bartók's stage works include a one-act opera and two ballets. His one major choral work, the *Cantata profana* (1930), based on a Hungarian legend, requires a double mixed chorus, tenor and baritone soloists, and a large orchestra.

Kossuth, an orchestral tone poem and Bartók's first major work for orchestra, was highly acclaimed at performances in England and in Budapest. The much later *Concerto for Orchestra* (1943) was his orchestral masterpiece and one of the great works of this century. Two other popular works, both written for smaller forces, round out his orchestral music—*Music for Strings, Percussion, and Celesta* (1936), and the *Divertimento for String Orchestra* (1939).

HIS STYLE

Throughout his life Bartók studied the folk music of Eastern Europe. The effects of his studies on his own compositions were profound, especially in his approach to tonality. Most Eastern European folk music is based on modes and scales that lie outside the familiar major-minor system, and Bartók realized the impossibility of using this material within the tonal system. He formed his own type of harmonic organization, one which could accommodate melodies not based on a major-minor tonality.

Bartók's studies also influenced his style of melodic writing, which sometimes has a folklike character. He rarely used actual folk songs in his compositions, but he understood how they were constructed and effectively imitated them.

The diverse, irregular rhythms of Hungarian folk music also had a significant impact on his work. In a single passage the meter may change almost from bar to bar, lending his music a strongly primitive rhythmic impulse. Syncopations and ostinato patterns are imaginatively employed as well.

Bartók's mature style is compact and economical. Often he derives his melodic material from just one or two very short motives and uses them extensively throughout a composition. He structures large-scale pieces cyclically, bringing back the same material in several movements. Bartók's writing is essentially contrapuntal, with greater emphasis on melodic line than on harmony. He frequently employs dissonances that range from relatively mild to exceedingly tense.

Traditional devices and forms are an important part of Bartók's style, and in this sense he can be called a Neoclassicist. He employed fugue, canon, and other contrapuntal procedures and also made use of the sonata-allegro principle. These formal schemes were modified to adapt to and accommodate other elements of Bartók's style.

Another aspect of earlier music that appears in Bartók's writing is the Baroque device of separating an ensemble into two antiphonal groups in order to make the contrapuntal lines more distinct. Bartók used this device in his outstanding *Music for Strings, Percussion, and Celesta*.

Music for Strings, Percussion, and Celesta was written in 1936 on commission for the celebration of the tenth anniversary of Switzerland's Basle Chamber Orchestra. It was Bartók's first major work after the Fifth String Quartet and displays the same kind of tightly organized structure evident in that work.

The piece is written for two separate string groups and two sets of percussion instruments, specified by the composer to be arranged in the following manner:

MUSIC FOR STRINGS, PERCUSSION, AND CELESTA
RECORD 6/SIDE 2

	Double Bass I	Double Bass II	
Cello I	Timpani	Bass Drum	Cello II
Viola I	Side Drums	Cymbals	Viola II
Violin II	Celesta	Xylophone	Violin IV
Violin I	Piano	Harp	Violin III

Conductor

This plan allows for many possible instrumental combinations; in addition, the choice of instruments such as the piano, harp, xylophone, and celesta creates the opportunity for exploiting fascinating instrumental effects and sonorities, an opportunity the composer used with great imagination.

FIRST MOVEMENT

The first movement (Andante tranquillo) is fugue-like, with the strings playing the major role. It is based upon the following subject with its four short phrases:

Example 19.10*

This melody is the basis for the entire first movement. After its first statement by muted violas, the piece proceeds with successive entrances of the melody, each time at the interval of the fifth higher or lower. The first entrance is on A, the second on E (a fifth above A), the third on D (a fifth below A), the fourth on B (a fifth above E), the fifth on G (a fifth below D), and so on until the most remote and climactic entrance on E-flat.

As each new voice part enters, the texture grows thicker and the dynamic level increases until the climactic point when the E-flat section is reached. After this climax, there is a short transition, based on the *inversion* of the first phrase, which leads to successive entrances on the inverted fugue subject:

Example 19.11

This part of the movement reverses the pattern of dynamics of the first part: there is a long dimenuendo to the end of the movement. The concluding portion uses both the original and the inverted forms of the second phrase of the theme, dying away to the pitch A which was the starting point:

Example 19.12

As previously noted, this movement is dominated by the strings, which work together as a homogeneous group. Only toward the end, after the climax, does the celesta enter playing an elaborate accompaniment to the strings.

SECOND MOVEMENT

The second movement is high-spirited (Allegro) and follows the basic outlines of sonata-allegro form. The first theme is characterized by the alternation of the two string groups answering back and forth. The second theme, which is clearly set off from the first, is rather delicate and playful:

Example 19.13

There is a full-fledged development section and a clear-cut recapitulation.

In addition to the strings, there is extensive use of the harp, the piano, and some of the percussion instruments in this highly rhythmic movement.

THIRD MOVEMENT

The slow third movement (Adagio) is an ABCBA form, with snatches of the theme from the first movement appearing between the various sections. The movement begins and ends with solo xylophone; glissandos on the piano and harp combine with interesting runs on the celesta to create evocative and unusual sonorous effects.

FOURTH MOVEMENT

The last movement is fast (Allegro molto) and hard-driving, with many contrasting sections. The most important materials are the dancelike

Example 19.14

and the return to a simplified and expanded version of the theme of the first movement in a slower tempo:

Example 19.15

The piece concludes with a dramatic coda based on the main thematic material in Example 19.14, ending fortissimo.

During the last ten years of his life Bartók did not compose a great deal of music, but the works he produced were of a very high order. *Music for Strings, Percussion, and Celesta* is perhaps the masterwork of that period of his life.

HINDEMITH (1895-1963)

Paul Hindemith (Hin'-duh-mit) was born in the town of Hanau, just outside Frankfurt, Germany. He began violin lessons at nine, learned to play other instruments, and was soon composing in a steady stream that was to make him among the most prolific of twentieth-century composers. At the Hoch Conservatory in Frankfurt he became close friends with the violin teacher Adolf Rebner, who helped him obtain a position as violinist in the Frankfurt Opera orchestra, which was conducted by Ludwig Rottenberg. In 1924, Hindemith married Rottenberg's daughter, Gertrude.

During his years with the opera orchestra, Hindemith gradually began to break with the highly chromatic styles of Wagner and Strauss. His song cycle *Das Marienleben* (*The Life of Mary,* 1923) was a landmark in his development as a composer, revealing a style devoid of Romantic traits. During the late 1920s he became interested in creating music that amateurs could not only listen to, but also play and sing. He began composing in a technically simple, melodically appealing style which came to be termed *Gebrauchsmusik* ("use music") because it was intended to be played (used) in the home by amateurs rather than by professional virtuosos.

Following the performance of his large-scale opera *Cardillac* at Dresden in 1926, Hindemith's reputation as a composer spread throughout Germany. The following year he took a teaching position at the Berlin Hochschule für Musik, which he held until 1935.

With the rise of the Nazi party in Germany in the 1930s, Hindemith found himself under attack as a "cultural Bolshevik" and as an associate of Jewish musicians. When the performance of his opera *Mathis der Maler*

Fig. 19.4 In addition to composing works in virtually all the traditional genres, Hindemith made an extremely valuable contribution as a teacher of composition.

(*Matthias the Painter,* 1932–1935) was banned in Germany, the premiere of this work took place in Zürich, Switzerland, in 1938.

Hindemith made his first appearance in America in 1937 and toured the country from 1938 to 1939. In 1940, when he was appointed to the music faculty of Yale University, he decided to settle in this country, becoming an American citizen six years later. He did not return to Germany until 1949, when he conducted the Berlin Philharmonic in a performance of his own works. In 1953 he moved back to Europe, teaching at the University of Zürich and conducting concerts throughout Germany and Austria. He died in Frankfurt on December 23, 1963, at the age of sixty-eight.

HINDEMITH'S WORK

Hindemith wrote in virtually all traditional genres of composition and contributed important works to the twentieth-century repertory of almost all commonly played musical instruments. His ten operas include, in addition to *Cardillac* and *Mathis der Maler,* several early one-act works, a marionette opera, a children's opera, and another large-scale work, *Die Harmonie der Welt* (*Cosmic Harmony, 1950–1957*).

His vocal works include art song collections, a series of short solo cantatas, canons, and a number of madrigals composed toward the end of his career. His most important large-scale choral-orchestral work is *When Lilacs Last in the Dooryard Bloom'd* (1946), an American requiem with text from Walt Whitman.

The chamber music includes a series of seven works for miscellaneous ensembles, each entitled *Kammermusik* (Chamber Music), sonatas for solo instruments, seven string quartets, and a number of duets and trios. His most substantial contribution to piano literature is the cycle of twelve fugues, *Ludus tonalis* (1943), a twentieth-century counterpart to Bach's *Well-Tempered Clavier.*

Hindemith's best-known orchestral compositions are the symphony *Mathis der Maler,* based on his opera of the same name, and the *Symphonic Metamorphosis on Themes by Weber* (1944). He also wrote concertos for piano, clarinet, horn, cello, violin, and viola. Included among his works are several composed for dance, of which *The Four Temperaments* is probably the most frequently performed.

SERGEI PROKOFIEV

A Russian composer whose development roughly paralleled that of Stravinsky was Sergei Prokofiev (Pro-koff'-yeff, 1891–1953). His early works are very dissonant and rhythmically exciting—characteristics also associated with Stravinsky's early period, although the two men were working quite independently. Prokofiev lived abroad for many years, first in America, where his outstanding opera, *The Love for Three Oranges,* had its premiere in 1921. During a subsequent stay in Paris, he wrote ballet scores for Diaghilev, as well as several symphonies and piano concertos.

Prokofiev returned to Russia in 1934 and worked at practical and propagandistic projects, including film scores, operas, and cantatas; he also continued to write symphonies, concertos, and sonatas. His music was frequently criticized by the Soviet regime, for reasons that are not totally clear to outsiders. He developed a very simple Neoclassical idiom, using traditional forms and accompaniments, with a strongly tonal orientation. The lyric qualities of his mature works are superb.

DMITRI SHOSTAKOVITCH

Another Russian composer who was even more deeply affected by the criticism of Soviet authorities was Dmitri Shostakovitch (1906–1975). His earliest works were Neoclassical and tonal, but his ironic sense of humor led him to use more dissonance and a more vigorous idiom. His First Symphony is virtually a parody of a Classical symphony.

Shostakovitch's opera *Lady Macbeth of the Mtsensk District* (1930–1932) was not favorably received, and he was attacked steadily by the Soviet regime until he evolved a new, more politically acceptable "heroic" style, first evident in his Fifth Symphony (1937). In all, Shostakovitch wrote fifteen symphonies as well as a variety of chamber works and a ballet. His Seventh Symphony ranks alongside the Fifth as one of his most important works.

BENJAMIN BRITTEN

The most outstanding English composer of the twentieth century was Benjamin Britten (1913–1976). In spite of a considerable output in instrumental music, Britten's best works were composed for voices or voices and instruments. Indeed, Britten is widely regarded as a master at setting English texts to music, in the tradition and, at times, the manner of his great English predecessor, Henry Purcell. His operas, particularly *Peter Grimes* (1945), are among the best twentieth-century works in the traditional operatic format.

Britten's style bears an original stamp. Superficially, his music is rather simple and appealing, with a wide variety of forms and procedures and an essentially tonal harmonic language. But beneath the surface lie complex and carefully worked out structures.

Fig. 19.5 Although Benjamin Britten composed a good deal of instrumental music, his finest compositions are those for voices, either solo or in chorus.

Britten's *War Requiem* (1963) is an outstanding example of the elaborate forces that may be involved. This work juxtaposes the Latin text of the Mass for the Dead with antiwar poems in English by Wilfred Owen, a young soldier-poet who wrote and died during World War I. This contrast is reflected in the orchestration: the traditional Latin text is performed by full orchestra, chorus, boys' choir and solo soprano; the English poetry is assigned to tenor and baritone soloists (representing soldiers) and a separate chamber orchestra. The styles employed range from Gregorian chant to fugue to aria. The result is a highly dramatic work depicting the horror of war in a unique and very moving way.

Almost all of Britten's major works involve voices, either solo or chorus. Some are on a large scale, particularly the *Spring Symphony* (1949), and *Ballad for Heroes* (1939), an unusually effective antiwar piece for large orchestra, chorus, and soloist. Britten also made important contributions to the literature of orchestrally accompanied song, including his *Serenade for Tenor, Horn, and Strings* (1943).

One of Britten's best-known works is *A Ceremony of Carols,* written in 1942. The piece was originally composed for boys' chorus (SSA) and harp but was later arranged for mixed chorus (SATB), also with harp. In it Britten welded together an exquisite selection of medieval carol texts in the form of choruses, a recitative, a solo movement, a duet, and an interlude for harp solo. All these pieces are framed by a processional and recessional consisting of an unaccompanied chant sung by the soprano section of the chorus at the beginning and end of the composition:

A CEREMONY OF CAROLS

*Example 19.16**

"This day Christ was born; this day the Savior appeared; this day the Angels sing on earth and the Archangels rejoice. This day the just exult saying: Glory to God in the highest. Alleluia!"

The general character of the piece is joyous and festive, qualities that have made *A Ceremony of Carols* an extremely popular piece, particularly at the Christmas season.

SUMMARY

Music since 1900 is characterized by an unprecedented diversity of styles and points of view. Three distinguishing features of modern music are its rhythmic complexity, its free use of dissonance, and its vaguely defined or nonexistent tonal center.

An important movement in music between the two world wars was Neoclassicism. Neoclassical composers believed musical composition should be approached systematically and rationally, with irrelevant emotions held in check. They varied the forms of the Baroque and Classical eras to develop a distinctly modern idiom.

The Russian-born composer Igor Stravinsky has been, along with Arnold Schoenberg, one of the two towering figures in twentieth-century music. His early works, Russian in flavor, combined glittering orchestration and unusual, aggressive rhythms. His Neoclassical style, dominant in Europe between the world wars, was austere and clear-textured. Stravinsky's creative energies never failed him, and in his later years he employed the twelve-tone technique in a number of compositions.

Béla Bartók, the leading composer to come out of Eastern Europe in this century, was profoundly influenced by Hungarian folk music. His mature style was compact, often dissonant, and rhythmically inventive.

Paul Hindemith, a German composer who immigrated to America, was important both as a composer and as a teacher of composition. He wrote in nearly all traditional genres of composition and for almost all commonly played musical instruments.

Other modern European composers who have contributed lasting works to the repertoire include the Russians Prokofiev and Shostakovitch and the Englishman Britten.

NEW TERMS

Neoclassicism
absolute music
primitivism

IN THEIR EFFORTS TO CREATE A NEW KIND OF "TONALITY" IT OC-curred to many twentieth-century composers that they might be able to avoid the traditional concept of tonality completely. But the idea of the tonal center was so fundamental to musical organization that it could not simply be dropped. Rather, it had to be replaced by an organizing principle of equal strength and validity. The search for such an alternative was the life work of several Viennese composers early in this century. Their work took place at the same time that Stravinsky, Bartók, Hindemith, and others were expanding the idea of tonality. These two simultaneous developments determined the course of musical composition for the first half of the century.

SCHOENBERG (1874–1951)

At the start of his career, Arnold Schoenberg (Shön'-behrg) was closely allied with late German Romanticism, although he moved farther from it than almost any of his contemporaries. Together with two of his students, Alban Berg and Anton von Webern, Schoenberg took the fateful step of rejecting the concept of tonality completely, and wrote in what is called an atonal style. He later developed a new system of musical organization to replace tonality which involves setting the twelve chromatic tones in a chosen order, and then using them in various ways. This system is called **serialism, twelve-tone technique,** or **dodecaphony.**

Almost single-handedly Arnold Schoenberg effected a radical and significant change in basic concepts of music. His development of the twelve-tone technique opened the door to new methods of composing and new ways of constructing harmonic relationships. He himself viewed his new method of composing not as a dramatic, revolutionary gesture against

Fig. 20.1 One of the most important and innovative figures in twentieth-century music, Schoenberg also enjoyed painting. This intense self-portrait reflects his association with the school of German Expressionism.

the past but as a logical consequence of nineteenth-century chromatic developments in harmony. He developed his method over many years through a number of compositions, each of which explores new techniques. Some of these techniques were to form part of his serial procedures.

Schoenberg was born into a Viennese middle-class family; although his parents both loved music, neither provided much guidance in his early training. While in grammar school he studied the violin and cello and was soon composing and playing in chamber ensembles. When Schoenberg was in his late teens, a friend, Alexander von Zemlinsky, who directed an amateur orchestral society, first interested him in serious musical study; and after working several years as a bank employee, Schoenberg decided in 1895 to embark on a musical career.

The two great influences in his early composition were the giants of late nineteenth-century German music: Brahms and Wagner. During the 1890s he wrote several string quartets and piano works and a small number of songs. In 1901 he married his friend's sister, Mathilde von Zemlinsky. Shortly afterward he was engaged as a theater conductor in Berlin. There he became acquainted with Richard Strauss, who helped him obtain a teaching position and expressed great interest in his work. In 1903 Schoenberg returned to Vienna to teach musical composition. Gustav Mahler became a supporter of his music, and, more importantly, he took on as students two younger men, Alban Berg and Anton von Webern. Both pupils would later adopt Schoenberg's twelve-tone methods, would develop them in their own individual ways, and Webern would influence decisively the future course of music (see Chapter 24).

During the first decade of the twentieth century, Schoenberg began turning away from the late Romantic style of his earlier works and gradually developed his new twelve-tone method. Although his name spread among composers and performers, public acclaim eluded him. His famous song cycle *Pierrot lunaire* (*Moonstruck Pierrot*), which drew invective from critics but praise from avant-garde sympathizers, employed a half-sung, half-spoken technique called **Sprechstimme** (literally, "speech voice").

Schoenberg's reputation was beginning to grow when his career was interrupted by World War I, in which he served with the Austrian army; but soon after he was again active as a composer, lecturer on theory, and teacher. The 1920s marked a new direction. He went to Berlin in 1925 to teach composition at the State Academy of the Arts, taking with him his second wife, Gertrude Kolisch. (His first wife had died in 1923.)

In 1933 Schoenberg's career again took another direction. When the Nazi party assumed power, Schoenberg, being a Jew, was dismissed from his post and emigrated first to France, then to the United States. Although his reputation as a teacher and as a "modernist" preceded him, he nevertheless had financial difficulty. After working in Boston and New York, he joined the faculty of U.C.L.A. He died in Los Angeles at the age of seventy-seven.

SCHOENBERG'S WORK

Schoenberg's work—amounting to fifty opus numbers, several early unpublished pieces, and three unfinished compositions—includes stage works, art songs, choral pieces, works for piano, a number of orchestral compositions, and an extensive variety of chamber music. His early works, up through the first years of the century, stand in the late German Romantic tradition of Wagner, Brahms, and Mahler. They are tonally based and use many of the Romantic forms. The tone poem *Verklärte Nacht* (*Transfigured Night,* 1899), written for string sextet and later revised for string orchestra, is based on a literary program and uses a recurring theme to link the sections of the work. The harmonic style is related to that of Wagner's *Tristan and Isolde.* His symphonic poem *Pelleas und Melisande* was inspired by the same Maeterlinck drama that interested Debussy. The symphonic cantata *Gurrelieder* (*Songs of Gurre,* 1900–1901) is a gigantic and complex work for soloists, chorus, and huge orchestra.

ATONALITY AND EXPRESSIONISM

Beginning in about 1905, Schoenberg evolved radically different procedures that were regarded by his contemporaries as quite revolutionary. Two different terms are often used to describe his new approach. The first, **atonality,** refers to the systematic avoidance of any kind of tonal center. This is accomplished by excluding simple, familiar chords, major or minor scales, and octave leaps. When these principles are combined with dissonance and a rapid succession of chords, the ear cannot find any stable point (tonic) to use as a center of reference. In this way the twelve tones of the chromatic scale are made equal, rather than consisting of seven "belonging" to the key of a piece and five others "not belonging."

As previously noted, Schoenberg considered his new harmonic style to be a logical extension of tendencies already apparent in late German Romanticism. In the music of Wagner and Strauss, brief atonal passages can be found, although they are embedded in a tonal context. Schoenberg simply increased the amount of dissonance and chromaticism in his music until the listener could no longer perceive the difference between stable tones ("belonging") and unstable tones ("not belonging"). Since dissonances were no longer resolved in the traditional manner, they became "emancipated." The ordering of successive intervals, not the traditional relationship of dissonance to consonance, became the chief organizing principle.

The second term used to describe Schoenberg's works in the period from 1905 to about 1912 is **Expressionism.** Borrowed from the field of art criticism, the term refers to a school of German artists and dramatists who tried to represent the artist's innermost experience. Often Expressionist artists used unusual, even revolutionary, methods—such as harsh colors and distortion of the human image —to achieve an intense emotional effect. The subject matter of Expressionism was modern humanity in its varied psychological states: isolated, irrational, rebellious, tense. The artist did not attempt to produce beautiful or realistic art, but only to penetrate and reveal inner feelings. Schoenberg shared the goals of the Expressionistic artists; his atonal music was the stylistic means of reaching those goals.

The problem that Schoenberg eventually had to face, having abandoned tonality, was the loss of the form-building properties that the old system had provided. Without tonal centers and modulations, the traditional forms could not really exist. Without such simple but useful devices as the dominant-tonic chord progression, there was no harmonic guide to help distinguish a cadence from any other point in a phrase.

At first Schoenberg found only temporary solutions. He wrote short pieces and depended heavily on outside material (either literary or dramatic) to impose form on the music. In addition, he used intricate motivic development and contrapuntal procedures to unify his "free" atonal compositions. These devices had been part of his Romantic style, but they became even more important as this Expressionistic style emerged. Some of his works from this middle period are characterized by the dominance of a particular interval. Others contain canons and ostinato figures.

Schoenberg creates incredible variety within each piece of his music. Rarely is the same texture maintained for more than a single phrase. Instead, contrapuntal patches are interspersed with accompanied melody. Rhythm and dynamics are also subject to the same rapid variation. Two consecutive phrases are rarely equal in length. Schoenberg almost never uses literal repetition or any other formal symmetry, even when a repeated text in vocal music invites such treatment.

An excellent example of Schoenberg's Expressionistic style is *Pierrot lunaire* (1912), a setting of twenty-one surrealistic poems for vocalist, piano, flute, clarinet, violin, and cello. Schoenberg provides for further variety by having some players switch to other instruments: piccolo, bass clarinet, and viola. The singer (a woman) uses the *Sprechstimme* technique. Both the rhythms and the pitches are precisely notated. The pitches, however, are points which the singer may center on, then fall away from. The effect of *Sprechstimme* in *Pierrot lunaire* is haunting and eerie.

DEVELOPMENT OF THE TWELVE-TONE METHOD

Schoenberg continued to be very much aware of the limitations his free atonal style placed on him; he wanted to write longer pieces, but lacked a formal framework on which to build them. Form was very important to Schoenberg. He believed that some underlying organization was essential, no matter what radical changes took place in the harmonic idiom.

Gradually he evolved a system he described as a "method of composing with twelve tones that are related only with one another, not to a central tone: a tonic." The rudiments of this method are simple: the composer arranges the twelve pitches of the chromatic scale in a particular order. This is known as a **tone row,** or **series,** or **set,** for a specific piece. The row can be transposed to any pitch level, and used upside down (*inversion*), backward (*retrograde*), or upside down and backward (*retrograde inversion*).

The original form of the row below is taken from the opening of the choral melody of Schoenberg's *A Survivor from Warsaw*.

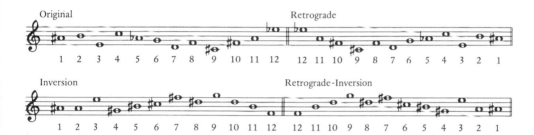

Example 20.1 ⃰

The notes of the series (or any of its variations) are sometimes used sequentially, both in full or in segments, to form a melody or theme, and are also used simultaneously in clusters to form chords. The system does not impose limits on rhythm, dynamics, or textures that the composer will choose, so it is not a mechanical music-producing method, as it might seem at first. A composer who writes with the serial technique is no more limited than one who chooses to write tonally. The basic tone row provides some coherence, in the same way that tonality does, but there is still room for tremendous variety.

Schoenberg had formulated his twelve-tone method by 1923, and he used it in most of his compositions thereafter. It was applied in part to the *Five Piano Pieces* (Opus 23, 1923) and the *Serenade for Seven Instruments and Bass Voice* (Opus 24, 1923). The *Suite for Piano* (Opus 25, 1924), which uses Baroque forms, and the *Wind Quintet* (Opus 26, 1924) use the system throughout.

No longer Expressionistic, the works written in the 1920s have a marked air of confidence and playfulness. A traditional spirit is also evident. In a way, Schoenberg could now be called a Neoclassicist. He used forms resembling Classical ones—theme and variations and sonata form, for instance—and contrasted his themes in a Classical manner, while continuing to write in a very dissonant idiom with serial techniques.

In 1928 Schoenberg completed the powerful *Variations for Orchestra* (Opus 31), a serial work for full orchestra (see pp. 370–372). He also used the twelve-tone system in a number of important works written in the United States during the 1930s and 1940s, including the Concerto for Violin and Orchestra (1936), the String Quartet No. 4 (1937), the Concerto for Piano and Orchestra (1942), and *A Survivor From Warsaw* (1947), a cantata for speaker, chorus, and orchestra. His death left uncompleted his major opera, *Moses und Aron* (begun in 1931).

⃰   Used by permission of Boelke-Bomart, Inc., Hillsdale, N.Y. 12529.

**VARIATIONS
FOR
ORCHESTRA
(OPUS 31)**
RECORD 7/SIDE 1

Variations for Orchestra is scored for a large orchestra with a full complement of winds, harp, celesta, mandolin, the usual strings, and a very extensive percussion section, including glockenspiel and xylophone. The piece consists of an introduction, a theme and nine variations, and a finale.

The basic series for this work is:

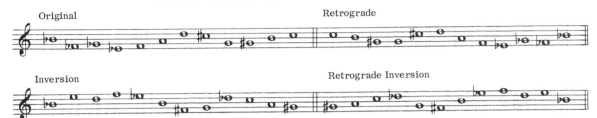

*Example 20.2 ***

The introduction presents this series gradually in its opening measures; it is not yet used thematically, since that would anticipate the function of the theme section. After a slow beginning and a more emphatic central section, a quiet closing rounds it off. The trombone introduces a motive that will be heard occasionally throughout the piece.

Example 20.3

In the German system for naming notes, our B-flat is called B, and our B is called H—thus these four notes spell BACH. Johann Sebastian Bach used this motive as the subject of one of his organ fugues, and other composers have been intrigued by it since. In *Variations for Orchestra,* the BACH motive is always treated motivically in fairly long note values.

The theme section introduces the row as a theme; it is played by the cellos with a soft chordal accompaniment. What sounds like one long melody is actually the row, first in its original form, then in retrograde inversion, then in retrograde, and finally in inversion. At the end of the movement it is treated contrapuntally, with the cellos playing the original version while the violins play its inversion (see Example 20.4).

In the variations that follow, the row is always present in a melodic form, but is not used with the same octaves or rhythms as in the theme, making it somewhat difficult to identify. Moreover, the entire row theme is not always the most important melodic material in each variation. Other motives also derived from the row are presented and developed; rhythmic ideas are elaborated; and varied instrumentations and contrapuntal textures are often the focus of attention. In a sense the conflict between the row as an underlying structural force (a substitute for tonality) and as thematic material is the basis of the piece.

One way to describe the variations is to locate the "theme" (meaning some continuous melodic variant of the basic series) and show how it is used. We can illustrate this most easily by giving the various rhythmic treatments of the theme in some of the variations (see Example 20.5).

---

*   Examples 20.2 through 20.6 are used by permission of Belmart Music Publishers, Los Angeles, Calif. 90049.

Example 20.4

Example 20.5

VARIATION I. The theme stays in the lowest bass instruments, with the full orchestra playing very short motives above.

VARIATION II. The inversion of the theme is presented in canon by the violin and oboe. The texture is complicated by simultaneous canons on other subjects. The movement is scored very lightly, for only solo instruments, which helps clarify the complex contrapuntal texture. The BACH motive is heard in the trombone.

VARIATION III. The theme is played mostly by the horns, but it is not particularly important. The first motivic material is a dotted arpeggio figure; a repeated-note group later turns out to be the central idea.

VARIATION IV. The harp, celesta, and mandolin play the theme as an accompaniment to contrapuntal wind and string parts. The instrumental colors are quite unusual because of the choice of instruments.

VARIATION V. The basses again have the theme, but attention focuses on the large leaps they make after each thematic note. These leaps are taken up by the other instruments and characterize the variation.

VARIATION VI. The theme is hidden in the solo part, but the more interesting material is first in the clarinet, and then in the other winds.

VARIATION VII. The piccolo and glockenspiel play the theme in a very high register and entirely off the beat. The winds are featured again, and the rapid changes of instrumental color are notable. Toward the end of this rather long variation, the rhythmic patterns are quite exciting.

VARIATION VIII. For the first time, the theme is not used melodically at the beginning of a variation. The texture provides the primary interest, with contrapuntal wind parts contrasted with rhythmic ostinatos in the strings. The theme appears in the flute and violin toward the end of the variation.

VARIATION IX. The theme itself is the dominant feature of this variation. It is treated contrapuntally at the beginning, with short interludes between presentations; later only fragments of it are used.

FINALE. The BACH motive opens the last movement and proves to be of great importance. It is interspersed with various versions of the row theme and several other motives derived from row material. There are many changes of tempo and texture in this concluding movement.

ALBAN BERG

Alban Berg (Behrg, 1885–1935) adopted most of Schoenberg's methods of construction but used them with a great deal of flexibility. His works allow for a sense of tonality and combine Schoenbergian techniques with established formal procedures from earlier musical periods, including the suite, the march, the rondo, and the passacaglia. His music has a warmth and lyricism that stems from the romantic tendencies in Schoenberg. In addition, such elements as his ability to sustain large forms and his use of large orchestras reinforce the romantic aspect of his style. As a result much of Berg's music is more accessible to the listener than some of Schoenberg's and most of Webern's.

Berg's principal works are his *Lyric Suite for String Quartet* (1926), his *Violin Concerto* (1935), and his two operas, *Lulu* (1929–1935, uncompleted) and *Wozzeck*. The latter is considered by many to be his greatest work.

Wozzeck was written between 1917 and 1921 and was unquestionably influenced **WOZZECK** by the environment created in Europe by World War I. In its psychological probing of the unconscious and its presentation of a nightmarish world, it is the finest manifestation of Expressionism in opera form.

The central character is Wozzeck, the soldier who represents "We poor people." He is belittled and abused by his superior, the captain; used as a hired guinea pig in medical "experiments" by his doctor; betrayed by his mistress, Marie; and eventually driven to murder and suicide by a completely hostile society.

Berg himself constructed the libretto, fashioning it from bits and pieces of a drama by Georg Bückner (1813–1837). Only a musician with substantial mastery of his craft could have formulated such a libretto! As designed by Berg, the opera has three acts which follow the scheme:

Act I   Exposition
Act II   Development
Act III Catastrophe

Each act consists of five scenes and is organized along the lines of a specific musical form. For example, Act II (the longest) takes the form of a symphony in five movements, the individual scenes of which are:

Sonata Movement (scene 1)
Fantasia and Fugue (scene 2)
Largo (scene 3)
Scherzo (scene 4)
Rondo with introduction (scene 5)

Acts I and III are organized along similar lines.

Actually there is continuous music throughout each act. The intervals between scenes are filled with short orchestral transitional passages which function either as a coda to the scene just finished or as an introduction to the ensuing scene.

Each of the musical structures (scenes) is used as the vehicle through which the plot of the opera is advanced and the spirit of the action is portrayed. The "delivery" of the lines of the libretto by the actor/singers and their stage actions take place within this musical framework.

The vocal style of *Wozzeck* depends heavily on the *Sprechstimme* technique, which in *Wozzeck* alternates with ordinary speech and conventional singing in an extremely expressive manner.

The prevailing mood of *Wozzeck* is one of cynicism, irony, outrageous helplessness, and depression. Partly in spite of this feeling and partly because of it, *Wozzeck* is an extremely exciting theater piece that speaks forcefully to our own troubled times.

Fig. 20.2 Like his teacher, Schoenberg, Webern achieved little recognition during his lifetime. Yet a decade after his death he came to be regarded as one of the principal influences on contemporary composers.

ANTON VON WEBERN

Anton von Webern (Vey'-behrn, 1883–1945) was also a pupil of Arnold Schoenberg in Vienna. While Berg came to represent a link to the past among the followers of Schoenberg, Webern represents a more radical denial of and departure from established compositional procedures and concepts. His mature works crystallize the serialist constructionist approach to musical composition inherent in the twelve-tone technique as originally postulated by Schoenberg.

While Berg was writing in long forms for large musical forces, Webern was striving for economy of material and extreme compactness of form. He was preoccupied with the idea that each individual note in a composition was in itself important; nothing was added for "general effect." As a result of this preoccupation, most of his works take on the quality of "miniatures." Indeed, Webern's music is the epitome of clarity, economy of material, spareness of texture, and brevity.

It is not surprising, then, that Webern wrote very little music and that all his works tend to be quite short, some individual pieces lasting less than a minute and some of his "largest" works not exceeding ten minutes. Recently his complete output was recorded on four long-playing records, which means that his entire creative effort produced perhaps four hours of music.

Webern's compositions are about equally divided between vocal and instrumental pieces. His vocal music includes collections of solo songs with various types of instrumental accompaniment, the choral work *Das Augenlicht* (*Light of the Eyes,* 1935), and two cantatas for soloists, chorus, and orchestra. The most important instrumental works are the *Symphony,* Opus 21 (1928) for nine solo instruments, String Quartet, Opus 28 (1938), the Concerto for Nine Instruments, Opus 24 (1934), and the Piano Variations, Opus 27 (1936).

Almost without exception, Webern's works are on the scale of chamber music, another manifestation of economy of means and compactness. His instrumentation often includes highly unorthodox combinations of instruments such as in his *Quartet,* Opus 22 (1930), which is scored for clarinet, saxophone, violin, and piano.

As we noted before, Webern's music depends heavily on serialism. His style is essentially contrapuntal and is marked by an exceptional sensitivity to instrumental color. Often a single melodic line, derived from a twelve-tone row, is divided among several instruments, each assigned only one or two notes at a time; the changes of timbre from instrument to instrument give the melody an added interest.

The beginning of the first movement of the *Symphonie,* Opus 21, demonstrates the spareness of Webern's style and the distribution of the melodic line over a number of instruments:

SYMPHONIE (OPUS 21)

Example 20.6*

Webern suffered the same lack of recognition by the general public during his lifetime as Schoenberg did, but his music, like that of his teacher, has become increasingly influential since World War II. In particular, in the last twenty years many young composers, captivated by the lean character of his style and his isolation of the single note as an important musical event, have adapted features of his music and expanded the techniques of serialism to suit their own purposes. It now seems inevitable that the twelve-tone technique initiated by Schoenberg and advanced by Berg and Webern will continue to be a powerful force in the world of music.

CHARACTERISTICS OF TWENTIETH-CENTURY MUSIC (TO WORLD WAR II)

Tonality	Major-minor system retained by some composers, but methods of establishing tonal centers altered; other composers employed atonal systems including serialism
Texture	Both homophonic and contrapuntal textures employed; variety of textures within a single work
Rhythm	Complex rhythms; rhythmic patterns used to build form; frequent absence of well-defined beat; frequent change of meter
Harmony	High dissonance levels; new methods of chord construction in addition to triadic harmony
Tone Color	Instruments sometimes played in extreme registers; unusual instruments, instrument groupings, and colors. Tone color a primary structural element, particularly in the music of Debussy
Melody	Melodic material sometimes derived from very short motives; melodies often not songlike
Dynamics	Dynamic extremes employed; rapid dynamic fluctuations
Ensembles	Wide variation in size of ensembles from very small to gigantic
New Organizational Procedures	Serialism (twelve-tone technique)
General Stylistic Trends	Impressionism Neoclassicism Expressionism
Vocal Style	Combination of ordinary speaking, conventional singing, and *Sprechstimme*

SUMMARY

The development of the atonal style was led by Arnold Schoenberg, a Viennese composer who, along with Igor Stravinsky, has been the dominant figure in twentieth-century music. Schoenberg rejected the concept of tonality completely and devised a new system, ultimately called serialism, to organize his works.

Schoenberg's early works are in the late Romantic tradition and are tonally based. During the first decade of the twentieth century he began to develop a "free" atonal style that systematically avoided any tonal center, thereby equalizing all twelve tones. He depended heavily on literary or dramatic material, motivic development, and contrapuntal procedures to impose form and organization. His works from 1905 to about 1912 are also described as Expressionistic, reflecting his association with the school of German artists and dramatists who were attempting through their art to represent the psychological experience of modern humanity.

Schoenberg was aware that the free atonal style placed certain limitations on his work. Tonality had provided a means of making structural distinctions. In its absence he needed to develop a formal framework on which to build. His solution was to arrange the twelve pitches of the chromatic scale in a particular order known as the tone row, series, or set for a specific piece. The twelve tones of the series could be used in sequence, forming a melody or theme, or simultaneously in groups to form chords. Furthermore, the system did not impose limitations on rhythm, dynamics, or texture. As a result the tone row provided coherence in the same way that tonality does, but still left room for great variety. Schoenberg had formulated his twelve-tone method by 1923 and used it in most of his compositions thereafter.

Although he received little recognition during his lifetime, Schoenberg has had a major influence on contemporary composition. Much of that influence has been transmitted through the music of his pupil and colleague Anton von Webern. Webern and Alban Berg represent the further development of two divergent aspects of Schoenberg's style: Webern the abstract constructionist, Berg the romanticist.

NEW TERMS

serialism (twelve-tone
   technique; dodecaphony)
Sprechstimme

atonality
Expressionism
tone row (series; set)

PART VII SUGGESTED LISTENING

Bartók, Béla

Mikrokosmos. A collection of piano pieces illustrating Bartók's compositional style from traditional nineteenth-century Hungarian harmonic structures and whole-tone scales to bitonality. Sets contain pieces ranging from the relatively simple to the fairly difficult.

Berg, Alban

Lulu. An uncompleted three-act opera illustrating the amalgamation of Wagnerian opera techniques with twelve-tone compositional techniques.

Britten, Benjamin

Serenade for Tenor Solo, Horn, and Strings. A cycle of English poems about night, death, and sleep, the *Serenade* is an expressive dialogue between tenor and horn. The "Nocturne" features duet bugle calls for the horn and voice.

Debussy, Claude

Pelléas et Mélisande. Opera in five acts based on a medieval legend. It epitomizes the subtlety of Impressionism—each act is a continuum of musical narrative employing leitmotives.

Hindemith, Paul

Das Marienleben. A cycle of fifteen songs written to poems by Rainer Maria Rilke arranged into four groups. Each is organized metrically and tonally while contributing underlying ideas to a unified whole. Hindemith subjected the cycle to many revisions, finally publishing a completed revision in 1948.

Prokofiev, Serge

Symphony No. 1 in D, Op. 25 (Classical Symphony). Prokofiev decided to write his first symphony in the style and spirit of Haydn. The work is both an appreciation and a parody of Classical style, using some very unclassical harmonies, wide leaps, and in the second movement, an accompaniment that limps on long after the melody has expired.

Ravel, Maurice

Daphnis and Chloë. Ravel's most ambitious work, this "ballet symphony" was commissioned for the Russian ballet. Ravel strove for a work that would be musically complete, not merely a vehicle for dancing.

Schoenberg, Arnold

A Survivor from Warsaw, Op. 46, for narrator, men's chorus, and orchestra. Schoenberg fashioned his text from reports of the Warsaw ghetto uprising after hearing that his niece had been murdered in a Nazi death camp. The narrator recites the account of horror in the first person against a dramatic orchestral background. In this 1947 work, a late example of Expressionism in the composer's twelve-tone output, the row is divided into units which function as fragments of melody and harmony. At the climax, the chorus breaks into the ancient Hebrew prayer *Shema Yisroel* (Hear, O Israel), the first clear melodic statement of the row. *A Survivor from Warsaw* is among Schoenberg's most gripping works, one of a series inspired by his experience as a Jew living through the twentieth-century nightmare.

Shostakovitch, Dmitri

Symphony No. 5. Unlike Shostakovitch's earlier symphonies, the Fifth is marked by its Neoclassical form and large orchestral sound. Shostakovitch wrote that "in the center of this composition—conceived lyrically from beginning to end—I saw a man with all his experiences."

Stravinsky, Igor

Octet for Wind Instruments. A Neoclassical work in two movements employing flute, clarinet, two bassoons, two trumpets, and two trombones. Evocative of concerto grosso form, it is contrapuntal in texture.

Webern, Anton

Symphony, Opus 21. After composing a series of extremely short pieces, Webern wrote this symphony in two movements: the first, in sonata-allegro form; the second, a theme and variations. Scored for clarinet, bass clarinet, two French horns, harp, and a small body of strings, it is a spare orchestration of strict counterpoint.

VIII
MUSIC IN AMERICA

Photographs and clippings on the door of Charles Ives's study create the effect of a collage. Ives was the first composer to employ collage extensively as a musical technique (see Chapter 24).

CHAPTER 21 | AMERICAN MUSIC

STRIKING CONTRASTS RUN THROUGH THE HISTORY OF MUSIC IN THE United States. Imitation of European models has contrasted with attempts to produce a more uniquely American idiom; conservative and radical strains have alternated or vied for dominance; concert music, jazz, and popular music have tended to go their separate ways, though occasionally cross-fertilizing. As America has grown in expanse and population, so has the breadth and significance of her musical expression. In the twentieth century, American music, written in the many different musical languages which characterize our multicultural nation, stands in the forefront of important and influential artistic movements throughout the world.

THE SEVENTEENTH CENTURY

The religious dissenters who settled New England in the early seventeenth century had come from a world rich in music and the other arts. The Pilgrims, for example, loved and practiced music, but had little time to spare for entertainment in their new land. Their music was functional and used mostly for worship, in church and at home. It consisted primarily of psalms and hymns, with tunes taken from older hymns or folk songs brought over from England and Holland.

The first book printed in the Colonies was a new rhymed translation of the psalms, called the *Bay Psalm Book* (1640), to which music was added in a 1698 edition. Its publication underscores the strong ties between music and religion in early America.

THE EIGHTEENTH CENTURY

Secular music began to flourish in the Colonies during the eighteenth century, particularly in such major cities as New York, Boston, Philadelphia, and Charleston.

Fig. 21.1 A page from the Bay Psalm Book, the first book printed in the American colonies.

Through shipping and trading, the people in these cities remained in close contact with the artistic life of Europe. As the cities prospered, the growing middle class acquired both the leisure and the money to support the arts.

Concerts in eighteenth-century America were not so serious or impressive as those in the major European cities. The most popular concert programs in America consisted of patriotic songs, opera airs, traditional folk songs, and dance tunes. Music publishers catered to amateurs and produced works that were modest in proportion and that demanded only moderate skill in performance.

Beginning in the 1730s, there were concerts, operas, and other musical events that featured immigrant musicians. These professionals worked both as performers and as "professors" of music. They taught music to gentlemen amateurs who, in turn, supported the rapid growth of music in America. The supporters included Thomas Jefferson, one of the outstanding patrons of music of his day and an amateur violinist himself, and Benjamin Franklin, who served capably as a performer, inventor of an instrument (the glass harmonica), and music critic. Another of the gentlemen amateurs, Francis Hopkinson (1737–1791), who wrote genteel songs, claimed to be the "first native of the United States who has produced a musical composition."

By 1770 there was a group of native American composers with enough in common to be considered a school. Led by William Billings (1746–1800), these composers produced music with a simple, rugged hymn style, angular, folklike melodies, and stark harmonies. Not feeling bound by the European traditions of composition, they created their own style. One of the favorite devices of Billings and his contemporaries was the "fuguing tune," a hymn or psalm tune with brief polyphonic sections that have imitative entrances. Billings and the others of this school felt that these pieces were "twenty times as powerful as the old slow tunes."

Unfortunately, however, this virile new style was soon abandoned, and native American music returned to a position of subservience to the European style. The original style created by the New England composers was considered crude by comparison with that of the European masters; and Americans were becoming self-conscious about their lack of sophistication and cultural heritage.

THE NINETEENTH CENTURY

The musical culture of nineteenth-century America was marked by two significant phenomena. The first was the division between what we now call "classical" and "popular" music. Classical music was meant either for serious study and listening or for religious purposes, while popular music aimed only to entertain. Earlier music had served both functions. For example, the eighteenth-century fuguing tunes were written for worship and enlightenment, but learning and singing them was also an enjoyable social function.

The second phenomenon of nineteenth-century music was the imitation of German music by American composers, a trend that became most evident after the Civil War. By that time the pattern of immigration to the United States had changed, as more people came from the European continent and fewer from Great Britain. The Europeans brought to America the ideas of the Romantic movement, which was strongest in Germany. Soon Romanticism influenced every area of American musical life.

AMERICAN COMPOSERS BEFORE THE CIVIL WAR

In the years preceding the Civil War, many extremely sentimental songs were written and published primarily for use by amateurs in their homes. The one great songwriter of the period did not follow in the European tradition, but wrote for the parlors and minstrel shows of America.

Stephen Foster (1826–1864) wrote music that appealed to a large segment of the American population—those who were from neither the sophisticated Eastern cities nor the frontier. He articulated the uneasy feelings of dislocation and transition in a rapidly changing country.

Although his formal musical training was not extensive, he had an unmistakable gift for melody. Many of his songs are filled with nostalgic yearning, often for an unattainable love; both the text and music of his best-known songs, like *I Dream of Jeanie,* are gentle and tender. Foster also wrote many songs for the minstrel shows that were a popular form of entertainment in the North, both before and after the Civil War. The music of minstrel shows had a robust quality that was missing from the household songs of the period. Dance tunes and songs using the dialects of black Americans were the basis of the shows, and Foster contributed many of the latter, including his well-known *Oh! Susanna* and *Camptown Races*.

While Foster wrote in a vernacular style and drew from uniquely American experience, composers of sacred music centered their attention on European styles. The Civil War and Reconstruction years were marked by a growing taste for hymns adapted from the music of the great European composers, from Palestrina to Mendelssohn. Lowell Mason (1792–1872) composed and adapted many such hymns. His efforts also brought music education into the public school curriculum for the first time.

Much American music—original compositions, arrangements of songs and dances, and sets of variations on well-known tunes—was written for the piano, the favorite instrument of the Romantic era. American piano builders became some of the best in the world. One of the most colorful and talented figures in

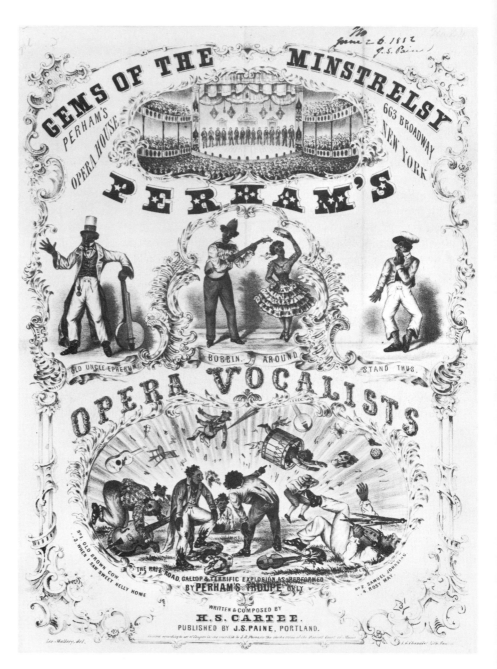

Fig. 21.2 The minstrel show was America's first form of musical theater. It evolved from performances by small groups of black entertainers on southern plantations. By the 1830s white professional entertainers had begun to copy the comedy, mannerisms, and folk music of the plantation showmen and to develop the minstrel show form, which reached its height around 1870. After 1875, the stereotyped, "comic" view of Negro song, speech, and humor replaced the earlier, relatively faithful portrayal. Ironically, as the artistic quality of the shows declined, they became even more popular. This 1882 music cover of "Gems of the Minstrelsy" illustrates the caricaturish image of blacks that became fixed in the consciousness of many white Americans.

American music before the Civil War was a virtuoso pianist from New Orleans, Louis Moreau Gottschalk (1829–1869), who adopted many of the mannerisms of Liszt. He composed numerous works for both piano and orchestra, many of exaggerated sentimentality, and also made use of such exotic musical materials as Afro-Caribbean rhythms and Creole melodies.

Most of the music performed by American orchestras was by European composers, although the works of the American George Bristow (1825–1898) were sometimes performed. Bristow wrote six symphonies in a style almost identical to Mendelssohn's. The New York Philharmonic, of which he was a member, was founded in 1842. A typical orchestral program in this period carefully mixed "heavy" music (single movements of symphonies, never complete ones) and lighter music (marches and overtures).

AFTER THE CIVIL WAR

From the end of the Civil War to World War I, German Romantic music had its greatest influence. Symphony orchestras were formed in many of the major cities, and large concert halls were built, including Carnegie Hall in New York (1891). Conservatories were established, and music departments appeared in colleges and universities.

A group of Romantic composers formed in Boston under John K. Paine (1839–1906), a conservative and serious craftsman who became the first professor of music at Harvard. Other talented members of the Boston group were Horatio Parker (1863–1919) of Yale and George Chadwick (1854–1931). These men composed instrumental and choral music: symphonies, sonatas, chamber music, and oratorios. Stylistically, they were closely allied with the early German Romantics, such as Schubert, Mendelssohn, and Schumann.

Edward MacDowell (1861–1908) also came under the influence of German Romanticism, but avoided the established instrumental forms in favor of program music. Having studied in Germany, he went on to achieve success there as a pianist, composer, and teacher. In contrast to the Boston group, MacDowell allied himself with the tradition of Wagner and Liszt. He wrote several tone poems for orchestra, a well-known piano concerto (in D minor), and many songs and choral pieces. But this American "tone poet" became primarily the composer of small character pieces for piano, most with programmatic titles. His *Woodland Sketches,* containing "To a Wild Rose" and "To a Water Lily," and *New England Idyls* are among his best-known works in this vein.

Late in the century a few American musicians began to react against the domination of German ideals and attitudes. Some American composers decided to make use of American Indian and Negro themes—a challenge put forth by Czech composer Antonín Dvořák on his visit to America from 1892 to 1895. Arthur Farwell (1872–1951) was an American composer who accepted Dvořák's challenge and concentrated on using Indian themes in his works. Those who reacted against the German influence also took interest in the new musical ideas from France and Russia. Charles T. Griffes (1884–1920), whose creative talents were cut short by his premature death, showed in his early works the influence of Debussy, Ravel, and Stravinsky. He also developed an interest in Oriental music, and his last works, especially the *Sonata for Piano* (1918, revised 1919) and the *Poem for Flute and Orchestra* (1919), contain the seeds of a synthesis of his various interests.

THE EARLY TWENTIETH CENTURY

During the first two decades of the twentieth century, as we have just noted, the German Romantic tradition continued to hold sway within the American musical "establishment"—among the concert-going public and in academic circles. Eventually, the influence of French Impressionism made some inroads via the music of Charles T. Griffes. Later, French traditions and the Neoclassicism of Stravinsky would be transmitted to American composers through influential French teachers and would supplant German attitudes.

But American musical pioneers were at the same time beginning to discover and invent new and radical kinds of music of their own, independently of and in some cases even before their European counterparts. From about 1900 to 1920, in such widely separated places as Danbury, Connecticut, and San Francisco, California, a few Americans were tinkering with an assortment of "ultramodern" sounds and methods of composition.

One of these bold figures was Charles E. Ives, the most extraordinary and original composer that America has produced. Not only did Ives use such advanced techniques as atonality, free dissonance, and extreme rhythmic complexity, he dipped into home-grown music as well. Indeed, his music contains elements drawn from the entire gamut of his musical and personal experience, from popular American songs and marches to hymn tunes to quotations from famous European classics. In a statement reflecting his open-minded approach, Ives said, "There can be nothing *'exclusive'* about a substantial art. It comes directly out of the heart of experience of life and thinking about life and living life." Thus, even within the same composition, Ives might shift from atonality to simple, hymnbook harmonies for evocative purposes. Ives, with his acceptance of all musical sources as valid and his rejection of dogmatic and exclusive methods, continues to influence composers here and beyond our borders.

IVES (1874–1954)

Charles Ives was raised in the small town of Danbury, Connecticut, where his father was town bandleader, church organist, music teacher, and composer. His father had an unusual interest in musical experimentation and a fascination with unconventional sounds, which he transmitted to his son. This was undoubtedly one of the most important musical influences in Ives's life.

The young Ives studied music at Yale and then launched a successful career in life insurance. He deliberately chose to earn his living in an enterprise separate from his composing on the theory that both efforts would be better for it, and he never regretted the decision. He composed furiously during evenings and weekends, storing his manuscripts in his barn. Ives's music was totally unknown until he published his *Concord Sonata,* a volume of songs, and a collection of essays in the early 1920s. Even then, his works were not readily accepted; only since World War II has his music become widely performed, published, and recorded. As his works became better known, Ives's influence increased, and successive generations of composers still draw inspiration from various aspects of his wide-ranging musical language. His work is considered to be so important among musicians and his popularity with the concert-going public is such that the one hundredth anniversary of his birth was widely celebrated in 1974.

The musical isolation in which Ives worked led to the development of an unusual philosophy of music. Ives idealized the strength and simple virtue of ordinary people. He had little regard for technical skill, either in composition or in performance, but placed high value on the spirit and earnestness with which amateurs sang and played their popular hymns and songs. The freedom that Ives permitted himself in the choice of musical materials he extended to performers of his works. Undismayed by an enthusiastic but inaccurate performance of *Three Places in New England* (1903–1914), Ives remarked approvingly, "Just like a town meeting—every man for himself. Wonderful how it came out!"

Fig. 21.3 Charles Ives, perhaps the boldest and most original of American composers, drew his musical elements and inspiration from the entire range of his musical and personal experience.

IVES'S WORK

Ives wrote several engaging orchestral works, including his four numbered symphonies, another symphony titled *New England Holidays,* and *Three Places in New England.* The latter contains the famous musical representation of two marching bands coming down Main Street on July Fourth, each playing in a different rhythm and key! Ives produced a considerable amount of chamber music as well, some for such traditional combinations as string quartet. But he also enjoyed creating new and unusual groupings of instruments. In *The Unanswered Question* (1906), a solo trumpet "asks the question" with an atonal melody, four flutes attempt an answer in successive flurries of confusion, all against a tonal background played by offstage strings. In *Hallowe'en* (1907?), for string quartet, piano, and optional bass drum, each of the strings plays in a different key. Ives also wrote several violin sonatas, piano sonatas, and other solos, and almost two hundred songs.

One of Ives's greatest works is the massive and fervent Second Piano Sonata (1909–1915). The sonata is an excellent illustration of Ives's interest in the New England Transcendentalists, of the rhythmic freedom found in his works, and of his characteristic use of quotations from famous classics, hymn tunes, revival songs, and band marches. Printed by Ives himself in 1919–1920 along with his six *Essays Before a Sonata,* this immensely difficult work remained generally unnoticed until 1939, when the American pianist John Kirkpatrick presented it at **SONATA NO. 2 (CONCORD SONATA)**

Town Hall in New York City. His performance, highly acclaimed by critics and the public, was perhaps more than anything else responsible for the long-delayed discovery of Ives's music.

Subtitled *Concord, Mass. 1840–60,* the sonata consists of four movements: "Emerson," "Hawthorne," "The Alcotts," and "Thoreau." In Ives's words:

The whole is an attempt to present one person's impression of the spirit of the transcendentalism that is associated in the minds of many with Concord, Mass., of over a half century ago. This is undertaken in impressionistic pictures of Emerson and Thoreau, a sketch of the Alcotts, and a scherzo *supposed to reflect a lighter quality which is often found in the fantastic side of Hawthorne. The first and last movements do not aim to give any programs of the life of any particular work of either Emerson or Thoreau, but, rather, composite pictures or impressions.**

As with so many of Ives's major works, much of the *Concord Sonata* evolved from earlier, often unfinished, pieces. One of his most ambitious projects was a series of *Men of Literature Overtures* for orchestra, which included works on Browning, Matthew Arnold, Emerson, and Hawthorne. The first two movements of the sonata are, in effect, a recomposition of the latter two overtures. The third movement is derived from the *Orchard House Overture,* another early symphonic work intended to evoke the home life of the Alcott family.

In a footnote near the end of the Epilogue to his *Essays Before a Sonata,* Ives describes his initial conception of each of the movements:

The first movement (Emerson) of the music which is the cause of all these words was first thought of (we believe) in terms of a large orchestra; the second (Hawthorne), in terms of a piano or a dozen pianos; the third (Alcotts), of an organ (or piano with voice or violin); and the last (Thoreau), in terms of strings, colored possibly with a flute or horn.†

RECORD 7/SIDE 2   FIRST MOVEMENT

"Emerson" comes closest to employing a traditional structure, using elements of a sonata-allegro scheme. Two motives are announced at the beginning: the first is lyrical in nature, sounding in the left hand

Example 21.1 ‡

---

*   From Charles Ives, *Essays Before a Sonata and Other Writings,* Howard Boatwright, ed. (New York: Norton, 1961), p. 1.
†   Ives, p. 84.
‡   Examples 21.1 through 21.8 are from Charles Ives, Second Piano Sonata. Copyright ℗ 1947 by Associated Music Publishers, Inc., New York. Used by permission.

and the second, more epic in spirit, is a direct quotation of the opening motives of Beethoven's Fifth Symphony. The original is notated

Example 21.2

and Ives has it appear first in the right hand, then in the left:

Example 21.3

The motive from Beethoven returns, in different settings, throughout the entire work, functioning as a unifying device.

The vast first movement unfolds as a series of contrasting "prose" and "verse" sections, to use Ives's own terminology. The two motives of the opening form the basis for the prose section (roughly analogous to the first-theme group of a sonata-allegro exposition), and a more extended, almost folklike melody initiates the verse (the second-theme group of an exposition):

Example 21.4

Like Beethoven, Ives begins developing his material as soon as it is stated. The epic and lyric motives pass through numerous transformations in rhythm, melodic contour, and harmonization. There is no key signature of definite tonal center, and the meter is highly irregular. The movement comes to a climax with the epic motive repeatedly enunciated fortissimo against the lyric motive in the bass. Then the texture thins and the pace slows. The movement gradually fades as soft statements of the motive from Beethoven are sounded against a background of faint, distant chords and a repeated, bell-like figure in the bass.

SECOND MOVEMENT

"Hawthorne" again makes use of the epic motive, but also introduces several other quotations. The "half-childlike, half-fairylike phantasmal realms"* of Hawthorne's imagination are suggested by the rapid, swirling figuration of the opening. The texture, now expanding, now contracting, is full of brilliant virtuoso effects. The epic motive enters in the right hand, fortissimo, and then suddenly the rapid-fire pace slackens as the hymn tune *Martyn* ("Jesus Lover of My Soul") quietly enters. Cut off by the scherzo figurations, it begins anew, ever more intense (see Example 21.5).

*   Ives, p. 42.

Example 21.5

This brief, churchlike reverie is again broken off with the return of the scherzo figuration. A jaunty march tune that Ives borrowed from an earlier work takes over:

Example 21.6

The march, in turn, is superseded by the complex syncopations of a ragtime. The pace gets faster and faster, the rhythms ever more complex, and toward the end a few bars of "Columbia, the Gem of the Ocean" make their way into the free-for-all.

THIRD MOVEMENT

The shortest and simplest of the movements, "The Alcotts," opens with a hymn-like version of the epic motive:

Example 21.7

But as the motive continues to expand, it becomes apparent that the opening is also that of another hymn tune, "Missionary Chant":

Example 21.8

In the juxtaposition of Beethoven and revival song, one flowing into the other, the two motives seem to suggest a musical Sunday afternoon at the Alcotts around "the little old spinet-piano Sophia Thoreau gave to the Alcott children, on which Beth played the old Scotch airs, and played at the Fifth Symphony."* The "old Scotch airs" dominate the movement, culminating in the return of Beethoven's Fifth.

FOURTH MOVEMENT

"Thoreau" is the most contemplative and dreamlike of the four movements. Bits and pieces of material heard earlier in the work are recapitulated, and suddenly —at the very end—Ives adds a separate line for solo flute. This odd intrusion of another solo instrument into the texture for so few measures reminds us again of Ives's often impractical approach to traditional concert forms. (There is an alternative version if no flute is used.) The flute's tonal melody is accompanied in the bass by a persistent, repeated figure which evokes timelessness. As the music slows and softens, it seems to evaporate, not resolving strongly into one key, but trailing off in several keys at the same time. Ives has hinted at his intent: "Every time I play it or turn to it, [the *Concord Sonata*] seems unfinished. . . . (I may always have the pleasure of not finishing it.)"

THE TWENTIES: OTHER "ULTRAMODERNISTS"

HENRY COWELL

Independently of Ives, other American modernists were working out their techniques at the same time. Henry Cowell (1897–1965), born near San Francisco, experimented with many radical compositional procedures which would later have considerable influence. Cowell's most famous device, found mainly in his piano music, is the **tone cluster.** This dense, indistinct sound, which Ives had also used in the *Concord Sonata* and elsewhere, can be produced by playing a large group of adjacent notes on the piano with the flat of the hand. It is said that Béla Bartók wrote Cowell asking permission to use this "invention" of his American colleague. Cowell wrote energetically about and published modern music as well, especially promoting the work of Charles Ives and Edgard Varèse.

EDGARD VARÈSE

Edgard Varèse (1883–1965) was born in Paris, but came to New York to live in 1915 and became one of the most innovative and influential composers of the twentieth century. Varèse challenged conservative musical traditions by defining music as "organized sound." This meant *all* sound, including some previously classified as nonmusical noises, such as Cowell's tone clusters.

Many of Varèse's compositions employ unusual combinations of instruments, which often play at the extremes of their registers. The musical idiom is character-

* Ives, p. 47.

ized by violent, screechingly dissonant, and blocklike chords spanning many octaves. Varèse's titles often reflect an interest in science: *Hyperprism* (1923), *Intégrales* (1925), *Ionisation* (1930–1933), and *Density 21.5* for solo flute (1936). The sound of the music tends to recall the noises of mechanized society. *Ionisation,* written for percussion ensemble, employs a huge battery of standard orchestral percussion and exotic instruments as well, such as the "lion's-roar" (a primitive kind of friction drum), and three sirens. The sirens illustrate Varèse's passion for expanding sound resources beyond those of the normal orchestra. Later, the development of more sophisticated electronic means was to inspire Varèse to write such masterpieces as *Déserts* (1949–1954) and *Poème électronique* (1957–1958).

"SYMPHONIC JAZZ"

The musically progressive and optimistic years between World War I and the beginning of the Depression also spawned an attempt by some composers to incorporate aspects of popular music into concert forms. The syncopated rhythms and "blue notes" of American jazz (Chapter 22) infected many European composers, including Stravinsky in his *Ragtime* (1918), Darius Milhaud in his *La création du monde* (1923), and Ravel in his Piano Concerto in G (1930–1931).

In America, the two main exponents of "symphonic jazz" were Aaron Copland, with his *Music for the Theater* (1925) and *Piano Concerto* (1926), and George Gershwin, with his *Rhapsody in Blue* (1924), *Concerto in F* (1925), and *An American in Paris* (1928).

THE THIRTIES AND FORTIES

Symphonic jazz was a transitory experiment, rather quickly abandoned by most composers who dabbled in it.* But in 1935 Gershwin, working in a different vein, produced an enduring work of genius, the folk opera *Porgy and Bess*.

GEORGE GERSHWIN'S *PORGY AND BESS*

George Gershwin (1898–1937) had become one of America's most successful songwriters and composers for the Broadway stage before he immersed himself in his finest achievement, *Porgy and Bess* (1933–1935). The work proved to be a near miraculous fusion of sophisticated popular songwriting and southern black folk styles, with the full trappings and dramatic force of opera.

Gershwin had long been influenced by black musicians. But in 1926 the composer read Du Bose Heyward's colorful parable of alienation, trouble, and futile striving, set in the ghetto of Charleston, South Carolina. He immediately asked for the rights to make the story into an opera. Many visits to the black communities of South Carolina's coastal islands provided the composer with first-hand in-

---

*   The idea of combining jazz elements and concert music reemerged in the mid-1950s, however. One hears jazz and "swing" in the brilliant musical show *West Side Story* by Leonard Bernstein (b. 1918). Another movement, spearheaded by Gunther Schuller (b. 1925), used more current improvisatory jazz styles. Schuller coined the term "Third Stream" for this music.

Fig. 21.4 Donnie Ray Albert (Porgy) and Clamma Dale (Bess) in the award-winning Houston Grand Opera production of Gershwin's *Porgy and Bess.*

spiration. (Actually, only the famous street-criers' songs are true folk material, transcribed by Gershwin himself.) The forms, the spirit, and the essence of this authentic music were molded into an elaborate and original orchestral fabric. The great songs, duets, and ensembles give the characters life and propel the action. The entire score, however, is infused with an almost supercharged emotion, and that singular "sound" has moved listeners throughout the world. Successful productions of Gershwin's original version of *Porgy and Bess* by the Houston Grand Opera toured the nation in 1977, and reaffirmed the theatrical impact of George Gershwin's masterpiece.

THE CONSERVATIVE TRADITION

The effects of the economic and social depression that followed the stock market crash of 1929 were reflected in the nation's concert halls. Isolationism and nationalism tended to inspire more conservative and inwardly directed musical idioms. *Porgy and Bess* represented one way to write a more consciously American-sounding music. Another way was to adopt modern atonal styles but to simplify them and to inject a deliberate emphasis on American folklore and local color. This effort became the preoccupation of a majority of composers during the mid-1930s and '40s. It was their belief that the cause of American music could best be served by streamlining the complex atonal idioms that had become prevalent in European music. The pungent tonalities and rhythmic drive of Stravinskian Neoclassicism served as a foundation on which to build.

COPLAND (b. 1900)

Aaron Copland was the first of a series of important American composers to study with the remarkable Mlle. Nadia Boulanger (b. 1887) in Paris. Setting Stravinsky as the example, she trained her pupils to develop their own personal styles. Although the rhythmic vitality and syncopation of American jazz continued to exert a subtle influence on many composers, Copland abandoned overt "symphonic jazz" and developed a more abstract, Neoclassical style. Among his works in this style are the brilliant *Piano Variations* (1930) and the rhythmically complex *Short Symphony* (1933).

By the mid-1930s, however, Copland began to be dissatisfied with the growing distance between the concert-going public and the contemporary composer. "I felt that it was worth the effort to see if I couldn't say what I had to say in the simplest terms possible," Copland wrote. Increasingly thereafter he drew on themes of regional America. His best-known scores are three ballets: *Billy the Kid* (1938) and *Rodeo* (1942) use actual cowboy songs; *Appalachian Spring* (1944) depicts life in rural Pennsylvania and is among the most beautiful and enduring representatives of Americana in our musical heritage.

Copland also wrote film scores during this

Fig. 21.5 One of Aaron Copland's abiding concerns has been to bridge the gap between the concert-going public and the modern composer.

period, among others *Of Mice and Men* (1939), *Our Town* (1940), and *The Red Pony* (1948). Several patriotic works, including the *Lincoln Portrait* (1942) and *Fanfare for the Common Man* (1942), were occasioned by the entry of the United States into World War II. Almost all these works used American subjects and were aimed at the wider audience provided by such media as film. Like Stravinsky, Copland turned to serial composition after 1950. The *Connotations for Orchestra* (1962) adapts the twelve-tone technique to his special musical style. For the past several decades Copland has spent much of his time conducting concerts of his own music all over the world.

Appalachian Spring, the last of Copland's three ballets on American frontier themes, was written on commission for Martha Graham's modern dance company. The work, choreographed by Miss Graham, premiered in October, 1944.

APPALACHIAN SPRING
RECORD 7/SIDE 2

Scored originally for a chamber orchestra of thirteen instruments, the ballet was later revised by Copland as a suite for symphony orchestra and is best known today in this form. The ballet itself is virtually plotless, having for its characters a young bride (originally danced by Miss Graham), her farmer husband-to-be, an older pioneering woman, and a preacher with his followers.

The music, evoking a simple, tender, and pastoral atmosphere, is distinctly American in its use of folklike themes suggesting barn dances, fiddle tunes, and revival hymns. Only one is actually a genuine folk tune: the Shaker song "Simple Gifts," which forms the basis for a set of five variations. Not only his melodic material, but also Copland's compositional techniques suggest a native American musical style. The orchestral texture is, by and large, open and transparent, with the different instrumental choirs—string, woodwind, brass, and percussion (chiefly piano and harp)—scored as individual units and juxtaposed with one another. The vigorous, four-square rhythmic patterns, particularly in the music for the revivalist preacher and his followers, could not have originated anywhere but in the folk music of the American frontier.

The orchestral suite falls into eight distinct sections, set off from one another by changes in tempo and meter. The opening section, marked "very slowly," introduces the characters, one by one. Over a luminous string background, solo woodwind and brass instruments enter one by one—paralleling the balletic action—with slowly rising and falling figures that outline different major triads. It is not until the solo flute and violin enter that these triadic figures coalesce into any kind of definite "theme":

Flute

mf cantabile
(Solo Violin doubles an octave higher.)

Example 21.9*

The serene mood of the introduction is suddenly broken by a vigorous, strongly accented theme sounded in unison in the strings and piano.

(*Continued on page 406.*)

---

*   Examples 21.9 through 21.14 are from Aaron Copland, *Appalachian Spring*. Copyright 1945 by Aaron Copland, renewed 1972. Reprinted by permission of Aaron Copland, copyright owner, and Boosey & Hawkes, Inc., sole publishers and licensees.

INTERLUDE | AMERICAN CULTURE BEFORE WORLD WAR II

In the seventeenth century Europeans colonized and settled the eastern seaboard of North America. By 1700, there were more than a million colonists scattered up and down the Atlantic coast, living mainly on farms, sometimes in villages, occasionally in trading towns like Boston, New York, or Charleston. In the eighteenth century the imperial health of England depended more and more on American shipbuilding and exports of agricultural commodities. To many Europeans the economic promise of the New World seemed limitless.

The cultural record of the American colonies is more spare. There is some rather naive local portraiture and some expressive tomb sculpture; the architecture, modeled on that of European masters like Palladio and Wren, is sometimes outstanding. On balance, however, there is little in American art of the seventeenth and eighteenth centuries to stand beside the masterwork across the Atlantic.

On the other hand, the American colonies had a rich local tradition in the crafts: even today the names Paul Revere and Duncan Phyfe suggest excellence in silversmithing and furniture-making. Likewise, native composers, mainly self-taught, traveled the countryside, organizing singing assemblies and getting tune-books published. These singing masters, of course, were most inclined toward choral music and hymn singing.

American painting came into its own in the late eighteenth century. The best American painters, though, had to leave the colonies and go to London to make their reputations. John Singleton Copley (1738–1815) moved to England in 1774, and Benjamin West (1738–1820) became President of the Royal Academy and Court Painter to George III. Purely American scenes did not become fashionable until the early nineteenth century. Then, painters of the untraveled West found a large and enthusiastic audience. George Caleb Bingham (1811–1879) painted scenes of flatboatmen, river ports, trappers, and local elections in Missouri. Hudson River landscapists like Thomas Cole (1801–1848) and Asher Durand (1796–1886) began a school of American nature painting that celebrated the wonder of the wilderness—in a more and more melodramatic way as the nineteenth century progressed. The paintings of later landscapists like Frederic Church (1826–1900) and Albert Bierstadt (1830–1902, Plate 35) were sometimes first displayed in the manner of the contemporary film premiere and were immensely popular, even if these works gave many Easterners a distorted and grandiloquent vision of Western topography.

In its pantheism and nature worship, early nineteenth-century American painting reflected elements of the Romantic movement. So also did literature, as Washington Irving, James Fenimore Cooper, and Edgar Allen Poe wrote tales of the wild, exotic, and supernatural. Not until 1830, however, did New England enter its greatest literary period. The brilliant speculations of Transcendentalist

Plate 35. *The Last of the Buffalo* (ca. 1885), by Albert Bierstadt. In the nineteenth century Americans living in Eastern cities provided artists with an enthusiastic audience for exotic and dramatic scenes of Western life and landscapes. In 1800 the American frontier was just beyond the Appalachians; by 1900 it was gone. (Courtesy Corcoran Gallery of Art; gift of Mrs. Albert Bierstadt.)

Plate 36. Augustus Saint-Gaudens's *Memorial to Robert Shaw,* a relief depicting a triumphant Civil War colonel and his black regiment, was erected in 1897 and reveals American taste for patriotic and commemorative sculpture at the end of the nineteenth century. (Courtesy Jean Boughton, Boston.)

Plate 37. As shown in his *Early Sunday Morning* (1930), Edward Hopper painted harsh, simplified forms in flat, bright light. Although his paintings have an "abstract" quality, Hopper remained distant from the experiments of European innovators like Picasso and Matisse. (Collection, Whitney Museum of American Art.)

Plate 38. Frank Lloyd Wright designed the Kaufman Hause at Bear Run, Pennsylvania (1936–1937), as an organic extension of nature. Massive cantilevers support the floors that hover above the waterfall; a skeleton of concrete, glass, and native rock further integrates the house with the landscape. (Courtesy Editorial Photocolor Archives.)

Ralph Waldo Emerson, the radical primitivism of Henry David Thoreau, and the thoughtful fiction of Nathaniel Hawthorne and Herman Melville created a rich literary environment of far-reaching significance.

Achievements in American music came late and were more modest. The most notable composer in the United States before the Civil War came out of the slightly vulgar realm of the minstrel show. Stephen Foster (1826–1864), a dreamer and outcast who destroyed himself with alcohol, wrote more than 200 songs, including tunes like "Camptown Races" and "Oh! Susanna" that have formed the bedrock of American popular music. The first American composer to achieve a reputation abroad was Edward MacDowell (1861–1908), who composed in the style of the German Romantics at a time when the Romantic mode was no longer in the European avant-garde. Even in the late nineteenth century most American composition continued to respond to European fashion. It was Charles Ives (1874–1954) who broke away from European tradition and helped to initiate an independent American avant-garde. Ives's extraordinarily original compositions were far ahead of their time, and it was not until World War II that his work gained wide critical acceptance. Since then his influence has been extensive, and composers today continue to draw inspiration from his bold experimentation.

When the colonies achieved independence in the late eighteenth century, the country had begun to outgrow its character as a collection of separate, often competing provinces and to move toward greater centralization. But it was not until the end of the Civil War (1865) that federal supremacy was assured. Then, with the rise of great railroad networks, with the emergence of new corporations that delivered manufactures to rapidly growing cities all over the continent, and with the settlement of the American interior from coast to coast, the United States became an urban, industrial power very different from the land of yeoman farmers that Thomas Jefferson had dreamed of at the beginning of the nineteenth century.

Significantly, American industrial captains of the nineteenth century collected art to decorate their great townhouses and country estates (Plate 40). Just as significantly, they were much more interested in buying Renaissance and Baroque work by established masters than in commissioning work that reflected American realities. Most American designers, especially architects, emulated (sometimes with slavish reverence) the models of the French academicians and l'École des Beaux-Arts (the prestigious French school of fine arts). A few far-sighted collectors bought the controversial work of the Impressionists; most connoisseurs, however, were attracted to the culturally "safe" style dictated by the well-entrenched art establishment in Paris. The distinction between "local color" and the "made-in-Europe" label was visible in music as well, as the upper class that built majestic concert halls and subscribed to operas and symphonies clearly demonstrated its preference for the imported styles.

At the turn of the century the favored painter in the United States was John Singer Sargent (1856–1925), whose handsome portraits of the landed, powerful, and financially secure were eagerly sought and displayed in the best New York and Boston townhouses. At the same time a very different style of art was being produced by the Ashcan School, so called after its raw, graphic scenes

Plate 39. *Janitor's Holiday,* by Paul Starrett Sample (1936). This gentle scene of a New England countryside is an example of the nostalgic regionalism of many American painters in the 1930s. Their work celebrated, often in sentimental fashion, purely American subjects. (Courtesy The Metropolitan Museum of Art; Arthur Hearn Fund, 1937.)

of proletarian New York. These paintings disturbed the average art patron, who felt that vulgarity and low life were not proper subjects for the painter. The European avant-garde was threatening, too. In 1913 a large exhibition of European art, including the Cubist work of Pablo Picasso and the Fauvist work of Henri Matisse, stupefied and revolted most of New York's influential critics —in the same way the Impressionists had scandalized Paris thirty years earlier. Nevertheless the Armory Show, as it was called, began to redirect American painting, and Europe's new modernism became a force that no serious painter could ignore.

Most American architecture of the early twentieth century was historical in concept, using a diverse vocabulary of styles that were revived from Antiquity, the Middle Ages, the Renaissance, and the Baroque. Two architects broke this mold, and in so doing, they created the prototypes for many of the buildings seen in America today. Louis Sullivan (1856–1924) rejected highly ornamented details when he built impressive skyscrapers whose lines clearly echoed their steel skeletons, and Frank Lloyd Wright (1869–1959) invented the low, relatively rustic residence that has since become a standard style of housing in suburban America (Plate 36).

Plate 40. The Breakers at Newport, Rhode Island (1893–1895), built by McKim, Mead, and White for the Vanderbilt family, was the grandest of all the palaces commissioned by American industrialists in the late nineteenth century. (Courtesy John Hopf.)

The building of cities slowed or halted during the Great Depression, although some projects, like Rockefeller Center in New York, went forward. In the 1930s the federal government, as part of its public works program, also commissioned murals and decorations for public buildings.. These were primarily in the regional style (Plate 39), of which Thomas Hart Benton and Grant Wood were leaders. Although the work of Benton and Wood was more abstract than earlier American art, it reflected a nostalgic realism that was uneasy with European experiments. Edward Hopper (1882–1967) understood the structural logic of Cubism, but his great talent lay in evoking the mystery inherent in commonplace aspects of American life (Plate 37). In the 1930s painters were also drawn to political subjects; some idealized the worker as the backbone and real hero of the American people.

Between the two world wars some American painters, especially in New York, were aware of concurrent French work; and in the 1930s the Museum of Modern Art was founded in New York. New York, however, did not outshine Paris until after 1945. Then the United States, which despite its commercial power had remained on the periphery of Western art, would become the cultural center of the Atlantic Community.

(*Continued from page 397.*)

Example 21.10

The action of the ballet now gets under way. The theme—initially built on the notes of an A-major triad—is soon broken down into smaller motives with the rhythmic figure  predominating.

Musical development intensifies as these motives are passed back and forth between different orchestral choirs and solo instruments. Constant changes in meter and shifts in rhythmic accents add to the increasing momentum of this section.

Then follows a *pas de deux* (a dance for two performers) for the bride and her husband-to-be, and their mixed feelings of tenderness and passion are expressed in a lyrical melody originating in the clarinet.

Example 21.11

The melody gradually expands and takes a definitive shape through numerous changes in tempo, culminating in a statement divided among the oboe, clarinet, and flute.

The revivalist preacher and his followers take over, announced by a cheerful tune that seems to have come right out of a country fiddlers' convention. Though heard first in the oboe and then the flute, the tune is not given fully until the entry of the violins.

Example 21.12

As in the second section, the rhythmic aspects of the tune soon prove to be more important than the melodic ones. The pace becomes more frenetic, cross-accents and syncopations soon predominate, and the section ends in a very Stravinskian manner with alternating meters of 2/4 and 5/8.

An extended solo for the bride follows, in which she expresses extremes of joy and fear, and exaltation at her coming motherhood. A presto theme forms the basis for most of this section,

Example 21.13

but toward the end a lyrical theme—very much like that of the earlier *pas de deux*—enters in the solo violin and oboe, gradually leading into a short recapitulation of the introduction.

A solo clarinet presents the melody of the Shaker song "Simple Gifts."

Example 21.14

The action of the ballet at this point, scenes of daily activity for the bride and her intended, seems perfectly reflected in the tune. The text of the song runs as follows:

> *'Tis the gift to be simple,*
> *'Tis the gift to be free,*
> *'Tis the gift to come down where we ought to be,*
> *And when we find ourselves in the place just right,*
> *'Twill be in the valley of love and delight.*
> *When true simplicity is gain'd,*
> *To bow and to bend we shan't be asham'd,*
> *To turn, turn will be our delight*
> *'Till by turning, turning, we come round right.*

The five variations following the statement of the tune present the melody in a variety of contrasting textures and accompanimental figures, often with new lines of counterpoint. At the end, the full orchestra blazes forth in a broad choralelike setting of the tune.

In the final section, the bride takes her place among her neighbors, and they depart quietly, leaving the young couple alone. Once again the luminous sonorities of the introduction return, and the work concludes in the atmosphere of serenity with which it began.

OTHER CONSERVATIVES

VIRGIL THOMSON

Virgil Thomson (b. 1896), after studying with Nadia Boulanger in Paris, turned to American hymns as one of his sources. He wrote in a melodic style, with humor and artful simplicity. His most important contributions are his three operas. *Four Saints in Three Acts* (1934), with a libretto by Gertrude Stein, is a charming work full of fantasy. *The Mother of Us All* (1947), also set to a Gertrude Stein text, draws morals from the life of Susan B. Anthony using hymnbook harmonies. *Lord Byron* (1968) is a further example of Thomson's infallible sense for setting American speech patterns to music.

ROY HARRIS

The music of Roy Harris (b. 1898), another Boulanger pupil, is characterized by chromatic but strongly lyric melodies, contrapuntal techniques, and an interest in Baroque procedures, such as fugue and ostinato. His Quintet for Piano and Strings (1936) and Symphony No. 3 (1938), both abstract instrumental pieces, are considered among his best compositions. Harris also has a strong interest in native American topics and musical materials, as evidenced in his *Folksong Symphony* (1940), his *Gettysburg Address Symphony* (1944), his choral settings of two texts by Walt Whitman, and many other pieces.

COMPOSER-EDUCATORS

Several important composers of this century have held positions as professors of music at American universities. One such composer was Walter Piston (1894–1976), yet another Boulanger pupil, who spent his entire career at Harvard. His approach was Neoclassical, using the traditional forms of instrumental music. His abstract but elegant style and high level of craftsmanship won him the respect of many of his fellow composers. Piston also wrote several widely used college texts on harmony, counterpoint, and orchestration.

Other composer-educators of the conservative tradition include Douglas Moore (1893–1969) at Columbia, Howard Hanson (b. 1896) at the Eastman School of Music, and William Schuman (b. 1910), for many years president of the Juilliard School and of Lincoln Center for the Performing Arts. Schuman is perhaps the best of the "American school" of symphonists. His nine symphonies are works of expressive power and original rhythmic vitality, and make expansive musical gestures from long, spun-out melodies and sumptuous orchestration.

NEOROMANTICS

Samuel Barber (b. 1910) has maintained a Neoromantic, lyric style throughout his career, with occasional touches of Neoclassicism. The popular *Adagio for Strings* (1936) illustrates an expressive, almost vocal contrapuntal style. Barber's two operas and many vocal works, especially *Dover Beach* (1933) for voice and string quartet and *Knoxville: Summer of 1915* (1948) for soprano and orchestra, attest to his skill in writing for the voice.

Gian Carlo Menotti (b. 1911), whose *Amahl and the Night Visitors* (1951) has become an American tradition at Christmas time, has made his career in opera. Born in Italy, but a resident of the United States for most of his creative life, Menotti follows the model of Puccini in both musical style and dramaturgy. His operas, the librettos for which he writes himself, deal with immediate experience that the average person can react to vividly in the theater.

AMERICAN SERIAL COMPOSERS

Some American composers had adopted the twelve-tone system even before Schoenberg came to the United States in 1933. American serialists remained a distinct minority during these years, but produced works of distinction.

Wallingford Riegger (1885–1961), who studied in Germany from 1907 to 1910, adapted serial procedures freely in such works as *Dichotomy* for chamber orchestra (1932). The Third Symphony (1948) uses a row for the opening movement's sonata form exposition, but abandons it in the development section. The last movement, a passacaglia and fugue, uses a seven-note chromatic theme rather than the full twelve-tone row.

Ruth Crawford Seeger (1901–1953) was one of the most remarkable American composers of the 1930s. Crawford, the stepmother of folksinger Pete Seeger, studied in Berlin and went on to invent her own serial systems. Each movement of her extraordinary String Quartet (1931) anticipates a technique heard thirty years later in works by Carter, Ligeti, and Messiaen. Crawford's socialist concerns are felt in the texts of several of her radical works. She later abandoned this atonal style in favor of transcribing and composing piano accompaniments to thousands of American folk songs. Many of these arrangements are still used today.

As we have already noted, after World War II the twelve-tone technique became accepted by many composers. Earlier it had been considered the special property of Schoenberg and the people working with him. After the war almost all the young composers in Europe and America used it, and some older composers adopted it too, including Copland, Sessions (see below), and Stravinsky. As Copland pointed out, twelve-tone writing is a technique, not a style; thus it can be used by composers with very different personal styles.

POSTWAR COMPOSERS: ROGER SESSIONS AND HIS STUDENTS

Roger Sessions (b. 1896) easily ranks alongside the most important European figures of his generation and remains one of the most highly respected composers in America today. Unlike many of his colleagues, Sessions never studied in Paris but he did spend several years in Italy and Germany. His works of the 1920s and '30s, including the First Symphony (1927), the First Piano Sonata (1930), and the Violin Concerto (1935), owed something to Stravinskian Neoclassicism, but had longer melodic lines and a more brooding intensity. Rich contrapuntal textures and a dynamic rhythmic drive have remained hallmarks of Sessions's style.

Sessions never deliberately strived for an "American" sound, believing instead that whatever an American composer produced was in every sense "American music." Rather than simplifying his style during the 1930s and '40s, Sessions wrote in an increasingly complex idiom. By 1953, he was employing a twelve-tone row; since then most of his works have employed serial methods. His eight symphonies (1927–1968), his two operas, *The Trial of Lucullus* (1947) and *Montezuma* (1941–1962), and his huge setting of Walt Whitman's *When Lilacs*

Fig. 21.6 Rich contrapuntal textures and a dynamic rhythmic drive are hallmarks of Roger Sessions's musical style.

Last in the Door-yard Bloom'd (1970) for soloists, chorus, and orchestra form an impressive legacy.

Sessions has exerted a powerful influence upon several generations of American composers. Among his students are some of the most important and influential figures in American music today: Miriam Gideon (b. 1906), Hugo Weisgall (b. 1912), Henry Weinberg (b. 1931), and Donald Martino (b. 1931).

Gideon and Weisgall, both students of Sessions during the late 1930s, were affected to some degree by the serial methods current in the 1940s and '50s, but took from these trends those aspects that served their own compositional purposes. Miriam Gideon has steadily produced a body of beautiful and finely etched works for voices and instruments. Her style is neither serial nor completely atonal. Instead, Gideon has developed an acute ability to handle complex chords clearly and tellingly. Her effective use of intimate instrumental combinations with voice is illustrated by *The Hound of Heaven* (1945) for voice, oboe, and string trio, and *The Seasons of Time* (1970) for voice, flute, cello, piano, and celesta. A novel conception is *The Condemned Playground* (1963) for soprano, tenor, and instruments, in which settings of poems in Latin and Japanese are preceded by settings in their English versions. Especially effective is the wispy, Haiku-like "Hiroshima."

Hugo Weisgall has forged his career writing freely atonal or serial operas and song cycles which deal with contemporary problems and ideas. Long vocal lines and an intimate knowledge of Hebrew service music exerted a strong influence on his writing for the voice. Capturing the rhythms of American speech is for Weisgall a primary occupation: the vocal lines themselves embody every nuance of emotion and make his characters come alive *musically* on the stage. Weisgall has few small pieces: each of his operas is a substantial one, based on the work of an important playright. Among them are *The Stronger* (1952, Strindberg), *The Tenor* (1950, Wedekind), *Six Characters in Search of an Author* (1956, Pirandello), *Purgatory* (1958, Yeats), and *The Hundred Nights* (1976, Yukio Mishima).

OTHER REPRESENTATIVE COMPOSERS

BLACK COMPOSERS

As American composers searched for national musical identity, American black composers of concert music struggled to be heard. Among those who have produced music of substance and vitality is Howard Swanson (b. 1909), who studied in Paris with Boulanger, then received attention when the great American contralto Marian Anderson performed Swanson's songs, which movingly capture the black experience in America. The award-winning *Short Symphony* (1948) was successful for a time; but Swanson has not yet been awarded the measure of recognition he deserves. Ulysses Kay (b. 1917) is among our best-known composers. His works in a variety of media embody a terse and fiery Neoclassicism, and rarely employ extramusical programs or texts. Carman Moore (b. 1936) was for several years an influential critic for *The Village Voice*. His recent *Wildfires and Field Songs* (1975) draws on a diverse palette of atonality, tone clusters, complex textures reminiscent of Ives, modern jazz improvisation, and other musical elements which reflect his black heritage.

JACOB DRUCKMAN

Jacob Druckman (b. 1928), who has recently emerged as an important figure on the American scene, reflects the diversity of inspiration and the theatrical bent of many composers of the 1960s and '70s. Druckman's music has always included attractive solo passages that exploit the idioms characteristic of the featured instruments. Since the 1960s this has been extended to giving solo players "scenes" to "act out" through musical and theatrical gestures. Examples are *Valentine* for solo contrabass (1969) and his ongoing *Animus* series (1966–), which pits soloists against prerecorded electronic tape. In *Windows* (1972), a Pulitzer Prize-winning composition, Druckman uses expertly managed orchestral masses to "open windows" onto elements from his own past, through quotation, stylized older idioms, and the like.

TWO INDEPENDENTS

Two of the best-known American composers today are Elliott Carter and George Crumb. Each has developed a personal style somewhat independently of the major movements discussed above. Their strikingly original work illustrates how two composers with entirely different points of view can create compelling music which attracts international attention.

CARTER (b. 1908)

Elliott Carter, one of the many Americans who studied with Boulanger in Paris, writes in a rhythmically charged Neoclassical style. With the first of his three string quartets (1951, 1959, 1971) he attracted international attention by his use of complex polyphonic textures evolving against several simultaneous layers of rhythm (perhaps an influence from Ives), and by achieving a fluid flow of sound, suggestive of rubato. In particular, he is known for developing a procedure called "metric modulation"—a means of easing smoothly from one tempo to another.

Unlike many composers who turned to serialism during the 1950s, Carter evolved his own free atonal style. This is illustrated by such large-scale works as the Double Concerto (1961), Piano Concerto (1966), Concerto for Orchestra (1969), and *A Symphony of Three Orchestras* (1976–1977).

Fig. 21.7 Elliott Carter's music is characterized by complex textures in simultaneous layers of rhythm and by a rubato-like rhythmic flow.

BRASS QUINTET Carter's Brass Quintet (1974), written for two trumpets, horn, and two trombones, is an example of his virtuoso treatment of instruments and the overlapping of complex, multilayered textures. There is no main theme, as such. Carter writes: "The entire work can be heard as one long, slow movement with interruptions." Thus, it opens with calm, long-held notes which are interrupted by the horn. As the piece progresses, various ideas are superimposed upon this "background" of slow music. After staccato chords build up the texture, a horn and bass trombone duet emerges. The slow music is distantly heard again, but is interrupted by a skittish duet in the trumpet and horn. Then the texture again becomes more active and dense. Above the slow music, scurrying figures in a trio of two trumpets and horn soon provide the accompaniment for a new, humorous duet between two trombones employing *glissandos*—those characteristic slides that trombones can make. The upper three parts of the score weave a soft, legato layer of texture, while underneath, the two trombones begin their own independent duet, a strand of free, rubato music (Example 21.15). By now the slow music has all but disappeared. The horn, after some struggle, manages to assert itself for an extended cadenza which is "cut off" by fortissimo octaves in the other four instruments. After yet another textural buildup, the quiet music of the opening returns in a more extended form; it breaks up one last time, and the piece ends in a flurry of trills.

*Example 21.15 * *

CRUMB (b. 1929)

Whereas Elliott Carter's music owes its overall sound to the manipulation of complicated strands of texture, the music of George Crumb focuses the listener's attention on minute and delicate shadings of instrumental color. Crumb's compositions draw heavily on extramusical atmosphere and theatrics. In the Ives tradition, the music tends to use seemingly unrelated musical elements (such as the juxtaposition of tonality with atonality) and employ quotation, all to serve dramatic or symbolic purposes.

The poetry of Federico Garcia Lorca has inspired many of Crumb's works, including the four books of *Madrigals* (1965–1969), written for soprano and small instrumental combinations, and *Ancient Voices of Children* (1970), written for mezzosoprano, boy soprano, and instruments. All of Crumb's recent music uses texts or programs: *Echoes of Time and the River* (1967) for orchestra, *Black Angels* (1970) for electrified string quartet, and *Star Child* (1977) for orchestra with soprano solo. The last of these is the composer's most Ivesian work to date.

Fig. 21.8 The compositions of George Crumb are marked by fascinating coloristic effects and theatrical touches.

---

* From Elliott Carter, *Brass Quintet*. © 1976 Associated Music Publishers, Inc., New York. Used by permission.

**VOICE OF
THE WHALE**
RECORD 8/SIDE 1

Vox Balaenae (*Voice of the Whale*) for Three Masked Players (1971) was inspired by the eerie vocal sounds made by the humpback whale. The three players, who should perform under deep-blue stage lighting, wear black masks. Crumb writes that "The masks, by effacing the sense of human projection, are intended to represent, symbolically, the powerful impersonal forces of nature."

Voice of the Whale is striking both for this theatrical touch and for the extraordinary coloristic effects produced from only three instruments: flute, cello, and piano. All are amplified electronically to enhance the unusual sounds. In addition, the players are required to play four tuned antique cymbals and to whistle as well. The work is carefully constructed along a simple three-part plan: a prologue, a set of variations, and an epilogue.

The prologue, headed "Vocalise (. . . for the beginning of time)," is Crumb's musical representation of the song of the humpback whale, played by the flute. The flutist sings into the instrument while playing and thus produces other-worldly sounds. Toward the end of this long, recitative-like solo, we hear a distorted parody of Richard Strauss's famous opening music for *Also Sprach Zarathustra*. Example 21.16 reproduces the composer's manuscript.

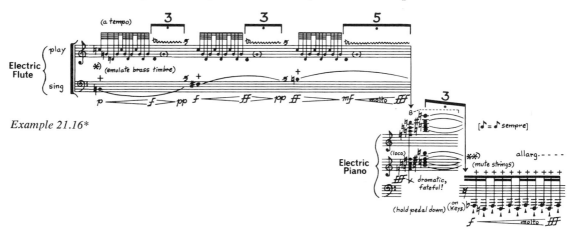

Example 21.16*

This parody is later heard again at the "Cenozoic" Variation (see below) to symbolize the emergence of human beings.

The main portion of the work is headed "Variations on Sea-Time." Here Crumb is making a musical pun, for in musical terminology, the syllable *si,* pronounced "see," refers to the note B, which is the note on which Crumb has based this work. The "Sea-Theme" is a calm, diatonic melody played in the high register by the cellist, and is accompanied by the unusual technique of strumming quietly on the piano strings.

Example 21.17

*   Examples 21.16 through 21.18 are from George Crumb, *Vox Balaenae*. Copyright © 1972 by C. F. Peters Corporation, New York. Reprinted by permission of the publisher.

This melody is repeated in shorter note values. Then it continues:

Example 21.18

Each variation that follows is given the title of a geological era: Archeozoic, Proterozoic, Paleozoic, Mesozoic, and Cenozoic.

The epilogue, entitled "Sea-Nocturne (. . . for the end of time)," brings back the "Sea-Theme," whistled by the flutist and cellist. But this time the piano accompanies it with a figuration in the pure tonality of B major, as the antique cymbals add brilliant touches of color and the music fades.

SUMMARY

American music in the seventeenth century was primarily religious in nature. Secular music began to flourish in the eighteenth century, when concerts, operas, and other musical events became popular. By 1770 a small "school" of American composers, led by William Billings, was producing music in a virile new style that was not bound by European traditions of composition.

Two important developments of the nineteenth century were the division between "popular" and "classical" (or concert) music and the tendency to imitate German Romantic composers. With a few exceptions, the German style held sway with the American musical establishment through the first two decades of the twentieth century. At the same time, a few American musical pioneers were experimenting with their own new and radical kinds of music.

The boldest and most original of the early twentieth-century "ultramodernists" was Charles Ives. He used advanced musical techniques and drew on such diverse sources as American songs and marches, hymn tunes, and quotations from European classics. His open-minded and nondogmatic approach to musical sources and techniques of composition has had tremendous influence. Modernist Edgard Varèse defined music as "organized sound" and challenged conventional notions of sonority with his use of nonmusical noises. Henry Cowell introduced his famous technique of "tone clusters." Each of these composers has also significantly influenced the course of modern music.

The musically progressive years between World War I and the beginning of the Depression spawned an attempt by some composers to incorporate elements of jazz music into their compositions. Although most of these composers soon abandoned their experiments in symphonic jazz, a later movement called "Third Stream" combined 1950s jazz styles with elements of concert music.

The Depression years of the 1930s, years of isolationism and nationalism, saw a majority of composers turn their attention to creating works in simpler styles based on American subjects. Aaron Copland, the leading exemplar of this "conservative" school, sought to write in an accessible style that could bridge the gap between the concert-going public and the contemporary composer.

The 1930s also saw a trend toward greater complexity, although it involved relatively few composers. Wallingford Riegger and Ruth Crawford Seeger produced works of distinction using twelve-tone technique. Roger Sessions wrote in an increasingly complex idiom during the 1930s and 1940s, and by 1953 was using a twelve-tone row.

Among the most strikingly original of American composers since 1950 are Elliott Carter and George Crumb. Carter's music is characterized by the manipulation of complicated strands of texture, while Crumb's compositions focus on instrumental color and theatrical atmosphere.

The last chapter of this book (Chapter 24) will discuss other current American composers who have had wide international influence. One of these, John Cage (b. 1912), has asserted in fact that bold American pathfinders have "made the twentieth century the American one."

NEW TERMS

tone cluster

CHAPTER 22 | JAZZ

JAZZ IS OFTEN CONSIDERED TO BE AMERICA'S GREATEST CONTRIBU-
tion to music. We don't know precisely where or when this uniquely American
music started. We are not sure of the origin of its strange name. But we do
know that jazz has become a truly universal music. Its message is direct, vital, and
immediate, enabling it to hurdle the usual cultural, linguistic, and political bar-
riers. Louis Armstrong, one of jazz's most famous exponents, once explained the
universality of jazz by saying, "What we play is life and the natural thing."

The essence of jazz is improvisation; much of the music is composed and arranged on the spot. The type and degree of improvisation vary with different jazz
styles, and improvisations can take several different forms. For example, an improvisation can be built upon a familiar melody which is varied and embellished
as the piece progresses, or it may be based on the underlying harmonic structure
of the song. A more radical approach than either of these is to remove all melodic
and harmonic restraints, thus allowing the performers to explore their own raw
musical and emotional ideas in totally free improvisations. Whatever form it
takes, the improvisational component of jazz accounts for much of its immediacy
and vitality.

BLACK FOLK MUSIC

Although the precise origin of jazz cannot be pinpointed, it is clear that its inspiration came from the experiences of black Americans in a difficult and frus-
trating environment and that musically it was influenced by both African and
European traditions.

Recall from Chapter 5 that in African culture there is no distinction between
music as "art," music as a leisure-time activity, and music functioning as part of
other activities, as there is in European culture. Instead, singing, dancing, and
drumming are part of daily tribal activity and are used for both spiritual and secu-

lar functions. Certain songs accompany specific activities, such as fishing, weaving, hunting, and worshipping; indeed, music in Africa is integral to every aspect of life.

We have seen, also, that the rhythmic organization of African music is more complex than that of European music. For example, the simultaneous use of several different rhythmic patterns (polyrhythms) is common in African music but has been relatively unexplored until recently in Western music. In addition, many African melodies are based on pentatonic (five tone) scale systems and therefore sound different from Western melodies.

When Africans who were brought to this country as slaves began to acquire aspects of American culture, particularly the Christian religion, a new music began to emerge. To the European harmonies of the Christian hymns, the Afro-Americans adapted aspects of African rhythm and scales as well as the vocal inflections that were basic to African language and music. Out of this merging of elements came the Negro spiritual, an expression of the suffering and hope of an oppressed people. Many of these religious songs followed a traditional African pattern of call and response, in which the leader sings a line first and is answered by a chorus, which comments in improvised verses on the leader's theme or on previous answers.

The improvised call-and-response pattern was also employed in work songs sung by the slaves as they labored in the fields or on the river barges. An important characteristic of the work song was its persistent rhythm. Often, the grunt of a man pushing a heavy weight or the blow of a hammer against a stone served to provide metrical precision. A good example of this rhythmic impetus can be found in the traditional work song, *Take This Hammer:*

> *"Take this hammer,* Huh!
> *Take it to the captain,* huh!
> *Take this hammer,* huh!
> *Take it to the captain,* huh!
> *Take this hammer,* huh!
> *Take it to the captain,*
> *Tell him I'm gone,*
> *Buddy, you can tell him I'm gone."*

The emotional content of black folk music, its use of improvisation, and its forceful rhythms are all aspects that figured importantly in the emergence of jazz's predecessor, the blues.

THE BLUES

The unique style of music known as the **blues** is the common strain running through virtually all American popular music. The style and phrasings of the blues can be found in the early music of the black churches, in country-and-western music, in songs by George Gershwin and other Broadway composers, and in current rock styles. But more than all else, the blues have influenced jazz styles, from the earliest to the most recent.

Fig. 22.1 Billie Holiday's vocal styling was strongly influenced by the instrumental styles of Lester Young and Louis Armstrong.

The blues are an intensely personal form of expression. Drawing on real experiences and deeply felt emotions such as loneliness, loss, and despair, the blues explore the frustrations of black American life.

By around 1900 the blues featured a highly structured style, with distinct forms for both the lyrics and the melodies. The standard lyrical pattern consisted of two rhyming lines of poetry with the first line repeated (aab) as in the following example:

> *Now listen baby, you so good and sweet,*
> *Now listen baby, you so good and sweet,*
> *I want to stay 'round you, if I have to beg in the street.*

The form of the blues is typically based on a twelve-bar harmonic progression in three phrases of four measures each. Only three chords are involved: tonic, dominant, and subdominant. The blues are usually played in 4/4 time. So-called **blue notes,** produced by flatting the third, fifth, or seventh notes of a major scale, are used extensively. These notes can be manipulated by allowing the performer to slide into them, rather than hitting them solidly. The result is "bent" or "glided" pitches that produce a highly distinctive sound.

Early blues were created by vocalists, but many instrumentalists soon adopted blues techniques and devices. One of the most influential blues vocalists and interpreters of this art was Bessie Smith (1895–1937), whose powerful, emotional, and poetic style is legendary. The musicians who accompanied her used their instruments to wail, sob, and growl in imitation of the pathos of her blues technique. Other fine vocalists who have sung blues include Ella Fitzgerald, Billie Holiday (see box), and Sarah Vaughan.

LADY SANG THE BLUES—BILLIE HOLIDAY

Women have usually played a part in jazz only as singers. Although there have been a few exceptions over the years (such as virtuoso pianist Mary Lou Williams and composer/bandleader Toshiko Akiyoshi), by far the widest avenue for women to enter the field has been as vocalists, and that remains the case even in our own "liberated" age.

Most of the leading jazz singers of the past few decades were greatly influenced by the classic female blues singers, such as Ma Rainey, Bessie Smith, and Ethel Waters. But the vocalist who brought the special art of the blues singer to its greatest heights and had the greatest influence on future jazz vocal styles was Billie Holiday (1915–1959).

Holiday was raised in the poorest section of Harlem, the daughter of a jazz guitarist with Fletcher Henderson's band who displayed little interest in Billie or her mother. She had a small, fragile voice and no musical training. Holiday got her start as a singer in 1933 at a club in Harlem, where her emotional rendition of "Body and Soul" had the customers in tears.

Shortly after she landed this job the eighteen-year-old Holiday was discovered by talent scout John Hammond (who later uncovered such talented contemporary performers as Aretha Franklin and Bob Dylan). Hammond arranged for her to record with Benny Goodman. Although these early records were disappointing, in 1936 she recorded with an all-star band that included Roy Eldridge, Ben Webster, Benny Goodman, and Lester Young. It was Young who gave her the nickname that stuck, "Lady Day." The 1936 recordings and subsequent ones, such as *Lady Day* (Columbia CL 637), *Golden Years,* Vol. 1 (Columbia C 3L 21), and *The Billie Holiday Story* (MCA 4006E), demonstrate eloquently the unique vocal style that became her trademark.

After "paying her dues" as a band singer, first with Count Basie and then—as the first black female singer in a white band—with Artie Shaw, Holiday made a breakthrough as a single attraction. Throughout the 1940s, her personal life began to deteriorate but her fame continued to spread. She performed such standards as "He's Funny That Way," "Crazy He Calls Me," and "Stormy Weather," and she also wrote her own material, including the deeply felt "God Bless The Child." The last became a pop hit in the late 1960s for the rock group Blood, Sweat and Tears. But by then Lady Day had passed from the scene, a victim of drug addiction, alcoholism, police harassment, and her own tragic self-destructiveness. Although she did record extensively for producer Norman Granz during the 1950s, in general her career as well as her personal life had been deteriorating steadily, and on July 17, 1959, she died at the age of 44.

The events that surrounded her premature death have added a sordid luster to the legend of Billie Holiday and to some extent have obscured the very real contributions that she made to jazz. Where most vocalists sang the music "straight," Holiday made each song her own, improvising on the basic melody, changing the beat of a phrase, investing the song with her unique inflections and emotional quality. As she herself once put it, "I don't think I'm really singing. I feel like I'm playing a horn. I try to improvise like Les Young, like Louis Armstrong, or someone else I admire. What comes out is what I feel."*

*   Dan Morganstern, *Jazz People* (New York, 1976), p. 240.

Occasionally the blues were performed without a vocalist, so that the distinctive sound and mood were created solely through the manipulation of a musical instrument. Ferdinand "Jelly Roll" Morton (1885–1941) was one of the most widely recognized blues pianists; his great contribution was to translate the "blues style" from the vocal idiom to the keyboard.

RAGTIME

Another early and popular relative of jazz was **ragtime,** a form that developed in the 1890s. Influenced by popular European dances, military marches, African dance music, and the cakewalks of minstrel shows, ragtime was composed piano music that used conventional harmony and classic forms. Its cheerful mood was

Fig. 22.2 Scott Joplin's rags earned him the title of "King of Ragtime."

in distinct contrast to the melancholy feeling of blues, and, unlike blues, ragtime was performed by blacks and whites alike.

In playing a rag, the performer's left hand maintained a steady, marchlike accompaniment, while the right hand played the melody, decorating it with runs and a variety of other ornamentations. Perhaps the most striking feature of ragtime, the one by which it is most easily recognized, is its syncopated rhythm; indeed, syncopation enjoyed its most consistent treatment in rag music. Although many people today have heard only fast, choppy versions of ragtime tunes, the music was intended to be played with a smooth, connected technique and not too fast.

One of the most distinguished exponents of ragtime was Scott Joplin (1869–1917), a classically trained pianist whose compositions, including the classic "Maple Leaf Rag" (1899), earned him the title "King of Ragtime." Recently there has been a considerable revival of Joplin's music in concert halls, on records, on Broadway, and in films such as *The Sting*. Other notable ragtime pianist-composers of the 1890s include James Scott, Tom Turpin, and Joseph Lamb.

JAZZ

Although jazz began to emerge wherever African and European music came into contact—which is to say, wherever black and white Americans came into contact—some places offered a more favorable climate for its growth than others. For a variety of reasons, the great cosmopolitan city of New Orleans has been granted the honorary title of the birthplace of jazz.

At the turn of the century, New Orleans possessed an international atmosphere relatively free of the racial bigotry that persisted in most of the Deep South. As a trading center located at the outlet of the Mississippi River into the Gulf of Mexico, New Orleans allowed elements of cultures as diverse as French, Spanish, Caribbean, Anglo-Saxon, and German to merge with the African traditions of both the Creoles (who were mulattoes with both African and French or Spanish blood) and the recently emancipated blacks. Perhaps as a result, jazz has always been characterized by its ability to assimilate whatever it found interesting or relevant without ever losing its own identity.

One of the earliest recognized jazz giants was a New Orleans cornetist named Buddy Bolden (1868–1931). Like many of his peers, Bolden was only a part-time musician, and he worked as a barber to support himself. At night Bolden and his fellow musicians often played at dances sponsored by one of the many black social clubs and fraternal organizations in the city, such as the Tammanys, the Original Swells, and the Jolly Boys. These clubs would hire bands for other important social functions as well, such as the funeral of a lodge brother. The custom of adding joyful music as the band marched back from a burial encouraged the creation of a swinging rhythm that greatly influenced early jazz. Buddy Bolden and "Jelly Roll" Morton were among the first to join the strains of this swinging music to the secular folk music of the rural southern blacks—the blues. Out of this union, accomplished in the black dance halls of New Orleans, came the new kind of music known as jazz.

Although the marching bands of the funeral processions were large, the bands which played strictly dance music were small. The typical instrumentation of such groups included a **front line** and a **rhythm section.** The front line was made up of a cornet, which carried the melodic lead, and a clarinet and a trombone, which supported it. The **rhythm section,** which supplied the harmonic and rhythmic accompaniment, consisted of drums, a guitar or banjo, a tuba or string bass, and sometimes a piano. The musicians used the style of playing that had evolved from imitating the early blues singers. This type of jazz is often called Dixieland. They were primarily self-taught and their improvisation was spontaneous; no one used written music. The players knew the tunes and their underlying chord sequences by memory; starting from this raw material, they improvised whatever variations struck their fancy. A classical musician might describe the process as "semiaccidental counterpoint." With each successive repetition of the tune (called a *chorus*) the variations became more elaborate and the original tune became harder to recognize.

The cornet, which played the melodic lead, was the dominant instrument in early jazz, and was usually played by the bandleader. Buddy Bolden was the first great cornet virtuoso. After Bolden, there were two major contenders for his title as King of Jazz: Freddie Keppard (1899–1933) and Joe Oliver (1885–1938). Keppard, who fronted the Original Creole, played louder than but not as subtly as Oliver, who subsequently replaced Bolden as the most influential jazz player of his time (he came to be known as "King" Oliver).

CHICAGO AND BEYOND

During World War I and the decade of the "Roaring Twenties," jazz migrated northward along with the black Americans who had created it, moving from the poor, rural South to the great urban industrial centers of the North. This migration was spurred in large part by the wartime demand for labor in the northern factories. Chief among the industrial cities to which blacks moved was Chicago, which soon replaced New Orleans as the seat of the jazz kingdom. Between 1910 and 1920, the black population of Chicago more than doubled, from about 40,000 to 100,000. By 1920, there were numerous New Orleans musicians living in the "Windy City."

Thanks in part to the many riverboats that regularly traveled the Mississippi, equipped not only with holds for cargo but also with saloons and dance halls where people could hear the "new sound," jazz spread over a wide geographic area. Naturally enough, as the music spread, it also began to change. In the North the style became a little more elaborate, the saxophone emerged as an important jazz instrument (it remains prominent today), and much greater emphasis was given to the role of the soloist. Whereas the heart of the New Orleans sound was an exciting *collective* improvisation, the Chicago sound was characterized by the assertion of the individual over the group, with a soloist soaring high above the rest of the band. By far the most important of the new jazz soloists was Louis Armstrong (1900–1971), a young cornetist from New Orleans who became the most influential stylist in the history of the idiom (see box).

LOUIS ARMSTRONG: THE FIRST JAZZ VIRTUOSO

Fig. 22.3 Trombonist James Young and cornetist Louis Armstrong end a number. Armstrong popularized individual soloist improvisation in the middle sections of each piece, leaving the beginning and end for ensemble playing.

If there is any one individual whose name is universally associated with jazz, it is Louis Armstrong (1900–1971). To those familiar with Louis only as the smiling, genial entertainer of his later, "Hello, Dolly" years, it is hard to imagine the enormity of his impact on the development of jazz. Armstrong's genius lay in his pioneering role in transforming jazz into a medium of personal expression.

Louis Armstrong was born in New Orleans on the first Fourth of July of the twentieth century. He was raised in a poor and unstable family, and soon became involved in the active street life of the city. At twelve he was sentenced as a juvenile offender and sent to the Colored Waifs' home. It was the director of the Waifs' Home Band who taught him to play the cornet.

After two years, Armstrong returned to the street, performing odd jobs and playing music whenever he got the chance. Eventually, the great Joe "King" Oliver took him under his wing. When Armstrong improved enough, Oliver sent him on jobs that he couldn't fill himself. At seventeen, Armstrong was firmly established as a competent New Orleans-style jazzman.

In 1919, Oliver moved to Chicago and Armstrong took his place as cornetist in the best band in New Orleans. Two years later, Armstrong received a telegram from Oliver asking him to join Oliver's band there. He accepted and soon became famous among that city's jazz players and fans as a genius with a natural harmonic gift. In 1923 he accepted another offer, this time from Fletcher Henderson's orchestra in New York.

When he left Henderson's orchestra, Armstrong went on to lead his own groups and to record extensively. Some of his best work was done with a group known as the Hot Five —which also featured Johnny St. Cyr, Kid Ory, Johnny Dodds, and Armstrong's second wife, Lil Hardin—and with a later band known as the Hot Seven.

In the 1940s Armstrong was featured on numerous radio shows and in films, and by the late 1950s "Ambassador Satch" and the Armstrong All-Stars were traveling the world as goodwill emissaries of the United States government. Toward the end of his life Armstrong became almost as prominent in that role as he had been earlier as a musician.

But it is Armstrong's influence on jazz musicians and singers that remains his most important contribution. Rhythmically his music was the embodiment of that elusive quality known as swing. His horn style, highly embellished, full of swoops and sudden dips and darts, has affected the performing style of all later cornet and trumpet players and of other instrumentalists as well, as is evidenced by Earl Hines's adaptation of Armstrong's style to the piano. His playing has also deeply influenced the vocal stylings of jazz singers like Billie Holiday and Ella Fitzgerald. Fine examples of Armstrong's recorded work are included on such albums as *The Louis Armstrong Story,* Vols. 1 and 2 (Col 851, 852) and *Louis Armstrong and Earl Hines,* 1928 (Smithsonian R002).

In exploring the possibilities of solo freedom, Armstrong utilized an integrated ensemble at the beginning and end of each piece, but reserved the middle sections for improvisations by soloists. Each member of the front line was given one chorus in which to improvise on either the theme or the harmonic structure of the piece while the rest of the band either rested or played background rhythms. With the ascendance of the individual soloist, the beat became much less pronounced than ever before. The result was a flowing sound that later came to be called *swing.*

As jazz gained in popularity during the 1920s, many white musicians began to take part in its development. One of the first of these was Leon "Bix" Beiderbecke (1903–1931), a virtuoso cornetist born in Davenport, Iowa. Another was bandleader Paul Whiteman (1890–1967), who in 1924 presented the first formal jazz concert. That concert featured the premiere of *Rhapsody in Blue,* a serious work by George Gershwin that incorporated jazz elements.

THE DEPRESSION YEARS

During the early years of the Depression, which began with the stock market crash of 1929, most clubowners didn't have enough money to hire a full-scale orchestra. As a result, the solo pianist came into vogue for a short time. The first important jazz piano styles were **stride** and **boogie-woogie.** In the stride style, the left hand alternated between a bass note and a chord played an octave or more above the bass, giving the effect of "striding" back and forth, while the right hand played the melody. The stride style, which was applied to blues, popular songs, and show tunes, allowed ample opportunity for improvisation.

Boogie-woogie was a blues piano style which used a rhythmic ostinato bass of eight notes to the measure in the left hand, while the right hand played a simple, often improvised melody. Typical left-hand patterns were

The percussive bass part gave the sound and feel of the left hand "walking" over the piano keys. For this reason boogie-woogie is sometimes called the "walkin' bass."

Among the finest of the early jazz pianists were James P. Johnson (1891–1955), Willie "The Lion" Smith (1893–1973), and Thomas "Fats" Waller (1904–1943). Another innovative jazz pianist was Earl "Fatha" Hines (b. 1905), who early in his career worked with Louis Armstrong. Hines was influenced by Armstrong's inventive cornet style, which he translated into the "trumpet style" for keyboard. In this style, the right hand played a melody line (much as a trumpet player or any single-line player might do) while the left hand played chords in flurries, punctuating and complementing the solo line. Pianists of the later bebop era drew from and expanded on the trumpet style of playing. (An excellent example of several jazz piano styles played by Count Basie is the selection "Moten Swing" on the *Smithsonian Collection of Classic Jazz,* P11893.)

THE BIG BAND ERA

By the mid-1930s, with the economy slowly recovering, larger ensembles began to make a comeback. Gradually jazz moved out of the saloons and into white as well as black ballrooms and dance halls. The big band sound, as it became known, soon reached an ever larger audience via radio. During this period New York, which had become the cultural and communications center of America, replaced Chicago as the major jazz city. Thus began the *swing* era, which lasted roughly from 1935 to 1950.

Swing featured big bands of perhaps fifteen to seventeen players, with the old New Orleans front line of cornet, clarinet, and trombone increased dramatically to include whole brass sections of trumpets and trombones, as well as woodwind sections of clarinets and saxophones. The rhythm section included piano, bass, guitar, and drums.

Stylistically the big bands evolved in two directions. One style, which was shaped primarily by black bandleaders, was built around the solo performer. In a departure from traditional jazz, which was mostly improvised, loose arrangements of pieces were written down. Yet these arrangements were often modified by the bandleader to showcase the special talents of individual performers. A characteristic technique of these bands was the use of a **riff,** a short melodic line, usually rhythmic, which can be repeated over and over to form either the main melody or the background for improvised solos. The musical repertoire included many blues tunes and many original compositions.

The first of a long line of talented black bandleaders was Fletcher Henderson, an important innovator in band arranging in the 1920s and Benny Goodman's chief arranger in the late 1930s. But perhaps the most original contributions to big band jazz were made by Edward Kennedy "Duke" Ellington (1899–1974), a bandleader/composer/pianist/arranger who brought out the best in his soloists with music so masterfully arranged that it created the effect if not always the fact of improvisation. During his long career, which spanned nearly half a century, he composed many popular standards ("Mood Indigo," "Take the 'A' Train," "It Don't Mean a Thing If You Ain't Got That Swing") as well as other works of great inventiveness, sophistication, and variety. Two other outstanding black musicians who gained fame in the swing era were William "Count" Basie, pianist and leader of a popular band, and saxophonist Lester Young, one of Basie's great soloists.

The other big band style is represented in the work of white bandleaders such as Benny Goodman, Harry James, Glenn Miller, Artie Shaw, and Tommy Dorsey, all of whom drew on the black style but modified it for their predominantly white audiences. Their intricate, special arrangements were calculated to achieve a consistent and "characteristic" sound. Often the leader was showcased as the star personality and sometimes as the star soloist. A few other "star" soloists might also be featured, but the main emphasis was on the overall sound of the band as a unit. The standard bill of fare served up by this type of big band consisted of smooth, polished arrangements of popular tunes. The aim was to please the listening and dancing audience, a goal that tended to produce music that was commercially successful but not artistically innovative.

BOP

At the height of the swing era, the bands had become too large to allow all potential soloists to perform. By the 1940s, many young jazz musicians had come to feel stifled by the subordination to a group effort that the big bands demanded. These young rebels began pushing for small groups that would offer more room for individual expression.

It was in special after-hours clubs that young, adventurous, experimental musicians like guitarist Charlie Christian (1919–1942), pianist Thelonious Monk (see box), and drummer Kenny Clarke (b. 1914) found the freedom to explore their personal potential. These and other musicians, notably trumpeter John "Dizzzy" Gillespie (b. 1917) and saxophonist Charlie "Bird" Parker (1920–1955), would work all night with the swing bands in Manhattan nightclubs and ballrooms, then ride north to Minton's Play House in the early morning to participate in "jam sessions" where they experimented with free-form solo work and harmonic improvisation. The new style they developed was given the name **bebop** (later shortened to simply **bop**). The bop combo consisted of one to three soloists supported by a rhythm section of drums and bass and sometimes piano or guitar.

Bop musicians sought to achieve a totally new sound by experimenting with various devices: wide leaps in melody, phrases of uneven lengths, and rhythmic variety. Kenny Clarke introduced an extraordinary rhythmic innovation with his technique of "dropping bombs"—that is, placing unanticipated bass drum accents before or after the beat. Almost singlehandedly, Clarke shifted the focus of jazz drumming away from the objective of simply keeping time. Now drummers

THELONIOUS MONK: THE HIGH PRIEST OF BOP

Fig. 22.4 Charles Mingus (bass), Roy Haynes (drums), Thelonious Monk (piano), and Charlie Parker (saxophone) performing in 1953.

Jazz musicians in general (and bop players in particular) have never been noted for their conformity. Even among such strongly individualistic personalities, however, pianist Thelonious Monk (b. 1917) stands out. Monk has always been his own man. Primarily a self-taught musician, he plays in a manner that is totally "wrong" in standard pianistic technique—his fingers are practically unbending—yet it somehow works for him. He pounds out his music in a syncopated, percussive style that is too unusual and individualistic for many; thus, the New York-bred musician has often had difficulty gaining employment, even in his hometown.

For years he worked only sporadically, playing obscure Harlem nightclubs and an ocsional "downtown" job arranged by fellow musicians and admirers like Coleman Hawkins. It was not until 1947, when Monk was already thirty, that he made his first recording with Blue Note Records. This and later recordings, such as *Genius of Modern Music,* Vols. 1 and 2 (Blue Note 81510, 81511) created a storm of critical comment, both pro and con, concerning Monk's unorthodox and unpredictable style, which utilized constant rhythmic variations and startling harmonic improvisations as well as an understated sense of humor.

Despite the success of his recordings, he nevertheless continued to have trouble finding steady work.

Yet Monk did enjoy the respect and admiration of his peers, including bandleader Miles Davis, who asked Monk to record with him in 1954 (though he insisted that Monk refrain from playing during his solos, since his style was too distracting). Finally, in the mid-1950s, Monk began to gain some measure of popular acceptance with regular gigs at the Five Spot Club in the Bowery, which became a haven for all those interested in exploring the challenges of the new music known as bop.

By 1964, Monk's career had progressed to the point that he was featured on the cover of *Time* magazine. Thelonious Monk had finally become established in the jazz world's hierarchy. Although his health has not been good in recent years, Monk made a triumphant return to the Newport Jazz Festival in 1975 and gave a brilliant Carnegie Hall recital in 1976.

worked around an implicit rather than a stated beat, and whatever timekeeping was necessary in the bop group usually fell to the bass player.

Another difference between bop and the jazz styles that preceded it was its exploration of chromatic harmonies, an innovation that expanded the range of harmonic possibilities.

Improvisation continued to be an integral part of bop. Among those who gained fame for their improvisations were Charlie Parker and Charlie Christian. Christian was a natural musician who first popularized the use of amplified guitar as a jazz instrument. In his improvisations, however, he inspired later horn players as much as later guitarists, because he did much of his solo work on a single string. Ironically, Christian died in 1942 at the age of 24, only three years after the public debut of the music he helped shape. Good examples of Christian's single-string solo work occur in "I Found a New Baby" and "Blues Sequence," both recorded with the Benny Goodman Sextet (*Smithsonian Collection of Classic Jazz,* P11894).

A NEW ATTITUDE

Besides being musically advanced, bop was one manifestation of a larger social protest movement whose members later became known as the "beat generation." Part of the "beat" attitude was an insistence on a "cool," detached manner. No longer did bandleaders extend the customary amenities to the audience, such as announcing song titles or hamming it up between tunes. The early bop players, though not outwardly rude to their audience, intended to make no concessions or commercial compromises with their music.

At least part of the detached attitude and the militant image of the bop musicians was due to changes in the way they saw themselves. At the same time as traditional swing music structure was being abandoned, many black musicians were undergoing a shift in consciousness. Whereas older black players had been forced to play the sometimes unwanted role of "entertainer" for the amusement of their predominantly white audience, the newer generation of players assumed a more self-assertive stance. As John Lewis of the Modern Jazz Quartet once put it:

This revolution, or whatever you want to call it, in the 1940's took place for many reasons, not only musical ones. . . . For the younger musicians, this was the way to react against the attitude that Negroes were supposed to entertain people. The new attitude was: "Either you listen to me on the basis of what I actually do or forget it." *

POST-BOP TO THE PRESENT

The years after World War II saw the evolution of a new type of jazz musician and a new jazz idiom. As a result of the G.I. Bill, higher education was made available to many ex-servicemen who could not otherwise afford college. Thus, many musicians who formerly would have learned their trade in saloons, dance halls, and hotel ballrooms were able to undertake formal musical training. Thousands of veterans studied their major instrument with classical teachers. They took courses in music theory, composition, and history and were exposed to a broad range of musical styles. Because many jazz musicians now had a broader musical background than their predecessors, jazz took on a more intellectual flavor in the 1950s. Referred to as "cool" jazz in New York and "progressive" jazz on the West Coast, the new style was played by small groups and used a combination of written arrangements and improvisations. In comparison with bop, it was economical and understated. Pianist Dave Brubeck, one of the principal exponents of progressive jazz, made excursions into odd-metered music in such compositions as "Take Five" (in 5/4 time) and "Blue Rondo à la Turk" (in 9/8 time). The Modern Jazz Quartet, under music director John Lewis, incorporated classical forms such as the rondo and fugue into jazz, even playing actual classical compositions with a jazz flavor.

Miles Davis (b. 1926), a trumpeter of extraordinary talents, has been at the forefront of virtually every post-bop jazz development, beginning with cool jazz and culminating in the furiously electronic jazz-rock fusion of the 1970s. In 1955 Davis led a bop quintet that featured saxophonist John Coltrane and an excellent rhythm section. Davis himself developed into a soloist of great lucidity, a master of understatement whose haunting tone quality quickly became the most recognizable in jazz. Such currently popular musicians as Herbie Hancock, Chick Corea, Keith Jarrett, and John McLaughlin are a few prominent alumni of Davis-led groups.

John Coltrane became an influential figure in his own right, moving beyond bebop to explore complex harmonies and long-neglected modal scale systems, and extending the tonal possibilities of the saxophone through his flights into extreme registers of the instrument. His efforts to expand the frontiers of jazz were shared by saxophonist Ornette Coleman, who broke with the Western tonal tradition,

---

* Nat Hentoff, *Jazz Is* (New York, Random House, 1976), pp. 259–260.

blending atonality and dissonance with free improvisation. Coleman's 1960 album *Free Jazz* (Atlantic 1364) lent a name to the emerging style.

Coleman and Coltrane were determined to liberate jazz forever from most traditional harmonic and tonal structures. Through the early 1960s their music became increasingly abstract, culminating in 1965 in Coltrane's raucous, almost unlistenable "free-jam" album called *Ascension* (Impulse A-95). In it Coltrane employed abrasive-sounding tone clusters, a wide assortment of pitches and timbres, and what has been called "sheets of sound" playing, which pelted like a furious rainstorm upon the ears of most listeners.

Since the 1960s, jazz has undergone a series of transformations. At the same time, it has regained a large degree of popular acceptance, after having lost many listeners who rejected the complexities of free jazz for the accessible rhythms of rock. Keyboard artist Herbie Hancock is currently one of the leaders in the merger of rock rhythms with jazz, a style that has come to be known as fusion or jazz-rock. His 1973 record *Head Hunters,* which sold nearly a million copies, started a stampede of performers to jazz-fusion. Pianist Keith Jarrett (b. 1945),

Fig. 22.5 Pianist Keith Jarrett's music—cool, temperate, melodic—contrasts sharply with Anthony Braxton's gutsy sound. But the two artists share a firm belief in improvisation.

by contrast, refuses to employ the host of electronic instruments that have become standard equipment for the jazz-rock keyboardist. Jarrett plays only traditional piano (now often called *acoustic* piano). Nevertheless, his improvisatory piano concerts have gained him enormous popular success, largely due to the extraordinary fluency and spontaneity of his playing.

Two other influential practitioners in the modern age of jazz are Dexter Gordon (b. 1923) and Anthony Braxton (b. 1945). Braxton, a scholarly composer and virtuoso saxophonist from Chicago who usually names his works after abstract geometric configurations, is the acknowledged leader of the current avant-garde. His difficult, demanding compositions are reminiscent of the free jazz work of John Coltrane and Ornette Coleman. Braxton also draws on older black forms such as the blues and ragtime. His playing can be heard on a number of excellent recordings, such as *The Montreux/Berlin Concerts* (Arista 5002).

Probably the best example of the current revival of interest in bop is the amount of attention lavished on saxophonist Dexter Gordon. After a long stay

Fig. 22.6 Perhaps the most innovative figure in jazz today, virtuoso saxophonist Anthony Braxton (shown here with a six-foot contrabass sax) creates original, visceral, and often bizarre sounds. His music reflects the influence of free jazz artists, especially Ornette Coleman.

in Denmark, Gordon returned to the United States in 1976 amid astounding critical and popular acclaim. The Columbia release *Homecoming* (Col PG34650) is a live recording of Gordon's group at the Village Vanguard in New York.

Although there is always some conflict between advocates of certain styles (such as that between keyboardists Hancock and Jarrett), today practitioners of many schools of jazz coexist peacefully. Indeed, the central fact about jazz today is its abundance and diversity. Despite the trend toward merging jazz with rock, the jazz mainstream is still vital, with traditional jazz, bebop, cool, and even big band all enjoying a revival of interest by a new generation of listeners. At the same time the avant-garde continues to explore the subtleties and complexities of this enduring American form.

SUMMARY

Perhaps the most significant American contribution to music is jazz, a musical language which grew out of the black experience in America. Its early forebears were the composed piano music known as ragtime and the lamenting vocal art known as the blues.

Traditional jazz, which featured collective improvisation, developed around 1900. The Chicago style of the 1920s, pioneered by Louis Armstrong, emphasized solo improvisation. The era of the big bands followed, as jazz took on mass appeal and moved into white as well as black dancehalls. During the 1940s some young jazz performers began to rebel against the restrictions on creativity that were imposed by big ensembles. They developed an innovative style for small combos called bebop.

The 1950s and '60s brought a new kind of jazz musician and more experimentation. Cool or progressive jazz and free jazz were among the styles explored. An important trend seen in the 1970s was the fusion of jazz styles with rock. In recent years there has also been a revival of interest in early styles of jazz.

NEW TERMS

blues	**rhythm section**	**bebop (bop)**
blue note	**stride**	**cool jazz**
ragtime	**boogie-woogie**	**(progressive jazz)**
front line	**riff**	**free jazz**

CHAPTER **23 | ROCK AND MUSICAL THEATER**

ROCK

WITH ROOTS IN SUCH DIVERSE AREAS AS THE RURAL SOUTH AND the urban North, the West Coast and the East, rock was the product of two independent and indigenous musical styles: black rhythm and blues, and white country and western. The merging of these two musical styles over several decades resulted in the creation of a national popular music, written for and purchased by a new generation of young Americans.

RHYTHM AND BLUES

Rhythm and blues is an outgrowth of jazz and black folk music. Initially it was performed exclusively in black communities in the South, but in the 1940s and '50s it spread to northern urban centers as more and more blacks migrated in search of employment. Early performers included Eddie Durham and the Kansas City Six (who were members of Count Basie's band) and Big Bill Broonzy, a Mississippi guitar player who relocated in Chicago. In 1938—a year before Charlie Christian first recorded with jazzman Benny Goodman—Durham became the first to record electric guitar solos.

Stylistically, rhythm and blues is characterized by loud, hard-driving sound, emotion-charged vocals, and insistent rhythm, with electric guitar and blues harp (harmonica) as key instruments. Such still-active performers as Muddy Waters, B. B. King, and Chuck Berry brought the style to its acknowledged peak in the mid-1950s.

COUNTRY AND WESTERN

Rock's other major source, **country and western,** achieved wide popularity long before rhythm and blues, primarily because it received more radio airtime and thereby reached a larger audience. As early as 1925, station WSM in Nashville broadcast the first programs of the now-famous "Grand Ole Opry," which was aimed at promoting the country and western sound. Performers like Jimmie Rodgers, the Delmore Brothers, and Bill Monroe gained large followings among working-class whites in the South.

Most of the musical qualities of the country sound are derived from southern folk songs preserved from the English/Scottish folk tradition of the Appalachian region. The songs are usually narratives, with melancholy vocals and simple, forthright harmonies and rhythms. The dynamic range of the singing is often limited, but is offset by the tradition of instrumental virtuosity, particularly on such stringed instruments as banjo, mandolin, and guitar.

The rise of the recording industry played a major role in the developing synthesis of white country and western with black rhythm and blues. By the mid-1930s records were a primary source of knowledge for such musicians as Jimmie Rodgers, and soon country performers were recording blues and dance tunes that were influenced by black styles.

ROCK 'N' ROLL PHASE ONE: ELVIS

By the early 1950s the rhythm and blues style finally began to gain access to the radio, and it soon found an audience outside the black community. For the most part, the new fans were young, energetic, and rebellious white teenagers, whose search for self-expression found an outlet in the strong rhythms and earthy feel of rhythm and blues.

One such rhythm and blues devotee was Mississippi-born Elvis Presley (1935–1977), who went on to become the "King of Rock 'n' Roll." Presley was raised in Tupelo, Mississippi, and spent his childhood listening to country artists as well as to white gospel groups. He also absorbed blues influences from the radio and from contact with local blacks. When he was thirteen, Presley's family moved to Memphis, Tennessee. Memphis was one of the first cities to open up its airwaves to black sounds. In 1950, recordings by blues artists like Chester ("Howlin' Wolf") Burnett and Sonny Boy Williamson were being played on station KWEM in West Memphis. At the same time, WDIA, the "mother station of the Negroes," was featuring B. B. King and Rufus Thomas. These and other blues artists had a profound effect on Presley's emerging style.

Another early influence on Elvis Presley was an independent record producer, Sam Phillips. Phillips owned a recording studio for "Negroes in the South who wanted to make a record [but] just had no place to go."* Within a short time, many black artists—among them, Howlin' Wolf Burnett, Walter Horton, Bobby "Blue" Bland, Junior Parker, and B. B. King—had made records in Phillips's studio.

Despite their quality, however, Phillips's records with these black artists never achieved commercial success. And Phillips thought he knew why. As his long-time secretary, Marion Kreisker, remembered it, Phillips said, "If I could find a white man who had the Negro sound and Negro feel, I could make a billion dollars."† In retrospect, it seems clear that Sam Phillips found exactly that

---

*   *The Rolling Stone Illustrated History of Rock & Roll,* ed. Jim Miller, (Rolling Stone Press: New York, 1976), p. 32.
†   Miller, p. 34.

Fig. 23.1 Soon after Elvis Presley became a national craze, black rock 'n' roll artists began to see their records catch on with white teenage audiences. Chuck Berry, Little Richard, and Fats Domino (pictured) were among the most popular performers in the fifties.

in Elvis Presley, although it turned out to be Presley and not Phillips who made "a billion dollars."

Around the same time as Presley began recording, rhythm and blues records began to be aired on white radio shows in major markets like New York and Chicago. A pioneer in the effort to promote this new music was disc jockey Alan Freed, who named the style "**rock 'n' roll.**" The name caught on immediately, and Freed later adopted it for his famous radio show, *Rock 'n' Roll Party,* carried on New York's powerful WINS.

Once the influential radio stations opened up to rock 'n' roll, it wasn't long before it became a national craze. Aided by exposure in the 1955 film *Blackboard Jungle,* Bill Haley and the Comets topped the pop charts with "Rock Around the Clock." A year later, Presley had his first hits with "Heartbreak Hotel" and "Don't Be Cruel," and the floodgates opened. In the years that followed, a number of other white southern rockers became popular, among them Jerry Lee Lewis ("Great Balls of Fire"), Carl Perkins ("Blue Suede Shoes"), and Buddy Holly ("That'll Be the Day"). Black artists Chuck Berry ("Maybelline"), Little Richard ("Tutti Frutti"), and Fats Domino ("Blueberry Hill") began to see their records "cross over" from the rhythm and blues charts and gain acceptance with the white audience, and the rock 'n' roll era was in full swing.

OTHER ROCK STYLES

From its roots in country and western and in rhythm and blues, rock developed in several directions, each reflecting a different set of influences. Among the most notable developments were two almost exclusively black styles—soul and the Motown sound—and one style, the "street corner" style, that was practiced by both black and white performers.

Soul and the Motown Sound Gospel-style singing, with its dynamic emotion, combined with blues, jazz, and rhythm and blues to form **soul** music. Soul had been popular for years with black audiences but didn't become popular with whites until the mid-1960s. The Rolling Stones and other groups who recorded black soul tunes introduced white Americans to the sounds of soul and made it easier for black artists to gain widespread acceptance. Among the most popular soul artists are Aretha Franklin ("Respect"), Otis Redding ("I Can't Turn You Loose"), James Brown ("Papa's Got a Brand New Bag"), and Wilson Pickett ("The Midnight Hour"). Soul is as much an attitude as a style, but it is always spirited, raw-edged music and frequently features wailing vocals and hard-driving rhythm and brass sections.

Another development in popular music of the 1960s was the Motown sound —so called because the headquarters of Motown Records was in Detroit, the "motor city." Berry Gordy, the head of Motown Records, was largely responsible for the development of Motown's musical personality, which is represented by groups like the Supremes ("Stop in the Name of Love") and the Temptations ("My Girl") and by solo performers like Stevie Wonder ("I Was Made to Love Her") and Marvin Gaye ("How Sweet It Is").

The difference between Motown and soul is the difference between satin and burlap. In contrast to the wailing, visceral sound of soul, the Motown sound features intricate, highly polished arrangements and relies on precise studio production for its smooth, elegant sound.

Street Corner Harmony Another rock style popular from the mid-1950s through the mid-1960s was "street corner" vocal harmony. This style was popularized by black groups such as Frankie Lymon and the Teenagers ("Why Do Fools Fall in Love?") and the Monotones ("Book of Love") and by white Italo-American groups like Dion and the Belmonts ("I Wonder Why") and the Four Seasons ("Sherry," "Big Girls Don't Cry"). The songs usually featured a lead singer backed by a group of vocalists in close harmony, often singing rhythmic syllables (doo-wa, shoo-be-doo) rather than words. The style was also popularized by a number of all-female groups, including the Shirelles ("Will You Still Love Me Tomorrow?") and the Chiffons ("He's So Fine").

Recordings of this type were often strictly controlled by the producer, and the songs usually followed a formula which the producer thought would "sell." The artist and the art were secondary and the results were far from innovative. The emphasis on commercial success was especially important in rock music in the 1950s and early 1960s. It became somewhat less important after the Beatles had proved that artistically innovative sounds could sell.

PHASE TWO: THE BEATLES

Concurrently with the development of the styles just described, rock 'n' roll began to develop in yet another direction. The impetus for this change came, not from American groups, but from four young musicians from Liverpool, England—the Beatles.

In the beginning, the Beatles did not depart from classic rock 'n' roll. Their early recordings included rhythm and blues hits like "Shake, Rattle, and Roll" and Chuck Berry's "Roll Over Beethoven." Their first American successes, such as "She Loves You" and "I Wanna Hold Your Hand," were in the standard rock 'n' roll format and gave little indication of the group's potential. The genius of the Beatles (particularly that of songwriters John Lennon and Paul McCartney) emerged when they began to experiment with the musical potential of the rock style. Urged by producer George Martin, they tried using more complex meters and adding orchestral and foreign instruments (such as sitar and tabla) to their compositions. The song "Eleanor Rigby," for example, was scored for cellos, a choice that lent a haunting, evocative sound to an otherwise pleasant but undistinguished melody.

One of the best examples of the Beatles' musical experimentation is their 1967 album *Sgt. Pepper's Lonely Hearts Club Band*. In this, the first "conceptual" or "song cycle" rock album, each song related to the next and to an overriding theme. The cycle included a range of diverse elements—an English music hall song ("When I'm Sixty-Four"), new "psychedelic" sounds using the latest electronic devices ("Lucy in the Sky with Diamonds"), large orchestras, Indian sitar and tabla ("Within You Without You"), and good, old-fashioned rock 'n' roll. In *Sgt. Pepper* the Beatles created the first rock album ever to be recognized as "art."

The Beatles were also among the first to consistently treat serious themes within the rock style. They were joined in this effort by poet/singer Bob Dylan and by their fellow Englishmen the Rolling Stones.

BOB DYLAN

Minnesota-born Bob Dylan (born Robert Zimmerman) first gained a following in the early 1960s as a folk singer emulating the work of the late Woody Guthrie. Dylan's protest songs, heard on such albums as *Highway 61 Revisited* and *Bringing It All Back Home,* had enormous appeal for young people involved in the struggle for civil rights for blacks and later in the growing protest over the war in Viet Nam. Not only Bob Dylan but also the Beatles, the Rolling Stones, and some "psychedelic" San Francisco-based groups—the Jefferson Airplane, the Grateful Dead, Big Brother and the Holding Company (featuring the late Janis Joplin on lead vocals)—all proved that rock could have significant social influence and at the same time achieve commercial success.

But Dylan did not remain only a social protest singer. In 1965 to the dismay of his loyal folk-music fans, he decided to convert from acoustic to electric guitar and to appear with an electric band. This decision, which was based to a large extent on the popular success of the Beatles, initially created a storm of contro-

Fig. 23.2 Janis Joplin's burning, frenetic rock style and freewheeling lifestyle personified the turbulent side of the generation of the sixties. Her career was cut short after only five years when she died of a heroin overdose at the age of 27.

versy, but his switch to electric eventually won him thousands of new listeners and created a new, more lyrical style that came to be known as "folk-rock."

PHASE THREE: RECENT TRENDS

Since the end of the 1960s, rock has continued to branch out in a number of different directions. One style, espoused primarily by Dylan's former backup musicians, who called themselves simply The Band, came to be called "country rock." It had a much softer sound than did the electric visions of Dylan in the 1960s. Country rock relied instead on crooning harmonies to evoke the simple country life—a theme that schoed the "back-to-the-land" movement of the early 1970s.

At the same time, a clangingly loud, electronic hard rock style known as "heavy metal" came into vogue. The primary instrument of heavy metal was the electric guitar, filtered through electronic warping devices and blasted through giant amplifiers.

Another rock style which is also produced using sophisticated electronic techniques is "disco." The appeal of the disco sound lies in its pulsating, insistent beat and danceable rhythms. The disco soundtrack from the 1977 film *Saturday Night Fever,* featuring many original songs by the Bee Gees, has become the best-selling record in history.

Another trend of the 1970s was so-called "glitter rock," whose practitioners painted their faces and posed as androgynous creatures. Leaders of the short-lived glitter rock phenomenon included Alice Cooper and David Bowie. The main intent of the music seemed to be to attract younger listeners by shocking the old, but it wasn't long before its leaders were absorbed into the mainstream.

"Our next mind-shattering song is a simple A—B—A form which relies on the rhythmic texture and variation of naive American marching music and Renaissance madrigals."

Edward Koren, Courtesy Harper's Magazine

Fig. 23.3 While the "older" generation of rock fans (many only in their early thirties) apparently prefer soft rock stylings, youngsters are flocking to see flashy hard rockers like Kiss.

Today rock 'n' roll (or, more succinctly **rock,** as all post-Beatles derivations have come to be known), once again faces a crossroad similar to that of the period immediately preceding the rise of the Beatles. While there is still experimentation, much of the originality that characterized the work of the Beatles has given way to an emphasis on commerical success. One of the most popular forms to emerge is the lyrical, subdued style known as "soft rock."

Soft rock began to gain a following in the early 1970s, when folk singer James Taylor achieved prominence with the lullabye-like tune "Sweet Baby James." Taylor's moody introspection also characterizes the work of soft-rock singer/songwriters Paul Simon, Joni Mitchell, and Jackson Browne.

At the same time rock continued to branch out and draw on other areas of music. Borrowing from classical music, the phenomenon of the "rock opera" emerged in the early 1970s. *Tommy,* by The Who, and *Jesus Christ Superstar,* by Andrew Lloyd Webber and Tim Rice, have been performed successfully with full orchestras in classical concert halls like Lincoln Center. Some groups, including Emerson, Lake, and Palmer, have based pieces on the music of classical composers or have included classical themes in their songs. "Variations on a Theme by Erik Satie," performed by Blood, Sweat and Tears, is an interesting effort in this direction.

To achieve new sounds rock performers have experimented with non-Western instruments and styles. They have also continued to experiment with electronics, adding synthesizers, computers, and electrified instruments of all kinds (violins and pianos included) as standard fixtures of the rock setting.

The rock audience of the late 1970s—hence rock itself—is split between young and old. The "old" in this case are largely the teenagers of the 1950s and '60s who grew up with rock music as a prime element of their culture. These "old folks" (most of whom are still only in their thirties) are opting in increasing numbers for soft rock.

The younger part of the rock audience, however, has continued to embrace harder rock stylings, many of which are as derivative as the soft-rock sounds attracting older listeners. "Punk rock," which is characterized by loud playing, outrageous dress, and ugly behavior, has emerged as an offshoot of glitter. And hard-rock groups like Aerosmith and Kiss have styled themselves after earlier English hard-rock groups.

Thus, rock today has become highly eclectic, often commercial, and more popular than ever. As we move into the 1980s it seems clear that rock, in one form or another, will continue to thrive.

MUSICAL THEATER

Musical theater occupies a unique position in American culture, lying somewhere between the commercially popular song and serious concert music. In many ways it may be considered a hybrid of the two styles.

Historically, the form of musical theater known as musical comedy evolved from the **musical revue** and the **operetta.** A musical revue is basically a series of unrelated singing and dancing numbers with no plot. An operetta, on the other hand, is a somewhat relaxed opera. The plot is usually light, often fanciful, and contains some spoken dialogue. The late nineteenth-century operettas of the Englishmen Gilbert and Sullivan (*H.M.S. Pinafore, The Mikado*) are typical of the genre.

Today's musical comedy (or musical, for short) combines plot, spoken dialogue, music, song, and dance. Its subject may be fanciful or serious, satirical or silly, and it often incorporates many types of music in a single production. Thus, solos, duets, ensemble numbers, dances, pop styles, and jazz are often present together in a single show. Since the mid-1960s, rock music and dance styles have also become firmly established in the musical.

Musical comedy, like opera and operetta, relies on certain conventions. Typically, characters will interrupt spoken conversations to express their feelings through song or to act out dramatic incidents through dance. To enjoy a musical, the members of an audience must suspend their ordinary sense of reality and allow themselves to be drawn into the world unfolding before them.

The first influential composers of the American musical theater were Victor Herbert, who was trained in Europe, George M. Cohan, and Jerome Kern. The work of these men helped shaped the musical comedy form that experienced its first flowering in the 1920s. Irving Berlin, George and Ira Gershwin, Oscar Hammerstein II, Lorenz Hart, and Cole Porter were among the composers and lyricists whose work gained them lasting recognition.

The shows of the 1920s featured popular musical styles, including ragtime and jazz. Jazz dancing was introduced to Broadway in an all-black show called *Shuffle Along* (1921). This effervescent musical, created by Noble Sissle and Eubie Blake, ran for over a year on Broadway, then went on tour throughout the

Fig. 23.4 *Oklahoma!,* by Rodgers and Hammerstein, marked a high point in the development of musical comedy. Pictured here is a dream sequence from an early production.

United States, breaking the color barrier at previously all-white theaters and paving the way for the production of many more black musicals.

As the 1920s moved to a close, the plots of some musicals became increasingly realistic and meaningful. One show that deserves special mention is *Show Boat,* written in 1927 by Jerome Kern and Oscar Hammerstein II. *Show Boat*'s sympathetic view of the social condition of blacks in the South was far ahead of its time, and certain songs from the musical, including "Ol' Man River," are still popular more than fifty years later.

The trend toward serious commentary in the Broadway musical accelerated in the 1930s, as America faced the reality of the Great Depression and the world moved inexorably toward war. One of the first of the more thoughtful musicals was the political satire *Of Thee I Sing,* by George and Ira Gershwin, which won a Pulitzer Prize in 1931. Irving Berlin's *Face the Music* appeared a year later with a theme concerning the economic depression. In *Three Penny Opera*—an English version of the musical they first produced in Germany—two Germans, the playwright Bertholt Brecht and the composer Kurt Weill, presented themes of global significance. The play, a modernization of John Gay's 1728 comedy *The Beggar's Opera,* was a Marxist attack on the social values of its audience.

Of course, not every show produced during the 1930s concerned itself with serious themes. There were many shows written purely as entertainment, including Jerome Kern's *Roberta,* with the still-recorded "Smoke Gets In Your Eyes," and Rodgers and Hart's *Babes in Arms.*

In the early 1940s dance became an ever more prominent element of the production and was interwoven with the story line of the musical. Musical comedy became a total theatrical form dependent on the delicate interrelation of story, music, lyrics, dance, scenery, and costumes. One of the high points in the development of this style was *Oklahoma!* (1943), composed by Richard Rodgers, with lyrics by Oscar Hammerstein II.

There are, of course, some musical theater composers who write their own lyrics. Irving Berlin, Cole Porter, and Stephen Sondheim are all examples of this special ability.

In the past twenty years, Broadway musicals have changed dramatically in an attempt to keep up with their audiences and the world at large. They have become increasingly more relevant to current problems and more experimental musically. A trailblazer in this modernization process was the epochal *West Side Story* (1957) by Leonard Bernstein and Stephen Sondheim. One of the most popular musicals ever made, *West Side Story* deals with gang warfare and racial tensions in New York City. Although the basic plot is little more than an updated version of Shakespeare's *Romeo and Juliet,* the music is, by the standards of previous musicals, extremely innovative. In numbers such as "The Dance at the Gym" for example, Bernstein employs irregular meters and dissonant harmonies.

A decade later, Gerome Ragni, James Rado, and Galt McDermott unleashed *Hair,* an "American Tribal Love-Rock Musical," on an unsuspecting public. *Hair,* very loosely the story of a young man's dilemma when he receives his draft notice, was described by critic Clive Barnes of the prestigious *New York Times* as "the first Broadway musical in some time to have the authentic voice of today rather than the day before yesterday." *Hair* was revolutionary in its use of rock music, its earthy lyrics (one song offers a list of sexual variations), and its twitting of the Establishment. Even more shocking than its overt protests against the Viet Nam war was its use of full frontal nudity (albeit briefly and tastefully by later standards). Perhaps because it was so controversial, *Hair* became enormously successful, spawning a number of imitators (*Grease* and *Salvation* among them) and being performed all over the world and in a host of languages.

In the 1970s the trend toward sophisticated, psychologically complex, and musically innovative shows continued. Michael Bennett's *A Chorus Line* probed the inner lives of dancers in the chorus line of a musical. Stephen Sondheim's *A Little Night Music* was inspired jointly by Mozart and the film maker Ingmar Bergman. From Mozart's *Eine Kleine Nachtmusik* Sondheim got the idea of setting all the music in waltz time; and from Bergman he got his plot, which revolves around several romantic intrigues.

At the same time, the 1970s witnessed the revival of numerous hits which dated back as far as the 1920s. Some new musicals such as *Annie,* based on the comic strip Little Orphan Annie, continued this nostalgic trend. And the all-black musical once again came into its own in such fresh and energetic productions as *The Wiz, Raisin,* and *Bubbling Brown Sugar.* Thus, the musical theater continues to offer a diversity of styles to entertain and occasionally to challenge American audiences.

SUMMARY

Rock music developed from a merger of black rhythm and blues and white country and western. In the mid-1950s, rock 'n' roll, as it became known, was popularized by Elvis Presley, whose sensual style attracted a huge audience of teenagers. From the late 1950s to the mid-1960s rock 'n' roll developed a number of offshoots, most notably the Motown sound, soul, and "street corner" harmony.

With the arrival of the Beatles in America in the early 1960s rock 'n' roll underwent a revolution. Soon abandoning the older format, the Beatles experimented with new meters and instruments and often wrote more thoughtful lyrics. Another young songwriter, Bob Dylan, expressed the social concerns of young people in his early music; later, he took up electric guitar and created a more lyrical style. In the 1970s rock became increasingly commercial and the rock audience increasingly divided between those who preferred soft rock and those who favored hard rock.

The American musical theater evolved from the musical revue and the operetta. While many musical comedies have been light and escapist in nature, others have explored serious themes and introduced musical innovations. Some landmark productions in this latter group are *Oklahoma!, West Side Story,* and *Hair.*

NEW TERMS

rhythm and blues
country and western
rock 'n' roll
soul

rock
musical revue
operetta

PART VIII SUGGESTED LISTENING

Bernstein, Leonard

Mass, "Theater Piece for Singers, Players, and Dancers" (1971–1972). This "mixed media" event brings together many facets of Bernstein's musical personality, drawing from his experience in the Broadway theater, from contact with more modern currents, and from a deep personal urge to "say something" to a wide audience.

Carter, Elliott

Concerto for Orchestra (1969). A work of immense textural and rhythmic complexity, the *Concerto* depicts the winds of change and renewal that sweep our country.

Copland, Aaron

Fanfare for the Common Man for brass and percussion (1942). Copland wrote this stirring patriotic piece as part of the war effort, then later incorporated it into the finale of his Third Symphony (1946).

Cowell, Henry

Piano Music (1912–1932). This unique assortment of daring pieces demonstrates the composer's "tone clusters" and the techniques of plucking, scraping, and strumming the piano strings.

Druckman, Jacob

Animus III (1969). Written for clarinet and a prepared electronic tape, this work explores combinations of live and prerecorded sound. The tape was created primarily from clarinet and voice sounds in various stages of transformation.

Gershwin, George

Rhapsody in Blue for piano and orchestra (1924). This famous example of "symphonic jazz" was given its premiere by the Paul Whiteman band and instantly captivated the musical world with what may be the most beloved American melody.

Ives, Charles

Three Places in New England. Each of the three movements of this often-played work illustrates a different facet of the composer's highly individualistic technique: the first (The "St. Gaudens" in Boston Common) presents a subtle and complex use of traditional American melodies; the second (Putnam's Camp, Redding, Connecticut) depicts a lively Fourth of July celebration, complete with colliding brass bands, and is one of Ives's most famous examples of polytempo; and the last (The Housatonic at Stockbridge) is a wonderfully evocative tone poem portraying a quiet-flowing New England river.

Martino, Donald

Notturno for chamber group with percussion (1973). This Pulitzer Prize-winning work has been described as "nocturnal theater of the soul." From its brilliant orchestral sounds one would never guess that the composer works in a carefully wrought serialism.

Sessions, Roger

Rhapsody for Orchestra (1970). This brooding, somber work represents this venerable composer's late orchestral style, descended from the Mahler and Schoenberg tradition.

Varèse, Edgard

Ionisation (1930–1933). This is one of the first pieces of Western music scored entirely for solo percussion instruments (including sirens, piano, gong, bongos, bass drums, maracas, and chimes). The piece builds upon the tensions between different tone colors and between sounds and silences.

Weisgall, Hugo

The Tenor, opera in one act (1950). A powerful story of love, death, and deception in the wings of an opera house comes to life through the vivid theatrical style of this American composer of opera.

A Brief Jazz Discography

Smithsonian Collection of Classic Jazz (P11891 to P11897).

Louis Armstrong, *The Louis Armstrong Story,* Vols. 1 and 2 (Columbia 851, 852); *Louis Armstrong and Earl Hines,* 1928 (Smithsonian R 002).

Charlie Christian, *Solo Flight* (Columbia G 30779).

Ornette Coleman, *Free Jazz* (Atlantic 1364).

John Coltrane, *A Love Supreme* (Impulse S-77); *Ascension* (Impulse A-95).

Miles Davis, *The Complete Birth of the Cool* (Capitol M-11026); *Kind of Blue* (Columbia PC 8163); *Bitches' Brew* (Columbia PG-26).

Duke Ellington, *This is Duke Ellington* (RCA VPM 6042); *Ellington at Newport* (Columbia CS 8468).

Coleman Hawkins and Lester Young, *Classic Tenors* (Flying Dutchman 10146).

Billie Holiday, *Lady Day* (Columbia CL 637); *The Golden Years,* Vol. 1 (Columbia C3L 21).

Thelonious Monk. *Genius of Modern Music,* Vols. 1 and 2 (Blue Note 82520 and 82511).

Charlie Parker. *The Savoy Recordings* (Savoy JC 2201).

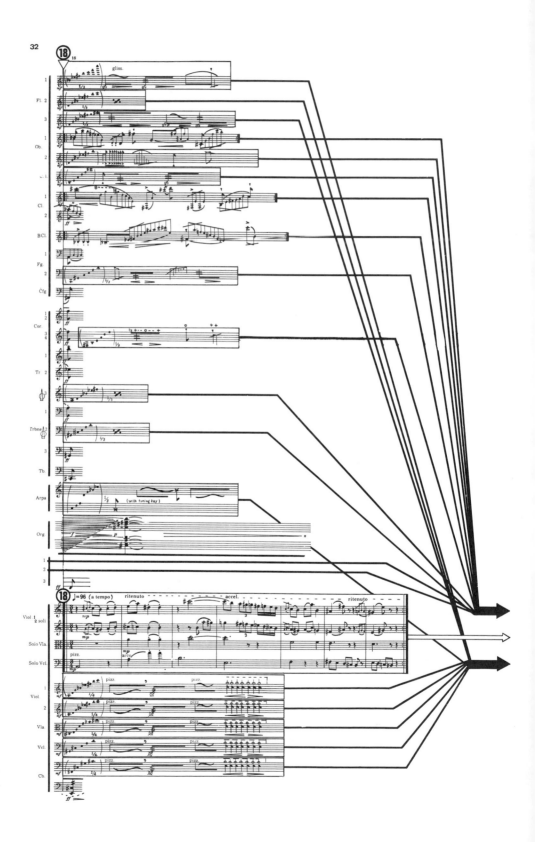

IX

MUSIC OF THE
LATE TWENTIETH CENTURY

A page of the score of *Windows,* by Jacob Druckman. (Copyright © 1974 by MCA Music, a division of MCA Inc., New York, N.Y. Used by permission. All rights reserved.)

CHAPTER **24** | **THE NEW MUSIC**

MUSIC WRITTEN SINCE THE END OF WORLD WAR II HAS CONTINUED and extended many of the trends having their origins in the first half of the century. These included atonality, serialism, rhythmic complexity, and the use of unconventional sounds—from environmental noise to electronically produced sound —as musical materials. But along with this continuation and further development, newer and yet more radical notions about the way music might be put together have become increasingly important, and the speed at which changes have evolved has accelerated.

Composers working during the 1950s and '60s tended to adopt one of two opposing approaches, or to choose a style that fell somewhere between the most extreme forms of them. The first approach is **total serialism**—the complete, predetermined, and ultrarational organization of every aspect of a composition. The second is **indeterminacy**—the free, unpremeditated, and irrational occurrence of musical events, which are deliberately meant to lie beyond the composer's ultimate control. Other current terms for indeterminacy are **chance music** and **aleatory music** (*alea* is Latin for game of dice).

BACKGROUND

Between the two world wars the two opposing musical positions among composers were on the one hand the new tonality and Neoclassicism, represented by Stravinsky, Bartók, and Hindemith, and on the other hand serialism and atonality, represented by Schoenberg, Berg, Webern, and their followers. In sheer numbers tonality and Neoclassicism were far ahead, encompassing most American composers. The dominance of the tonally oriented side was strengthened by the populist and nationalist political movements of the 1930s and by the sinister suppression of any kind of music that hinted at atonality throughout Nazi-occupied Europe and Stalinist Russia.

Within a few years of the end of World War II, however, the situation had changed completely. Many composers who under Nazi domination had been denied opportunities to hear the works of Schoenberg, Berg, and Webern immediately immersed themselves in this exciting, unfamiliar music. Neoclassicism dropped out of favor, and the twelve-tone technique became the central interest of young composers. Even Stravinsky, whose opera *The Rake's Progress* represented the epitome of Neoclassicism, performed an about-face that astounded the musical world: he began to study twelve-tone music, especially that of Webern, and began to experiment with various aspects of serialism, at first incorporating the techniques into his tonally based works of the mid-1950s. At about the same time, other well-established composers developed similar interests in serialism, including Aaron Copland, Roger Sessions, and Luigi Dallapiccola (1904–1975), Italy's most important twentieth-century composer.

TOTAL SERIALISM

The French composer Pierre Boulez has described the feelings of the younger postwar generation of composers: "After the war we all felt that music, like the world around us, was in a state of chaos. Our problem was to make a new musical language. . . . We went through a period of seeking out total control over music." Recall from Chapter 20 that Schoenberg's original serial techniques applied only to pitch relationships and imposed no limitations on rhythm, dynamics, or textures. Further, his musical style lay in post-Romantic Expressionism. Schoenberg's association with the "old tradition" seemed to the younger generation confirmed by his occasional reversion to tonality from the 1930s onward. Anton Webern, on the other hand, composed lean, uncluttered, and icily compact music; he abandoned the traditional lyric approach to melody in favor of a technique called **pointillism,*** in which the texture is built up from isolated tones or chords; and he actually extended systems of order beyond the domain of pitch. "Schoenberg is dead" trumpeted the title of Boulez's famous polemical article of 1952. It was now Webern who was alive among the European avant-garde.

Actually, the first to adapt serial procedures to all the aspects of a musical composition was the American composer Milton Babbitt (b. 1916). Babbitt extended Schoenberg's most rigorous systems of organizing tones to the systematization of durations, tempos, dynamics, articulations, and timbre. *Three Compositions* for piano (1947), *Compositions for Four Instruments* (1947–1948), and *Composition for Twelve Instruments* (1949) are landmarks of total serialism, and exemplify the clean, objective, and often pointillistic texture common to much music written through the 1960s.

At almost the same time the French composer Olivier Messiaen (b. 1908) was experimenting with total organization and in 1949 produced the étude *Mode de valeurs et d'intensités* (Scale of Durations and Dynamics) for piano. Messiaen's musical language, however, draws on such diverse materials as Stravin-

---

*   The term comes from the visual arts, and refers to the Post-Impressionist technique of applying color with dots or short strokes, as exemplified in the work of Georges Seurat in the 1880s.

Fig. 24.1 The music of Pierre Boulez was deeply influenced by the ideas of his teacher, Olivier Messiaen. Boulez's serial compositions and his conducting of twentieth-century orchestral works exhibit precision, clarity, and control.

skian rhythms, Debussian harmonies, Hindu rhythmic procedures, Gregorian chant, and actual bird songs meticulously transcribed from field trips, as well as on Webernian serialism. Although Messiaen was one of the few European musicians who taught serial methods after the war, he regarded them as just one among many possible approaches. His students, Boulez and Karlheinz Stockhausen, however, dived into total serialism with a vengeance, and became, along with the American John Cage (who possesses a radically different point of view), the most important figures on the international contemporary music scene.

PIERRE BOULEZ

Pierre Boulez (Boo-lez', b. 1925), like Babbitt, had studied mathematics as a young man. Precision, clarity, and ultrarational control are exemplified in the almost mathematically calculated and totally serialized *Structures I* for two pianos (1952) and *Le marteau sans maître* (The Hammer without a Master) for alto and six instruments (1955). This control, which can also be heard in his definitive performances of twentieth-century orchestral masterpieces, reins in what the composer himself admits is a furious and "hysterical" temperament. In contrast to the jagged pointillism of these works, delicate harmonic and instrumental color can be heard in others, such as the three *Improvisations sur Mallarmé* which Boulez incorporated into his very "French-sounding" large-scale orchestral work *Pli selon pli* (*Fold upon Fold,* 1957–1962).

KARLHEINZ STOCKHAUSEN

Karlheinz Stockhausen (b. 1928) absorbed himself in the extended serialism and pointillism of Webern, but almost immediately evolved ways by which Webern's tiny, jewel-like structures could be expanded to create larger gestures and forms. Stockhausen's conceptions became more highly organized, more dense, and more "Germanic" in character, reaching the huge proportions of *Gruppen* (Groups) for three orchestras (1955–1957), *Carré* (Square) for four choruses and four orchestras (1959–1960), and *Momente* for soprano, four choral groups, and thirteen instrumentalists (1962–1964), performances of which can last as long as two hours.

Fig. 24.2 Karlheinz Stockhausen, one of the foremost exponents of total serialism, has also made use of chance elements and minimalist techniques.

OTHER SERIAL COMPOSERS OF THE 1950S

Prominent composers of the 1950s who now began to produce serial works were the Hungarian György Ligeti (b. 1923), the Italians Luigi Nono (b. 1924) and Luciano Berio (b. 1925), the American Gunther Schuller (b. 1925), and the Belgian Henri Pousseur (b. 1929).

Boulez, in his statement about postwar attitudes at the beginning of this section, goes on to say that "What we were doing by total serialism was to annihilate the will of the composer in favor of a predetermined system." In other words, by objectively choosing the series of pitches, durations, tempos, dynamics, and articulations *before* actually beginning to compose, composers released themselves to a considerable extent from the necessity of making choices during composition itself. Total serialism in its most extreme form could be described as rather like a machine programmed in advance which, once set in motion, goes its own way to produce what some people feel is inherently rigid and mechanical music.

INDETERMINACY

In indeterminant, chance, or aleatory music, the composer deliberately abstains from exercising control over the composition process. Unlike the totally planned constructions of the serialists, indeterminant works call on the performers to make many decisions, so they are unpredictable before any given performance, or else they are the product of using chance operations during composition to obtain a random series of musical events. The chance operations, or aleatory procedures, that have been used include throwing dice, tossing coins, plotting star charts, and tracing imperfections on music paper. A basic premise of indeterminacy is that all the sounds or silences that may occur at any given moment are important in themselves and may automatically be called music.

JOHN CAGE

The undisputed leader in indeterminant music is the American composer John Cage (b. 1912). Cage follows in the American experimental tradition of Ives, Cowell, and Varèse. Both Ives and Cowell, with whom Cage studied in the 1930s, had in certain works anticipated the later full-blown appearance of indeterminacy. Other important musical ideas which influenced Cage were Ives's free combination of contrasting musical materials, Cowell's interest in Oriental cultures and in percussion, and Varèse's enthusiastic acceptance of "noise" elements as usable building blocks for composition.

Cage's early interest in percussion, during the 1930s, led him to his "prepared piano" music of the 1940s, in which delicately percussive sounds were produced by introducing foreign objects onto the strings of the piano. Such works as the *Sonatas and Interludes* for prepared piano (1946–1948) and the Concerto for Prepared Piano and Chamber Orchestra (1951) sound like Javanese gamelan music. His appreciation of the Oriental esthetics of Zen Buddhism led him to think in terms of the removal of self from the compositional process. The Chinese

Fig. 24.3 John Cage's experiments in indeterminacy have had enormous impact on the new music. Many current composers, including leading serialists, have adopted aspects of this "music of chance."

I Ching (Book of Changes) provided chance operations for *Music of Changes* for piano (1951); the map of the heavens provided the note heads for *Atlas eclipticalis* (1961–1962). This work, the sound of which is uncannily similar to the pointillism of total serialists, consists of 86 instrumental parts (there is no score) "to be played in whole or part, any duration, in any ensemble, chamber or orchestral."

The role of silence and of the unpredictable background noises that are always present is most radically embodied in *4'33"*, Cage's classic example of pure nonmusic (1952). The piece consists entirely of environmental sounds: a pianist sits quietly at an open piano for four minutes and thirty-three seconds, then leaves the stage. The point of this gesture is to focus attention on the sounds around us and also to provoke the audience to make its own music. This fulfills the premise that any sound or no sound at all is as valid or "good" as any other.

Cage's pieces are all radically different from one another, but they have this in common: they are programmed activities with certain boundaries set by the composer. He limits his control over the outcome of the piece and no way predicts it. Like the wind blowing a mobile and thereby changing its shape, the performers make decisions on the spur of the moment. Thus, rational control is avoided. This "every man for himself" attitude toward the role of performers reminds us of Ives's enthusiastic approval of an unruly performance of *Three Places in New England*.

Cage's impact has been great. Boulez, Stockhausen, Berio, and other serialists have adopted aspects of indeterminacy to varying degrees. In fact, much of the music written today stems from Cage's explorations into the very essence of the meaning of music.

ELECTRONIC MUSIC

Music produced by electronic means can employ musical techniques as diverse as serialism and indeterminacy; it can consist of original compositions in the style of any period, or it can be the works of old masters "realized" on electronic instruments, such as the "Switched-on Bach" recording of Walter Carlos (b. 1939). Indeed, electronic music is as varied as music produced by nonelectronic means. Varèse, Cowell, and others dreamed of electronic instruments that could produce *any* sound their imagination suggested. The percussion music composed by Varèse, Cowell, and Cage during the 1930s was symptomatic of their desire to free the raw materials of music from the limitations of traditional instrumentation.

The first step in the development of the phenomenon known today as electronic music took place in 1948 at the studios of the French National Radio. Sounds were tape-recorded, then altered mechanically or electronically, and finally combined into organized pieces. The product was known as **musique concrète.** Any sounds may be used in *musique concrète,* including street noise, sounds from nature, human singing and speech, and unusual sounds from conventional instruments, all of which may be distorted, recombined, or put through echo chambers. After prerecording, sound alteration, cutting, and splicing are finished, the piece has been both composed and performed by the composer in a fixed and accurate version. In addition, the unlimited dynamic range available through electronic means and the striking spatial effects obtained by placing loudspeakers around the concert hall have revolutionized the concert-going experience. Masterpieces of *musique concrète* are Stockhausen's *Gesang der Jünglinge* (Song of the Youths, 1956), Varèse's *Poème électronique* (1958), and Berio's *Omaggio à Joyce* (Homage to Joyce, 1958) and *Visage* (1961).

Because the medium of tape offered composers complete and accurate control over the final "performance," it attracted total serialists such as Babbitt and Stockhausen, whose rhythms, articulation, and abrupt changes in dynamics had become incredibly difficult to execute in live performances. These composers, however, were not satisfied with the "found sound" employed in *musique concrète.* The next logical step was the use of electronically produced sounds. With tone-producing machines—or synthesizers—not only could familiar sounds be duplicated synthetically (as was already done to some extent by the electronic church organ), but entirely new sounds could be invented, with the potential of realizing fully the dreams of Varèse. Important synthesized electronic works by serial composers are Stockhausen's pioneering *Electronic Studies I* and *II* (1953–1954); Babbitt's *Composition for Synthesizer* (1961–1963), *Ensembles for Synthesizer* (1967), and *Occasional Variations* (1973); and *Time's Encomium* (1969) by Charles Wuorinen (b. 1938), which won the 1970 Pulitzer Prize. Today, computers can facilitate the instantaneous production of sounds, can put them together with absolute accuracy according to the composer's desires, or can, for the aleatory composer, produce random events. *HPSCHD* (1969), a collaborative effort by Cage and Lejaren Hiller (b. 1924), uses fifty-one computer-generated sound tapes in conjunction with seven live harpsichordists and fifty-two slide projectors. The technological age continues to enrich composers' materials, options, and working habits.

Fig. 24.4 Milton Babbitt at the huge RCA Mark II Synthesizer. In several important works, including the rigorously serial *Philomel*, Babbitt has pitted a singer against recorded sound.

Fig. 24.5 One of the first of its kind in the world, the prestigious Columbia-Princeton Electronic Music Center is a vital center for electronic music. Pictured in the Center are (l. to r.) Milton Babbitt, Mario Davidovsky, Vladimir Ussachevsky, Pril Smily, Alice Shields, and Otto Luening.

Composers of electronic music have not abandoned live performance. In fact, the manipulation of synthesizers and sound alteration devices during concerts has become standard practice among many rock groups. Among composers of concert music, too, the combination of live musicians and taped sounds has become a highly refined and effective medium. Otto Luening (b. 1900) and Vladimir Ussachevsky (b. 1911) of Columbia University, as well as Edgard Varèse himself, were the first to explore this relationship. Varèse used such a combination in his *Déserts* (completed in 1954), in which music for winds, brass, and percussion alternates with taped *musique concrète*. Babbitt's *Vision and Prayer* (1961) and *Philomel* (1963–1964) pit a singer against recorded sounds. Mario Davidovsky (b. 1934) with his series of *Synchronisms* (1963–1977) and Jacob Druckman (b. 1928) with his *Animus* series have created brilliant works for soloists or various groups of live performers and prerecorded tape. In addition, live musicians are being asked to attach microphones to their instruments so as to enhance or distort certain novel playing techniques through amplifiers.

COLLAGE

The technique of juxtaposing independent styles or seemingly unrelated sound sources is known as **collage,** a term borrowed from the visual arts. The first important composer to use collage techniques extensively was Ives, during the first decades of the twentieth century. Many of Ives's most remarkable orchestral works feature the simultaneous or successive appearances of contrasting styles, some borrowed, some his own. Alban Berg, the twelve-tone composer, occasionally quoted for symbolic reasons from Bach, Wagner, and street songs; and Messiaen quoted from Gregorian chant and bird calls.

Recently, however, collage has gone hand in hand with wholesale quotation of traditional or classical music from the past or present. The American George Rochberg (b. 1918) was one of the first composers to incorporate large segments from the music of others into his own; Rochberg's Third Symphony, "A Twentieth-Century Passion" (1968), is the most radical in this regard, quoting huge passages from Schütz, Beethoven, and Mahler. Henri Pousseur's operatic fantasy *Votre Faust* (1967), the *Baroque Variations* (1967) of Lukas Foss (b. 1922), and many of Berio's recent works employ various kinds of collage and quotation.

The ability to manipulate tape in the electronic studio has given composers limitless possibilities to graft together or superimpose diverse musical elements. Such a work as Stockhausen's *Hymnen* (Hymns) for tape and/or four players and/or orchestra and/or colored lights (1969), draws on the national anthems of many countries. Many works of *musique concrète* are also examples of collage.

VIRTUOSITY, COMPLEXITY, AND THE PERFORMER'S ROLE

Over the past few centuries the continuing search for new expressive means has tended to produce music of ever-increasing complexity. In addition, the glorification of virtuosity for its own sake, a tendency fostered most notably during the Romantic era, has continued and is still with us today. As a result of these two trends, as well as the radical new esthetic positions taken by the avant-garde since World War II, demands on performers have been pushed to seemingly superhuman extremes. Performers have nevertheless made the effort to keep pace, and in this century there has emerged a new breed of virtuoso whose technical mastery is equal to the requirements of the new music.

Characteristic difficulties in the performance of recent music are rhythmic complexity, pointillistic textures which require a single peformer to shift directly from one extreme register to another, rapid alternations in articulation of dynamics, and the production of sounds that are alien to conventional performing methods. The musical examples discussed in Chapter 21, on American music, illustrate representative virtuoso performance techniques. In Elliott Carter's *Brass Quintet* the rhythmic difficulties result from the composer's need to differentiate contrasting layers of musical material without the assistance of a perceptible beat. In George Crumb's *Vox Balaenae* the performers must not only master parts that are technically difficult in the conventional sense, but must also execute special sound effects—singing into their instruments, whistling, playing extra percussion —and work with microphones and amplifiers, all in a theatrical setting.

The rigorously serial and often pointillistic style of Milton Babbitt's *Philomel* presents formidable obstacles for the virtuoso singer—an extreme vocal range, rhythmic complexities, abrupt changes of register and dynamics, and accurate following of electronic cues for precisely indicated coordination with the taped part.

Few sopranos other than the remarkable Bethany Beardslee, for whom *Philomel* was written, have tackled this immensely difficult work.

In much indeterminant music, performers are expected to go beyond performance and enter into the creative process itself. Sometimes they are required to improvise freely, sometimes to improvise within limits spelled out with varying degrees of precision by the composer in a kind of "controlled chance."

One of the greatest challenges for the new virtuoso lies in acquiring the ability to "hear" today's atonal musical language and complicated rhythms with the same ease as many of us "hear" tonal music and conventional rhythm. This ability, which requires years of experience, is essential if an individual performer's part is to fit smoothly and accurately into the total fabric. Thus, performance of the new music requires more than technical brilliance; an aural sensitivity to the new language—perhaps the most difficult aspect to master—may be the most important prerequisite to an effective performance.

NEW NOTATION FOR NEW IDEAS

The fact that traditional notational practice has, in general, been adequate to serve composers through about two and a half centuries of drastic style changes testifies to its flexibility. In the twentieth century, however, the sounds that composers have imagined have become more complex. New symbols have had to be invented or old ones redefined to make clearer the details of the composers' intentions. The increasing need for attention to tiny details, plus the bewilderment of so many performers in the face of the accelerated pace of new musical developments, has led to the use of ever-larger numbers of notational markings. In many twentieth-century scores it is not unusual to find a specific marking for the dynamics, the articulation, and the shading—written out in precise note values—of almost *every* note in a given measure.

As we have seen, in the music of the twentieth century many composers have tried to eliminate the use of a steady beat and to substitute calculatedly irregular rhythms. In the late 1940s and the 1950s the notation of these complex rhythms became increasingly difficult for both composers and performers. Also, it became evident that in dense textures, the effect upon the listener was one of randomness or arbitrariness, rather than of a highly organized event, as intended by the composer. Could not almost the same result be achieved by allowing performers the freedom to produce actual random rhythms or pitches on the spur of the moment? One answer was the development of graphic notation—a vaguer, more open-ended, and often blatantly pictorial method of notating music. The development of graphic notation has gone hand in hand with that of indeterminacy and interest in performer improvisation. As the composers of indeterminate music seek to give over various details of their compositions to chance, the performers necessarily assume greater degrees of creative imagination or responsibility for appropriate realizations of graphic indications. An example of graphic notation can be seen in Fig. 24.6, pp. 472–473.

In addition to these pictorial forms of notation, a host of new symbols have been invented by composers to deal with ever-expanding instrumental and vocal performance techniques. (The example on p. 448 combines conventional notation with the composer's own symbols.) Despite some important attempts in the past several years to standardize them, new symbols continue to be invented by composers who have come to identify their music with their own special notational systems. This often means they must preface their scores with long explanations to enable performers to learn the piece.

Some composers go one step further than this and, instead of producing what looks like a musical score, give nothing but a set of written directions. This might be called the epitome of indeterminacy, since activities rather than musical material are suggested to the performers, who then actually make the music.

MINIMALISM

Although complexity seems to be the word most often associated with twentieth-century music, periodic movements in favor of simplicity have arisen in reaction to complexity in musical styles and to the accompanying explosion in sheer amount of musical information to be mastered.

Recall that in the early part of the century, in Paris, reaction to overblown late nineteenth-century Romanticism clustered around the work of Erik Satie, who deliberately wrote in a diatonic, simplistic, and "unserious" style. In the 1930s, the German composer Carl Orff (b. 1895) evolved a serious, primitivistic style, based on steady, hammering rhythms and simple diatonic harmony, which is evident in such works as his cantata *Carmina Burana* (1937).

More recently, the extreme tonal and rhythmic complexities of post-Webern styles have led to yet another movement toward simplicity which has been referred to as **minimalism.** This has been largely an American phenomenon—an outgrowth of Cage's encouragement of pluralism and of current interest in Oriental music. Steve Reich (b. 1936) has summed up the movement by his debatable prediction that "the pulse and the drone will re-emerge as basic sources of new music." In the music of the minimalists we hear endless repetitions of diatonic note patterns in even, insistent rhythms. Patterns change only gradually over long time spans, and the listener loses a sense of "real time" due to concentration on the hypnotically slow pace. Typical of the minimalist approach is *In C* for any number of instruments (1964), by Terry Riley (b. 1935), which presents players with a series of fragments based on a "tonic" C in an underlying steady beat. Recent examples of minimalism include Reich's *Four Organs* (1970) and *Drumming* (1971); Stockhausen's *Stimmung* (1968)—a composition for six vocalists who for almost an hour "tune up" on a single chord vocalizing a *mantra* (a sacred word used for chanting in the Hindu religion); and such huge "mixed media" events as *Einstein on the Beach* (1975) by Philip Glass (b. 1937).

FOUR REPRESENTATIVE VOCAL WORKS

Each of the following vocal works represents an important current technique and at the same time uses the human voice in a significant and exciting way.

This short work for soprano and tape was written to be an encore piece for the brilliant American soprano Bethany Beardslee. The vocal portion was written in 1970, and the tape part was synthesized in 1974. The title refers to *phonemes*— the smallest sound units of speech. Babbitt has arranged 24 consonant sounds and 12 vowel sounds into a "text" that itself forms part of the comprehensive serial organization. (The phonemes are not arranged into words.) The work is a virtuoso piece for the singer, requiring a two-octave range, the ability to manage the wide leaps of its pointillistic texture, and split-second timing. Clarity, objectivity, and elegance continue to be hallmarks of Babbitt's style.

MILTON BABBITT: PHONEMENA (1970, 1974) *RECORD 8/SIDE 1*

The title of this work for eight voices and orchestra does not designate the Baroque form called the sinfonia; rather, it refers to the root meaning of the word— "sounding together." The voices of the singers are meant to blend in with the orchestra, as well as to stand out in virtuoso vocal styles. The particularly beautiful second section, called "O King," is an elegaic tribute to the memory of Dr. Martin Luther King, Jr. The text here consists only of the slain Nobel Prize-winner's name, in a slow, chantlike harmonic unfolding. The third section is a remarkable example of collage. The basis of this exciting piece is the Scherzo movement of Mahler's "Resurrection" Symphony (No. 2, 1888–1894), which forms a kind of musical backdrop. Onto this Berio grafts spoken quotations from Samuel Beckett and James Joyce, political graffiti from the Paris student insurrection of 1968, and bits of random conversations. In addition, snippets of Berio's own musical works are woven into the complex vocal and orchestral texture. The score is completely written out, an astonishing feat of workmanship.

LUCIANO BERIO: SINFONIA (1968)

At one time Ligeti was a strict serial composer, but he eventually began to feel that the technique was leading too far away from clear distinction of pitches and rhythms. His *Requiem,* scored for soprano and mezzosoprano solo, two mixed choruses, and orchestra, uses the orchestra and choruses in dense and shifting bands of blurring tone clusters, rather than in clear-cut chords or melodies. The score is carefully written out to sound irregular and indistinct. Only selected portions of the traditional Latin text are used. The clusters in the Kyrie (rather well known from its inclusion in Stanley Kubrick's film *2001*) build from a single quiet note toward a series of fortissimo climaxes before dying away again to a single tone. This hair-raising effect illustrates how composers can make voices and instruments sound almost "electronic" without actually resorting to mechanical aids.

GYÖRGY LIGETI: REQUIEM (1963–1965)

This indeterminate "happening" is actually two separate compositions, each with a separately published score. "The *Aria*," writes the composer, "may be sung in whole or in part to provide a program of a determined time-length, alone or with the *Fontana Mix* or with any parts of the *Concert*" (one of Cage's large-scale indeterminate works). The text of the *Aria* contains words and sounds from five languages (Armenian, Russian, Italian, French, and English), strung together in apparently random order. The score is a procession of squiggly lines which indicate the approximate up and down movement of the voice (see Fig. 24.6). The lines are shaded with various colors to correspond to any ten different styles of

JOHN CAGE: ARIA (1958) WITH FONTANA MIX (1958)

(*Continued on page 472.*)

INTERLUDE | RECENT DIRECTIONS IN MODERN CULTURE

The most notable quality of Western society since the Renaissance, and especially during the last 200 years, has been an on-going, apparently inexorable process of change. It is nearly impossible for an American of the twentieth century to imagine the roughness and poverty of a world before machine production; it is difficult to comprehend the stability, predictability, and pallor of most pre-industrial lives. That contemporary social scientists are deeply concerned about the impact of accelerating change on the behavior of individuals is not surprising. Change in the late twentieth century both excites with its possibilities and frightens with its ripping away of the familiar.

The diverse ideas and techniques explored by avant-garde artists over the past one hundred years have been confusing for many lay people, for whom the restless search for the new and different has made it hard to distinguish between worthy departure and slick gimmickry. Moreover, it seems that art in the twentieth century has become more and more divorced from nature and daily experience. Experimental painting and music, for example, have in many cases become so subtly abstract and theoretical that they have alienated a large section of the public. In the 1950s the public was likely to ridicule or disregard them. However, since then many of these works have gained critical acceptance, and consequently the public in the 1970s has become more worried or intimidated than hostile. Thus, in the last generation historians and commentators have spoken more and more frequently of a division between "high" and "pop" culture.

The direction taken by advanced painting since 1945 grows out of the movements seen during the first years of the twentieth century: by World War I Cubism was well established in Paris, and Kandinsky had introduced nonrepresentational abstraction. In the 1930s and 1940s, with the wholesale emigration of European artists from war-torn countries, New York replaced Paris as the art center of the world. After World War II a group of painters began working in a chaotic, gestural style called Abstract Expressionism—a kind of painting radically different from Fauvism and Cubism, the principal schools of earlier avant-garde design. The leader of the Abstract Expressionist school was Jackson Pollock (1912–1956), who developed a method of making huge works by pouring, splattering, and dripping paint onto the surface of the canvas (Plate 43). Others who painted in this highly felt, often violent manner, in which the process *of painting was meant to display the passions of the artist, were Willem de Kooning (b. 1904) and Franz Kline (1910–1962). Some Abstract Expressionists, particularly Mark Rothko (1903–1970), adopted a more meditative, transcendental approach, working with luminous color rather than explosive brushwork.*

Plate 41. Barnett Newman's *Broken Obelisk* (1963–1967) is a meeting of pyramid and upended obelisk, broken off to suggest the incompleteness of humanity's spiritual search. This elegantly conceived sculpture is hauntingly powerful. (Collection, The Museum of Modern Art, New York.)

The Abstract Expressionists were at first considered outrageous. Later, they were revered for making the United States the leading force in Western art and for dispelling once and for all any sense of American subservience to European design. Ironically, as the style gained a larger and more enthusiastic audience, some other painters were becoming impatient with the high seriousness and lofty ideals of the new masters. In the late 1950s Pop Art burst onto the New York scene. Although Pop was by no means a homogeneous movement, it was across the board a reaction to abstraction, choosing for its subjects familiar and trivial objects from modern life and depicting them with a kind of tongue-in-cheek humor. Andy Warhol (b. 1931), the flashiest and most irreverent of the school, "did" soup cans, electric chairs, and popular celebrities (Plate 44). Roy Lichtenstein worked in a style that was suggested by comic books. In 1967, Pop artist Claes Oldenburg (b. 1929) wrote, "I am for an art that embroils itself with the everyday crap and still comes out on top . . . I am for an art that comes in a can or washes up on shore."

In the last ten years American painting and sculpture have displayed styles that range from the wholly abstract to the super-realistic (Plates 41, 45). Some artists in the 1970s even declared that images are irrelevant and tried to develop a "conceptual art" based on words rather than objects. Minimal Art, a highly distilled art of basic shapes and intentive geometries, has emerged as one reaction to the visual extravagances of Abstract Expressionism and Pop. Devoid of passion or irony, it is elementally simple and even icily cerebral. Examples of Minimal Art are canvases of single colors or sculptures in the forms of cubes and spheres.

Plate 42. Le Corbusier's church at Ronchamp, France (1950–1955), departs radically from the International style, exploiting the variety of shapes and textures made possible by steel-reinforced concrete. (Courtesy Giraudon: Art Reference Bureau, © S.P.A.D.E.M. 1978.)

Contemporary music has been equally diverse in the forms of its expression, and some composers have challenged long-accepted notions about the nature of music itself. John Cage's indeterminate music, for example, is an attempt to limit the role of the composer in determining the musical events, thus allowing the performer, as well as unpredicable elements, to create the music. Other composers, notably Boulez and Stockhausen, extended the serial techniques of Webern in an attempt to gain complete control over all aspects of a work. Minimalist composers, like their counterparts in the visual arts, have sought simplicity and a return to the basics in their music. And new means of sound production—particularly electronic media—have expanded the range of dynamic and tonal possibilities far beyond conventional boundaries.

Recent architecture has been less eccentric and extreme than either music or painting—mainly because of the functional requirements of any good building. In the last decade the International style has come under increasing fire from critics who consider it sterile and antihuman. Particularly since architects have encountered the costs of climate control and maintenance in glass-and-steel towers and have become more sensitive to the monotony of these giant rectilinear boxes, new buildings of ingenious shape and use of space have been designed (Plate 46). Likewise, renovation and restoration of old buildings has become more common. Philip Johnson, the most intelligent and capable proponent of the International style, recently said, "We no longer belong to the International style. It doesn't interest us; those blank, bare boxes are boring now. Less isn't more; more is more." Le Corbusier (1887–1965), probably the premier architect of the

Plate 43. Jackson Pollock became the leader of the Abstract Expressionists in the late 1940s. *Grayed Rainbow* (1953), measuring 72″ by 96″, is an example of the style he developed. He tacked canvas to the floor and then dripped, spilled, and threw color so he could "walk around it, work from the four sides and literally be *in* the painting." (Courtesy Art Institute of Chicago; gift of the Society for Contemporary Art, 1955.)

Plate 44. *Elvis I and II,* by Andy Warhol (1964). Warhol, a superstar of Pop art, takes his inspiration from the banal, trivial, and tawdry, and sometimes focuses on the images of media gods and goddesses such as Elvis, Marilyn, and Jackie. (Courtesy Art Gallery of Ontario, Toronto; gift from the Women's Committee Fund, 1966.)

Plate 45. Duane Hanson's super-realistic sculpture of painted plastic deals with everyday subjects, as in *Couple with Shopping Bags* (1976). His objective, says critic John Canaday, is to "confront us with familiar material isolated in a way that forces us to see it with an intensity that habit has dulled in our daily contexts." (Courtesy O. K. Harris Works of Art.)

Plate 46. The sliced trapezoids of Philip Johnson's Pennzoil Palace (Houston, 1975) illustrate the visual interest that can be created in architecture based on the International style. (Courtesy Richard W. Payne.)

Plate 47. In recent years photography has come to be recognized as a medium of immense potential. Shown here is Ansel Adams's *Moon and Half Dome, Yosemite National Park, California* (1960). Adams (b. 1902) was one of the earliest photographers to raise the technical and pictorial quality of the photograph to the level of art. (Courtesy Ansel Adams.)

twentieth century, began to move away from an austere, hyperrational architecture as early as the 1950s (Plate 42). Nevertheless, the impact of glass-and-steel and reinforced concrete building has already radically transformed the appearance and nature of cities all over the world.

Common to all art forms today is their internationalism. In this age of instant communication, no longer does a style develop in an art center like Paris or New York from which it slowly spreads to other centers. In music, for example, composers, conductors, and performers frequently participate in events in many parts of the world, thus facilitating the rapid assimilation of new ideas. Avant-garde artists and composers are unified chiefly by their search for new means of expression and the public reception has been mixed. Much of the audience for new works of art and music is, however, eclectic in its tastes and broad-minded. Therefore, the challenge of the late twentieth century is to refine standards of criticism and to make sense out of esthetic chaos. While the great artist has always had extraordinary powers of intuition, artists find it no easier than anyone else to resolve the paradoxes of modern life. But by expressing their sensations and visions—even if their expression is difficult to comprehend —they reflect eloquently the complexities and contradictions of the present age.

THE ARIA MAY BE SUNG IN WHOLE OR IN PART TO PROVIDE A PROGRAM OF A DETERMINED TIME-LENGTH, ALONE OR WITH THE <u>FONTANA MIX</u> OR WITH ANY PARTS OF THE <u>CONCERT</u>.

THE NOTATION REPRESENTS TIME HORIZONTALLY, PITCH VERTICALLY, ROUGHLY SUGGESTED RATHER THAN ACCURATELY DESCRIBED. THE MATERIAL, WHEN COMPOSED, WAS CONSIDERED SUFFICIENT FOR A TEN MINUTE PERFORMANCE (PAGE = 30 SECONDS); HOWEVER, A PAGE MAY BE PERFORMED IN A LONGER OR SHORTER TIME-PERIOD.

THE VOCAL LINES ARE DRAWN IN BLACK, WITH OR WITHOUT PARALLEL DOTTED LINES, OR IN ONE OR MORE OF 8 COLORS. THESE DIFFERENCES REPRESENT 10 STYLES OF SINGING. ANY 10 STYLES MAY BE USED AND ANY CORRESPONDANCE BETWEEN COLOR AND STYLE MAY BE ESTABLISHED. THE ONE USED BY MISS BERBERIAN IS: DARK BLUE = JAZZ; RED = CONTRALTO (AND CONTRALTO LYRIC); BLACK WITH PARALLEL DOTTED LINE = SPRECHSTIMME; BLACK = DRAMATIC; PURPLE = MARLENE DIETRICH; YELLOW = COLORATURA (AND COLORATURA LYRIC); GREEN = FOLK; ORANGE = ORIENTAL; LIGHT BLUE = BABY; BROWN = NASAL.

THE BLACK SQUARES ARE ANY NOISES ('UNMUSICAL' USE OF THE VOICE, AUXILIARY PERCUSSION, MECHANICAL OR ELECTRONIC DEVICES). THE ONES CHOSEN BY MISS BERBERIAN IN THE ORDER THEY APPEAR ARE: TSK, TSK; FOOTSTOMP; BIRD ROLL; SNAP, SNAP (FINGERS), CLAP; BARK (DOG); PAINED INHALATION; PEACEFUL EXHALATION; HOOT OF DISDAIN; TONGUE CLICK; EXCLAMATION OF DISGUST; OF ANGER; SCREAM (HAVING SEEN A MOUSE); UGH (AS SUGGESTING AN AMERICAN INDIAN); HA, HA (LAUGHTER); EXPRESSION OF SEXUAL PLEASURE.

THE TEXT EMPLOYS VOWELS AND CONSONANTS AND WORDS FROM 5 LANGUAGES: ARMENIAN, RUSSIAN, ITALIAN, FRENCH, AND ENGLISH.

ALL ASPECTS OF A PERFORMANCE (DYNAMICS, ETC.) WHICH ARE NOT NOTATED MAY BE FREELY DETERMINED BY THE SINGER.

Fig. 24.6 Cage's prefatory statement to *Aria* and a page of the score. Colors used on the page shown are indicated in the key at right. (Copyright © 1960 by Henmar Press, Inc. Sole selling agents C. F. Peters Corporation.)

(*Continued from page 463.*) singing which the singer may choose. Cathy Berberian, for whom *Aria* was written, chose such styles as jazz (dark blue), *Sprechstimme* (black dotted line), and coloratura (yellow) for her interpretation. The score of *Fontana Mix* is also ingeniously indeterminate, consisting of transparent sheets with various lines that look like road maps. These sheets may be superimposed on one another in a number of ways to create ever-changing patterns that suggest various kinds of electronic realization. The variety that is displayed in different recorded performances of this work dramatically illustrates the importance of performer input in Cage's music.

SUMMARY

Music written since World War II has continued and extended many of the trends of the first half of the century, including atonality, serialism, rhythmic complexity, and the use of unconventional sounds. At the same time new schools of thought have

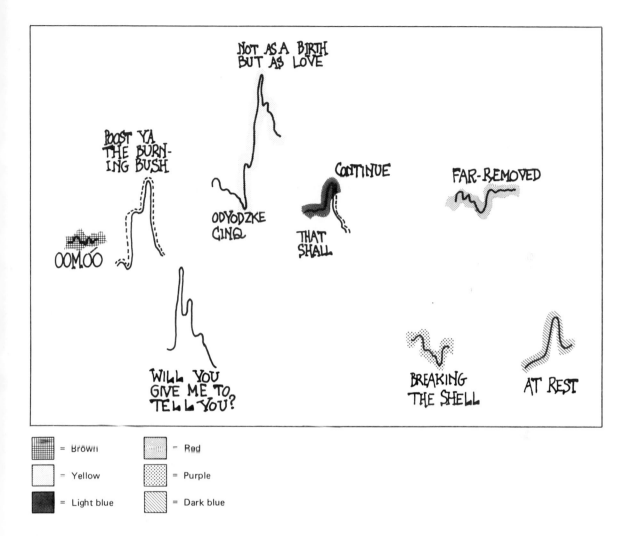

NOT AS A BIRTH BUT AS LOVE

BOOST YA THE BURNING BUSH

CONTINUE

FAR-REMOVED

ODYODZKE CINQ

THAT SHALL

OOMOO

WILL YOU GIVE ME TO TELL YOU?

BREAKING THE SHELL

AT REST

⊞ = Brown		▒ = Red	
☐ = Yellow		⊡ = Purple	
■ = Light blue		⬚ = Dark blue	

emerged which have in some cases radically altered the roles of composer and performer and even challenged accepted notions about the nature of music itself. Two of the most important mid-century developments are total serialism and indeterminacy.

The desire of postwar composers for complete control over every aspect of their music was a significant factor in the emergence of total serialism. Schoenberg had already applied his serial procedures to pitch relationships but had imposed no limitations on rhythm, dynamics, or textures. Webern, on the other hand, extended systems of order beyond the realm of pitch. It was his lean, pointillistic style that became the central interest for young composers. The foremost experimenters with total serialism have been Milton Babbitt, Olivier Messiaen, and his students Pierre Boulez and Karlheinz Stockhausen.

Indeterminant, chance, or aleatory music was developed primarily by John Cage. His goal has been to limit rational control over the outcome of his pieces, allowing unpredictable elements to become part of the musical fabric and encouraging performers of his works to take an active role in the creative process by making decisions on the spur of the moment.

Concurrent with experiments in total serialism and indeterminacy has been the development of electronic music. At first sounds were tape recorded, altered mechanically or electronically, and combined into organized pieces that were known as *musique concrète*. The next step was to use synthesizers which could not only duplicate familiar sounds but also "invent" entirely new sounds. Today computers facilitate the work of composers of electronic music. In concert music electronically generated sounds are often pitted against or combined with live performers.

Another twentieth-century technique, collage, was first employed extensively by Charles Ives. Recently the collage technique has been extended to wholesale quotation of music from the past and present.

While the bulk of twentieth-century music is tonally and rhythmically complex, periodic movements in favor of simplicity have arisen. The recent minimalist movement, for example, seeks to return music to its simplest, most basic elements.

NEW TERMS

total serialism

indeterminacy (chance music, aleatory music)

pointillism

musique concrète

collage

minimalism

PART IX SUGGESTED LISTENING

Babbitt, Milton

Philomel (1963–1964). The text of this work is by poet John Hollander, and is drawn from Greek myth; Babbitt's ingenious setting is scored for live soprano, prerecorded soprano, and synthesized sounds. *Philomel* defies the notion that total serialism produces music that is any less communicative than that produced by other techniques.

Boulez, Pierre

Improvisation sur Mallarmé II, "Une dentelle s'abolit" (A piece of lace disappears, 1958). Boulez incorporated this ten-minute piece, written for soprano and nine keyboard and percussion players, into his large-scale *Pli selon pli* (1957–1962). Both versions illustrate the composer's tempering of pointillism with lacy, bell-like sounds and almost Debussian colors.

Cage, John

Concerto for Prepared Piano and Chamber Orchestra (1951). The delicate percussive sounds of Javanese gamelan music inspired Cage's "preparation" of the piano. Chance operations determined many of the musical events.

Dallapiccola, Luigi

Sicut umbra for mezzosoprano and twelve instruments (1970). A lyric, Italian temperament colors the serial works of this great composer, whose free-sounding rhythms are calculated to avoid a steady beat.

Davidovsky, Mario

Synchronisms No. 6 for piano and electronic sounds (1970). The intimate interaction of the piano soloist and tape part are the brilliant achievement of this Argentinian-born composer, now living in the United States.

Messiaen, Olivier

Turangalîla-Symphonie for piano, ondes Martenot, and orchestra (1946–1948). This immense and extravagant work employs many of the composer's stylistic traits, including sumptuous harmony, personalized uses of serial and ostinato procedures, and bird calls (especially in the sixth movement—"The garden of the sleep of love"). The piano and the electronic instrument known as the ondes Martenot are given featured roles.

Penderecki, Krzysztof

Threnody for the Victims of Hiroshima (1960). Scored for fifty-two strings, this work is a study in experimental string sonorities; the thematic material consists of tone clusters and harmonic overtones combined within an essentially polyphonic structure.

Riley, Terry

In C for any combination of instruments (1964). This attractive example of minimalism is open to performance by almost everyone, for the "score," consisting of small fragments of melody played over and over, is printed right on the record album.

Stockhausen, Karlheinz

Gesang der Jünglinge (*Song of the Youths* 1955–1956). A landmark "electroacoustical" work, combining sung sounds with electronically produced sounds. The sung sounds—though often distorted in various ways—become comprehensible words from time to time. The text is based on the Biblical account of Shadrach, Meshach, and Abednego being cast into the fiery furnace (Daniel 3).

Subotnick, Morton

Silver Apples of the Moon, electronic sounds on tape (1967). One of several albums commissioned specifically for recordings, this work illustrates the composer's rich and colorful palette of electronically produced sounds.

SUGGESTED READING

(An asterisk denotes books published in paperback.)

GENERAL READING LIST

Apel, Willi. *Harvard Dictionary of Music,* 2nd ed. rev. Cambridge, Mass.: Harvard University Press, 1973. A concise historical and bibliographical handbook of terminology, concepts, and essay subjects. Each major entry has a working definition, history, and bibliography. (Nonbiographical)

Apel, Willi, and R. T. Daniel, *The Harvard Brief Dictionary of Music.* Cambridge, Mass.: Harvard University Press, 1970. A succinct version of the *Harvard Dictionary of Music.*

Cannon, Beekman C., Alvin H. Johnson, and William G. Waite. *The Art of Music: A Short History of Musical Styles and Ideas.* New York: Crowell, 1960. A general introduction to the history of music for readers with little musical background.

Crocker, Richard L. *A History of Musical Style.* New York: McGraw-Hill, 1966. Emphasis on the evolution of characteristic musical styles within major historical periods.

*Einstein, Alfred. *A Short History of Music.* New York: Knopf, 1954; New York: Random House, 1954 (paper). One of the best concise histories of music, this work is a nontechnical chronological survey of important composers and musical genres from the Middle Ages through the nineteenth century.

Grout, Donald Jay. *A History of Western Music,* rev. ed. New York: Norton, 1973. An excellent college-level text, with thorough coverage of European music from the end of antiquity through the early twentieth century.

**Grove's Dictionary of Music and Musicians,* 5th ed. (ed. Eric Blom), 10 vols. New York: St. Martin's Press, 1970. An authoritative, comprehensive, and easy-to-use reference work with a British music emphasis. Many biographical and period essays are considered classics.

Kinsky, George. *A History of Music in Pictures.* St. Clair Shores, Mich.: Scholarly Press, 1971. The standard one-volume pictorial history of music, arranged chronologically from antiquity to the early twentieth century.

Lang, Paul Henry. *Music in Western Civilization.* New York: Norton, 1940. A highly influential work which discusses music in the context of political, cultural, and social trends in Western civilization from ancient Greece through the nineteenth century.

*Strunk, Oliver, ed. *Source Readings in Music History,* 5 vols. New York: Norton, 1965. Each volume (Antiquity and Middle Ages, Renaissance, Baroque, Classic, Romantic) collects the writings of theorists, composers, teachers, critics, and musicians arranged in chronological order under topics.

Genres

*Cuyler, Louise Elvira. *The Symphony*. New York: Harcourt Brace Jovanovich, 1973. Traces the two-hundred-year development of the symphony, citing and analyzing the most important, representative compositions from each period by country and composer.

Grout, Donald Jay. *A Short History of Opera*, 2nd ed. New York: Columbia University Press, 1965. The standard English-language history of opera, this book surveys the most significant works and the major developments in operatic style from its beginnings through the early twentieth century.

Hartmann, Rudolph. *Opera*. New York: Morrow, 1977. Beautifully produced book that links photographs of recent celebrated productions and interviews with designers and stage directors.

*Stevens, Denis, ed. *A History of Song*, rev. ed. New York: Norton, 1970. A technical, historical, and geographic survey of secular song in Western countries with criticism and analysis.

Ulrich, Homer. *Chamber Music*. New York: Columbia University Press, 1966. Ulrich defines and analyzes the growth of chamber music to 1930, using the works of Haydn, Mozart, Beethoven, and the Romantics as the core. Contemporary chamber music is also discussed.

PART I: FUNDAMENTALS OF MUSIC

A. GENERAL WORKS

*Cooper, Grosvenor W. *Learning to Listen*. Chicago: University of Chicago Press, 1962. A compact survey of musical elements and concepts, including chapters on rudiments of theory and notation, rhythm, harmony, form, and style.

*Copland, Aaron. *What to Listen for in Music*. New York: New American Library, 1964. A highly useful introductory guide to the elements of music, including chapters on basic structural forms (fugue, variation, sonata-allegro).

*Erikson, Robert. *The Structure of Music: A Listener's Guide*. Westport, Conn.: Greenwood Press, 1977. Explores the nature of harmony, melody, and counterpoint from a nontechnical point of view.

B. MUSICAL INSTRUMENTS AND ORCHESTRATION

*Baines, Anthony, ed. *Musical Instruments through the Ages*. New York: Walker & Co., 1975; Baltimore: Penguin, 1962 (paper). A brief chronological survey of the development of instruments and their performance capabilities.

*Carse, Adam. *The History of Orchestration*. New York: Dover, 1964. A largely nontechnical survey of the orchestra and the art of orchestration from the sixteenth century through the late nineteenth century.

Sachs, Curt. *The History of Musical Instruments*. New York: Norton, 1940. An exhaustive evolutionary survey of instruments by history (from antiquity), period, country, and function.

PART II: THE MUSIC OF WORLD CULTURES

Collaer, Paul, ed. *Music of the Americas: An Illustrated Music Ethnology of the Eskimo and American Indian Peoples*. New York: Praeger, 1971. A survey of the music and instruments of North and South American Indians and Eskimos.

Hofmann, Charles. *American Indians Sing*. New York: The John Day Company, 1967. A study of the thought, religion, and culture of American Indians as revealed through their music, dances, and ceremonies. Well illustrated and very readable.

*Malm, William P. *Music Cultures of the Pacific, the Near East, and Asia*, 2d ed. Englewood Cliffs, N.J.: Prentice-Hall, 1977. Well illustrated with both drawings and musical selections, this volume explores the anthropological, historical, and musical aspects of the subject cultures.

McAllester, David P., ed. *Readings in Ethnomusicology*. New York-London: Johnson Reprint Corp., 1971. A collection of essays on the major emphases in ethnomusicological research including: definition of the field, notation and classification of material, historical interpretations, functional interpretations, and regional studies.

*Nettl, Bruno. *Folk and Traditional Music of the Western Continents*, 2nd ed. Englewood Cliffs, N.J.: Prentice-Hall, 1973. Describes in some detail representative folk music of Europe, America, and Africa south of the Sahara. The more general introductory chapters are especially valuable.

Nettl, Bruno, and Helen Myers. Folk Music in the United States: An Introduction, *3rd ed. Detroit: Wayne State University Press, 1976. An introduction to characteristics of folk music, its history, instruments, and singers.

Warren, Dr. Fred, and Lee Warren. *Music of Africa: An Introduction.* Englewood Cliffs, N.J.: Prentice-Hall, 1970. A lively account of African vocal and instrumental music.

PART III: MEDIEVAL AND RENAISSANCE MUSIC

Dart, Thurston. The Interpretation of Music. *Atlantic Highlands, N.J.: Humanities Press, 1969. New York: Harper & Row, 1963 (paper). A survey of performance practices in early music. Chapters on the Middle Ages and the Renaissance discuss the use of early instruments, methods of performing vocal pieces, and the various religious, ceremonial, and social occasions for which music was composed.

Reese, Gustave. *Music in the Middle Ages.* New York: Norton, 1940. A systematic and exhaustive study of periods and schools of medieval music. A scholarly, lucid, and readable work.

————. *Music in the Renaissance.* New York: Norton, 1959. A meticulous, basic reference work, fully documented with biographies, pictorial illustration, and technical discussion.

Robertson, Alec, and Denis Stevens, eds. The Pelican History of Music, Vol. I: Ancient Forms to Polyphony. *Baltimore: Penguin Books, 1961. A collection of essays on early non-Western and European musical developments up to the fifteenth century. European topics include Gregorian chant, the earliest types of polyphony, and the music of Machaut and his generation.

————. *The Pelican History of Music, Vol. II: Renaissance and Baroque.* Baltimore: Penguin Books, 1964. Also a collection of essays. The Renaissance section emphasizes the place of music in society. The discussion of musical performance in the sixteenth century is excellent.

PART IV: MUSIC OF THE BAROQUE ERA

A. GENERAL WORKS

Bukofzer, Manfred F. *Music in the Baroque Era.* New York: Norton, 1947. A comprehensive history of the important musical developments in the Baroque period.

Jacobs, Arthur, ed. *Choral Music.* Magnolia, Mass.: Peter Smith, 1977. A collection of essays, five of which deal with choral music of the Baroque era.

B. INDIVIDUAL COMPOSERS

Bach

Geiringer, Karl, and Irene Geiringer. *Johann Sebastian Bach: The Culmination of an Era.* New York: Oxford University Press, 1966. The most up-to-date biography in English, incorporating the large amount of new research on Bach done since World War II.

Handel

Dean, Winton. *Handel's Dramatic Oratorios and Masques.* London: Oxford University Press, 1959. A thoroughly researched study of a number of Handel's major vocal works.

Lang, Paul Henry. *Georg Frederic Handel.* New York: Norton, 1966. Emphasizes the social and cultural background of the times and the musical antecedents upon which Handel built.

PART V: MUSIC OF THE CLASSICAL ERA

A. GENERAL WORKS

Blume, Friedrich. Classic and Romantic Music, *trans. by M. D. Herter. New York: Norton, 1970. Blume analyzes the changing use of rhythm, harmony, thematic development, and concept of sound, arguing the issues of absolute vs. program music, and contrasts the nationalism of the Romantic era following Beethoven with the forces behind the Classic era.

Pauly, Reinhard G. Music in the Classic Period, *2nd ed. Englewood Cliffs, N.J.: Prentice-Hall, 1973. A concise survey of the period in two parts, the first tracing the evolution of the Classical style from the Rococo through Haydn and Mozart, the second discussing the principal forms and genres of the period.

B. INDIVIDUAL COMPOSERS

Beethoven

*Grove, George. *Beethoven and His Nine Symphonies.* New York: Dover, 1962. Grove traces Beethoven's musical development, progressing through symphonies and minuets, illuminating them with letters and anecdotes as well as a semi-technical discussion of the music.

*Thayer, Alexander Wheelock. *Life of Beethoven.* Princeton: Princeton University Press, 1970 (paperback); Mattapan, Mass.: Gamut Music, 1966 (hard cover). The standard biography of Beethoven; remarkably comprehensive and detailed.

Haydn

*Geiringer, Karl. *Haydn: A Creative Life in Music.* Berkeley: University of California Press, 1968. An excellent survey covering the composer's life and his works.

Mozart

*Einstein, Alfred. *Mozart: His Character, His Work.* New York: Oxford University Press, 1965. A thoughtful, leisurely study of the composer, his character, musical development, and works.

PART VI: MUSIC OF THE ROMANTIC ERA

A. GENERAL WORKS

*Blume, Friedrich. *Classic and Romantic Music,* trans. by M. D. Herter. New York: Norton, 1970. See annotation under General Works listed for Part V.

Einstein, Alfred. *Music in the Romantic Era.* New York: Norton, 1947. Basic for the student wanting to comprehend the generating and sustaining forces of the Romantic period.

Abraham, Gerald. *Slavonic and Romantic Music.* New York: St. Martin's Press, 1968. A series of essays providing informative data on nationalistic composers.

B. INDIVIDUAL COMPOSERS

Berlioz

*Berlioz, Hector. *Evenings with the Orchestra,* trans. by Jacques Barzun. Chicago: University of Chicago Press, 1973. Thoughts on contemporaneous musical ephemera. Delightful to read.

————. *Memoirs,* new edition (edited and translated by David Cairns). New York: Norton, 1975. Cairns's impeccable scholarship provides a contemporary description through footnotes and appendixes, enhancing the memoirs. Includes a glossary of personalities, source list, and bibliography.

Brahms

James, Burnett. *Brahms: A Critical Study.* New York: Praeger, 1972. A standard biography, assessing Brahms's artistic achievements and emphasizing his progressive tendencies and influence on Schoenberg, Webern, and Sibelius.

Chopin

Melville, Derek. *Chopin: A Biography, with a Survey of Books, Editions, and Recordings.* Hamden, Conn.: Shoe String, 1977. A concise biography tracing Chopin's musical development and works.

Dvořák

Clapham, John. *Antonín Dvořák, Musician and Craftsman.* New York: St. Martin's Press, 1966. A scholarly, comprehensive survey using Czech material, previously unpublished, for a close analysis of Dvořák's craft of composition. Includes biographical text, illustrations, and musical examples.

Liszt

Pereyni, Eleanor. *Liszt: The Artist as Romantic Hero.* New York: Little, Brown, 1974. A psychological exploration of Liszt in the framework of the Romantic movement, probing the literary, musical, and social influences on Liszt's symphonic poems. Illustrated with comprehensive chronology.

Mendelssohn

Werner, Eric. *Mendelssohn: A New Image of the Composer and His Age.* Glencoe: The Free Press,

1963. The comprehensive biography of Mendelssohn, containing many excerpts from the composer's correspondence not commonly available.

Mussorgsky

Calvocoressi, Michel Dimitri. *Mussorgsky.* New York: Collier, 1962. A definitive study tracing all major works and many lesser compositions, describing and analyzing them in nontechnical language against the cultural background and musical climate of the age. A chapter on technique and style is included.

Schubert

*****Einstein, Alfred.** *Schubert: A Musical Portrait.* New York: Vienna House, 1976. Einstein follows Schubert's creative development year by year, with a semitechnical analysis of the music.

Schumann

Schumann, Robert. *On Music and Musicians.* Boston: Longwood Press, 1977. A lively collection of articles from Schumann's musical review, *Neue Zeitschrift für Musik,* these often humorous pieces discuss the merits of Beethoven, Bach, Schubert, etc., offer advice to composers and maxims for young musicians.

Tchaikovsky

*****Abraham, Gerald, ed.** *The Music of Tchaikovsky.* New York: Norton, 1974. Eminent music critics analyze the music by genre: chamber music, symphonies, songs, ballets, etc. With a chronology and musical examples.

*****Osborne, Charles.** *The Complete Operas of Verdi.* New York: Knopf, 1970; New York: DaCapo, 1977 (paper). Lively prose and fine scholarship illuminate this discussion of Verdi's twenty-six operas, the Requiem, and other musical pieces, each given a literary and historical background to complement a play-by-play synopsis and nontechnical discussion of the music.

Wagner

*****Gutman, Robert.** *Richard Wagner: The Man, His Mind, and His Music.* New York: Harcourt Brace Jovanovich, 1974. This provocative, nontechnical biography examines the nationalism and racism from which Wagner drew his most powerful symbols.

PART VII: MUSIC OF THE EARLY TWENTIETH CENTURY

A. GENERAL WORKS

Austin, William. *Music in the 20th Century: From Debussy through Stravinsky.* New York: Norton, 1966. A detailed survey of modern music that is an essential reference source for comprehending the forces affecting it.

*****Salzman, Eric.** *Twentieth-Century Music: An Introduction,* 2nd ed. Englewood Cliffs, N.J.: Prentice-Hall, 1974. A comprehensive survey of contemporary music.

B. INDIVIDUAL COMPOSERS

Bartók

*****Stevens, Halsey.** *The Life and Music of Béla Bartók.* rev. ed. New York: Oxford University Press, 1967. This most important work on Bartók in English is divided into two sections: a biographical study and a categorized, subjective analysis of his music.

Berg

*****Reich, Willi.** *Alban Berg,* trans. by Cornelius Cardew. New York: Vienna House, 1974. An informative study of the life and works of Berg.

Debussy

Debussy, Claude. *Debussy on Music.* Collected and introduced by François Lesure; translated and edited by Richard Langham Smith. New York: Knopf, 1977. A comprehensive collection of Debussy's lively musical criticism and interviews (written under the pseudonym M. Croche) liberally laced with annotations and anecdotes by Smith.

Hindemith

*****Kemp, Ian.** *Hindemith.* New York: Oxford University Press, 1970. Concentrating on Hindemith's creative achievements, Kemp lucidly charts the main stages of stylistic progress, choosing representative works, movements, and quoted excerpts.

Schoenberg

*****Rosen, Charles.** *Arnold Schoenberg.* New York: Viking, 1975; New York: Penguin, 1975 (paper). This study of stylistic phases (essentially nonbiographical) elucidates Schoenberg's composing technique and artistic philosophy through an exposition of musical ideas.

Schoenberg, Arnold. *Letters,* ed. by E. Stein and E. Kaiser. New York: St. Martin's Press, 1965. Schoenberg discusses art, his works, friends, and events in this selection of letters which shape a vivid portrait of artistic development. Extensively footnoted.

Stravinsky

*****Lang, Paul Henry, ed.** *Stravinsky: A New Appraisal of His Work.* New York: Norton, 1963. A group of essays by accepted authorities on twentieth-century music. Positive criticism of Stravinsky's music, describing effects of his music on modern compositional styles.

Webern

Kolneder, Walter. *Anton Webern: An Introduction to His Works.* Berkeley: University of California Press, 1968. Based on university lectures and radio talks by the author, this study stresses the importance of Webern's stylistic origins and traditional roots to an understanding of his subsequent development.

PART VIII: MUSIC IN AMERICA

A. GENERAL WORKS

*****Amram, David.** *Vibrations: The Adventures and Musical Times of David Amram.* New York: Penguin, 1971. A composer and musicologist of wide-ranging interests, the author explores, through personal reminiscence, the meeting between jazz, street music, rock, and classical music to produce a form unique to the 1960s and '70s.

Chase, Gilbert, ed. *America's Music: From the Pilgrims to the Present,* rev. ed. New York: McGraw-Hill, 1966. A comprehensive survey of American music from colonial times through the 1960s. Of particular interest is the final chapter, "The Scene in the Sixties."

*****Copland, Aaron.** *The New Music: 1900–1960.* New York: Norton, 1968. A collection of essays on important stylistic trends and composers in Europe and America. The American section includes chapters on Ives, Harris, and Thomson.

Hitchcock, F. Wiley, ed. *Music in the United States: A Historical Introduction,* 2nd ed. Englewood Cliffs, N.J.: Prentice-Hall, 1974. An excellent and concise survey of American music. Particularly fine are the chapters on nineteenth-century popular music and Charles Ives.

Lowens, Irving. *Music and Musicians in Early America.* New York: Norton, 1964. A delightfully written collection of short studies concentrating on the colonial and Federalist periods.

Machlis, Joseph. *American Composers of Our Time.* New York: Crowell, 1963. Short, interesting vignettes on the lives and musical activities of sixteen American composers ranging from Edward MacDowell to Lukas Foss.

Southern, Eileen. *The Music of Black Americans.* New York: Norton, 1970. A lengthy survey of folksongs, popular vocal and dance music, religious, theatrical, and concert music against the context of social and political development, with analyses of characteristic musical forms and a discography.

B. JAZZ AND ROCK

Feather, Leonard. *The Encyclopedia of Jazz,* rev. ed. New York: Horizon, 1960. Feather's widely praised work has two thousand biographies, recommended records and essay articles ("Anatomy of Jazz," "Guide to Jazz History," "Jazz and Classical Music"), as well as photographs and technical definitions.

*****Garland, Phyl.** *The Sound of Soul: The History of Black Music.* New York: Contemporary Books, 1969. A detailed, sensitive study of the roots and forms of black music in America. A masterfully stated discussion of the music of the early years serves as a prelude to a more extended treatment of the major "soul" singers of recent years.

*****Jones, Leroi.** *Blues People.* New York: Morrow, 1971. Jones places the entire continuum of black music in the context of cultural history, following changes in musical style by social and economic events. An excellent and intriguing thesis.

Morgenstern, Dan. *Jazz People.* New York: Abrams, 1976. Combines an excellent tracing of the origins and subsequent history of jazz with a number of finely etched personality profiles. Includes graceful and insinuating photographs by Ole Brask.

————. *Rolling Stone Illustrated History of Rock and Roll.* Rolling Stone Press, New York: Random House, 1976. A critical history, bringing together the work of the finest rock writers in a pictorial record of the history of rock 'n' roll, soul, and rock and blues. Unique photos and discographies.

*Shapiro, Nat, and Nat Hentoff, eds. *Hear Me Talkin' to Ya.* New York: Dover, 1966. A collection of first-person reminiscences by many major figures from the richest years of jazz history.

*Williams, Martin. *The Jazz Tradition.* New York: Mentor, 1971. A clear and vivid narrative of developments in jazz from the early 1920s through the 1960s, with discussions of leading jazz figures from "Jelly Roll" Morton through Ornette Coleman.

C. INDIVIDUAL COMPOSERS

Copland

Dobrin, Arnold. *Aaron Copland: His Life and Times.* New York: Crowell, 1967. A short biographical sketch, including general discussion of the composer's ideas and musical activities.

Gershwin

Jablonski, Edward, and Lawrence Stewart. *The Gershwin Years.* New York: Doubleday, 1973. A pictorial biography of the composer-lyricist brother team of George and Ira Gershwin with critical bibliography, Gershwin compositions, discography, and performance notes.

Ives

*Cowell, Henry, and Sidney Cowell. *Charles Ives and His Music.* New York: Oxford University Press, 1969. A biography of Ives written by two close friends of the composer. Approximately half of the book is devoted to a study of Ives's musical style and major works with many quotations from the composer that are not found elsewhere.

*Perlis, Vivian. *Charles Ives Remembered: An Oral History.* New Haven: Yale University Press, 1974 (hard cover); New York: Norton, 1976 (paper). An illustrated oral biography of fifty-eight interviews with friends and musicians, with Ives's music discussed both anecdotally and analytically.

PART IX: MUSIC OF THE LATE TWENTIETH CENTURY

A. PERIODICAL LITERATURE

The most important source of information on contemporary music is periodical literature. Significant periodicals devoted to contemporary and avant-garde compositions are *Perspectives of New Music* (published by Princeton University Press) and *Die Reihe* ("The Row," a German periodical published in translation by Theodore Presser Company), *The Score* (London), the *Journal of Music Theory* (New Haven), and the *Music Quarterly* (New York).

Babbitt, Milton. "Who Cares if You Listen?" *High Fidelity,* Vol. VIII, No. 2 (February, 1958). A personal and unusual statement by one of America's most influential composers defending his concepts of an esoteric and "cerebral" style of composition.

B. GENERAL WORKS

*Lang, Paul Henry, and Nathan Broder, eds. *Contemporary Music in Europe: A Comprehensive Survey.* New York: Norton, 1965; 1968 (paper). This group of essays discusses postwar musical trends in each of the major European countries.

*Salzman, Eric. *Twentieth Century Music: An Introduction.* Englewood Cliffs, N.J.: Prentice-Hall, 1967. This excellent and concise survey includes valuable chapters on avant-garde music through the early 1960s.

C. INDIVIDUAL COMPOSERS

Boulez

Peyser, Joan. *Pierre Boulez.* New York: Schirmer Books, 1976. A chatty, controversial profile of the avant-garde composer, populated with famous friends and artistic figures, and enlivened by accounts of clashes of will and infighting.

Cage

*Cage, John. *Silence.* Middletown, Conn.: Wesleyan Press, 1961. A collection of writings on experimental music, techniques of composition, and other miscellaneous topics. An invaluable source for the author's ideas on chance music.

SOURCE ACKNOWLEDGMENTS

Excerpts from the works listed below are reproduced by permission of the publishers, whose cooperation is gratefully acknowledged.

Claude Debussy: *Prélude à l'après-midi d'un faune,* by permission of C. F. Peters Corporation, New York.

Igor Stravinsky: *The Rite of Spring,* by permission of Boosey & Hawkes, Inc. (Copyright 1921 by Edition Russe de Musique. Copyright assigned 1947 to Boosey & Hawkes, Inc.)

Igor Stravinsky: *Symphony of Psalms,* by permission of Boosey & Hawkes, Inc. (Copyright 1931 by Edition Russe de Musique. Renewed 1958. Copyright and renewal assigned to Boosey & Hawkes, Inc. Revised Edition Copyright 1948 by Boosey & Hawkes, Inc.)

Béla Bartók: *Music for Strings, Percussion, and Celesta,* by permission of Boosey & Hawkes, Inc. (Copyright 1937 by Universal Edition. Renewed 1964. Copyright and renewal assigned to Boosey & Hawkes, Inc. for the U.S.A.)

Benjamin Britten: *A Ceremony of Carols,* by permission of Boosey & Hawkes, Inc. (Copyright 1943 by Boosey & Co., Ltd. Renewed 1970.)

Arnold Schoenberg: *Variations for Orchestra,* by permission of Belmont Music Publishers, Los Angeles, California 90049.

Arnold Schoenberg: *A Survivor from Warsaw,* by permission of Boelke-Bomart, Inc., Hillsdale, New York 12529.

Anton Webern: *Symphonie,* Opus 21, by permission of European American Music Distributors Corporation. (Copyright 1929 by Universal Edition. Renewed 1956. All rights for the U.S.A. and Canada controlled exclusively by European American Music Distributors Corporation.)

Charles Ives: Second Piano Sonata, by permission of Associated Music Publishers Inc., New York. (Copyright © 1947 by Associated Music Publishers, Inc.)

Aaron Copland, *Appalachian Spring,* by permission of Aaron Copland, copyright owner, and Boosey & Hawkes, Inc., sole publishers and licensees. (Copyright 1945 by Aaron Copland, renewed 1972.)

Elliott Carter: *Brass Quintet,* by permission of Associated Music Publishers, Inc., New York. (Copyright © 1976 by Associated Music Publishers, Inc.)

George Crumb: *Vox Balaenae,* by permission of C. F. Peters Corporation, New York. (Copyright © 1972 by C. F. Peters Corporation.)

Jacob Druckman: *Windows,* by permission of MCA Music, a division of MCA Inc., New York. (Copyright © 1974 by MCA Music. All rights reserved.)

John Cage: *Aria,* by permission of C. F. Peters Corporation, New York. (Copyright © 1960 by Henmar Press, Inc. Sole selling agents C. F. Peters Corporation.)

Other illustrative materials were supplied by a large number of individuals and institutions. The sources for quotations, cartoons, and photographs of art objects are in general given on the page where the material appears. In addition, credit is due to the following for photographs used on the pages listed.

Facing page 1, Harbutt/Magnum
33 (left), Janet Knott/Boston Globe Library

33 (right), United Press International
34 (left), copyright © 1975 Stephen J. Sherman
34 (right), David Ryan/Boston Globe Library
36 (top left), James Holland/Stock Boston
36 (top right), Owen Franken/Stock Boston
36 (bottom), C. Manos/Magnum
38 (top left), Christa Armstrong/Photo Researchers
38 (top right), copyright © 1976 Stephen J. Sherman
38 (bottom left), Bill Curtis/Boston Globe Library
38 (bottom right) copyright © 1978 Michael Philip Manheim
40, Ludwig Industries
41 (left), Baldwin Piano and Organ Co.
41 (right), Susan E. Meyer
42, Wide World Photos
44 (top), Peter Schaaf
44 (bottom), copyright © 1978 Christopher R. Harris
47, Richard Braaten
50, The Peabody Museum, Harvard University, photo by Hillel Burger
57, Rapho/Photo Researchers
58, Jan Lukas/Photo Researchers
64, Hewett, UNICEF/SYGMA
66 (top), Marc and Evelyne Bernheim/Woodfin Camp
66 (bottom), The Peabody Museum, Harvard University, photo by Hillel Burger
67, Marc and Evelyne Bernheim/Woodfin Camp
68, The Peabody Museum, Harvard University, photo by Hillel Burger
74, Historical Pictures Service
78, Boston Globe Library
83, Culver Pictures, Inc.
100, Scala/Editorial Photocolor Archives
106, by permission of the British Library
114, Historical Pictures Service
132, Ulrike Welsch/Boston Globe Library
139, The Bettmann Archive
142, Historical Pictures Service
143, The Bettmann Archive
156, The British Museum, London
163, 173, Historical Pictures Service
174, The Bettmann Archive
189, copyright © Beth Bergman
202, Historical Pictures Service
204, The Bettmann Archive
222, Historical Pictures Service
223, 227, 232, 235, The Bettmann Archive
242, 245, Historical Pictures Service
247, 250, The Bettmann Archive
253, 259, Historical Pictures Service
273, The Bettmann Archive
274, Martha Swope
279, The Bettmann Archive
281, Snark/Editorial Photocolor Archives
285, 293, The Bettmann Archive
306, Historical Pictures Service
308, copyright © 1978 Beth Bergman
312, Historical Pictures Service
313, copyright © 1977 G. C. Izenour Archive
316, Historical Pictures Service
322, André Meyer Collection, Paris, © S.P.A.D.E.M. 1978
326, from F. Lesure, *Debussy on Music* (Alfred A. Knopf)
346, Albright-Knox Art Gallery, Buffalo, N. Y., Fellows for Life of 1926 Fund
347, 355, Historical Pictures Service
360, 362, The Bettmann Archive
366, Belmont Music Publishers
374, The Bettmann Archive
380, Lee Friedlander
384, Historical Pictures Service
386, 389, The Bettmann Archive
395, Martha Swope
396, Eugene Cook
410, Lloyd Eldon Saunders, The University of Chicago
412, Associated Music Publishers, Inc.
413, C. F. Peters Corporation
419, Fred Lyon/Photo Researchers
421, Terry Waldo, courtesy of Hawthorne Books
424, Dain/Magnum
428, Bob Parent
431, 432, copyright © 1976 by Stephen J. Sherman
436, Brown Brothers
439, Editorial Photocolor Archives
441, Waring Abbott/SYGMA
443, The Bettmann Archive
453, Newsweek/Robert McElroy
454, Gerhard Gscheidle/Magnum
456, Rhoda Nathans, courtesy of Artservices
458, courtesy of Milton Babbitt, Princeton University
459, Vernon L. Smith/Scope Associates

GLOSSARY

A Cappella Designating choral music without instrumental accompaniment.

Absolute Music Music that is entirely free of extramusical references or ideas.

Accompanied Recitative A type of recitative in which the voice is accompanied by instruments in addition to continuo.

Alternation A principle for building musical form in which a main section (A) alternates with contrasting sections (B, C, D, etc.). Ternary form (ABA) is a simple example.

Answer In a fugue, the restatement of the subject by a new voice part in the key of the dominant.

Aria A composition for solo voice and instrumental accompaniment.

Arioso A vocal style that is midway between recitative and aria. Its meter is less flexible than that of recitative, but its form is much simpler and more flexible than that of the aria.

Arpeggio (ar-pej'-ee-oh) A chord whose tones are played one after another in rapid succession rather than simultaneously.

Art Song A musical setting of a poem for solo voice and piano. The German words *lied* (song) and *lieder* (plural) became the standard terms for this type of song.

Atonal Lacking a recognizable tonal center or tonic.

Augmentation A rhythmic variation in which the original note values of a theme are increased.

Ballad (Vocal) A narrative poem set to music.

Ballade (Instrumental) A relatively large, free-form instrumental work. The term was apparently used first by Chopin.

Barline The vertical line which separates the notes in one measure from those in the next.

Basso Continuo, Continuo Continuous bass. A bass part performed by (1) a keyboard player who improvises harmony above the given bass notes, and (2) a string player—usually cello or viola da gamba—who reinforces the bass line.

Basso Ostinato A short melodic phrase that is repeated continually as a bass line, above which one or more voices have contrasting material.

Battery The percussion section of an orchestra.

Bebop (Bop) A jazz style which emphasizes small ensembles, harmonic innovation, unusual chord structures, an implicit beat, and a "hard" sound.

Bel Canto "Beautiful song." A vocal technique emphasizing beauty and purity of tone and agility in executing various ornamental details.

Binary Form A basic musical form consisting of two contrasting sections (A B), both sections often being repeated (A A B B); the two sections are in related keys.

Blue Note In blues and jazz music, any of the notes produced by flatting the third, fifth, or seventh notes of a major scale.

Blues A lamenting, melancholy song characterized by a three-line lyrical pattern in AAB form, a twelve-bar harmonic progression, and the continual use of "blue notes."

Boogie-Woogie A blues piano style which uses a rhythmic ostinato bass in the left hand while the right hand plays a simple, often improvised melody.

Bridge In a musical composition, a section that connects two themes.

Cadence A point of rest at the end of a passage, section, or complete work that gives the music a sense of convincing conclusion. Also, a melodic or harmonic progression that gives the feeling of conclusion.

Cadenza A section of music, usually in a concerto, played in an improvisatory style by a solo performer without orchestral accompaniment.

Call and Response A song style found in many West African cultures (and black American folk music) in which phrases sung by a leader alternate with responding phrases sung by a chorus.

Canon A contrapuntal technique in which a melody in one part is strictly imitated by another voice or voices.

Cantata A choral work, usually on a sacred subject and frequently built upon a chorale tune, combining aria, recitative, chorus, and instrumental accompaniment.

Chaconne (sha-konh') A keyboard form popular in the Baroque period that employed given melodic material and made use of basso ostinato. Similar to passacaglia.

Chamber Music Music written for a small group of instruments, with one player to a part.

Chanson (shahn-son') French for "song." A type of Renaissance secular vocal music.

Character Piece A work portraying a single mood, emotion, or idea.

Chorale A German hymn, often used as a unifying theme for a cantata.

Chord A combination of three or more tones sounded simultaneously. See also *arpeggio*.

Chorus, Choir A vocal ensemble consisting of several voice parts with four or five or more singers in each section. Also, a section of the orchestra comprising certain types of instruments, such as a *brass choir*.

Chromatic Designating melodic movement by half steps.

Chromatic Scale The scale containing all twelve tones within the interval of an octave.

Church Modes A system of eight scales forming the tonal foundation for Gregorian chant and for polyphony up to the Baroque era.

Clef Sign A sign placed at the beginning of a staff to indicate the exact pitch of the notes.

Coda The concluding section of a musical work or individual movement, often leading to a final climax and coupled with an increase in tempo.

Collage The technique of juxtaposing independent musical styles or apparently unrelated sound sources within a composition.

Concert Overture A one-movement self-contained orchestral concert piece, often in sonata-allegro form.

Concerto A work for one or more solo instruments and orchestra.

Concerto Grosso A multimovement work for instruments in which a solo group called the *concertino* and a full ensemble called the *ripieno* are pitted against each other.

Consonance A quality of an interval, chord, or harmony that imparts a sense of stability, repose, or finality.

Continuo See *basso continuo*.

Cool Jazz A restrained, controlled jazz style that developed during the 1950s.

Counterpoint A musical texture consisting of two or more equal and independent melodic lines sounding simultaneously. See also *polyphony*.

Countersubject In a fugue, new melodic material stated in counterpoint with the subject.

Country and Western A form of white popular music derived from the English/Scottish folk tradition of the Appalachian region and from cowboy ballads.

Cyclical Treatment A unifying technique of long musical works in which the same thematic material recurs in succeeding movements.

Da Capo "From the beginning." Indicates that a piece is to be repeated in its entirety or to a point marked *fine* ("end").

Development In a general sense, the elaboration of musical material through various procedures.

Diminution A rhythmic variation in which the original note values of a theme are shortened.

Dissonance A quality of an interval, chord, or harmony that gives a sense of tension and movement.

Dodecaphony See *twelve-tone technique.*

Dominant The fifth note of a given scale or the chord built upon it (dominant chord); it is the note that most actively "seeks" or creates the expectation of the tonic note.

Drone A stationary tone or tones of constant pitch played throughout a piece or section of a piece.

Dynamics Degrees of loudness or softness.

Edge-Blown Describing a woodwind technique in which the player funnels a narrow stream of air to the opposite edge of the mouth hole.

End-Blown Describing a woodwind technique in which the air is blown into a mouthpiece.

Episode In a fugue, a transitional passage based on material derived from the subject or based on new material, leading to a new statement of the subject.

Equal Temperament A method of tuning instruments so that all half steps within an octave are exactly the same size.

Étude A study piece for piano concentrating on a single technical problem.

Exposition The first section in sonata-allegro form, containing the statement of the principal themes. Also, the first section in a fugue, in which the principal theme or subject is presented imitatively.

Expressionism An artistic school of the early twentieth century which attempted to represent the psychological and emotional experience of modern humanity.

Fantasia An improvised keyboard piece characterized by virtuosity in composition and performance; popular during the Baroque era. Also, a virtuoso piece for lute; popular during the Renaissance.

Fermata (⌢) A notational symbol which indicates that a note is to be sounded longer than its normal time value; the exact length being left to the discretion of the performer.

Figured Bass, Thorough Bass A shorthand method of notating an accompanimental part. Numbers are placed under the bass notes to indicate the intervals to be sounded above the bass notes. See also *basso continuo.*

Flat (♭) A notational sign indicating that a pitch is to be lowered by a half step.

Form The aspect of music involving the overall structuring and organization of music.

French Overture A style characteristic of the first movement of a Baroque suite, in which a slow, stately section with dotted rhythms is followed by a brisk, fast section.

Frequency The rate at which a sounding body vibrates, determining the pitch of a musical sound.

Front Line In jazz bands, the instruments that carry the melodic material.

Fugue A type of imitative polyphony based on the development of a single theme or subject.

Grand Opera A type of Romantic opera which concentrated on the spectacular elements of the production.

Gregorian Chant The music that accompanies the Roman Catholic Liturgy, consisting of monophonic, single-line melodies sung without instrumental accompaniment.

Half Step, Semitone One half of a whole step; the smallest interval in traditional Western music.

Harmonic Progression A series of harmonies.

Harmony A composite sound made up of two or more tones of different pitch that sound simultaneously.

Heterophony Performance of a single melody by two or more individuals who add their own rhythmic or melodic modifications.

Homophony A musical texture in which one voice predominates melodically, the other parts blending into an accompaniment providing harmonic support.

Idée fixe (ee-day feeks') A single, recurring motive; e.g., in Berlioz's *Symphony fantastique,* a musical idea representing the hero's beloved that recurs throughout the piece.

Imitation The repetition, in close succession, of a melody by another voice or voices within a contrapuntal texture.

Impressionism A late nineteenth-century artistic movement which sought to capture the visual impression rather than the literal reality of a subject. Also, in music, a style belonging primarily to Claude Debussy, characterized by an emphasis on mood and atmosphere, sensuous tone colors, elegance and beauty of sound.

Improvisation The practice of "making up" music and performing it on the spot without first having written it down.

Incidental Music Music written to accompany a play.

Indeterminacy, Aleatory, or Chance Music Music in which the composer sets out to remove the decision-making process from his or her own control. Chance operations such as throwing dice are employed to obtain a random series of musical events.

Interval The distance in pitch between any two tones.

Inversion Modification of a theme by reversing the direction of the intervals, with ascending intervals replaced by descending intervals and vice versa.

Key Tonality; the relationship of tones to a central tone, the tonic.

Key Signature The group of sharps or flats placed at the beginning of each staff to indicate which notes are to be raised or lowered a half step. The particular combination of sharps or flats indicates the key of a composition.

Ledger Lines Short horizontal lines added above or below the staff to indicate notes that are too high or too low to be placed within the staff.

Legato (le-ga′-toh) "Linked, tied." Indicating a smooth, even style of performance, with each note connected to the next.

Leitmotiv (lite-mo-teef′) "Leading motive." A musical motive representing a particular character, object, idea, or emotional state. Used especially in Wagner's operas.

Libretto The text of an opera or similar extended dramatic musical work.

Lied, Lieder (leet′; lead′-er) "Song." See *art song*.

Lyric Opera A type of French Romantic opera that relied on beautiful melodies for its effect.

Madrigal A polyphonic vocal piece set to a short poem; it originated during the Renaissance.

Major Scale A scale having a pattern of whole and half steps, with the half steps falling between the third and fourth and between the seventh and eighth tones of the scale.

Mazurka In Romantic music, a small piano piece based on the Polish dance form. Prominent in the works of Chopin.

Measure A unit of time organization consisting of a fixed number of beats. Measures are separated from one another by vertical barlines on the staff.

Measured Rhythm Regulated rhythm in which precise time values are related to each other.

Melismatic Designating a melodic phrase in which one syllable of text is spread over several notes.

Melody A basic musical element consisting of a series of pitches of particular duration that sound one after another.

Meter The organization of rhythmic pulses or beats into equal, recurring groups.

Metronome A mechanical device used to set the exact tempo of a musical work.

Microtone An interval smaller than a half step.

Minimalism A late twentieth-century movement which seeks to return music to its simplest, most basic elements.

Minor Scale A scale having a pattern of whole and half steps, with the half steps falling between the second and third and between the sixth and seventh tones of the scale.

Minuet and Trio A form employed in the third movement of Classical symphonies, cast in a stately triple meter and ternary form (ABA).

Modulation Gradual or rapid change from one key to another within a composition.

Monodic Style Designates a type of accompanied solo song that evolved in Italy around 1600 in reaction to the complex polyphonic style of the late Renaissance. Its principal characteristics are (1) a recitativelike vocal line, (2) an arioso with basso continuo accompaniment.

Monophony A musical texture consisting of a single melodic line without accompanying material, as in Gregorian chant.

Motet A polyphonic choral work set to a sacred text.

Motive A short melodic or rhythmic figure that reappears frequently throughout a work or section of a work as a unifying device.

Movement An independent section of a longer composition.

Musique Concrète "Concrete music." A musical style originating in France about 1948; its technique consists of recording natural or "concrete" sounds, altering the sounds by various electronic means, and then combining them into organized pieces.

Natural (♮) A notational symbol indicating that a pitch that has been sharped or flatted is to be restored to its basic pitch.

Neoclassicism In music of the early twentieth century, the philosophy that musical composition should be approached with objectivity and restraint. Neoclassical composers were attracted to the textures and forms of the Baroque and Classical periods.

Nocturne "Night piece." A character piece for piano, of melancholy moods, with expressive melodies sounding over an arpeggiated accompaniment.

Octave An interval between two pitches in which the higher pitch vibrates at twice the frequency of the lower. When sounded simultaneously, the two pitches sound very much alike.

Opera A drama set to music and made up of vocal pieces such as recitatives, arias, duets, trios, and ensembles with orchestral accompaniment, and orchestral overtures and interludes. Scenery, stage action, and costuming are employed.

Opéra Comique (Comic Opera) A type of French Romantic opera distinguished by its use of spoken dialogue rather than sung recitative. Many operas in this form had serious plots.

Oratorio An extended choral work made up of recitatives, arias, and choruses, *without* customing, stage action, or scenery.

Orchestration The arrangement of a musical composition for performance by an orchestra. Also, utilization of orchestral instruments for expressive and structural purposes.

Organum The earliest type of medieval polyphonic music.

Ostinato (ohs-tih-nah′-toh) A musical phrase repeated persistently at the same pitch.

Overture The orchestral introduction to a musical dramatic work.

Passacaglia (pah-sah-kahl′-ya) A keyboard form popular in the Baroque period that employed a basso ostinato of four to eight measures. Similar to chaconne.

Pedal Point A long-held tone, usually in the bass, sounding through changing harmonies in other parts.

Pentatonic Scale A five-tone scale. Various pentatonic scales are commonly employed in non-Western music.

Phrase A musical unit consisting of several measures.

Pitch The highness or lowness of a musical tone, determined by the frequency of vibration of the sounding body.

Pizzicato (pit-see-kah′-toh) A performance technique in which stringed instruments such as the violin are plucked with the fingers instead of bowed.

Plainsong, Plainchant See *Gregorian chant*.

Pointillism A term borrowed from the visual arts and used to describe a melodic line made from isolated tones or chords.

Polonaise In Romantic music, a small piano piece based on the Polish dance form.

Polyphony Many voices. A texture combining two or more independent melodies heard simultaneously; generally synonymous with counterpoint.

Polyrhythm Two or more contrasting and independent rhythms used at the same time.

Prelude A free-form piece that may introduce another piece or stand alone.

Primitivism In music, the use of frenzied, irregular rhythms and percussive effects to evoke a feeling of primitive power, as in Stravinsky's *The Rite of Spring*.

Program Music Instrumental music associated with a nonmusical idea, this idea often being stated in the title or in an explanatory program note.

Raga One of the ancient melodic patterns employed in Indian music.

Ragtime A composed music of the 1890s, usually for piano, characterized by steady, marchlike accompaniment in the left hand and a decorated, syncopated melody in the right hand.

Recapitulation The third section of sonata-allegro form, which restates the entire exposition in the tonic key.

Recitative (res-see-tah-teev′) A form of "singing speech" in which the rhythm is dictated by the natural inflection of the words.

Rest A notational sign denoting the duration of silence.

Rhythm The element of music that encompasses all aspects of musical time.

Rhythm and Blues A form of black popular music which blends elements of jazz and the blues.

Rhythm Section In jazz bands, the instruments that supply the harmonic and rhythmic accompaniment.

Ricercar (ree-chayr-kahr′) A type of Renaissance lute music, often polyphonic, that demonstrated the virtuosity of the performer.

Riff A short melodic line, usually rhythmic, which can be repeated over and over to form either the main melody or the background for improvised solos.

Ritornello (ree-tor-nel′-lo) "Return." A characteristic form for the first and sometimes the last movement of the Baroque concerto grosso. The thematic material given to the ripieno returns between the passages played by the soloists.

Rock 'n' Roll (Rock) Popular music characterized by a heavy beat, electronically amplified instruments, simple melodies, and often using elements from country music and the blues.

Roll A sound produced by rapid strokes of drumsticks on a drumhead.

Rondo An extended alternating form often employed in the fourth movement of Classical symphonies; generally spirited and playful in character.

Root The bottom tone of any triad.

Rubato (roo-bah′-toh) "Robbed." A term indicating that a performer may treat the tempo with a certain amount of freedom, shortening the duration of some beats and correspondingly lengthening others.

Scale The arrangement of adjacent tones in an order of ascending or descending pitches.

Scherzo (skehr′-tso) "Joke." A sprightly, humorous instrumental piece, swift in tempo; developed by Beethoven to replace the minuet.

Secco Recitative (sek′-ko res-see-tah-teev′) A recitative with only continuo accompaniment.

Sharp (♯) A notational sign indicating that a pitch is to be raised by a half step.

Singspiel (zing′-shpeel) German comic opera that employed spoken dialogue.

Solo Concerto A multimovement Baroque work differing from concerto grosso in that the concer-

tino consists of only one instrument (most often the violin or piano).

Sonata An instrumental work consisting of three or four contrasting movements.

Sonata-Allegro Form A musical form encompassing one movement of a composition and consisting of three sections—exposition, development, and recapitulation—the last often followed by a coda.

Song Cycle A series of art songs that tell a story.

Soul A spirited, raw-edged form of rock music that features wailing vocals and hard-driving rhythm and brass sections.

Sprechstimme (shprek′-shtim-meh) "Speech voice." A vocal technique in which a pitch is half sung, half spoken. Developed by Arnold Schoenberg.

Staccato (sta-kah′-to) "Detached." Indicating a style of performance in which each note is played in a short, crisp manner.

Staff A graph, consisting of five lines and four intermediate spaces, on which music is notated.

Stopping Changing the pitch of, for example, a violin string by pressing the string against the fingerboard.

Stretto A type of imitation in which each successive voice enters before the phrase is completed in the previous voice; usually employed in fugues or fugal textures.

Stride A jazz piano style in which the left hand alternates between a bass note and a chord played an octave or more above the bass, giving the effect of "striding" back and forth, while the right hand plays the melody.

String Quartet A chamber ensemble consisting of a first and a second violin, a viola, and a cello. Also, the form which is a sonata for these instruments.

Strophic Designating a song in which all verses of text are sung to the same music.

Style Broadly, the manner of expression that distinguishes a particular work, composer, historical period, or artistic school.

Subject In a fugue, the principal theme, introduced first in a single voice and then imitated in other voices, returning frequently during the course of the composition.

Suite A series of instrumental movements, each based on a particular dance rhythm.

Syllabic Designating a musical phrase in which each syllable of text is given one note.

Symphony A sonata for orchestra.

Syncopation A deliberate disturbance of the normal metrical pulse, produced by shifting the accent from a normally strong beat to a weak beat.

Tala One of the ancient rhythmic patterns employed in Indian music.

Tempo The speed at which a piece of music moves.

Ternary Form A basic musical form consisting of three sections, ABA, the final A section being a repetition or slight variation of the first.

Terraced Dynamics Sudden shifts in dynamic levels (e.g., from loud to soft or soft to loud) characteristic of Baroque music.

Texture The relationship between the horizontal (melodic) and vertical (harmonic) aspects of a piece of music. The principal classifications are monophony, homophony, and polyphony.

Theme A musical idea that serves as a starting point for development of a composition or section of a composition.

Theme and Variations A form based on a single theme and its subsequent repetition, with each new statement varied in some way from the original.

Theme Transformation The practice of varying a single theme or melody through the different sections of a piece; this procedure was used especially in Romantic tone poems.

Thorough Bass See *figured bass*.

Through-Composed A term applied to songs in which new music is used for each successive verse.

Time Signature A numerical sign placed at the beginning of a composition to indicate the meter.

Toccata (ta-kah′-ta) A Baroque keyboard piece full of scale passages, rapid runs and trills, and massive chords.

Tonality The relationship of tones to a central tone called the tonic. See also *key*.

Tone A pitch having a steady, constant frequency.

Tone Cluster A chord produced by playing a large group of adjacent notes on the piano with the flat of the hand. The resulting sound is dense and indistinct.

Tone Color, Timbre The characteristic quality, or "color," of a musical sound as produced by a specific instrument or voice, or by a combination of instruments.

Tone Poem, Symphonic Poem A single-movement programmatic work, relatively long and very free in form, usually involving a dramatic plot or literary idea.

Tonic The tonal center. The tone which acts as a musical home base, or point of rest and finality, in a piece of music.

Total Serialism The complete, predetermined, and ultrarational systemization of every aspect of a composition: pitch, tempo, dynamics, articulations, and timbre.

Transcription An arrangement of a composition for a medium other than that for which it was originally written.

Tremolo A "trembling" effect produced on string instruments when the bow is moved rapidly back and forth across the strings.

Triad A combination of three tones (chord) built on the interval of the third.

Twelve-Tone Technique, Serialism, Dodecaphony A system of composition developed by Arnold Schoenberg which consists of arranging the twelve pitches of the chromatic scale in a particular order (known as a tone row, series, or set).

Verismo (vay-reez′-mo) "Realism." An Italian operatic point of view favoring realistic subjects taken from everyday, often lower-class, life.

Vibrato (vi-brah′-toh) A slight fluctuation in pitch which increases the "warmth" of a tone.

Virtuoso Designating a performer or performance characterized by outstanding technical skill.

Voice (Voice Part) A melodic line, either vocal or instrumental, in a contrapuntal piece such as a fugue.

Whole Step, Whole Tone An interval of two consecutive half steps.

Whole Tone Scale The scale in which the octave is divided into six consecutive whole steps.

Wind Ensemble A small-scale band composed primarily of wind and percussion instruments and intended for indoor performance.

Word Painting Representation of the literal meaning of a text through musical means (e.g., singers' voices imitating the sounds of birds).

INDEX

MUSICAL EVENTS	DATE	COMPOSERS

ROMANTIC

Liszt's *Les préludes* (1854)
Wagner's *Tristan und Isolde* (1859)
Balakirev, Cui, Borodin, Rimsky-Korsakov,
and Mussorgsky form the "Five" (1862)

First Wagner Festival held at Bayreuth (1876)
Edison invents the phonograph (1877)

New York Metropolitan Opera founded (1883)
Development of French Impressionistic music
Dvořák conducts first performance of
"New World Symphony" (1893)
Debussy's *Prélude à l'après-midi d'un faune* (1894)

1875

Alexander Borodin (1834–1887)
Georges Bizet (1838–1875)
Modest Mussorgsky (1839–1881)
Peter Ilyich Tchaikovsky (1840–1893)
Antonín Dvořák (1841–1904)
Edvard Grieg (1843–1907)
Gabriel Fauré (1845–1924)
Giacomo Puccini (1858–1924)
Gustav Mahler (1860–1911)
Edward MacDowell (1861–1908)
Frederick Delius (1862–1934)
Claude Achille Debussy (1862–1918)
Richard Strauss (1864–1949)

TWENTIETH CENTURY

1900

German expressionism, represented chiefly by
Schoenberg and Berg, developed
before World War I

Jean Sibelius (1865–1957)
Erik Satie (1866–1925)
Ralph Vaughan Williams (1872–1958)
Arnold Schoenberg (1874–1951)
Charles Ives (1874–1954)
Maurice Ravel (1875–1937)
Manuel de Falla (1876–1946)
Ottorino Respighi (1879–1936)
Béla Bartók (1881–1945)
Zoltán Kodály (1882–1967)

Stravinsky's *The Rite of Spring* (1913)
Schoenberg announces his method of
composing with twelve tones (1922)
First performance of Gershwin's
Rhapsody in Blue (1924)
American jazz influences composers in the 1920s
N.Y. Philharmonic Orchestra first broadcast
over radio (1928)

1925

Igor Stravinsky (1882–1971)
Anton von Webern (1883–1945)
Charles T. Griffes (1884–1920)
Alban Berg (1885–1935)
Wallingford Riegger (1885–1961)
Edgard Varèse (1885–1965)
Sergei Prokofiev (1891–1953)
Darius Milhaud (1892–1974)
Paul Hindemith (1895–1963)
Virgil Thomson (b. 1896)
Roger Sessions (b. 1896)

First performance of Ives's Second
Piano Sonata (1939)
Many European composers emigrate to the United
States during the 1930s and early 1940s, including
Schoenberg, Stravinsky, Hindemith, and Bartók

Henry Cowell (1897–1965)
George Gershwin (1898–1937)
Roy Harris (b. 1898)
Aaron Copland (b. 1900)
Ruth Crawford Seeger (1901–1953)
Miriam Gideon (b. 1906)
Dimitri Shostakovich (1906–1975)
Olivier Messiaen (b. 1908)
Elliott Carter (b. 1908)

Copland's *Appalachian Spring* choreographed
by Martha Graham (1944)
Early experiments in electronic music; devel-
opment of *musique concrète* in Paris (1948)
Introduction of long-playing records (1948)
American experiments in electronic music at
Columbia University (1952)
John Cage develops chance music in the 1950s
Stockhausen's *Gesang der Jünglinge* (1956)
Boulez's *Improvisations sur Mallarmé* (1958)
Druckman's *Animus* Series (1966–   )
Rochberg's Third Symphony, using technique
of collage (1968)
Leonard Bernstein's *Mass* is opening work at
Kennedy Center in Washington, D.C. (1972)

1950

Howard Swanson (b. 1909)
Samuel Barber (b. 1910)
William Schuman (b. 1910)
Gian Carlo Menotti (b. 1911)
John Cage (b. 1912)
Hugo Weisgall (b. 1912)
Benjamin Britten (1913–1976)
Milton Babbitt (b. 1916)
Ulysses Kay (b. 1917)
George Rochberg (b. 1918)
Lukas Foss (b. 1922)

1975

Györgi Ligeti (b. 1923)
Pierre Boulez (b. 1925)
Gunther Schuller (b. 1925)
Karlheinz Stockhausen (b. 1928)
Jacob Druckman (b. 1928)
George Crumb (b. 1929)